CRIMINOLOGICAL APPROACHES TO INTERNATIONAL CRIMINAL LAW

This volume is one of the few books to explain in-depth the international crimes behind the scenes of substantive or procedural law. The contributors place a particular focus on what motivates participation in international crime, how perpetrators, witnesses and victims see their predicament and how international crimes should be investigated at local and international level, with an emphasis on context. The book engages these questions with a broad interdisciplinary approach that is accessible to both lawyers and non-lawyers alike. It discusses international crime through the lens of anthropology, neuroscience, psychology, state crime theory and information systems theory and draws upon relevant investigative experience from experts in international and domestic law prosecutions.

ILIAS BANTEKAS is Professor of Law, Brunel University, School of Law

EMMANOUELA MYLONAKI is Senior Lecturer in Law at South Bank University, Department of Law

CRIMINOLOGICAL APPROACHES TO INTERNATIONAL CRIMINAL LAW

Edited by

ILIAS BANTEKAS

and

EMMANOUELA MYLONAKI

CAMBRIDGE
UNIVERSITY PRESS

CAMBRIDGE
UNIVERSITY PRESS

University Printing House, Cambridge CB2 8BS, United Kingdom

Cambridge University Press is part of the University of Cambridge.

It furthers the University's mission by disseminating knowledge in the pursuit of education, learning and research at the highest international levels of excellence.

www.cambridge.org
Information on this title: www.cambridge.org/9781107060036

First published 2014

Printed in the United Kingdom by Clays, St Ives plc

A catalogue record for this publication is available from the British Library
Library of Congress Cataloging-in-Publication Data
Criminological approaches to international criminal law / edited by Ilias Bantekas, Emmanuela Mylonaki.
pages cm
ISBN 978-1-107-06003-6 (Hardback)
1. International criminal law. I. Bantekas, Ilias, editor. II. Mylonaki, Emmanuela, editor.
KZ7050.C73 2014
345–dc23 2014021239

ISBN 978-1-107-06003-6 Hardback

CONTENTS

FIGURES

TABLES

CONTRIBUTORS

ANDY AITCHISON is lecturer in criminology at the School of Law, Edinburgh University and founding co-director of the MSc Global Crime, Justice and Security. His main research interests lie in criminology and the politics of criminal justice. Andy's main works to date examine the development of criminal justice institutions in states in transition from authoritarian government and violent conflict. Findings are presented in various publications including *Making the Transition: International Intervention, State-building and Criminal Justice Reform in Bosnia and Herzegovina* (2011). Andy is currently researching police as perpetrators of international crimes in the former Yugoslavia and has presented preliminary papers on the topic at British and European criminological meetings. Formerly, Andy lectured in social policy at the University of Edinburgh School of Social and Political Science and worked as a researcher for Cardiff University and the UK Home Office.

HENRIK ANCKARSÄTER is professor of forensic psychiatry at the University of Gothenburg and senior consultant at Sahlgren's University Hospital in Gothenburg. He has been visiting professor at the universities of Lund and Paris XII, is a scientific expert at several governmental bodies, board director of the International Academy of Law and Mental Health, author of more than one hundred peer-reviewed papers in psychiatry and forensic psychiatry and several book chapters and other publications. His main research interests are child neuropsychiatry, adult personality disorders and forensic psychiatric epistemology. Dr Anckarsäter was one of the founders of the Centre of Ethics, Law and Mental Health at the University of Gothenburg and has initiated a range of cross-disciplinary studies, including the Gothenburg Forensic Neuropsychiatry Project, the Child and Adolescent Twin Study in Sweden (CATSS, currently the world's largest twin study on child and adolescent psychiatry) and a large-scale collaboration between philosophy of science and forensic psychiatry (FILUR).

ILIAS BANTEKAS is professor of international law at Brunel Law School and associate fellow at the Institute of Advanced Legal Studies of the University of London. He has advised international organisations, such as UNDP, UNODC and OSCE, law firms, barristers and governments on matters of international law, international criminal law, financial crime, international development banks, human rights and foreign debt. His principal works include *International Criminal Law* (4th edn, 2010), *International Law* (2013, with E. Papastavridis), *International Arbitration* (2015) and *International Human Rights Law and Practice* (Cambridge University Press, 2013, with L. Oette).

TOVA BENNET is a doctoral student in criminal law at Lund University, Sweden. Her thesis focuses on the prerequisites for attributing criminal responsibility.

BRIAN CUTLER serves as professor and associate Dean of the Faculty of Social Science and Humanities at the University of Ontario Institute of Technology. He is past president of the American Psychology-Law Society and past Editor-in-Chief of the *Journal of Law and Human Behavior*. Dr Cutler recently edited *Conviction of the Innocent: Lessons from Psychological Research* (2012) and *Reform of Eyewitness Identification Procedures* (2013), both published by the American Psychological Association Press. He serves as a consultant and expert witness in cases involving eyewitness identification and false confessions.

DR DIONYSIOS DEMETIS is a lecturer in management systems at Hull University Business School. He holds a PhD on anti-money laundering (AML) and information systems from the London School of Economics (LSE), where he taught information systems management, information security and research methods. He is a member of the Scientific Board of the Geolab Institute at the Ionian University in Corfu and was an Adjunct Professor for the Thomas Jefferson School of Law in California (San Diego) where he lectured on international compliance, AML, the Bank Secrecy Act (BSA) and research methods for LLM/JSD students. He is the author of two books and a number of journal publications, and his book on AML entitled *Technology and Anti-Money Laundering: A Systems Theory and Risk-based Approach* (2010) is the first book to provide a coherent theoretical structure for AML research and practice based on systems theory. While at the LSE, he contributed widely to a number of research deliverables for the European Commission, but most importantly to the domains of AML and countering the financing of terrorism for the Spotlight EU project, as well as the GATE EU Project. He has acted as a convener of the steering group for the Future of Identity for the Information Society (FIDIS) and has presented widely on AML and information systems across Europe. His core research interests include AML, systems theory and information systems.

DERMOT GROOME is currently a Senior Prosecuting Trial Attorney at the Office of the Prosecutor of the International Criminal Tribunal for the former Yugoslavia (ICTY) and a Distinguished Fellow of International Criminal Law at Pennsylvania State University School of Law. He is a former New York City prosecutor. He has led the investigation and prosecution of several ICTY cases. He is currently leading the prosecution of the case against Ratko Mladić. He served as a legal adviser with the International Human Rights Law Group and as a consultant for the OHCHR. He regularly lectures at the International Institute of Criminal Investigation and is the author of the *Handbook of Human Rights Investigation* (1st edn, 2001; 2nd edn, 2011).

KRISTIAN LASSLETT is a lecturer in criminology at the University of Ulster and a member of the International State Crime Initiative Executive Board. He is editor of the *State Crime Testimony Project* and joint editor-in-chief of *State Crime*. Kristian has conducted extensive field research in Australia, Papua New Guinea and the United States, and has published papers on state crime and criminological theory in leading international journals. His first book *State Crime on the Margins of Empire* is forthcoming. Presently, Kristian is carrying out research on land grabbing, corruption and civil society in Papua New Guinea.

ROD LINDSAY graduated from the University of Alberta (1982) and has researched eyewitness issues at Queen's University, Canada, since that date. He has testified as an expert on eyewitness issues in both criminal and civil cases. He was a member of the Technical Working Group for Eyewitness Evidence (US National Institute of Justice) responsible for the American national guidelines and has extensive experience training legal professionals, including judges, police, prosecutors and lawyers. Dr Lindsay co-edited the *Handbook of Eyewitness Psychology* (2007).

AMISSI M. MANIRABONA is assistant professor at the Faculty of Law of the University of Montreal where he teaches courses in various fields, including national and international criminal law. He is also a researcher at the International Centre for Comparative Criminology (ICCC) at the University of Montreal. Prior to his current position he was a postdoctoral researcher at the ICCC as well as an Aisenstadt Fellow at McGill University, Faculty of Law.

JEFFREY STEVENSON MURER is a lecturer on collective violence and a research fellow at the Centre for the Study of Terrorism and Political Violence, University of St Andrews, Scotland. In his research he explores the process of large group identity formation and the roles that violence plays in performing and communicating that identity. Previously, he was the principal investigator of the European Study of Youth Mobilisation, a three-year, multi-sited study funded by the British Council, which explored the motivations for social action among young people in Central and Nordic Europe, and their attitudes toward, and participation in, political violence. In other research he has explored the roles of violence in the political transitions following the fall of Communism in Central Europe, in the wars of the break-up of Yugoslavia, and in the independence and religious struggles in the Caucasus region. He has held many research fellowship awards, including as a national fellow of the American Psychoanalytic Association between 2006 and 2007, and is currently a research lecturer at the Scottish Institute for Policing and a member of the Young Academy of the Royal Society of Edinburgh.

EMMANOUELA MYLONAKI is senior lecturer in criminology at London South Bank University and director of its Postgraduate Programme. She has published widely on the intersection between criminology and (international) criminal law and has advised several private and public organisations on anti-terrorist policies and strategies.

THOMAS NILSSON is a licensed psychologist and a senior lecturer in Forensic Psychology at the University of Gothenburg, Sweden. He has worked as a psychologist at the National Board of Forensic Medicine, conducting court-ordered forensic psychiatric assessments. His main research interests focus on risk assessments and factors associated with negative outcomes of mentally disordered criminal offenders.

OLAOLUWA OLUSANYA is currently a lecturer at the Department of Law and Criminology, Aberystwyth University, UK. His most recent work has appeared in journals such as the *British Journal of Criminology*, *New Criminal Law Review*, *Psychiatry, Psychology and Law* and *Critical Criminology*. He is a member of several associations, including the British Society of Criminology, the British Sociological Association, the American Sociological Association, the American Society of Criminology and the Society for the Study of Symbolic Interaction (SSSI). His most recent book is entitled *Emotions, Decision-Making and Mass Atrocities through the Lens of the Macro-Micro Integrated Theoretical Model* (2014). He is currently working on a book project entitled *Understanding War Crimes*.

SUSANNA RADOVIC is senior lecturer in theoretical philosophy and director of the Centre for Ethics, Law and Mental Health, University of Gothenburg, Sweden. Her main research interests focus on the concept of accountability and its application in criminal law, as well as on delusions and false beliefs. She has published a textbook on accountability.

JONATHAN J. RUSCH is Deputy Chief of Strategy and Policy at the US Department of Justice, Fraud Section, where he previously held the post of counsel for fraud prevention and senior litigation counsel. Prior to this he was director and acting director of the US Department of Treasury, Office of Financial Enforcement. Between 1984 and 1986 he served on the US President's Commission on Organised Crime and practised with Cleary, Gottlieb, Steen and Hamilton. He is an adjunct professor of law at Georgetown University Law School.

ANDREW SMITH is a doctoral candidate at Queen's University, Canada. His doctoral research examines the use of multiple show-ups for single perpetrator crimes and is funded by the Social Science and Humanities Research Council of Canada. In related research, he is studying multiple perpetrator crimes and show-ups. He is primarily interested in examining eyewitness-related issues, as well as factors affecting juror decision-making. He has published in both psychology and law-related journals.

JO-ANNE WEMMERS is a full professor at the School of Criminology of the University of Montreal as well as head of the research group Victimology and Restorative Justice at the International Centre for Comparative Criminology. She has published widely in the areas of victimology, international criminal law and restorative justice. Her books include *Therapeutic Jurisprudence and Victim Participation in Justice:*

International Perspectives (2011), *Introduction à la victimologie* (2003), *Caring for Victims of Crime* (1999) and *Victims in the Criminal Justice System* (1996). Former secretary general of the World Society of Victimology, she is currently editor-in-chief of the French language journal *Criminologie*, as well as editor of the *International Review of Victimology* and the *Journal international de victimologie.*

PREFACE

You know that an edited book has the potential for contributing something to knowledge when all the contributors tell you that they are challenged by the questions posed, even if the subject matter of their chapter is close to their scholarly or professional expertise. None of the contributors alone, including the editors, possesses expertise on all the areas covered in this book. We have asked contributors to offer perspectives on psychiatry, psychology, forensic science, anthropology, law, organisational behaviour and several other areas, and it is natural that none of us could predict from the outset what each chapter would look like or what conclusions would be reached. We did not ask that contributors confirm or deny existing theories, practices, policies, etc., with the aim of reaching a particular line of thinking. What we were certain of was that international criminal justice should not be confined to what lawyers alone say but should become as interdisciplinary as possible, because law is clearly only one element in this process. We were not convinced, for example, that the extensive debates on *mens rea* currently occupying international criminal law scholarship (especially following the *Lubanga* case) could only be answered by criminal law theorists, but thought that at the very least psychiatry and neuroscience should inform the current debate. Equally, it was felt that international criminal justice scholarship had narrowed its scope so much (with its centre of gravity being on the so-called core crimes) that it had lost sight of conduct producing more victims as compared to average war crimes. State crime theory is just one example where lawyers have lost the bigger picture.

When we set out to organise the contents of this book we did not necessarily aim at constructing a general theory of international criminology. Our purpose was to ask selected experts how they thought established knowledge in their disciplines could be adapted to international (or transnational) crimes, if at all. This book is therefore a first attempt towards expanding the boundaries of international criminal law in order to realise its full potential. It is hoped that this will inspire others, including judges, academics, counsel and policy makers, to develop these ideas further through new research and practice. We hope that this is merely the first step towards something much bigger.

We would like to thank all contributors for their hard work, as well as the staff at Cambridge University Press for their professionalism and high standards throughout the production of this book.

Introduction: an interdisciplinary criminology of international criminal law

ILIAS BANTEKAS

Some reasons for the absence of interdisciplinarity in international criminal proceedings

Whereas the fusion of international criminal law with other disciplines is much more obvious in the context of academic research, principally because of the inroads made by non-legal scholars, the application of these disciplines to international criminal proceedings is rare. One explanation for this is the practical function of international tribunals whose role is to dispense justice to 'real' people. As a result, and given the tight deadlines within which tribunals must process a huge amount of evidence and conduct trial proceedings, they may well claim that they do not have the luxury of experimenting with other disciplines. If this was indeed a valid explanation, tribunals could very well make use of the vast existing literature – as is the case with the reliability of traumatised eye witnesses[1] – in order to make persuasive arguments concerning the pitfalls of testimony provided by those directly affected by hostilities and violent crimes.[2] Equally, the tribunals could apply indisputable findings from the natural and medical sciences demonstrating the stresses on human physiology arising from combat. Explanations for the absence of interdisciplinarity in international trials should clearly be sought elsewhere.[3]

[1] See, for example, B. L. Cutler, S. D. Penrod, *Mistaken Identification: The Eyewitness, Psychology and the Law* (Cambridge University Press, 1995).

[2] See N. A. Combs, *Fact-Finding without Facts: The Uncertain Evidentiary Foundations of International Criminal Convictions* (Cambridge University Press, 2011) at 63–105, which explores the decline and pitfalls of oral testimony specifically in the context of international criminal proceedings.

[3] To be fair, the ICTY in its early work did seek some expert testimony on evidence reliability, particularly from the late W. A. Wagenaar. See www.icty.org/x/cases/kupreskic/trans/en/990603it.htm. See also www.ictytranscripts.org/trials/kupreskic/990603it.htm. Subsequent chambers, however, made little use of these findings.

The judicial chambers of international criminal tribunals ultimately validate and dictate in what manner the prosecution and defence will present their evidence, including the methods by which such evidence will be presented. By way of illustration, if the judges of a particular tribunal encouraged the application of neuroscience in order to ascertain the mental condition of those claiming exculpatory defences (e.g., duress) then no doubt all future litigants would hire the assistance of neuroscientists and relevant legal arguments would depend on scientific data. In this manner, and in that particular context, the law's construction would be made dependent on extra-legal considerations. As a result, the dynamics of the parties' arguments would shift from legal to extra-legal. At present, such a shift is a fiction in international criminal proceedings (with, it has to be said, some exceptions), but not in other fields of legal inquiry. Neuroscience, for example, plays a central role in the application of an infant's attachment to its parents and the family courts of several nations attribute great significance to attachment theory in their determination of custody and visitation rights.[4]

Why is it, then, that national courts are ultimately receptive to scientific developments in fields such as family and criminal law – not without their fair share of resistance – whereas international criminal tribunals are generally disinclined to consider these at any length? Some personal reflections will be offered to explain this phenomenon, albeit by no means can they holistically disentangle this very complex state of affairs. National courts, as permanent institutions grounded in nation states, are continuously engaged with powerful stakeholders and institutions that exert significant influence upon them, which they cannot lightly ignore. By way of illustration, bar associations, universities, alumni, published research in local or international eminent journals, research by civil society and media coverage are organisations and factors that sway the courts' opinion on several matters, particularly if said matters are not politically contested. The science behind the battered wife syndrome, which is not politically charged, is far more acceptable than the science

[4] See the pioneering work of J. Bowlby, *Attachment* (revised edition, Pimlico, 1997). For an application in family proceedings, see especially, C. George, M. B. Isaacs and R. S. Marvin, 'Incorporating Attachment Assessment into Custody Evaluations: The Case of a 2-Year Old and her Parents', (2011) 49 *Family Court Review* 483 and A. Schore and J. McIntosh, 'Family Law and the Neuroscience of Attachment: Part I', (2011) 49 *Family Court Review* 501.

underlying abortions, which remains politically contested principally along religious lines.

These 'pressure groups' are absent in the judicial politics of international criminal tribunals, where the principal stakeholders are the organs that created them and, in some cases, the victim population – especially where the tribunal is operating on the territory of the inflicted state. Given that in the vast majority of cases the victim population is largely illiterate and destitute there would be no direct interest in scientific advances outside the courtroom. Local populations would only take issue with the potential impact of particular scientific data on their commonly perceived notions of justice, which are understandably coloured by bias and clan affiliation (e.g., acquittal of an accused on account of his mental state). International bar associations are institutionally weak and members generally view their case loads before international tribunals through a temporary lens; universities and alumni exert little influence given the disparity in the ethnic composition of chambers; the only journals of influence upon the judges are law-related as this is their domain and, as has already been explained, the vast majority of writings on international criminal law in legal journals are not interdisciplinary; the agenda of civil society (at least that of the heavily funded and transnational non-governmental organisations (NGOs)) is largely geared towards anti-impunity (including lawfare) and is disinterested in the introduction of interdisciplinary approaches; and media coverage of the work of international tribunals by the large networks is minimal and hence the judges do not feel any media pressure as such. It is only the local media of the inflicted nations that report extensively, but this hardly exerts significant pressure on foreign judges who do not converse in the local language and see their judicial post as a temporary appointment and perhaps as a step to a subsequent post which is definitely unaffected by local media.

The second explanation for the absence of an interdisciplinary dimension in the work of international tribunals is simply the lack of expertise by lawyers in other sciences and disciplines.[5] One need only recollect how complex law itself has become, forcing lawyers to become specialists in narrow areas. This is true even in the academic sphere where forays into neighbouring legal disciplines are exceptional for fear of failure and rejection of one's writings. This 'closed' and distorted form of scholarship

[5] This is not necessarily true for those with a US-style legal education who will have undertaken a first degree unrelated to law.

breeds confirmation bias and blocks the emergence of new ideas and methodologies by 'outsiders'.[6] However, the absence of science and humanities in the operation of international tribunals' judicial reasoning is not the result of ignorance on the part of the judges (i.e., ignorance as to the exact science). No judge is expected to follow scientific developments or obliged to infuse law with science. Rather, in their dispensation of justice, judges must (in theory) be open to all those factors that serve justice in the best possible way. Hence, they must invite, rather than oppose, expert opinion on matters that affect the types of human conduct they are determining, in the same manner they employ military analysts to inform themselves of the military structure of the warring parties (e.g., in order to ascertain command hierarchies for the purpose of determining command responsibility). Judges must breed a culture of scientific exchange, inviting expert reports from eminent scientists and should call upon their sponsors to establish a scientific entity that will be charged with the following tasks:

(1) contextual study of each situation (historical, sociological and anthropological);
(2) consult the court and the parties on the available scientific evidence and authorities in respect of a particular issue (i.e., what is the dominant theory on the effects of post-traumatic stress disorder (PTSD) on soldiers in the field); and
(3) arrange for leading experts to offer expert determinations on said issues and assist the court in making sense of scientific data.[7]

The third factor inhibiting international judges' reluctance to introduce extra-legal elements into their judicial reasoning concerns their apprehension of the effects that science may have on judicial outcomes. By way of illustration, if a court had embraced neuroscience which had conclusively

[6] Confirmation bias entails the publication of works endorsed by editors of journals and book series, while rejecting other perhaps better works with which they are not in agreement. For an early empirical exposition of the problem, see J. Mahoney, 'Publication Prejudices: An Experimental Study of Confirmatory Bias in the Peer Review System', (1977) 1 *Cognitive Therapy and Research* 161.

[7] One of the biggest problems in science is the vast diffusion of lab-based results and the lack of inter-connectedness. Biologists, for example, typically study the operation of minute elements in human cells. Although their results are unique they are not directly (or necessarily) related to any particular disease. In the maze of very particular biological discoveries much is lost to medical researchers who are unable to connect every result to a disease.

demonstrated that combat-weary soldiers, whose physiology had been severely strained, possessed few cognitive powers, it would have no alternative but to determine that the culprits exhibited a diminished intention compared to the typical *mens rea* requirements of the criminal law. Hence, if non-legal sciences are kept as far removed as possible from the judicial reasoning process the courts decrease the risk of reliance on subjectivity. It is not, of course, that international judges desire unjust outcomes; rather, it is natural to fear that science (including criminological theories) is susceptible to absolute and irreversible results which subsequent judicial reasoning cannot escape without severe criticism. That judges may become slaves to scientific 'truths', dressed in an immutable facade, is as dangerous as uncontrolled judicial subjectivism that is altogether sceptical towards science and criminological thinking. However, no scientific advancement can ever substitute sound judicial reasoning, because the determination of justice in a particular case requires good use of one's inner faculties. Science can never achieve justice without the intervention of rational faculties. Hence, judges may ultimately decide that the application of a universally accepted theory to the facts of a particular case does not produce just outcomes. Practice has shown that in the few instances where international criminal tribunals have sought expert advice on non-legal issues – as in the anthropological construction of genocide – they did so with a view to reaching a just result.[8]

Transplanting criminology into the realm of international crimes?

The principal difference between ordinary (domestic) crime and international crime is context. Ordinary crime involves deviant conduct in a given societal setting that is subject to a degree of control by the local authorities. International crimes, on the other hand, particularly so-called core crimes (genocide, crimes against humanity and war crimes) occur in situations of lawlessness and breakdown of authority. Most transnational crimes, therefore, such as organised crime and terrorism, are akin to ordinary crime as far as their context is concerned. As a result of this diffused context between ordinary and international crimes it is not possible simply to transplant existing criminological theories to explain deviant conduct in the international realm.[9] The evolution and

[8] Anthropology has generally played a minor role at the ICTY, save for the construction of the pertinent groups susceptible to genocide. See Chapter 9.

[9] See Chapter 1.

application of criminological theories has been largely premised on the notion that criminal conduct is the result of several complex factors; some are attributable to the individual as such (e.g., biological and mental problems and dispositions, aggression theories), but many exist outside the individual and concern his or her interaction with society. Differential association theory, social disorganisation and sub-cultural theory are but a few of the theories that were developed to explain the link between socio-economic circumstances and deviance. Most importantly, criminology has never really dealt with atrocity crimes and the dynamics behind these (such as power relations, broader geostrategic interests etc.), having principally focused on individual deviance.[10]

A criminology of international criminal law, therefore, gives rise to two important questions, namely: (1) Are existing theories on the links between society and deviance still relevant in explaining international crimes, given that in most cases core international crimes occur as a result of the political decisions of a few individuals; and (2) to what extent do we need a new (or perhaps adapted) criminology to address crimes in situations of lawlessness (as in the case of armed conflict), semi-lawlessness (such as piracy and terrorism in failed states) and mass spontaneity (if indeed such spontaneity actually exists) of the type associated with genocide and crimes against humanity independent of armed conflicts?

As to the first question, little empirical research has been conducted to explain why individuals who are not ordinarily exposed to delinquent and deviant behaviour (as per existing criminological theories) exhibit brutal attributes in the context of mass criminality. In the Rwandan genocide even priests participated in the killings, neighbours massacred neighbours and, in the former Yugoslavia, ordinary people turned into heinous torturers. Of course, given that not everyone transforms into a sadistic murderer when mass conflict erupts it is evident that mass criminality and lawlessness do not suddenly awake a latent deviance in all those caught up in it, especially those in positions of power over others. In the *Erdemović* case, for example, the accused, a conscript in the Bosnian-Serb army, refused to execute unarmed civilians in *Srebrenića* as did most of his peers. Equally, most Germans rejected Nazi ideology even if they felt powerless to actively resist it. Criminologists have only recently begun to examine such phenomena,[11] albeit a consistent theory

[10] See the discussion of atrocity crimes in Chapter 1.

[11] D. Maier-Katkin, D. Mears and T. J. Bernard, 'Towards a Criminology of Crimes against Humanity', (2009) 13 *Theoretical Criminology* 227. A. Smeulers and R. Haveman (eds.),

backed by empirical evidence is missing, as relevant discussions so far have been largely theoretical and of a reconnaissance nature into the realm of international criminal law.[12] It is certainly worth undertaking a detailed social and psychological profiling of all those mid- to lower-level executioners convicted by international and domestic tribunals in the context of the Yugoslav, Rwandese and Sierra Leone conflicts. Such a study would highlight particular traits common among the perpetrators, their associations prior to the outbreak of hostilities, quality of family life, income distribution, influences from external sources, etc., which, in turn, would possibly point to characteristics shared among the observed group. Hence, the answer to the first question is that criminology does indeed have a role to play in the assessment of characters and their societal interaction prior to the triggering of mass criminality. This process must be adapted to the exigencies of the international crimes under consideration, since the transplantation of existing theories as such is probably inappropriate, albeit certainly the starting point for any subsequent discussion.

As to the second question, significant empirical work has been undertaken by psychiatrists on the physiology and cognitive faculties of those involved in combat.[13] In a study completed at the close of World War II on US infantry who had fought in northern Europe it was demonstrated that after a period of sixty days of continuous combat, 98 per cent of troops would suffer from a psychological condition, such as acute anxiety, combat exhaustion or depression, whereas the remaining 2 per cent developed an 'aggressive psychopathic personality' on the basis of which they could endure long periods of combat without any of the aforementioned symptoms common to the majority of their comrades.[14] Even so, we are still unaware of the effects of combat or non-organised violence on civilians-turned-combatants, or the impact of one's socio-economic history in the context of lawlessness. Equally, anthropological

Supranational Criminology: Towards a Criminology of International Crimes (Intersentia, 2008), have called for the establishment of a 'supranational criminology' for the purpose of examining mass international crimes.

[12] See, for example, N. Theodorakis and D. P. Farrington, 'Emerging Challenges for Criminology: Drawing the Margins for Crimes against Humanity', (2013) 6 *International Journal of Criminology and Sociological Theory* 1150.

[13] D. Grossman and L. Christensen, *On Combat: The Psychology and Physiology of Deadly Conflict in War and in Peace* (PPCT Research Publications, 2008).

[14] R. L. Swank and W. E. Marchand, 'Combat Neuroses, Development of Combat Exhaustion', (1946) 55 *Archives of Neurology and Psychiatry* 236, at 244.

data reflecting the views among the warring factions of a conflict are typically collected after the eruption of violence and, as a result, we possess a foggy picture as to the social relationships between victims and attackers at various temporal periods prior to the outbreak of hostilities. If we did possess such data, by means of early warning mechanisms, criminologists would be able to assess at what point in time social relations deteriorate. This would provide them with an opportunity to pinpoint those factors that exacerbate or ignite the change of circumstances, such as acute propaganda, high concentration of criminal elements in positions of authority, or other factors. Criminologists could then inform policy makers but also come to grips with those factors that trigger large social meltdowns that lead to mass unrest and criminality.[15]

It is clear, therefore, that the transplantation of existing criminological theories into the realm of international crimes – save for most transnational crimes – is inappropriate for addressing the multifaceted dimensions of these offences and their particular contexts. The social, anthropological and psychological context of international crimes demands new methodological approaches and new theories that link the individual to mass spontaneous phenomena.

Designing an appropriate research agenda

The organisation of the chapters in this book reflects a very specific thinking about what should be encompassed in a supranational (or international) criminology. This author does not view the aforementioned core crimes as the only international crimes, as they do not exist in isolation of other so-called transnational crimes,[16] such as terrorism, organised crime, corruption etc., which almost exclusively feed, to a larger or smaller degree, international conflicts and mass criminality.[17]

[15] In the Rwandese conflict, propaganda was a major tool in the hands of the *genocidaires* and at some point all transmission by radio was blocked through concerted international effort. See J. F. Metzl, 'Rwandan Genocide and the International Law of Radio Jamming', (1997) 91 *American Journal of International Law* 628.

[16] For a discussion as to their distinction, see I. Bantekas, *International Criminal Law* (4th edn, Hart, 2010), at 9.

[17] 'A Comprehensive Report of the Security Council-appointed Panel of Experts on the Illegal Exploitation of Natural Resources and other Forms of Wealth of the Democratic Republic of the Congo underlined the direct or indirect implication of 157 corporations, the operations of which fueled the purchase of arms, the perpetration of war crimes and crimes against humanity and the exploitation of Congo's natural resources to the detriment of its people.' Letter dated 23 October 2003 from the Secretary-General

Going a step further, terrorism and corruption, among other crimes, have been found to produce the same effects as war crimes and crimes against humanity.[18] As a result, while victimologists do undertake research on the effects of particular international crimes,[19] they are typically concerned with objective criteria, such as mortality rates and particular criminal incidences. Four broad phases are identified in a criminological study of international crime, namely:

(1) establishing context and understanding criminal conduct from multiple perspectives;
(2) investigation of crime by examination of available evidence;
(3) collaboration and enforcement through the use of appropriate and legitimate techniques; and
(4) transitional justice.

The first three phases are directly relevant to the work of international criminal tribunals, whereas the fourth concerns policy makers. By comparison, context is largely irrelevant to domestic criminal proceedings and there is no equivalent to transitional justice other than a generalised crime policy. Moreover, the degree of collaboration among institutions in a single nation is far more effective, less complex or cumbersome as compared to cooperation between states or institutions at the international level.

Anthropology and state crime studies reveal practical and theoretical approaches to context which are not obvious to the enforcer of law. In the Sierra Leone conflict, admission of cannibalism by the culprits was found to possess an altogether metaphorical meaning,[20] whereas accidental deaths caused by an earthquake may be attributed to the negligence of the state through its failure to enforce the highest standards of diligence upon its construction industry.[21] Neuroscience and psychology offer useful insights into the context of an armed conflict and explain from a clinical perspective the conduct of the persons involved in mass criminality.[22]

addressed to the President of the Security Council, UN Doc S/2003/1027 (2003), paras. 10–13.

18 A. Cassese, 'The Multifaceted Notion of Terrorism in International Law', (2006) 4 *Journal of International Criminal Justice* 933.

19 As is the case with Chapter 12 of this book, which examines victimisation in the context of armed conflicts and war crimes.

20 See Chapter 9. 21 See Chapter 3. 22 See Chapters 8 and 10.

Examination of evidence is the bread and butter of criminal proceedings. A detailed study of context will have already provided a solid basis for reading the available evidence. Although the methodology will largely remain the same, there are crucial differences between the construction of evidence before international criminal tribunals and other courts. International tribunals typically prosecute senior figures and, as a result, prosecutors therein must link the criminal conduct of mid- and lower-level executioners to their source and inspiration. Moreover, eye witnesses may be in the thousands and forensic evidence will be extensive, including scores of rape and mutilated victims, displaced communities and mass graves. Victims and witnesses will have to return home at the end of their testimony, perhaps in close proximity to the friends and allies of the person they testified against. Unlike ordinary crime the majority of the culprits will perceive their role from a gallant lens, reinforced by notions of nationalism, patriotism, religious mission etc., which naturally dissolves their sense of guilt, even in respect of the most heinous crimes. This is further augmented by popular perception of the culprits' heroic image and their contribution to the group as such. As a result, oral testimony in mass criminality cases may be misleading due to the fact that an entire class of witnesses colours events, even heinous acts, according to its particular view and does not attach the requisite degree of importance to conduct as do the prosecutor or the judges. Equally, although much research has taken place on urban gangs and domestic organised criminal groups, as well as terrorist organisations, little work has been undertaken on the organisational aspects of mass crime organisations of the type involved in the context of the International Criminal Tribunal for the former Yugoslavia (ICTY), International Criminal Tribunal for Rwanda (ICTR) and the Sierra Leone Special Court (SLSC).[23] International tribunals have used abstract and, to a large degree, arbitrary legalistic criteria to explain participation in 'groups' engaged in genocide and crimes against humanity and have, as a result, developed concepts such as joint criminal enterprise (JCE) in order to achieve justice. These concepts have not, however, been tested from a criminological perspective and, hence, there is uncertainty as to whether participants share the same goals, motivations or intentions.

The theme on collaboration and enforcement concerns the field of transnational criminal law and not the work of international criminal

[23] See O. Olusanya, 'A Macro–Micro Integrated Theoretical Model of Mass Participation in Genocide', (2013) 53 *British Journal of Criminology* 27.

tribunals. Here our concern is with strategies and policies of prevention and of making the best possible use of technology to detect crime in circumstances where the culprits make a concerted effort to cover their tracks. For example, lawyers involved in piracy prosecutions are missing that part of the puzzle which seeks to understand the motivations behind large-scale piracy off the coast of Somalia and the policies involved to contain, deter and eliminate the phenomenon as a whole. Given that piracy *jure gentium* has a direct impact on the global shipping industry and has itself become a very lucrative enterprise that sustains a nation[24] – as is the plundering of a country's natural resources by warlords – it is evident that the relevant policies are international in nature. Moreover, the use of technology is underestimated in the context of transnational criminological approaches. Its utility is virtually endless, so here we concern ourselves with a particular application of information systems theory (IST) to terrorist financing, organised crime and money laundering, the detection of which by financial institutions (that are obliged to act as gatekeepers, among others) is extremely difficult.[25] They are burdened with a duty to report all suspicious transactions (above a particular monetary threshold) and it is understandable that this is a massive task given the number of daily transactions processed by financial institutions across the world. Without the assistance of information systems (IS) this task would resemble looking for a needle in a haystack. These sort of algorithmic-based databases are crucial to stemming the flow of finances to criminal organisations and are ultimately an important tool not only for UN Security Council-based sanctions committees, but also for relevant freezing policies against all warlords and leaders engaged in mass crimes against their people.

Finally, in recent years, starting with the UN-backed Latin American truth commissions of the 1980s and continuing with the aftermath of the Yugoslav and Rwandese conflicts, part of the emphasis of the international community has shifted from punishment to restorative justice.[26] There are cogent reasons for encompassing transitional justice in the realm of criminology, rather than treating it as merely an element of

[24] See E. Papastavridis, 'Piracy off Somalia: The Emperors and the Thieves of the Oceans in the 21st Century', in A. Abass (ed.), *Protecting Human Security in Africa* (Oxford University Press, 2010), at 122.

[25] See Chapter 7.

[26] See P. B. Hayner, *Unspeakable Truths: Transitional Justice and the Challenge of Truth Commissions* (2nd edn, Routledge, 2011).

international politics. It is unthinkable that criminologists and policy makers in the criminal justice field would not devise a system of containment and deterrence in the aftermath of a protracted and violent civil conflict where heated passions and sentiments naturally persist. This can only be achieved through a long-term combination of retributive and restorative justice actions that are designed and executed at the highest level. Here, we examine the position of the victim in transitional justice mechanisms and the adaptation of victimology to international crimes.[27] Although the criminological dimension of transitional justice depends on external funding, the success of any policy, as such, principally rests on the will of the international community. The latter's political pressure on the local parties to uphold their obligations constitute a significant aspect of any such policy.

These four phases to a criminologically informed investigation of international crimes require a variety of expertise in the humanities, technological, social and medical fields. No single scholar can undertake the task on his or her own. Although not all these phases will be relevant to a judge, prosecutor or defence counsel before an international or domestic tribunal dealing with international crimes, they should inform every international criminal justice policy initiated by intergovernmental organisations or coalitions of states.

A discussion of the chapters in this book

Chapter 1, by Andy Aitchison, responds to the question: 'What can criminological theory contribute to scholarship in international criminal law?' Before answering that question, the chapter recognises criminology as a relative latecomer to the study of atrocity, highlighting the apparent incongruity of a discipline with a strong mainstream theoretical and methodological focus at the individual level on the one hand, and a set of phenomena characterised by systematic organisation and mass participation. John Hagan and Wim Huisman are presented as exemplars of the current criminology of atrocity, identifying respectively the value of a sociological, structural criminology and the applicability of frameworks derived from research on organised forms of criminality. Three further areas of criminology are explored as a potential basis for further development. A Durkheimian perspective suggests merit in examining the

[27] See Chapter 12.

uneven development of a 'global society'. A victimological approach points to the benefit of comparative analysis of atrocities and of contexts marked by entrenched cleavages and inequalities but which do not feature atrocity. Finally, techniques of neutralisation are examined as an example of a perpetrator-oriented framework. This highlights the need for caution in utilising more individual-level analyses. Careful attention to social processes means that an alternative terminology of temporary deviant normative orders is more appropriate than the neutralisation of a conventional morality. Criminological theory is beginning to make a contribution to international criminal law scholarship and has the potential to develop this further.

Chapter 2, by Emmanouela Mylonaki, examines the application of social science research methods to the study of international crimes and international criminal law. Traditionally, criminologists have focused on common crime and violence, rejecting the idea that violations of international criminal law offer substantial theoretical and practical interest to the discipline of criminology. However, the evolution of international crimes and the frequency of crimes such as international terrorism, genocide and crimes against humanity present important intellectual challenges for criminological theory and research. By studying the causes and motives of those involved either as perpetrators or victims, the situations in which such crimes are committed, and their inherent dynamics, criminologists can unravel many of the complexities in the development and proliferation of such activities across the world and by doing so avoid any irreversible short term legalistic solutions.

There are several major research tools available to traditional criminology, such as field research and survey research. Each one of these poses particular difficulties. For example, field research presents physical dangers, while survey research is complex because it would be difficult to obtain anything but availability samples. Chapter 2 focuses on the practical application of empirical research methods in international criminal law by providing insights into the process of gaining access to sources and the different ways in which data can be collected and analysed for research on international crime and international criminal justice. In particular, the chapter deals with quantitative and qualitative research methods. It examines the extent to which criminological research methods can assist in explaining the persistence of international crimes and suggests how criminological research methods could inform the central issues of crime in the international context. The chapter is divided into two sections. The first highlights the relevance of the application of criminological research methods to the study of international crimes and gross violations of human rights and reinforces the arguments for the inclusion of the notion of international crimes within the realm of empirical research. The second demonstrates the practical application of quantitative and qualitative research methods in the study of international crimes and indicates the areas where empirical research is relevant.

Chapter 3, by Kristian Lasslett, discusses the notion of state crime. In a challenge to orthodox criminological understandings of what constitutes crime, and who can legitimately sanction wrongful behaviour, over the past two decades criminologists have paid increasing attention to crimes committed by states and the movements of resistance that emerge in opposition to deviant state practice. At the heart of this new criminological sub-discipline is an interest in the social configurations which cause states to exceed accepted rules of conduct and the factors that prompt victims and civil society to define these actions as criminal and then actualise censure through acts of sanction. In order to acquaint readers with critical features of the emerging terrain in state crime studies, Chapter 3 begins by examining the particular conceptual frameworks criminologists employ to define state crime – particular attention being paid to criteria-based and process-driven approaches. It suggests that although the former framework illuminates breaches of normative criteria, the latter approach is more attuned to the practical processes of historical struggle that stigmatise state practices as criminal. Attention is then turned to criminology's growing interest in the forms of social resistance state crime prompts. It is suggested that this stream of inquiry offers a conduit through which to consider the broader economic, political and ideological fault-lines upon which state crime and resistance rest, a conduit that allows scholars to concretise understandings of why states exceed certain normative boundaries and why communities of resistance are strategically disposed to stigmatise these actions as criminal. Finally, the chapter considers the different theoretical traditions criminologists have employed to understand these fault-lines, looking in particular at the strengths and limitations of positivist versus Marxist approaches. It is concluded that state crime studies offer a powerful vantage point through which to inquire into, and articulate, the way different configurations of civil society produce, through struggle, normative boundaries which states must adhere to, and then enact sanctions when these boundaries are exceeded, in addition to illuminating the factors that inspire states to exceed these normative boundaries and eschew subsequent stigmatising labels, looking at the potential this complex social exchange has for producing emancipatory forms of social change.

Chapter 4, by Jonathan Rusch, discusses the problems and techniques associated with the investigation of complex crimes, the vast majority of which are either transnational or international in nature. Successful criminal investigation requires the use of lawful investigative methods to gather evidence that is available to investigators and appropriate for the type of evidence needed. Because certain types of crime are notably more complex than others, police or investigative agencies need to use a wider array of investigative methods and techniques to be successful at investigating those crimes. Chapter 4 first describes the leading characteristics of complex crime:

(1) groups committing the same types of crime over an extended period;
(2) geographic and functional dispersion of operations;
(3) targeting of multiple victims;
(4) use of false or fraudulent statements and withholding of material information in furtherance of crime;
(5) counter-intelligence and counter-surveillance measures and measures to obstruct investigations; and
(6) threatened or actual violence.

It then identifies and examines the principal investigative methods and techniques that law enforcement agencies use to investigate complex crime. These include:

(1) interviews of witnesses;
(2) surveillance;
(3) acquisition of documentary evidence;
(4) testimony of eyewitness or third-party witnesses;
(5) use of confidential informants and criminal participants;
(6) use of undercover agents; and
(7) electronic surveillance.

The chapter provides examples from a number of criminal operations – with particular reference to drug trafficking organisations (DTOs), organised-crime groups and mass-marketing fraud and other economic-crime networks – to explain the relevance and value of each of these methods and techniques. It also examines various international conventions and domestic legal measures by which nations conducting investigations of complex crime can secure cooperation from other nations to obtain evidence of complex crime.

Chapter 5, by Dermot Groome, examines the collection, administration and use of evidence in mass crime cases, particularly from the perspective of the prosecutorial team. International crimes are most often the result of collective action and may involve the co-opting of state institutions for criminal purposes. Domestic crimes can be elevated to international crimes when committed on a widespread or systematic basis as part of an attack on a civilian population. Identifying and collecting the evidence necessary to establish this additional element presents challenges that are different from domestic prosecutions. Chapter 5 examines the search for evidence establishing international crimes; the conceptual and practical differences between collecting evidence for international, transnational and national crimes; and the relationship between international courts and states in possession of relevant evidence. It considers different sources of potential evidence, including legislative materials, minutes of state organisations and statements of senior political leaders. The chapter examines all of these issues in the context of adjudicating both individual and state criminal responsibility.

Chapter 6, by Brian Cutler, Rod Lindsay and Andrew Smith, focuses on the role and psychology of eyewitnesses in international criminal trials. In recent decades, global recognition of wrongful convictions has increased. DNA-based evidence conclusively confirms that wrongful convictions do occur. Catalogues of known wrongful convictions find that mistaken eyewitness identification is the antecedent most commonly associated with wrongful conviction.[28] Approximately 50 per cent of known wrongful convictions were preceded by mistaken eyewitness identification.[29] Although alleged perpetrators of international crimes are often known to eyewitnesses, identification errors may still occur. Errors in memory may occur at the time of perception or anytime thereafter. In Chapter 6, the authors examine the identifications of Clément Kayishema and Obed Ruzindana, both of whom were convicted of genocide at the ICTR.[30] The authors believe that the eyewitness evidence is compelling on the whole and do not suggest that either

[28] S. R. Gross and M. Shaffer, 'Exonerations in the United States, 1989–2012: Report by the National Registry of Exonerations', (2012) 1, The National Registry of Exonerations, available at www.law.umich.edu/special/exoneration/Documents/exonerations_us_1989_2012_full_report.pdf;A. M. Smith and B. L. Cutler, 'Introduction: Identification Procedures and Conviction of the Innocent', in B. L. Cutler (ed.) *Reform of Eyewitness Identification Procedures* (APA, 2013).

[29] Ibid.

[30] *ICTR Prosecutor* v. *Kayishema and Ruzindana*, judgment (21 May 1999).

Kayishema or Ruzindana is innocent of genocide; however, the case provides several opportunities to discuss the conditions under which identification accuracy is likely and provides a framework for discussion of several potential errors in memory. The authors begin their analysis by questioning the utility – or lack thereof – of in-dock identifications.[31] In further discussion of the case, they consider eyewitness and target characteristics including memory for in-group versus out-group persons, the age of the eyewitness, source misattributions and fatigue. They also consider event characteristics, such as stress and perpetrator visibility (e.g., lighting, distance and disguise), and how, under conditions of low visibility, expectancies may guide correct or incorrect recognition. They go on to consider the length of exposure and the delay between witnessing the event and remembering. Subsequently, they discuss the potential for post-event information to alter the eyewitness's memory of the perpetrator. In doing so, they examine the moderators, including age and attention, and the sources of post-event information, including additional eyewitnesses and interviewer suggestion. Finally, they conclude the chapter with a review of best-practice interviewing techniques.

Chapter 7, by Dionysios Demetis, examines a variety of IS influences on the prevention and detection of criminal behaviour. First, the chapter delineates the basic information principles that surround the technological manipulation of large datasets. These essentially constitute databases that are profiled, algorithmically manipulated and used in order to distil actionable information for preventing criminal behaviour. Basic principles of profiling and data mining are described, while implications that stem from the phenomenon of data growth are analysed. Data growth is important, as the central problem of using IS for preventing criminal activity is anchored on the mass of data that requires processing, manipulation, categorization and analysis. These processes construct the basis upon which different data types become computationally malleable and form the ground that gives rise to the power of algorithms. The complexity that emerges out of the interaction of technology with its socio-economic and political context becomes further deconstructed with the use of examples. The role of international-level IS influences is discussed through a brief analysis of Europol's information systems. Furthermore, the chapter focuses on the domain of *money laundering* in order to describe the impact technology has had on flagging suspicious

[31] Ibid., para. 457.

activity. As a result of this analysis, general themes in the organisation of technology and criminality are highlighted, while a theoretical framework is presented that deconstructs the most important dimensions in the profiling of suspicious behaviour with the aim of synthesizing these into a coherent structure.

Chapter 8, by Olaoluwa Olysanya, examines the dynamics of participation in mass violence through the perspective of the macro–micro integrated theoretical model (MMITM). Extreme forms of collective violence, such as genocide and crimes against humanity, involve organised and goal-directed one-sided acts of violence by members of an aggressor group against members of a targeted group in order to achieve specific objectives. Logic would dictate that variables such as group size, task type (e.g., committing murder or torture), group climate and group cohesion will have an impact on effectuating collective violence. The reality is that perpetrators of genocide and crimes against humanity, especially at the outset, represent a highly heterogeneous group with different beliefs, emotions and attitudes towards members of a targeted group. In essence: 'the good the bad and the ugly'. These three disparate subgroups, despite their differences, at some point in the course of destructive events, appear to work together to achieve a common criminal objective. From this perspective, it becomes important to recognise that collective violence involves associations between three distinct subgroups of individuals whose journey into collective violence can be traced back to disparate origins. How are these disparate groups of people brought together for the duration of a specific, time-limited criminal project? How do we evaluate the fit of each individual in terms of his or her likelihood of following each offending trajectory? How do we trace these distinct offending trajectories? And how is evil unknowingly perpetrated by the 'good', who clearly constitute the majority of perpetrators? These issues have been largely ignored by criminologists. Also, there is some doubt as to whether criminological theories that were originally designed to explain domestic crimes can be extended to explain organised and goal-directed large-scale acts of violence. The MMITM was developed to explain the latter category of crimes. Chapter 8 aims to demonstrate how the MMITM can help shed light on these complex issues.

Chapter 9, by the present author, discusses the theoretical as well as the practical application of anthropology and its methods in the field of international criminal justice. For far too long the prosecution of serious international crimes, particularly genocide and crimes against humanity, was undertaken without any research on the context or the culture of the actors involved. The work of the ICTR has shown that legal definitions and concepts are inconsistent with established knowledge in anthropology, the humanities and medical sciences. As a result, the construction of existing treaties by judges dealing with international crimes can only be achieved by reference to culture. However, given that culture is local, constituting a phenomenon which cannot be understood by outsiders without significant anthropological research, it is evident that international prosecutions of crimes require contextual analysis. The author offers numerous examples whereby the courts implicitly conceded the inadequacy of existing law or otherwise realised (or not, as the case may be) that the literal translation of words and sentences from one language to another fails to encapsulate or convey other shared meanings behind those words. It must become imperative for international tribunals to hire anthropologists knowledgeable in the cultures under investigation before any case reaches the bench.

Chapter 10, by Henrik Anckarsäter, Tova Bennet, Thomas Nilsson and Susanna Radovic, examines the perspective of neuroscience and psychiatry on international criminality. It is now firmly established that mental disorders – just as social disadvantages – have probabilistic relationships with crimes. Established risk factors for violent crimes include first, and most importantly, previous criminal behaviour of the individual, but also gender, age at onset, substance abuse, attention-deficit hyperactivity disorder (ADHD) and antisocial personality disorder. The current state of knowledge includes very few, if any, systematic studies of psychiatric factors on perpetrators of international crimes. International crimes differ from general violent criminality in several respects. They are more often performed in a social context of perpetrators rather than alone and are dependent on societal power structures. They would be thought to be more related to ideologies and thought content rather than driven by personal gain. This means that for forensic psychiatry the general importance of childhood-onset conduct disorder, substance abuse and ADHD or similar diagnoses of impulsivity will probably not be central in the context of international crime. Instead, disorders of social dynamics and thought content will come to the forefront.

The authors start by giving a brief presentation of the insanity defence in the context of the International Criminal Court (ICC), and then move on to discuss whether an insanity defence should be included in international law. They further discuss on what grounds a person should be acquitted due to insanity when it comes to mass atrocity crimes. In this context they especially focus on thought disorders. The classic disorder of thought content is paranoia. In autism spectrum disorders, thought content is also affected but in a different way. Generally, autism, like paranoia, is thought to decrease the possibility of successful social interaction, but may confer 'charisma' to individuals operating in strictly hierarchical organisations. The social disability in autism specifically hampers reciprocal interaction, but may not be evident in command interaction.

Chapter 11, by Jeffrey Stevenson Murer, explores the motivations for joining violent groups across a range of circumstances. In particular, the chapter explores the similarities in the role of violence as a marker of identity within groups as diverse as street gangs and ethnic communities. Frequently, membership in violent groups is explained in terms of individual material gain or the attainment of individual fame in very rationalist and individualistic terms. These violent encounters or employments of violence by young people are often defined as being interpersonal in nature; that is, the motivation to use or not use violence is held by a single individual, expressing individual agency in making a choice whether or not to deploy violence. This focus on individual choice and motivation has likewise been extended to studies of terrorism and rationalist interpretations for the motivation to participate in civil wars or other armed conflicts. Indeed, many of these studies treat joining these violent groups and the deployment of violent acts as being antisocial, as if the choice to engage in violence is one wholly against social norms or social values. However, much can be gained by seeing these groups in completely the opposite light: gangs, communal factions, militias, even terrorist organisations can be seen as highly social environments, especially for those who feel that they have limited opportunities for social capital accumulation or mobility within larger society, or indeed have even been expelled from a mainstream social mobility milieu altogether. Within such social milieus violence is but one form of social action among a whole range of social acts; or, to put it more succinctly, in such circumstances violence itself is a social act. Chapter 11 examines the performative qualities of violence and the role that violence plays in the experience of belonging in large groups and in collective identity formation.

Chapter 12, by Jo-Anne Wemmers and Amissi Manirabona, examines the victimology of war crimes. Despite the growing number of studies in victimology in recent years, relatively little attention has been paid to the development of classification systems in this field. Chapter 12 reviews existing typologies and points at their primary limitation, namely their narrow definition of victims. Increasingly, we have come to realise that crime not only impacts the individual who is the direct target of a crime but can also affect their family, friends and community. Moreover, following the creation of the ICC, which typically deals with mass victimisation such as war crimes, it is clear that classical models which focus on one victim fail to take into account the complexity of wartime victimisation and its effects. A typology of victims is proposed based on the victims' emotional or psychological proximity to the crime. The value of this typology is that it allows us to identify the different types of consequences which different categories of wartime victims may experience and, therefore, better identify their needs. Using this typology the authors address the needs of wartime victims with respect to reparation. The chapter closes with recommendations for reparation in the context of the ICC.

1

Criminological theory and international crimes: examining the potential

ANDY AITCHISON

Introduction

This chapter asks what criminological theory can add to scholarship in international criminal law. After initial interest in the first half of the twentieth century, criminological attention shifted away from the activities covered by an emerging international criminal law and it is not until the 1990s that a criminological scholarship of atrocity begins to develop in earnest. As criminology is a late arrival in a field already well covered by scholarship in law, history, political science, sociology and psychology, the exercise calls for humility and openness.[1] Criminology is no stranger to working in fields already populated by other disciplines and is characterised by its 'incessant raiding' of these,[2] and the resultant lack of 'autonomy' and outward looking attitudes have been put forward as a strength.[3] Beyond a respectful humility in the face of existing scholarship in the field, using criminological theory in relation to atrocity requires a degree of humility in the face of events. The assumptions and starting points of several strands of criminological theory are fundamentally challenged by the systematic and mass-participatory nature of many episodes of violence falling within the remit of international criminal law. In examining the 'canon', much is to be questioned, adapted or abandoned. Thus, criminologists should seek to retain the relatively open borders of the discipline, using resources already absorbed and developed where appropriate, but absorbing and developing new perspectives and knowledge through encounters with others. While

[1] On the disciplinary 'scattering' of knowledge, see A. Smeulers, 'Collective Violence and International Criminal Justice', in A. Smeulers (ed.) *Collective Violence and International Criminal Justice: An Interdisciplinary Approach* (Intersentia, 2010) 6.

[2] D. Garland, 'Of Crimes and Criminals: The Development of Criminology in Britain', in M. Maguire, R. Morgan and R. Reiner (eds.) *The Oxford Handbook of Criminology* (Oxford University Press, 1994) 26.

[3] D. Garland, 'Criminology's Place in the Academic Field', in M. Bosworth and C. Hoyle (eds.) *What is Criminology?* (Oxford University Press, 2011) 299.

recognising a longstanding gap in criminology, the chapter takes two prominent examples of criminologists working on crimes under international law to show the value of applying particular strands of theoretical criminology. Following this, the chapter explores three further strands from the 'back catalogue' of criminological theory that highlight further potential contributions to scholarship in the field of international criminal law and some of the challenges in realising these.

Although criminologists may be comfortable with relatively open boundaries, the willingness to absorb from other disciplines does not mean an uncritical acceptance of those disciplines' restrictions. A number of criminologists are wary of being tied too firmly to the borders set by a legal framework and seek to maintain a certain distance from what is characterised as a 'strictly' legal scholarship.[4] In relation to international criminal law this might be reflected in a more open terminology of mass or atrocity crimes as opposed to a strict adherence to studying only those acts covered by the 'core' crimes of international law,[5] or in an explicitly constructivist approach to understanding the origins and limitations of the dominant definitions of such crimes.[6] The chapter uses the terminology of atrocity crime to refer to large scale, systematic and collective acts of violence, but returns to examine the term as a dynamic category below. Before identifying the potential contribution of criminological theory in atrocity scholarship the chapter examines criminologists' late entry into the field.

Atrocity crimes: a criminological blind spot?

The gap in criminology where atrocity crimes might stand has long been noted. In 1970, Lopez-Rey wrote of criminological neglect of a range of crimes committed in official roles, identifying these as 'a form of

[4] For a discussion on the relationship between criminological and criminal law scholarship, see N. Lacey and L. Zedner, 'Legal Constructions of Crime', in M. Maguire, R. Morgan and R. Reiner (eds.) *The Oxford Handbook of Criminology* (5th edn, Oxford University Press, 2012).

[5] The terminology of atrocity law and atrocity crimes is introduced by diplomat and lawyer D. Scheffer in 'The Future of Atrocity Law', (2002) 32 *Suffolk Transnational Law Review* 389, and has been taken up by numerous criminologists. For example, developments in the European Society of Criminology include a dedicated issue of the society journal, S. Karstedt and S. Parmentier (eds.) *Atrocity Crimes and Transitional Justice* (2012) 9 special issue of *European Journal of Criminology*, and the recently established working group on Atrocity Crimes and Transitional Justice.

[6] A. Woolford, 'Making Genocide Unthinkable: Three Guidelines for a Critical Criminology of Genocide', (2006) 14 *Critical Criminology* 99.

Table 1.1: *Thomson-Reuters classification of journal articles, topic search 'Genocide' 1944–2012*

		Social Science		Criminology and Penology	
	All	N	%	N	%
1944–99	488	304	62.3	74	15.2
2000–12	1162	848	73.0	154	13.3

Note: The data are derived by using 'refine' tools to narrow down all results to articles, and then to the subject categories as defined by *Web of Knowledge*. To maintain consistency, a further process of manual sifting was conducted on records from after 2003 when the database starts to pick up edited books.

organised crime'.[7] More recently, alongside an increased willingness to examine crimes committed under the auspices of the state,[8] a number of authors have noted the marginal position of war crimes and genocide within the field of criminology. Some actively seek to address this using criminological tools or frameworks to understand the processes behind atrocities.[9] Others have a more general concern with the health of the discipline,[10] or with its capacity to reflect crime as enacted and experienced across large parts of the world.[11] To illustrate the gap, the following section examines criminological engagement with genocide, using a database of published work.

Table 1.1 summarises two periods of articles on the topic of genocide derived from the Thomson-Reuters Web of Knowledge database. The first, 1944–1999, covers the period from Raphael Lemkin's coining

7 M. Lopez-Rey, *Crime: An Analytical Approach* (Routledge and Kegan Paul, 1970) at 39–40.

8 R. Coleman, J. Sim, S. Tombs and D. Whyte (eds.), *State, Power, Crime* (Sage, 2009).

9 A. Alvarez, *Governments, Citizens, and Genocide: A Comparative and Interdisciplinary Approach* (Indiana University Press, 2001); D. Maier-Katkin, D. Mears and T. Bernard, 'Towards a Criminology of Crimes against Humanity', (2009) 13 *Theoretical Criminology* 227; S. Tanner and M. Mulone, 'Private Security and Armed Conflict', (2013) 53 *British Journal of Criminology* 41.

10 I. Clegg and J. Whetton, 'In Search of a Third World Criminology', in L. Noaks, M. Levi and M. Maguire (eds.), *Contemporary Issues in Criminology* (University of Wales Press, 1995); Garland, above note 3.

11 K. Aas, 'The Earth is One but the World is Not: Criminological Theory and its Geopolitical Divisions', (2012) 16 *Theoretical Criminology* 12; M. Eisner, 'The Uses of Violence: An Examination of Some Cross Cutting Issues', (2009) 3 *International Journal of Conflict and Violence* 42.

Table 1.2: *Manual categorisation of 'Criminology and Penology' articles 1944–2012*

	1944–1999		2000–2012	
Journal grouping	N	%	N	%
Psych-sciences	20	27.0	34	22.1
Medical (excluding psych)	23	31.1	33	21.4
Criminology	2	2.7	23	14.9
Genocide and Holocaust studies	5	6.8	12	7.8
General cross-disciplinary	2	2.7	10	6.5
Sciences – general, cross-disciplinary, other	4	5.4	8	5.2
Development	5	6.8	1	0.6
Others	13	17.6	33	21.4

of the term 'genocide' to the end of the twentieth century. The second covers the current century as far as 2012. It is notable that there is a general growth of criminological, social science and general scholarship on genocide identified by the database, shifting, for example, from an average of just over one criminological or penological article a year in the twentieth century to thirteen per year at the start of the twenty-first. Table 1.1 also shows a consistent share of genocide scholarship classed as criminological, accounting for roughly one in seven of the published articles. However, a further analysis of the output classed as 'criminology and penology' shows the diversity of such material.

Table 1.2 shows that within those articles classed as criminology and penology a consistently large group is published in journals where the primary disciplinary affiliation is to medicine, including public health, as well as psychology and psychiatry. Across the two periods these papers account for 58 and 44 per cent of output respectively. Those in named criminology journals account for only two papers from 1944 to 1999 and appear in the final two years of the period, after the establishment of ad hoc tribunals for international crimes in the former Yugoslavia and Rwanda.[12] By the second period, papers appearing in criminology journals account for roughly one in seven of the total, covering ten journals

[12] A. Brannigan, 'Criminology and the Holocaust: Xenophobia, Evolution, and Genocide', (1998) 44 *Crime & Delinquency*; C. Cunneen, 'Criminology, Genocide and the Forced Removal of Indigenous Children from their Families', (1999) 32 *Australia and New Zealand Journal of Criminology* 124.

and a number of special issues.[13] This suggests that criminology, through certain disciplinary forums, is making a greater contribution to the study of genocide as an example of atrocity crime.

Finally, using web-searches, a study of the institutional affiliations[14] of the first named authors of the papers identified by Thomson-Reuters as 'Criminology and Penology' in the period 2000 to 2012 shows a range of disciplinary backgrounds. Affiliations were identified for 149 of 154 first-named authors. Of these, sixteen (11 per cent) had a named affiliation to criminology or criminal justice.[15] Medicine and psychology continue to be the main contributors, accounting for 42 per cent of first authors (n=63), with a further five authors indicating a cross-disciplinary affiliation including medicine or psychology. This brief examination of one set of published sources shows that while criminology has been relatively slow to include genocide as a mainstream disciplinary concern, work is taking place to close the resulting gap. It is also evident that, beyond named criminology journals, the broader 'criminological' output remains characteristically transdisciplinary, drawing on contributions from a range of institutional and intellectual sources. It is worth reflecting on the historical gap in criminology, as it may suggest limitations in and challenges to a criminological approach to international crimes.

Explaining criminology's absence

Alvarez lists a number of explanations for criminological neglect of genocide, including the sheer magnitude of the crimes.[16] Arguably, none of these is insurmountable. Mannheim is clear that while the Holocaust is rightly analysed as a part of world history, the 'size and numbers' do not alter the fact that there is a criminological and legal dimension to the events,[17] and, while Neubacher identifies a reluctance to treat mass

[13] The journals are *Archiv für Kriminologie*; *Australian and New Zealand Journal of Criminology*; *British Journal of Criminology*; *Crime, Law and Social Change*; *Criminology*; *Déviance et Société*; *European Journal of Criminology*; *Homicide Studies*; *Monatsschrift für Kriminologie und Strafrechtsreform*; and *Theoretical Criminology*.

[14] As indicated first and foremost by a named position (chair, lectureship), or secondly by department name as indicated on the published output or online.

[15] Criminology (10), criminal justice (2), criminology and criminal justice (2), sociology and criminal justice (1), law and criminology (1).

[16] Alvarez, above note 9, at 4–7.

[17] H. Mannheim, *Comparative Criminology*, Vol. 2 (Routledge and Kegan Paul, 1965) at 564.

crimes in the same category as ordinary crimes,[18] such categorisation is not an inevitable consequence of engaging with criminological theory. Here I focus on three particular concerns: parochialism; the relationship between criminology and the state; and an emphasis on analysing individuals and their pathologies.

While much criminological research may be restricted to developing explanatory frameworks for crime and deviance in one jurisdiction, Rafter identifies international collaboration and correspondence in the early days of the discipline.[19] International networks are now facilitated and institutionalised through conferences, exchanges and funding arrangements. Nonetheless, a specific sense of parochialism continues to pervade the literature appealing for a more serious criminological engagement with international crimes. Aas captures this, drawing on Morrison, pointing to a failure of 'territorial imagination' in a discipline limiting itself to 'pacified domestic spaces'.[20] In one sense, this is explicable in terms of the practical difficulties of conducting research in an insecure environment as opposed to limits to the criminological imagination, but John Hagan and colleagues have shown that criminologists can contribute to effective documentation and analysis of mass violence through careful survey and interview work with victims.[21] The practicalities of empirical research aside, Aas identifies a sense of theoretical disinterest in contexts which are 'not like us'.[22] There are sound methodological reasons for limiting comparisons to countries with a limited range and extent of differences, but there may be further theoretical reasons why criminologists have been reluctant to venture into less civilised or pacified spaces.[23] If atrocity crimes take place in uncivilised or unpacified spaces, then criminology may be rendered irrelevant by the absence of the kind of rules and structures from which the discipline

[18] F. Neubacher, 'How Can it Happen that Horrendous State Crimes are Perpetrated? An Overview of Criminological Theories?', (2006) 4 *Journal of International Criminal Justice* 787.

[19] N. Rafter, 'Origins of Criminology', in M. Bosworth and C. Hoyle (eds.) *What is Criminology?* (Oxford University Press, 2011) at 145–6.

[20] Aas, above note 11, at 12.

[21] For example, J. Hagan, 'Prosecuting Ethnic Cleansing and Mass Atrocity in the former Yugoslavia and Darfur', (2009) 10 *Journal of Scandinavian Studies in Criminology and Crime Prevention* 26; J. Hagan, W. Rymond-Richmond and P. Parker, 'The Criminology of Genocide: The Death and Rape of Darfur', (2005) 43 *Criminology* 525.

[22] Aas, above note 11, at 9.

[23] T. Landman, *Issues and Methods in Comparative Politics: An Introduction* (2nd edn, Routledge, 2003).

draws some of its coherence. Yet, atrocity crimes are made possible by features of pacification, including the concentration of force and by cooperation predicated on social rules and structures. Elias examines elements of a breakdown of pacification in Weimar Germany, but not a total breakdown.[24] Were it so, the Nazi capture and development of the state apparatus that was essential to their projects of extermination would not have been possible. Equally, as Nazi power extended eastwards it encountered not only military resistance but also a large, unarmed and vulnerable civilian population, characteristic of pacified space.

States are clearly implicated in atrocity crime, but the extent to which this is problematic for criminological theory given posited relationships between criminology and the state is questionable.[25] As Bosworth and Hoyle note, the relationship between criminology and the state varies historically and geographically and is neither fixed nor inevitable.[26] Even the milder critique that positivist criminological perspectives are limited by their reliance on state definitions of crime leaves a wide space for criminological endeavours given the development of international law based on state practice and consensus and codified in international instruments.[27] Moreover, the framework of state crime provided by Green and Ward gives a tight definition based on objective measures for state crime, but opens a wider concept of deviance for investigation without strict reliance on codified rules.[28] Their concept of deviance combines a wider sense of *perceived* illegitimacy, which can be defined from above or below, with social disapproval indicated through pejorative labelling and actors' awareness of the sanctionability of the conduct.[29]

While the state is the prime suspect in atrocity crime, the individual is identified as the focal point of much criminological theory and

[24] N. Elias, *The Germans: Power Struggles and the Development of Habitus in the 19th and 20th Centuries* (Columbia University Press, 1996).

[25] C. Sumner, 'Crime, Justice and Underdevelopment: Beyond Modernisation Theory', in C. Sumner (ed.), *Crime, Justice and Underdevelopment* (Heinemann, 1982) at 28; Garland, above note 2, at 31 ff.

[26] M. Bosworth and C. Hoyle, 'What is Criminology? An Introduction', in M. Bosworth and C. Hoyle (eds.), *What is Criminology?* (Oxford University Press, 2011) at 2.

[27] C. Cunneen, 'Postcolonial Perspectives on Criminology', in M. Bosworth and C. Hoyle (eds.), *What is Criminology?* (Oxford University Press, 2011) at 253.

[28] P. Green and T. Ward, 'State Crime, Human Rights, and the Limits of Criminology', (2000) 27 *Social Justice* 110.

[29] Ibid., at 105 and 109. The potentially relevant audiences for legitimacy are also internal and external, see ibid., at 110.

methods.[30] This individualism sits uncomfortably with crimes characterised as systematic and based on widespread or mass participation and complicity. However, to work back analytically to the individual level need not involve dismissing structures as part of a rounded explanation (see below on Van Baar and Huisman's multi-level analysis of Topf and Sons). Nonetheless, criminology has focused heavily on deviance and so crimes of mass participation in which perpetrators are not criminalised within their most immediate social setting represent something of a challenge.[31] As institutions of human rights and international criminal law become a more established feature of global governance, associated behavioural norms may become more forceful and more conventional criminological analyses may become more useful. Criminology is far from homogenous, as befits a discipline which owes much of its origins and structuring features to other disciplines. As such, the challenges identified above are not absolute obstacles and the path dependency observed elsewhere can be broken.[32]

While there is a historical criminological gap, it is not a complete absence. As far back as Durkheim – often among the first social theorists introduced to criminology students – questions of war and deviance have been analysed. In his analysis of German conduct in the war of 1914–1918, Durkheim considers the 'aggressive temper ... contempt of international laws ... systematic savagery ... and deliberate cruelties' of Germany.[33] He concludes that a unified state is able to overcome the heterogeneity of civil society, gathering human forces and directing them towards a supreme end.[34] Following on from Durkheim, leading criminologists in Britain and the USA turned their attention to war.[35] Mannheim shows a clear awareness of the dangers of moving from a focus on the individual to dealing with groups and societies but nonetheless is able to proceed to examine the criminological toolkit in

[30] B. Bowling, 'Transnational Criminology and the Globalization of Harm Production', in M. Bosworth and C. Hoyle (eds.), *What is Criminology?* (Oxford University Press, 2011) at 373.

[31] Neubacher, above note 18, at 788–9.

[32] Maier-Katkin, Mears and Bernard, above note 9, at 230.

[33] E. Durkheim, *Germany above All: German Mentality and War* (Librairie Armand Colin, 1915) at 3.

[34] Ibid., at 34 and 45.

[35] S. Glueck, *War Criminals: Their Prosecution and Punishment* (Alfred A. Knopf, 1944); H. Mannheim, *War and Crime* (Watts and Co, 1941); on Radzinowicz, see Maier-Katkin, Mears and Bernard, above note 9.

order to attempt to explain the aggressive actions of Germany.[36] Glueck, although widely recognised as a pioneering criminologist focusing on the use of empirical research to study juvenile delinquency,[37] also wrote in his capacity as a member of the Commission on Trial and Punishment of War Criminals. While Mannheim closes with a consideration of what to do to rehabilitate deviant states,[38] Glueck comes closer to the concerns of international criminal law, focusing on the challenge of dealing with individuals at a range of levels of authority.[39]

The emerging criminology of atrocity

The earliest criminological studies were neglected for some time, perhaps because they were unable to show any decisive value in criminological analysis in the emerging field of international criminal law. It is notable that even today, while these are often identified as early criminological forays into the field of international crimes, they are rarely cited in support of the development of particular theories or analytical frameworks.[40] Rather, the recent criminological work on international crimes adapts a range of criminological scholarship to make sense of crimes that go far beyond the more 'ordinary' concerns of the discipline. The following section illustrates this by way of two prominent examples.

John Hagan: process and structure in Sudan

One of the most prolific writers on the criminology of atrocity is John Hagan. His independent scholarship and collaboration with a number of co-authors appear in explicitly criminological publications,[41] but also in

[36] Mannheim, above note 35, at 23 and 26.

[37] A good overview of his collaborative work with his wife can be found in S. Glueck and E. Glueck, *Ventures in Criminology* (Tavistock, 1964).

[38] Mannheim, above note 35, at 196 ff.

[39] Glueck and Glueck, above note 37, at 171 ff.

[40] J. Hagan and S. Greer, 'Making War Criminal', (2002) 40 *Criminology* 231.

[41] J. Hagan, 'The Unaccountable Genocide: A Case Study of the US State Department and US Accountability Office in Calculating the Darfur Death Toll', in A. Smeulers and R. Haveman (eds.), *Supranational Criminology: Towards a Criminology of International Crimes* (Intersentia, 2008); Hagan, above note 21; J. Hagan, J. Kaiser, D. Rothenberg, A. Hanson and P. Parker, 'Atrocity Victimization and the Costs of Economic Crimes in the Battle for Baghdad and Iraq', (2012) 9 *European Journal of Criminology* 481; Hagan, Rymond-Richmond and Parker, above note 21.

journals in the field of socio-legal studies,[42] public health,[43] sociology and the more general social sciences.[44] Hagan's chair is in law and sociology, rather than criminology, but his ability to work with, and speak to, a range of scholars united in their concern with international crimes and international criminal justice make him an exemplar of the kind of cross-disciplinary criminological scholarship identified in the introduction to this chapter. Before his work on atrocity crimes he was already keen to prevent the negative effects of creating criminology as a separate, 'fully autonomous discipline',[45] and he continues to push for the synthesis of different approaches to inquiry.[46] His work encompasses those criminological endeavours that seek to delimit, describe and explain the phenomenon of crime and those which seek to scrutinise the institutions and acts of criminal justice in their social settings.[47] The following section will engage with a subsection of Hagan's body of work to identify the theoretical contributions that he and his colleagues have made to scholarship in international criminal law.[48]

[42] J. Hagan, R. Brooks and T. Haugh, 'Reasonable Grounds Evidence Involving Sexual Violence in Darfur', (2010) 35 *Law and Social Inquiry* 881; S. Kutnjak-Ivković and J. Hagan, 'The Politics of Punishment and the Siege of Sarajevo: Toward a Conflict Theory of Perceived International (In)justice', (2006) 40 *Law and Society Review* 369.

[43] J. Hagan, W. Rymond-Richmond and A. Palloni, 'Racial Targeting of Sexual Violence in Darfur', (2009) 99 *American Journal of Public Health* 1386.

[44] J. Hagan and J. Kaiser, 'The Displaced and Dispossessed of Darfur: Explaining the Sources of a Continuing State-led Genocide', (2011) 62 *British Journal of Sociology* 1; J. Hagan and S. Kutnjak-Ivković, 'War Crimes, Democracy and the Rule of Law in Belgrade, The former Yugoslavia and Beyond', (2006) 605 *Annals of the American Academy of Political and Social Science* 125; J. Hagan and R. Levi, 'Crimes of War and the Force of Law', (2005) 83 *Social Forces* 1499; J. Hagan and R. Levi, 'Justiciability as Field Effect: When Sociology Meets Human Rights', (2007) 22 *Sociological Forum* 372; J. Hagan and W. Rymond-Richmond, 'The Collective Dynamics of Racial Dehumanization and Genocidal Victimization in Darfur', (2008) 73 *American Sociological Review* 875; J. Hagan, H. Schoenfeld and A. Palloni, 'The Science of Human Rights, War Crimes and Humanitarian Emergencies', (2006) 32 *Annual Review of Sociology* 329.

[45] J. Hagan, *Structural Criminology* (Polity, 1988) at 257.

[46] Hagan, Schoenfeld and Palloni, above note 44, at 329.

[47] The former is developed in an analysis of Darfur (e.g., Hagan, Rymond-Richmond and Parker, above note 21); the latter focuses on the International Criminal Tribunal for the former Yugoslavia (e.g., Kutnjak-Ivković and Hagan, above note 42) and is not included here. Current work focuses on Iraq (Hagan, Kaiser, Rothenberg, Hanson and Parker, above note 41) and again, is not examined here.

[48] The focus on Hagan and others' contributions in terms of theory will not dwell on the considerable volume of material on the development of specific methodological innovations as criminological and social research methods are handled separately. See Chapter 2 of this book.

A large part of Hagan's collaborative work on Darfur has been dedicated to describing the nature of events in the region, building up a rich picture of the joint attacks on black, African Sudanese[49] settlements in Darfur by Sudanese government forces and *Janjaweed* militia, including racially denigrating language, killings, rape and sexual violence and the destruction of homes, livestock and water sources.[50] While this descriptive endeavour provides material for explanatory theory, it also serves to develop a correction to a limited understanding of genocide, which focuses primarily on killing.[51] Hagan and Kaiser identify, in the case of Darfur, a range of activities which contribute to creating conditions of life calculated to contribute towards destruction of particular groups of Darfuris, and point to Lemkin's development of the concept of genocide in support of this. This wider concern with conditions of life, as much as direct acts of violence, is evident in Lemkin's earliest work around the 1933 International Conference for the Unification of Criminal Law in Madrid, when he proposed a new international crime of barbarity, which included action against the economic existence of members of a collective motivated by hatred or intended to exterminate that collective,[52] and survives in the language of the Genocide Convention of 1948.[53] In the intervening years these elements of the as yet unnamed crime of genocide were recognised at the highest level in the emerging institutions of the then international community. At the end of 1935, James McDonald, League of Nations' High Commissioner for Refugees, protested against an ever more intensive set of legislative, administrative and party actions against German Jews, describing the 'catastrophic development of conditions' as an ostracism from social relations with other Germans, and through exclusion, 'a systematic attempt at starvation'.[54] A more comprehensive legal and criminological definition of genocide as a

[49] For a full account of the complexities of Sudanese and Darfuri identity, see A. Madibbo, 'Conflict and the Conceptions of Identities in the Sudan', (2012) 60 *Current Sociology* 302.

[50] Hagan and Kaiser, above note 44, at 18; J. Hagan and W. Rymond-Richmond, 'The Mean Streets of the Global Village: Crimes of Exclusion in the United States and Darfur', (2007) 8 *Journal of Scandinavian Studies in Criminology and Crime Prevention* 62.

[51] Hagan and Kaiser, above note 44, at 3.

[52] R. Lemkin, 'Genocide as a Crime under International Law', (1947) 41 *American Journal of International Law* 146.

[53] Article 2(c) includes, among the acts intended to partially or wholly destroy a protected group, inflicting 'conditions of life calculated to bring about its physical destruction'.

[54] E. Stowell, 'Intercession against the Persecution of Jews', (1936) 30 *American Journal of International Law* 102.

composite crime that is pursued through a range of strategies is important for explanatory theory accounting for genocide in terms of unfolding processes. Where international political factors are permissive, this presents openings for earlier preventive action, but also suggests avenues for prosecution in which evidence may be less contested and controversial.[55]

Hagan and his colleagues have observed strong correlations between the use of racial epithets and the most excessive forms of physical and sexual violence and resultant displacement of populations in combined Sudanese military and *Janjaweed* paramilitary attacks on Darfuri settlements.[56] Hagan identifies the role of dehumanisation in facilitating group-based violence, highlighting parallels with Nazi developments of existing anti-Semitic tropes, anti-Tutsi discourse in Rwanda and the use of discriminatory terminology by Serb authorities in different parts of the former Yugoslavia. Mann is correct in noting that while the language is consistently degrading and denigrating, marking out groups for exclusion, it is not necessarily dehumanising and dehumanisation is not a necessary condition of genocide.[57] The language used is important to Hagan as a sign of both motivation (hatred) and intent (extermination), but also as part of explaining the destructive impact of the attacks. He draws on Katz to show the role of curses and denigrations in providing the attacker with a sense of righteousness and shows how they serve to exclude black Darfuris from Sudanese society and, in Fein's terms, the universe of normative protection.[58]

One reading of Katz's work in *The Seductions of Crime* suggests some limits to its translation of mass atrocities. His work on homicide suggests a relatively arbitrary link between the putative perpetrator's project or purpose and the ultimate outcome in a given situation. His analysis of processes whereby 'righteous rage' is developed and a

[55] On this and its relation to case law surrounding massacres and displacements in the Srebrenica area of Bosnia and Herzegovina, see Hagan and Kaiser, above note 44, at 3. While the facts of displacement may be less open to contestation on account of the immediate evidence of refugees and internally displaced people, the interpretation of such facts as evidence of genocide is open to challenge.

[56] Hagan, Brooks and Haugh, above note 42, at 909; Hagan and Kaiser, above note 44, at 15, and reiterated in J. Hagan and J. Kaiser, 'Forms of Genocidal Destruction: A Response to Commentators', (2011) 62 *British Journal of Sociology* 63; Hagan, Rymond-Richmond and Palloni, above note 43, at 1390.

[57] M. Mann, 'Processes of Murderous Cleansing/Genocide: Comment on Hagan and Kaiser', (2011) 62 *British Journal of Sociology* 44.

[58] Hagan and Rymond-Richmond, above note 44, at 876–7.

victim is marked out is part of an analysis of the actions of non-predatory assailants.[59] Transposing this onto a systematic attack with a pre-defined victim group is not straightforward. Here, the righteous anger is built into a longer time frame. Collins presents an alternative analysis of the emotional dimension of participation in mass atrocity, starting from an assumption that most attempts at violence are abortive, inaccurate or incompetent and are frequently accompanied by bluster and gesture.[60] Collins identifies several 'pathways' to violence. Among the most common is to attack the weak, where weakness is understood as both a situational as well as a structural factor.[61] This has been taken up in an analysis of the massacre and mass expulsion from Srebrenica in which bluster and bluff were instrumental to perpetrator group solidarity, emotional momentum and dominance, while rendering victims passive, subordinate and vulnerable.[62] Some of the immediate interactions in Collins' and Klusemann's micro-level situational analysis of unfolding processes of violence demonstrate perpetrators drawing on an image of victims in line with longer term processes of subordination, marginalisation and exclusion. This interaction between the immediate micro-level and societal macro-level is recognised in Hagan and Rymond-Richmond's work on Darfur.[63] In the case of Darfur, these unite a top-down Arab-supremacist ideology pursued by the central state with the bottom-up concentration of pejorative racial epithets.[64] This fits with Hagan's longstanding project of developing a sociological, structural criminology with a focus on power relations and looking at the role of individual and corporate actors in generating domination.[65]

59 J. Katz, *The Seductions of Crime* (Basic Books, 1988) at 17–18.

60 R. Collins, 'Micro and macro Theories of Violence', (2009) 3 *International Journal of Conflict and Violence* 9, at 10–11; on firearms and posturing, as opposed to killing, see also D. Grossman, *On Killing: the Psychological Cost of Learning to Kill in War and Society* (Little, Brown and Company, 1995) 9, at 17 ff.

61 Collins, above note 60, at 11.

62 S. Klusemann, 'Massacres as Process: A Micro-sociological Theory of Internal Patterns of Mass Atrocities', (2012) 9 *European Journal of Criminology* 468, at 469–70.

63 Hagan and Rymond-Richmond, above note 44, at 878.

64 Although the use of racial epithets and derogatory language may accompany action against atrocity. For examples in relation to anti-Semitism among Polish rescuers, see N. Tec, 'Polish Anti-Semitism and the Rescuing of Jews', (1986) 20 *East European Quarterly* 305 ff.

The macro-level analysis points towards the development of exclusion and is present in dimensions of Hagan's work which point back to processes of Arabisation and exclusion of black Africans in the Sudanese state since the 1980s.[66] This is characteristic of the development of a polarised plural society with ever more entrenched cleavages,[67] and, in Fein's terminology points to the increasing exclusion of black Darfuris from 'the universe of obligation of the dominant group'.[68] Further features come into Hagan's analysis of the longer term structural features behind genocide in Darfur, including historical constructions of a local elite during Anglo-Egyptian colonisation;[69] regional politics and Libya's armament of Arab herders at the height of Gaddafi's pan-Arabist policies;[70] the internal politics of Sudan, the 1989 coup and a shift towards more forceful authoritarianism;[71] and pressures on land and water resources arising from a combination of environmental and political factors.[72] Given Hagan's interests in a structural criminology, there is more that can be added here. Alongside his call for greater attention to the 'structural and systemic sources of conflict and violence', Krever provides a re-analysis of the Yugoslav conflicts of the 1990s.[73] At the crux of his account is the austerity and declining living standards which followed on from International Monetary Fund-led restructuring and economic liberalisation. The pace of these changes fuelled republican nationalism and undermined minority rights while occurring in a time frame that left little opportunity for cross-republic political organisation. The analysis does not discount the role and responsibility of particular actors within Yugoslavia, but highlights the way in which international institutions 'profoundly shape' and are

[65] Hagan, above note 45, at 2, 9.

[66] On exclusion from defence forces, Hagan and Kaiser, above note 44, at 5; on the presentation of a threat from black Darfuris, Hagan and Rymond-Richmond, above note 50, at 65; on denigration of black African culture and on Arabisation of the civil service, Hagan and Rymond-Richmond, above note 44, at 880–1.

[67] One of Kuper's conditions conducive to genocide, see L. Kuper, *Genocide: Its Political Use in the Twentieth Century* (Yale University Press, 1981) at 187 ff.

[68] H. Fein, 'Genocide: A Sociological Perspective', (1990) 38 *Current Sociology* 34.

[69] Hagan and Kaiser, above note 44, at 4.

[70] Hagan and Rymond-Richmond, above note 44, at 881.

[71] Ibid. The relative lack of limits on non-democratic governments is identified as a facilitating factor by H. Fein, 'Accounting for Genocide after 1945: Theories and Some Findings', (1993) 1 *International Journal on Minority Group Rights* 98.

[72] Hagan and Kaiser, above note 44, at 5.

[73] T. Krever, 'International Criminal Law: An Ideology Critique', (2013) 26 *Leiden Journal of International Law* 702.

'centrally implicated' in a situation of increased 'inflammability of social relations'.[74]

In the context of Sudan, Verhoeven's analysis implicates colonial and post-colonial structures designed to exploit the country's agricultural potential.[75] While Verhoeven is writing with the intention of recapturing a sense of human agency in accounts of the conflict, he gives a rich account of some of the structural factors that complement Hagan's work on Darfur. His work is an effort to connect 'local, national and global political economy, power struggles and discursive hegemonies'.[76] From Anglo-Egyptian exploitation of cotton fields, supported by tariffs to protect British manufacturing, through the Second World War and subsequent attempts to benefit from food prices, Sudan has developed agricultural policies that leave the country dependent on its position in a global market, on foreign investment and which have favoured riverain and urban elites.[77] In concert with Abdul-Jalil and Unruh's historical account of changes in law and governance in relation to land in Darfur, Verhoeven's work adds flesh to one of the strands of Hagan and his colleagues' already rich analysis.[78] This shows that when allied with area studies and scholarship from those areas in which atrocity crimes take place a structural criminology can build a more comprehensive account incorporating agency alongside international political economy and international and domestic politics.

[74] Ibid., at 715–17. The complex political structure of the former Yugoslavia means that there is no quick way to sum up the political context of republics, autonomous provinces and, cutting across these, nationalities and peoples. Clearly, cross-republic political organisation was possible and is evident in Serb moves to secede from Croatia upon its independence, similar efforts in Bosnia and Herzegovina, and Croat secessionist moves in Bosnia and Herzegovina. For a background to the local political structure and republican powers, particularly after the 1974 constitution, see D. Jović, *Yugoslavia: A State that Withered Away* (Purdue University Press, 2009), especially chapters 2 and 3, and for a discussion on categories of identity, see T. Bringa, *Being Muslim the Bosnian Way: Identity and Community in a Central Bosnian Village* (Princeton University Press, 1995) at 21–2 and 25–6.

[75] H. Verhoeven, 'Climate Change, Conflict and Development in Sudan: Global Neo-Malthusianism Narratives and Local Power Struggles', (2011) 42 *Development and Change* 679.

[76] Ibid., at 684. [77] Ibid., at 686 ff.

[78] M. Abdul-Jalil and J. Unruh, 'Land Rights under Stress in Darfur: A Volatile Dynamic of the Conflict', (2013) 32 *War and Society* 156. This account suggests a complex relationship between *Janjaweed* militia and Sudanese government forces, where the latter accompany the former to ensure that the government's military objectives are met, rather than simply the land seizure attributed to the former, see 157.

Strain, association and rationality in Nazi Germany

The work of Wim Huisman, again in collaboration with others, shows recent developments in criminology, which identify the value of bringing together broad analytic frameworks from social science with specific criminological theories.[79] In Huisman's work these are applied to explain the contribution of commercial actors in episodes of mass atrocity and international crimes. This makes a contribution to an existing strand of historical analysis of the Holocaust which seeks to avoid reductionism[80] by developing accounts of the conditions and interests most relevant to specific categories of actors including doctors,[81] bureaucrats[82] and industrialists.[83] Huisman's work builds on his scholarship in the field of organisational crime and focuses on the role of commercial enterprise in international crimes in Iraq and Sierra Leone[84] and Nazi-controlled Europe,[85] as well as providing a wider overview of the relationship between commercial actors and international crimes.[86]

In examining the contribution of Topf and Sons, producer of crematoria and other equipment for Nazi concentration and extermination camps, Van Baar and Huisman adopt three levels of analysis: the individual at the micro-level, the organisation at the meso-level and the state and political economy at the macro-level.[87] They do not include – and may have good reasons for not doing so – the international level incorporated elsewhere, which can also include a political economy

[79] W. Huisman, 'Corporations and International Crimes', in A. Smeulers and R. Haveman (eds.), *Supranational Criminology: Towards a Criminology of International Crimes* (Intersentia, 2008); W. Huisman, *Business as Usual* (Eleven International Publishing, 2010); W. Huisman and E. van Sliedregt, 'Rogue Traders: Dutch Businessmen, International Crimes and Corporate Complicity', (2010) 8 *Journal of International Criminal Justice* 803; A. van Baar and W. Huisman, 'The Oven Builders of the Holocaust: A Case Study of Corporate Complicity in International Crimes', (2012) 52 *British Journal of Criminology* 1033.

[80] D. Bloxham, 'Organized Mass Murder: Structure, Participation and Motivation in Comparative Perspective', (2008) 22 *Holocaust and Genocide Studies* 204.

[81] C. Browning, 'Genocide and Public Health: German Doctors and Polish Jews, 1939–41', (1988) 3 *Holocaust and Genocide Studies* 21.

[82] C. Browning, *The Path to Genocide* (Cambridge University Press: 1992) at 125 ff. Also, Bloxham, above note 80.

[83] Various contributions in G. Feldman and W. Seibel (eds.), *Networks of Nazi Persecution: Bureaucracy, Business and the Organization of the Holocaust* (Berghahn, 2005).

[84] Huisman and van Sliedregt, above note 79.

[85] Van Baar and Huisman, above note 79.

[86] Huisman, *Business as Usual*, above note 79.

[87] Van Baar and Huisman, above note 79, at 1036.

dimension.[88] While these four levels may serve useful purposes for analysis, they should not be taken as hard empirical dividing lines or strict hierarchies. Organisations found at the meso-level of analysis do not simply sit beneath states, but are increasingly likely to operate in an international environment and are as likely to act upon states as they are to be acted upon by them.[89] Within this framework, Van Baar and Huisman draw on strain theory, differential association and criminological interpretations of rational choice theory to populate a matrix composed of the three levels of analysis and three explanatory dimensions: motivation, opportunity and control.[90]

While Van Baar and Huisman are not as explicit in mapping their subsequent analysis into this matrix as were Kramer, Michalowski and Kauzlarich in their discussion of state-corporate crime, from which the framework is derived,[91] a reading of the case study of Topf and Sons does suggest that certain cells can usefully be populated to illustrate the value of particular theoretical strands in criminology (see Table 1.3). These are necessary to establish how apparently otherwise law-abiding, 'ordinary' engineers and businessmen come to breach a moral code which is reflected not only in prohibitions and inhibitions around murder, but

[88] See, e.g., D. Rothe and C. Mullins, 'Genocide, War Crimes and Crimes against Humanity in Central Africa: A Criminological Explanation', in A. Smeulers and R. Haveman (eds.), *Supranational Criminology: Towards a Criminology of International Crimes* (Intersentia, 2008) 137 ff. A discussion below of Durkheimian perspectives considers the level of global society in more detail. In the case of van Baar and Huisman, above note 79, they are analysing a relatively autarchic state, and so the international level may be less relevant for that reason too.

[89] As evident in Huisman and van Sliedregt, above note 79.

[90] Strain theory proposes a range of reactions to a disjuncture between culturally defined goals and the capacity to achieve these through permissible means. Of particular interest to criminologists are 'innovation', where alternative means to socially valued goals are sought, and 'rebellion', involving a rejection and replacement of means and goals. See R. Merton, 'Social Structure and Anomie', (1938) 3 *American Sociological Review* 672. Differential association seeks to account for behaviours learned through regular contact with different groups. See E. Sutherland, 'White Collar Criminality', (1940) 5 *American Sociological Review* 1, for his hypothesis on learning through association in professional environments. For an early example of the renaissance of rational choice theory in criminology, see R. Clarke and D. Cornish, 'Modelling Offenders' Decisions: A Framework for Research and Policy', in T. Michael and N. Morris (eds.), *Crime and Justice: An Annual Review of Research*, Vol. 6 (University of Chicago Press, 1985) at 147 ff.

[91] R. Kramer, R. Michalowski and D. Kauzlarich, 'The Origins and Development of the Concept and Theory of State-corporate Crime', (2002) 48 *Crime and Delinquency* 274, table 1.

Table 1.3: *Plotting Van Baar and Huisman's criminological analysis of Topf and Sons*

	A Motivation	B Opportunity	C Control
1 Individual, micro	Engineers: innovation, pride in work; owners: survival of family enterprise.	Party membership supports commercial opportunities; head engineer's personal connections with the SS.	
2 Enterprise, meso	Organisational culture favouring innovation.	Business with SS; access to resources.	Social transmission of norms relating to technical rather than moral responsibility.
3 State and sector, macro	Culture and morality of efficiency; sectoral culture of *Qualitätsarbeit*; sectoral competition.	Nazi policy and procurement; closed economy, autarchy limits opportunity structure.	'Reversed normative framework' state control encourages complicity.

even in the more mundane domestic legal codes regulating the operation of crematoria in line with standards of human dignity.[92] Firstly, cell C1 of Table 1.3, which handles individual level controls, remains empty. In part this fits with Van Baar and Huisman's observation that the absence of normal formal controls is characteristic of mass atrocities, where the state has no interest in discouraging certain forms of illegal conduct and so the lack of individual control fits with the negation of moral responsibility at the corporate level (Table 1.3, cell C2) and the absence of restraints imposed by the state (Table 1.3, cell C3). Column B of Table 1.3

[92] Van Baar and Huisman, above note 79, at 1037.

represents an opportunity structure dictated by the closed economy and totalitarian rule in Germany that points towards the rational elements in the actions of leading figures in Topf and Sons, notably the Topf brothers, who joined the party around the time of the Nazi rise to power with a view to avoiding the confiscation of the firm.[93] The rationality of such actions only makes sense in relation to the underlying motivations provided in column A of Table 1.3, that is to say that they only make sense as rationales towards particular goals, in this case the survival of Topf and Sons' family enterprise and its good name as an innovative producer of high-quality goods. The combination of opportunities to sustain socially recognised goals with illegal means in a competitive environment points to strain theory. It also suggests a qualification of the useful term 'reversed normative framework' that is located in Table 1.3, cell C3. The morality of efficiency and the sectoral culture focusing on quality are not part of the normative reversal, rather they are attached to new normative goals supported by a totalitarian party and state apparatus. The power of temporary 'deviant normative order' may be temporary, but it can support a range of behaviours that would not fit in with entirely disrupted conventions.[94]

Towards the close of the analysis of Topf and Sons, Van Baar and Huisman explore one further area of criminological theory, that of the importance of techniques through which the force of conventional social controls is neutralised. This can be tied in to motivations of offenders, but the evidence of neutralisations during the course of the war are limited to a few euphemisms and evasions,[95] while there is evidence of openness about the function and nature of the ovens[96] and Topf and Sons' role in their production.[97] Rather, the characteristic neutralisations seem to emerge post hoc.[98] A fuller discussion of the challenges analysing neutralisations is found below.

Mining the criminological archives

The previous section focused on two examples of criminologists actively engaged in analysing atrocity crimes including, but not limited to, genocide. It is evident that strands of criminological theory, developed in

[93] Ibid., at 1039, but this is a claim made by one of the brothers *after* the war.
[94] Maier-Katkin, Mears and Bernard, above note 9, at 237.
[95] Van Baar and Huisman, above note 79, at 1044.
[96] Ibid., at 1038. [97] Ibid., at 1044. [98] Ibid., at 1044–5.

criminologists' characteristic interactions with, or from positions within, other foundational disciplines, offer complementary insights into structures, processes and actions underlying atrocity. Rather than proceed further to give a complete 'state of the art' account of criminology's contribution to scholarship in this area to date, the following section will revisit elements of criminological theory in order to identify further potential contributions. This will not result in a general or unified criminological theory of atrocity, rather a selection of criminological 'leads' which might be followed up and integrated into, or discarded from, atrocity scholarship.

The shocked conscience and Durkheimian perspectives

As noted in the introduction, a criminological approach can introduce a degree of conceptual independence, allowing the development of categories for their analytical rather than their legal value. There may still be common ground here, and interaction between criminologists focusing on describing and explaining atrocity and legal scholars focused on definitions which make such actions justiciable may be fruitful. Current criminological work using the terminology of atrocity crime draws its inspiration from the work of lawyer and diplomat David Scheffer.[99] Broadly speaking, Scheffer writes to stress the importance of legality in protecting US national security and exercising global leadership. More specifically he is conducting an exercise in conceptual tidying in an area characterised by multiple legal origins, a series of ad hoc actions and based on diverse treaties and customary practices. The labels atrocity crime and atrocity law are intended as blunt terms, understandable to a lay audience,[100] and valuable in promoting early intervention.[101]

To understand atrocity crime as a subset of a wider category of crime and to set it apart from crime that might be termed ordinary requires some form of conceptual differentiation. Scheffer gives a fivefold set of criteria, some of which are tied to specific bodies of law, whereas others focus on the scale of any crime and on the role of leadership and planning.[102]

[99] Scheffer, above note 5; for examples of criminological uses see Hagan, above note 21, at 26; S. Karstedt, 'Contextualizing Mass Atrocity Crimes: Moving towards a Relational Approach', (2013) 9 *Annual Review of Law and Social Science* 387; Karstedt and Parmentier, above note 5; N. Rafter and S. Walklate, 'Genocide and the Dynamics of Victimization: Some Observations on Armenia', (2012) 9 *European Journal of Criminology* 515.

[100] Scheffer, above note 5, at 398 and 418. [101] Ibid., at 420. [102] Ibid., at 399–400.

In terms of the scale of crimes, Scheffer emphasises a sense of scale developed over time as part of an enduring and linked set of actions.[103] By also identifying the scale of shock and the associated response he points in the direction of Durkheim.[104] Taking crime as a 'social fact', Durkheim focused on the punitive social reaction. He was cautious to stress that this definition was a working one and that it could not claim to say anything about the 'essence of reality', rather it serves as an externally visible symptom of the underlying phenomenon that we seek to understand.[105] His analysis depends upon a consistent relationship between the characteristic symptom and the object of enquiry.[106] Durkheim's use of 'essence' contrasts with the dynamic concept of crime implied by a punitive social reaction. The behaviours which attract such reactions vary temporally and spatially.[107] To take Durkheim's approach further, to attempt to specify the external or surface symptoms of atrocity crime suggests either a special kind of condemnation or a combination of condemnation and some other factor. The language which is used to describe atrocity crimes has a strong Durkheimian edge to it. The first UN resolution to accept the act of genocide as a crime states that it 'shocks the conscience of mankind' and its punishment is a matter of international concern,[108] while in the second protocol, of 1977, to the Geneva Conventions the preamble identifies the 'public conscience' as providing protection to the human person.[109] The ad hoc tribunals for Yugoslavia and Rwanda do not feature such terms in their statutes, nor in their founding resolutions,[110] but the preamble to the

103 Ibid., at 400–1. 104 Ibid., at 400.

105 E. Durkheim, *The Rules of Sociological Method* (Free Press, 1964) at 42.

106 Ibid., at 43.

107 Ibid., at 69. Durkheim puts forward a hypothetical society of saints in which acts likely to be forgiven elsewhere would generate a scandal with punitive consequences.

108 UN General Assembly Resolution 96(1), 11 December 1946. The language of a universal conscience being defied or outraged, or of profound shock is present in a number of the draft documents for the 1948 Convention, but the preamble to the final text drops this and refers to condemnation by the civilised world. UN Economic and Social Council, Resolution 77(V), 6 August 1947; Draft Convention on the Crime of Genocide: note by the Secretary General A/362, 25 August 1947; Report of the Ad hoc Committee on Genocide and the Draft Convention drawn up by the Committee E/794, 5 April–10 May 1948; Convention on the Prevention and Punishment of the Crime of Genocide, 9 December 1948.

109 Protocol II, 8 June 1977.

110 Yugoslavia: UN Security Council, Resolution 808, 22 February 1993 and Resolution 827, 25 May 1993, and Statute of the International Criminal Tribunal for the former Yugoslavia. Rwanda: UN Security Council, Resolution 995, 8 November 1994 and Statute of the International Criminal Tribunal for Rwanda.

Rome Statute of the International Criminal Court again identifies 'atrocities that deeply shock the conscience of humanity'.

While the language may be Durkheimian the context of its application is different in an important way. Broadly speaking, Durkheim, when writing in a less historical or anthropological mode is largely, if implicitly, talking about national, state-based societies. Nonetheless, Turner notes that Durkheim anticipates 'the idea of political globalization on the basis of a universalistic notion of humanity'.[111] Durkheim saw this as being located in something of a distant future, although he recognised his contemporaries' advocacy of European confederation as something of a staging post.[112] But the organisation of humanity as one society is not the only way in which a universal conscience might be achieved. Durkheim writes of a 'silent' form of patriotism, focused on the internal affairs of a state and society rather than exterior expansion.[113] In such a situation the discrepancies between national morals and human morals would be reduced so that the citizen's civic duties are aligned with the general obligations of humanity. Such developments in human morals need not proceed evenly, but certainly give some grounds for analysing atrocity crime as those collective acts of violence which are deemed most shocking, attract international attention and condemnation and are subject to efforts at punishment, whether through domestic or international courts.

While the language surrounding atrocity crime is in a Durkheimian register, the action which backs it up is sporadic. Elsewhere, drawing on Chalk and Jonassohn and Charny, I present twenty-six episodes between 1933 and 1999 that have been characterised, in academic literature, as genocide.[114] Of these, a limited number have seen a concerted international effort to punish, suggesting a conscience that is inconsistent and slow to move.[115] This suggests that while there may be many indications

[111] B. Turner, 'Preface to the Second Edition', In E. Durkheim, *Professional Ethics and Civic Morals* (2nd edn, Routledge, 1992) at xxxv.

[112] E. Durkheim, *Professional Ethics and Civic Morals* (2nd edn, Routledge, 1992) at 74. Elsewhere he recognises increasing interdependence of European nations leading to a greater degree of self-consciousness as a society (E. Durkheim, *The Division of Labour in Society* (Free Press, 1964) at 121 and 405), and in his discussion of federal states, recognises the possibility of nested-levels of political society (*Professional Ethics and Civil Morals*, at 47).

[113] Ibid., at 75.

[114] A. Aitchison, 'Genocide and Ethnic Cleansing', in F. Brookman, M. Maguire, H. Pierpoint and T. Bennett (eds.), *Handbook on Crime* (Willan, 2010) at 777–8.

[115] Continental Europe 1933–45, Yugoslavia 1992 onwards, and Rwanda 1994 are the most obvious international attempts to apply punishment; one could add international assistance to domestic tribunals in the cases of East Timor and Cambodia.

of an emerging global society, it has remained, throughout the twentieth century, in a condition which fits Durkheim's account of a society lacking stability. Under such circumstances social discipline is 'easy to escape', the existence of the society is felt only intermittently and the society 'can communicate only a very feeble influence to the precepts it lays down'.[116] An on-going Durkheimian analysis of atrocity crimes would explore the extent to which global society is thickening, the evenness of such processes across the globe and, through their articulations of an offended human conscience, the extent to which the various manifestations of international criminal law contribute in turn to any thickening and development of global solidarity.

Although Durkheim often speaks in terms of morals and emotions, any such analysis must not neglect the economic dimensions of his accounts of solidarity achieved through interdependence. Not only does this suggest that the economic interdependence of states in a context of global markets might support a qualified thickening of global social solidarity, the varying positions of regions and populations in relation to those global markets may be part of an account of how inclusive such solidarity actually is – a possible variable in how protected from, or vulnerable to, atrocities, particular groups are. This is far from straightforward, as the 'frequent contact' required to maintain a lively public opinion[117] is less obvious on a global scale and may be more indicative of what Durkheim characterises as 'simple relations of *mutualism*'.[118]

Victim focused perspectives

The coherence of a working category of atrocity crimes comes in part from the nature of the victims. They are victimised not on account of their individual features or actions, but rather their inclusion in a socially meaningful category. This is not to exclude the possibility of individual offenders acting against individual victims on account of personal motivations or grievances. Alvarez talks about the 'dreadful intimacy' of genocidal actions in contexts where there is a pre-existing connection between perpetrator and victim[119] and Kalyvas gives an account of selective and intimate violence in the context of the Greek

[116] Durkheim, *Professional Ethics*, above note 112, at 8. [117] Ibid., at 10.
[118] Durkheim, *Division of Labour*, above note 112, at 282 (emphasis in the original).
[119] Alvarez, above note 9, at 20.

civil war.[120] These are made possible only in the context of more widespread attacks in which the relevant criteria for victimhood are defined through social processes, and individual experiences of victimhood are intelligible through those wider processes as much as on a personal level. This is evident at the beginning of moves towards identifying and criminalising crimes against humanity and genocide.[121] Focusing specifically on genocide, Bauer adopts a relatively restricted set of parameters for the categories on which groups are defined, namely, national, ethnic or racial groups.[122] In part this is justified in terms of fidelity to the roots of the term genocide, but it is also stated in terms of members of such groups having certain inescapable attributes defined at birth.[123] As a category, atrocity crime is less tied to the etymological origins of the word *genocide*, but the value of Bauer's emphasis on the lack of an avenue of escape for victims through their own ability to define themselves out of the victim group remains important. As perpetrators are relatively powerful, their definitions of a victim group can close off avenues of escape regardless of an individual's inherited characteristics. Chalk and Jonassohn's definition of genocide takes this into account and suggests the need for close attention to the processes whereby victim groups are defined, marked and targeted.[124]

Rafter and Walklate have recently identified the merit in drawing from the sub-field of victimology to support the analysis of atrocity crime. The work seeks to rebalance the criminology of atrocity, which has largely been focused on perpetrators, but does not focus exclusively on victims, rather on victims and the social relations, including those between victims and perpetrators, in genocidal settings.[125] Building on earlier victimological work they introduce a concept of *victimality*, a variable reflecting the potential for becoming a victim, and provide revised interpretations of victim precipitation in which the victim group 'strikes a blow in the sequence of events that immediately lead to genocide'

[120] S. Kalyvas, *The Logic of Violence in Civil War* (Cambridge University Press, 2006) chapters 7 and 10.

[121] Lemkin, above note 52, at 146.

[122] Y. Bauer, 'Comparison of Genocides', in L. Chorbajian and G. Shirinian (eds.), *Studies in Comparative Genocide* (Macmillan, 1999) at 34. For a brief discussion of sociological understandings of victim groups, see Aitchison, above note 114, at 772–4.

[123] Bauer, above note 122, at 35.

[124] F. Chalk and K. Jonassohn, *The History and Sociology of Genocide: Analyses and Case Studies* (Yale University Press, 1990) at 10 and 23.

[125] Rafter and Walklate, above note 99, at 517.

and victim proneness as a measure of the likelihood of repeated victimisation.[126] In examining the case of the Armenians through this lens, Rafter and Walklate identify a range of relevant characteristics, including the lack of national statehood, a second class form of citizenship, calls for greater autonomy and protection in the Ottoman Empire and alliances outside the Empire in support of these. These are set in the context of changes in the shrinking Ottoman state, where Armenians stood as an obstacle to the realisation of pan-Islamist goals and subsequently Turkish nationalist goals.[127] The perspective they bring calls for further systematic comparative work, not simply to identify regularities, rather, in keeping with Walklate's critique of positivist victimology, to build an understanding of the processes whereby such regularities are reproduced.[128] A fully developed victimological account would extend its comparative reach to those societies where subordination and entrenched inequalities do not develop into genocide, but still include lesser atrocities.[129]

Perpetrators and neutralisations

In more perpetrator-focused accounts of atrocity there are examples of usage of criminological theories concerning techniques of neutralisation. The theory was initially developed as a reaction to accounts of oppositional delinquent subcultures,[130] and suggests that delinquents are rarely opposed to dominant, conventional cultures on a consistent and comprehensive basis. This is evidenced by the delinquents' experience of guilt or shame, by the adoption of conventional heroes for adulation and by other elements in their moral code.[131] A range of justifications is identified as

126 Ibid., at 517–18. Given the reputation for victim blaming that earlier victimological research acquired, Rafter and Walklate are cautious to put distance between precipitation and blameworthiness.

127 Ibid., at 519–20.

128 S. Walklate, *Understanding Criminology: Current Theoretical Debates* (Open University Press, 1998) at 116.

129 See Kuper, above note 67, chapter 10, on non-genocidal societies which nonetheless feature many of the social relations identified by Rafter and Walklate.

130 G. Sykes and D. Matza, 'Techniques of Neutralization: A Theory of Delinquency', (1957) 22 *American Sociological Review* 664. Matza makes clear in later writings that the theory is also a reaction against positivistic attempts to find deterministic causes of crime, whether in biological or social conditions, suggesting that the theoretical focus on permissive factors are of prime importance, D. Matza, *Delinquency and Drift* (John Wiley, 1964) 3.

131 Sykes and Matza, above note 130, at 665.

providing post hoc protection from the discomfort of self-blame and as permissive factors in offending by neutralising particular social controls in situ.[132] Taking on the idea of neutralisation as a selective phenomenon, Agnew infers variation across types of crime and situations and so suggests a finer grained analysis, taking violence as his focus.[133] He also identifies the methodological difficulty in differentiating between pre-crime permissiveness and post hoc rationalisation.[134] In atrocity scholarship this has been identified as a particular problem at the level of individual perpetrators, given a reliance on after-the-fact defences.[135]

Permissive neutralisations may be generated and sustained by social processes within particular milieu. Evidence exists of contemporary provision of neutralisations by state authorities. Neubacher analyses Himmler's October 1943 speech to assembled *SS-Gruppenführer* and finds thirteen examples of neutralisation.[136] As well as such high-level speeches, state-based propaganda in the run up to atrocities is a likely source of neutralisations of obstructive conventional moralities. Different types of neutralisation may have varying levels of currency with perpetrators in different roles. Himmler's speech to the military identified appeals to higher loyalties stressing the 'difficult duty'[137] and similar appeals are made in Major Trapp's address to his militarised police battalion before the massacre of the Jews of Józefów.[138] Thus, state and intermediary organisations can play a role in developing context-specific neutralisations, whether for engineers (see discussion of Van Baar and Huisman, above), doctors,[139] or any other participant. The credibility of some neutralisations deserves to be interrogated. For example, Trapp's account of the Jews of Józefów as a threat to be struck at sits uneasily with an order for immediate execution of children and the elderly.

Alvarez proposes a sixth technique, the denial of victimisation through the denial of humanity, but it has already been noted that denigration and degradation need not go as far as dehumanisation.[140] But certain

[132] Ibid., at 667–9. The paper outlines five techniques: denial of responsibility, denial of injury, denial of victim, condemning condemners and appealing to higher loyalties
[133] R. Agnew, 'The Techniques of Neutralization and Violence', (1994) 32 *Criminology* 536.
[134] Ibid., at 556. [135] Alvarez, above note 9, at 116.
[136] Neubacher, above note 18, at 797. [137] Ibid., at 796, especially note 32 therein.
[138] C. Browning, *Ordinary Men: Reserve Police Battalion 101 and the Final Solution in Poland* (Penguin, 2001) at 2.
[139] Browning, above note 81, at 21. Here he notes how doctors' contributions to the *final solution* are re-categorised as a response to a (self-induced) public health dilemma.
[140] Alvarez, above note 9, at 125.

accounts of atrocity suggest that the contexts are so far removed from an anti-atrocity morality that there is little requirement for a permissive neutralisation. Morrison's account of genocide tourism photographs taken by German soldiers and police officers, and his comparison of similar photographs taken during the Japanese occupation of China, is ambiguous in terms of how it may relate to neutralisations and conventional morality. The photographs are characterised as akin to tourist snaps, but both German and Japanese accounts show an awareness of a conventional morality.[141] The German photographers sought to limit the circulation of the images beyond a trusted group, and Morrison quotes a Japanese soldier's diary saying that if such things had happened in Japan, 'it would be an enormous incident'.[142] Ultimately, any application of the theory of techniques of neutralisation to atrocity crimes encounters the same challenge as any other criminological theory of deviance. In the face of distant sources of moral condemnation, atrocity events are characterised by '*conformity* to very immediate and powerful social expectations' after which convention may be restored.[143] This may be especially true of, but not unique to, expeditionary atrocities, where perpetrators are far removed from their normal environment.

Concluding remarks

This chapter began with a reflection on the open boundaries of criminology reflected in a breakdown of published work classified as criminological and penological. Accepting blurred and shifting borders as a feature of the criminological landscape, it is clear that criminologists are showing increased interest in crimes of atrocity. In doing so, they find common ground with other scholars of international criminal law and crimes of atrocity. This chapter is a necessarily partial account of the actual and potential contribution of criminology in dialogue with other disciplines. By setting illustrative examples of recent scholarship alongside an exploratory review of diverse strands of theory and their

141 W. Morrison, 'Reflections with Memories: Everyday Photography Capturing Genocide', (2004) 8 *Theoretical Criminology* 343. This merits some comparison with the photographs and postcards of public torture lynchings in the American South during the first third of the twentieth century, as analysed by D. Garland, 'Penal Excess and Surplus Meaning: Public Torture Lynchings in Twentieth-Century America', (2005) 39 *Law and Society Review* 793, 794–5.

142 Morrison, above note 141, at 343 and 351.

143 Maier-Katkin, Mears and Bernard, above note 9, at 237 (emphasis added).

application to the problem of atrocity crime, the chapter suggests that criminological theory can help to understand the processes leading to atrocity. This chapter avoided making a commitment to a unified or general criminological theory of atrocity, but connections are evident in some of the strands identified above. Adapting Durkheim to examine an emerging and uneven global society begs the question as to how societies and groups experiencing atrocity are integrated into that society. Both the victimological and structural positions represented by Rafter and Walklate, and Hagan, are suggestive of this. They identify the connection of Armenians to Christian powers outside the Ottoman Empire and the position of Darfur within the Sudanese economy and, in turn, Sudan within a global economy. A sociological criminology, sensitive to historical context and change, and to political and economic structures, is no easy undertaking, but can draw support from, and ultimately contribute something back to, atrocity scholarship across a range of disciplines. The open borders of criminology make it well suited to absorb ideas from elsewhere, but also mean that once those ideas are further developed they should find it easier to find purchase outside the discipline.

2

The relevance and application of empirical research methods to the study of international crimes

EMMANOUELA MYLONAKI

Introduction

The international criminalization of genocide, crimes against humanity and war crimes has been followed by a vast amount of published work on the legal instruments and institutions dealing with such crimes and the procedural aspects of their prosecution at national and international level. Most of the relevant work relies on secondary data analysis rather than the collection of primary data and the use of criminological research methods. In fact, the discipline of criminology has traditionally excluded violations of international criminal law from its scope,[1] restricting itself to common crime and violence such as homicide, gang crime, domestic violence and other types of ordinary (national) criminal activity.[2] It is only recently that criminologists have gradually started paying attention to international crimes and calling for the development of a new sub-branch of criminological research, a so-called international criminology, with the aim of examining crime and justice beyond national boundaries.[3] The examination of international crimes through criminological lenses has resulted in broadening the horizons of the research methods employed in order to fully appreciate the nature of international crimes. This is evident in the various studies conducted to address – on a quantitative level – the prevalence of international crimes, the etiology of

[1] G. Yacoubin, 'The (In)significance of Genocidal Behavior to the Discipline of Criminology', (2000) 34 *Crime, Law & Social Change* 7; see also A. Brannigan, 'Criminology and the Holocaust: Xenophobia, Evolution, and Genocide', (1998) 44 *Crime and Delinquency* 257.

[2] M. Bosworth and C. Hoyle, *What's Criminology?* (Oxford University Press, 2011) at 36.

[3] A. Smeulers, 'Criminology in a State of Denial – Towards a Criminology of International Crimes: Supranational Criminology', in A. Smeulers and R. Haveman, (eds.), *Supranational Criminology: Towards a Criminology of International Crimes* (Intersentia, 2008) at 3–26; F. Neubacher, 'How Can it Happen that Horrendous State Crimes are Perpetrated? An Overview of Criminological Theories', (2006) 4 *Journal of International Criminal Justice* 787.

offending at a micro and macro level,[4] the impact of the offence on the victim and the legal reaction to international criminality.[5]

This chapter focuses on the application of criminological empirical research methods to the study of international crimes by providing insights into the different ways in which data can be collected for research thereto. It is not the aim of the chapter to produce a full account of the various social science research methods but only to identify particular problems potentially encountered by anyone conducting research on international crimes, especially as this relates to data collection for qualitative or quantitative analysis. The chapter is divided into two principal sections. The first highlights the relevance of the application of criminological research methods to the study of international crimes and gross violations of human rights and reinforces the arguments for the inclusion of the notion of international crimes within the realm of empirical research. The second demonstrates the practical application of quantitative and qualitative research methods in the study of international crimes and indicates the areas where empirical research is relevant. It should be stressed from the outset that the chapter is concerned with criminological empirical research methods – involving the systematic use of qualitative and quantitative methods – rather than criminological research methodology which refers to a broader theoretical framework.[6]

The relevance of criminological research methods to the study of international crimes

It is true that emanations of violence such as genocide and crimes against humanity establish a variety of interesting prisms; political/international relations,[7] legal and, with the plethora of current scientific and social methods, many others. While political science and legal research are mostly concerned with analysing the various institutions and procedures set up to deal with international crimes, such as the creation of international criminal tribunals, the notion of the individual as perpetrator or as victim, the incidence of mass criminality and the number of offences committed are better addressed from a social science methodological

4 Smeulers and Haveman, above note 3, at 78. 5 Ibid.

6 J. Cresswell and P. Clark, *Designing and Conducting Mixed Methods Research* (London Sage, 2007) at 4; L. Reychler and T. Paffenholz (eds.), *Peace-building: A Field Guide* (Lynne Rienner Publishers, 2001).

7 Ibid.

perspective. It is only recently that the value of social science research methods has been appreciated for its ability to provide clearer insights into the realm of international crimes. Perhaps the delay is due to the arguments that have traditionally been put forward by criminologists against the inclusion of international crimes within the realm of criminological studies.

The conceptual differences between traditional criminality and international criminality rest at the heart of the arguments against the application of empirical research methods to the study of international crimes. The fact that mass offences against civilians perpetrated in war time are committed on most occasions under governmental command or, at least, some involvement by the state renders them not only an act of the individual perpetrator(s) – who becomes a prescribed deviant[8] – but also an act encompassed within the sphere of extraordinary international criminality. This new dimension of criminal activity conflicts with the traditional criminological view whereby the state as legislator prevents and punishes crime. Likewise, it has been argued that the discipline of criminology, which is concerned with the notion of 'common crime' as this is clearly defined in various jurisdictions, cannot examine concepts which are either non-defined or contain political elements which make definitions vague.[9]

These arguments notwithstanding, the concern of the international community with serious international crimes has led to the adoption of several multilateral treaties criminalizing said conduct and providing relevant definitions. By way of illustration, the Regulations attached to Hague Convention IV of 1907 specify which conduct gives rise to war criminality and, in equal manner, Article 2 of the 1948 Genocide Convention defines this offence as consisting of:

> any of the following acts committed with intent to destroy, in whole or in part, a national, ethnical, racial or religious group, as such: killing members of the group; causing serious bodily or mental harm to members of the group; deliberately inflicting on the group conditions of life calculated to bring about its physical destruction in whole or in part; imposing measures intended to prevent births within the group; [and] forcibly transferring children of the group to another group.

Despite the shortcomings of this articulation of genocide, the mere fact that the particular conduct is prescribed as a crime under the terms of a

[8] Smeulers and Haveman, above note 3, at 233–65.

[9] Yacoubin, above note 1, at 8.

binding treaty supports the argument for its inclusion in the criminological research agenda.[10]

Similarly, the definition of crimes against humanity is codified, among others, in Article 7 of the Rome Statute of the International Criminal Court (ICC). The notion encompasses crimes such as murder, extermination, rape, persecution and all other inhumane acts of a similar character (wilfully causing great suffering, or serious injury to body or to mental or physical health), committed 'as part of a widespread or systematic attack directed against any civilian population, with knowledge of the attack'. The clear reference to murder, rape and violence – even of a large scale – which constitute traditional forms of criminality reinforces the aforementioned argument.

The traditional tools of criminological research have been regarded as inappropriate for the study of international crimes due to the methodological challenges they typically pose.[11] There are several major research tools available to criminologists, namely field research, survey research and experiments.[12] The physical dangers inherent in field research and the complex process of survey research have been suggested as the main arguments against the application of social science research in the case of international crimes. As the subsequent sections demonstrate these arguments are not supported by current research practice. Besides the use of experiments, which are not readily relevant to the study of international crimes, the application of qualitative and quantitative research methods – despite the difficulties involved – is not only possible but certainly worthwhile. No doubt, the recognition as to the relevance of criminology to the study of international crimes has encouraged legal scholars and social scientists gradually to employ social science research methodologies to the study of international crimes.[13]

Of course, research on international crimes with particular reference to the measurement of offences has been conducted by epidemiologists using statistical methods to measure the number of casualties. However, as Hagan suggests, the majority of available research is undertaken by public health workers rather than criminologists and evidence that a war

[10] F. Chalk, 'Definitions of Genocide and their Implications for Prediction and Prevention', (1989) 2 *Holocaust and Genocide Studies* 149.

[11] D. Lisak and P. M. Miller, 'Repeat Rape and Multiple Offending among Undetected Rapists', (2002) 17 *Violence and Victims* 73.

[12] See, generally, R. Taylor, *Research Methods in Criminal Justice* (McGraw-Hill, 1994).

[13] A. M. Drumbl, 'Towards a Criminology of International Crimes', (2003) 19 *Ohio State Journal on Dispute Resolution* 263.

crime has been committed is simply a by-product rather than the focus of relevant studies.[14] There might very well be 'a tendency [among] health-oriented researchers to underreport violent deaths in what these researchers designate as complex humanitarian emergencies'. Therefore, there is a need for legal and criminology scholars to better adapt social science research methods to international crimes in order to synthesize and entrench four particular thematic areas.[15] The first concerns prevalence of crime. Finding out the number of offences committed in a specific region and within a particular time frame is important for estimating the number of victims but also the patterns of offending. Given that not all gross violations of human rights amount to international crimes it is important to investigate a particular case in order to reach the conclusion that genocide has actually taken place. Measuring patterns of violence and the scale of offending leads to an identification of patterns of offending which can satisfy the elements of several international crimes, such as genocide and crimes against humanity. By way of illustration, an investigation in the patterns of sexual violence during conflict can determine the extent to which rape and other forms of sexual violence can be termed widespread or systematic or can be regarded as a deliberate and systematic plan to kill and destroy a group in whole or in part.

In the *Akayesu* case, the International Criminal Tribunal for Rwanda (ICTR) took the unprecedented step of holding that systematic rape committed with the intent to destroy a particular group is encompassed within the statutory definition of 'genocide'.[16] Measuring the scale of offending and the nature of the offence leads to an identification of patterns of offending which can be useful for linking offences to perpetrators and thus making effective prosecution possible.[17] In fact, anonymous and confidential evidence can be employed in order to establish the scale and pattern of mass rape. Despite the legal objection against the use of survey evidence in international criminal trials due to its hearsay dimension, there is no generally accepted prohibition concerning the use of hearsay evidence. Likewise, hearsay evidence can produce reliable and valid sources of information, which is excluded only where it is assessed as unreliable.

[14] J. Hagan and P. Parker, 'The Criminology of Genocide: The Death and Rape in Darfur', (2005) 43 *Criminology* 525.

[15] Ibid.

[16] *ICTR Prosecutor* v. *Akayesu*, Trial Judgment (2 September 1998), paras. 688 and 731; *ICTY Prosecutor* v. Karadzic, amended indictment (28 April 2000), para. 17b; *ICTY Prosecutor* v. *Mladic*, indictment (10 October 2002), paras. 25a and 34b.

[17] Smeulers and Haveman, above note 3, at 80.

Besides its utility in studying the incidence of international crimes, social research methods can advance our knowledge as to the etiology of offending at a micro level by allowing us to examine the motives of the offender and his or her profile. This can be accomplished by conducting interviews with perpetrators or by using documents such as court files which provide insights on the motives of the perpetrators. Legal reactions or responses to international crimes constitute further areas of study allowing researchers to focus on procedural justice legal processes, legal outcome and the effectiveness of legal interventions.[18]

It should finally be noted that in the aftermath of an armed conflict the number of individuals involved and the political outcomes usually give rise to demands for an accurate historical record. This process has been found to promote a significant degree of reconciliation.[19] One of the key issues is the search for truth, i.e. to bring the facts about past crimes to the surface, or at least as many facts as possible. Reconciliation and truth is also crucial for society as a whole, since it shapes further political and social debates and transformations. Orentlicher argues in favour of 'the right to truth' for victims in a manner that gives rise to legal implications.[20] Several UN bodies, among others, have concluded that the right to truth about gross or serious human rights violations is an inalienable and autonomous right that is linked to the duty and obligation of the state to protect and guarantee human rights, to conduct effective investigations and to guarantee effective remedies and reparations.[21]

Researching international crimes

Although the interest of the researcher and the question under investigation are the factors guiding the selection of one's research method there are two main approaches for researching international crimes and gross violations of human rights from a qualitative and quantitative

[18] Ibid.

[19] S. Parmentier, 'Global Justice in the Aftermath of Mass Violence: The Role of the International Criminal Court in Dealing with Political Crimes', (2003) 41 *International Annals of Criminology* 203.

[20] Report of the Independent Expert to Update the Set of Principles to Combat Impunity (Diane Orentlicher), UN Doc. E/CN.4/2005/102 (18 February 2005).

[21] Human Rights Council Res A/HRC/RES/12/12 (12 October 2009) on the right to the truth; Report of the UNHCHR on the Right to Truth, UN Doc. A/HRC/15/33 (28 July 2010); Report of the UNHCHR, Study on the Right to Truth, UN Doc. E/CN.4/2006/91 (8 February 2006).

methodological perspective. Quantitative research aims at establishing the number of offences committed in a certain place and at a specific time and provides numerical data on the distribution of crime through the collection of a representative sample. The sample collection is produced by the use of victimization surveys and the use of data already obtained. In the case of victimization surveys the researcher uses samples in order to draw conclusions in respect of the general population with a view to assessing the incidence of conflict and the number of offences committed. This is commonly used when the researcher is interested in describing particular occurrences of international crimes.

On the other hand, non-statistical methods involve the collection of qualitative data through interviews with persons involved in international crimes whether as victims or perpetrators. The objective of data collection is to determine in the form of a narrative what really happened, who was involved and what were the consequences of one's involvement. The collection of qualitative data poses particular difficulties, particularly in terms of accessing people in order to conduct the interviews, in addition to the emotive nature of international crimes.[22] Interviews are (typically) structured conversations. Observation, involving an actual examination and breakdown of actions and interactions among people, is an approach to data collection that seems rather straightforward but which is actually a very challenging method for gathering systematic information about individual conduct, social interaction, places and things.[23] Let us now proceed to examine particular research methods that have been used in order to describe and document international human rights violations.

Measuring international crime

As already mentioned, there are many reasons why knowing the precise number of victims is important. From a prosecutorial perspective it determines the classification of the conduct. Although none of the relevant genocide or crime against humanity provisions in the statutes of international tribunals specifies the number or proportion of victims required for a genocide charge, it is generally assumed that the number needs to be significant.

Perhaps more relevant to the study of international crimes in terms of understanding its nature and prevalence is the use of quantitative

[22] S. Kleinman and M. Copp, *Emotions and Fieldwork* (Sage, 1993).

[23] B. Bruce, *Qualitative Research Methods for the Social Sciences* (Pearson, 2007).

research methods for assessing victimization. Studying the prevalence of international crimes requires detailed research on the mortality rates, which comprises both direct and indirect mortality, that is, deaths attributable to conditions generated by the conflict, such as breakdown of health services.[24] The traditional tools for data collection on crime incidence(s) include official sources, census data, victim surveys or use of secondary data.[25] The use of official sources is a common way of data collection in order to measure crime at a national level. This is a method by which data are collected from official bodies such as the police which provide statistical information on crime occurrence. However, not all crimes are recorded by the police. This is known as the dark figure of crime, a term adopted by criminologists to describe the amount of unreported crime.[26] The main problem with the dark figure is that it challenges the validity of official statistics. The challenges for recording international criminality are further compounded by the lack of a dedicated reporting body (this role is typically played by the police and dedicated statistical organizations in domestic criminal justice systems) as well as by manipulation through official state reports (typically the territorial state) of relevant events and numbers.[27] In an attempt to escape prosecution for international criminal activity the state's authorities may play a major role in hiding evidence of killings, rape and other acts of a criminal character.[28] This notwithstanding, several commentators have argued that some states are willing to paint an accurate picture,[29] but it is doubtful that this paradigm applies to countries in transition from conflict, particularly where the incumbent government was a party to the conflict. One further way by which the researcher might collect data on the number of persons killed or disappeared is by reference to census data.[30] A census is often construed as being opposite to a sample as everyone is surveyed rather than a fraction.[31]

[24] A. Smeulers (ed.), *Collective Violence and International Criminal Justice: An Interdisciplinary Approach* (Intersentia, 2010) at 283.

[25] Ibid. [26] Ibid.

[27] A. Brusk, 'The Politics of Measurement: the Contested Count of the Disappeared in Argentina', (1994) 16 *Human Rights Quarterly* 676; R. Goldstein, 'The Limitations of Using Quantitative Data in Studying Human Rights Abuses', (1986) 8 *Human Rights Quarterly* 607.

[28] Smeulers and Haveman, above note 3, at 82.

[29] S. Poe, and C. Carey, 'How are These Pictures Different? A Quantitative Comparison of the US State Department and Amnesty International Human Rights Reports, 1976–1995', (2001) 23 *Human Rights Quarterly* 650.

[30] Smeulers and Haveman, above note 3, at 83. [31] Ibid.

The problem is that many countries where gross violations of human rights are taking place do not possess proper census information. However, this is not overly crucial. For example, in a study conducted by Verwimp in 2004 on death and survival during the 1994 genocide in Rwanda,[32] the target group's situation was compared with data collected in a pre-genocide survey in Rwanda's Kibuye province. In this manner, the researcher was able to draw a fairly accurate account of the mortality rates in that particular province. Verwimp used a database produced from a house-to-house survey of victims by the organization of genocide survivors, Ibuka. From a total of 59,050 victims of the genocide, data were collected on age, sex, occupation, commune of residence before the genocide, as well as place and date of death.[33]

Likewise, someone trying to estimate the number of people who lost their life as a result of a particular conflict can:

(1) start from the size of the population before the conflict;
(2) estimate a counterfactual population size after the conflict has ended on the basis of the initial population and a population growth rate; and
(3) finally, subtract from that the actual post-conflict population size in order to arrive at an estimate of overall mortality.[34]

As Bijleveld notes, the problem arises when we lack reliable numbers for the starting population and the final population size, suggesting that the researcher will have to resort to assumptions. According to Bijleveld, one way the researcher might be able to deal with the problem is to avoid fixed point estimates and instead resort to intervals.[35] The suggestion – somewhat arbitrarily conceived, according to this author – is that one may use the population data of a neighbouring country in order to estimate the pre-conflict and post-conflict population of the target nation and hence arrive at a probable mortality rate on account of the war. The final tally will also take into consideration the neighbouring country's population growth, which will naturally decline in the target state. This method is subject to several limitations, not least the absence of adequate censuses in developing nations, wherein most conflicts take place, as well as the disparity in financial, wellbeing and other indicators even across neighbouring nations. Such a methodology would also not sit well with international criminal tribunals, which would avoid using its results for fear of being labelled illegitimate.

[32] D. Verwimp, 'Death and Survival during the 1994 Genocide in Rwanda', (2004) 58 *Population Studies* 233.

[33] Ibid. [34] Smeulers, above note 24, at 283. [35] Ibid., at 285.

An additional method to estimate physical harm (and implicitly mortality) is through the use of victim surveys which ask people whether they have been the victim of a crime. This method has various advantages. Victimization surveys can obtain information on crimes which have not been reported to the police (or monitored by intergovernmental bodies in the case of international crimes) or which have not been recorded by the authorities. Many studies have examined mortality rates using victim surveys. Victim surveys typically encompass questions on the respondents' personal victimization as well as that of family members.[36] In a survey with a nationwide character, Deportere reported the findings of a mortality survey in West Darfur, Sudan, for the period between 2003 and 2004, demonstrating that the mortality rates were much higher than the emergency benchmark.[37] The researcher gathered data from four internally displaced persons (IDP) camps in Darfur, namely Zalingei, Murnei, Niertiti and El Geneina by using a two-stage cluster sampling method to identify households within the camp. He then interviewed the head of the household in order to gather information on:

(1) deaths that had occurred during the recall period;
(2) the age, time of year (month), location, cause of death;
(3) month of arrival at the camp;
(4) reasons for leaving the village; and
(5) the age and sex of the household members.[38]

By using this sampling strategy the researcher then interviewed the following number of subjects from each camp: 460 households at Zalingei (representing 2,386 people); 912 households in Murnei (representing 4,754 people); 903 households in Niertiti (representing 5,188 people); and 900 households in El Geneina (representing 5,191 people). Once data were collected the researcher carried out two types of analysis:

(1) mortality rate: the number of deaths per day, per 10,000 people; and
(2) risk of violent death of adult men and women relative to children under fifteen years old.

Surveys such as the above have important and well-described limitations. When mortality rates are high entire households may disappear

[36] Smeulers and Haveman, above note 3, at 83.
[37] E. Deportere, F. Checchi, F. Broillet, S. Gerstl, A. Minetti, O. Gavraud, V. Briet, J. Pahl, I. Defourny, M. Tatay and V. Brown, 'Violence and Mortality in West Darfur, Sudan (2003–4): Epidemiological Evidence from Four Surveys', (2004) 364 *The Lancet* 1315.
[38] Ibid.

(survival bias) leading to underestimates. Likewise, survivor bias is a limitation of victim surveys as entire households might have disappeared. In order to overcome this problem the researcher needs to employ a cluster sampling design.[39] Research has shown that it is important to include a large number of clusters.[40]

Of course, collecting the numbers of casualties might not in itself seem an interesting task for a socio-legal researcher. However, knowing the number of deaths can lead to the conceptualization of a particular case of international criminality by identifying patterns of offending. Likewise, survey research can contribute to the contextualization of international crimes. The research conducted by Hagan and Rymond-Richmond in 2009 is an example of the use of survey data demonstrating how collective action may be incited on racial grounds, confirming that the events in Darfur demonstrate a pattern of genocide, assuming that the victims are found to constitute a distinct racial group, or at least are viewed as such by the perpetrators.[41] In fact, Hagan and Rymond-Richmond's analysis of the data allowed them to argue that the timing, location and circumstances surrounding attacks on hundreds of thousands of Darfuri villagers since 2003, as well as the specific nature and scale of those attacks, involving killings, rape, other forms of sexual violence, racial insults and confiscation or contamination of property and natural resources, amounted to an intentional state-sponsored genocide.[42] For Hagan and Rymond-Richmond, the evidence of collective racial intent is the missing piece for defining the atrocities of Darfur as genocide: the individual and collective (including government) racial intent constitutes genocidal *mens rea* on the part of the Sudanese government and *Janjaweed* militia.

Such research can provide the basis for ascertaining traces or fully-fledged evidence of genocide as it occurs, clearing the way for prosecution in the interest of international justice. The main data source was the atrocities documentation survey commission in 2004 by the US Department of State, which interviewed randomly chosen Darfuri refugees in Chad. From interviews with 1,136 refugees – a statistically valid sample of the 2.2 million Darfuris affected by the violence – interviewers coded up to twenty crime incidents per household in sufficient detail to support potential courtroom claims. The atrocities documentation survey (ADS) refugee interviews

[39] Smeulers and Haveman, above note 3, at 83. [40] Ibid.

[41] R. Matsueda, 'Toward a New Criminology of Genocide: Theory, Method, and Politics', (2009) 13 *Theoretical Criminology* 495.

[42] Ibid.

showed that: 81 per cent of respondents reported that their village was destroyed; 80 per cent that their livestock was stolen; 67 per cent had witnessed or experienced aerial bombing, 61 per cent reported the killing of a family member and 33 per cent reported hearing racial epithets during attacks. Hagan performed a statistical analysis on the ADS interviews. By using research tools standard in sociology and criminology (such as survey research, field research) he extracted and quantified data from the interviews allowing him to identify patterns of violence. By performing hierarchical linear modelling on these statistics the researcher was able to document the nature, timing and circumstances of the attacks and most importantly to determine the intent of the attackers. The statistical analysis revealed that racial epithets were more likely to be heard when government militia leaders were present at the attacks. The identification of intent is central to determining the occurrence of genocide and in the eventual prosecution of those responsible.

The estimation of mortality rates was equally key in the aftermath of the Kosovo conflict. Ball and Asher employed a method known as multiple systems analysis in order to ascertain the number who had died between March and June 1999, at the height of oppression.[43] Their work was in fact part of an effort to determine whether the regime of Slobodan Milosevic had orchestrated the alleged forced migration and killings of ethnic Albanians during the crucial time. The idea was that they would be called in as expert witnesses in the prosecution's case against the former Yugoslav leader. Their study consisted of a statistical survey measuring patterns of death and migration in relation to NATO airstrikes and the military activities of the Kosovo Liberation Army. This was assessed against similar data from the ethnic Albanian community. The researchers employed multiple system estimation to decipher their data. Much of this was readily available from a plethora of sources, namely:

(1) an ABA survey with 1,674 interviews with ethnic Albanian refugees;[44]
(2) exhumations carried out on behalf of the International Criminal Tribunal for the former Yugoslavia (ICTY) by multinational forces using the latest forensic technology;

[43] P. Ball and J. Asher, 'Statistics and Slobodan: Using Data Analysis and Statistics in the War Crimes Trial of Former President Milosevic', (2002) 15 *Chance* 17.

[44] Refugees were interviewed through a questionnaire allowing a narrative description of events, which allowed the respondents to converse and tell their story rather than simply to respond briefly to standard questions.

(3) surveys by non-governmental organizations (NGOs), again through narrative-based questionnaires whose purpose clearly is not to elicit the kind of information that would be useful to the prosecutorial authorities. A Human Rights Watch survey covered 337 interviews and a total of 1,717 incidents; and
(4) surveys by intergovernmental organizations.[45]

Studying perpetrators

Studies on perpetrators attempt to explain why certain people offend, what are their individual characteristics, all with a view to understanding why ordinary people commit gross violations of human rights. Studying the etiology of international crimes can reveal motives and background characteristics of the perpetrators and it is an area where both qualitative and quantitative research may be relevant. In social science research this can be done by conducting offender interviews, or collecting information from court files. For example, Verwimp's research regarding the profile of perpetrators in Rwanda was a quantitative study of the economic profile of perpetrators based on administrative records and using multivariate analysis techniques.[46]

Qualitative studies are also relevant in researching perpetrators and, despite the difficulties involved in conducting ethnographic research on international crimes, it is a method that has proven to produce valuable results. Ethnographic research means that the researcher 'gets close' to people's everyday experiences 'through exposure to or involvement in the day-to-day or routine activities of participants in the research setting'.[47] A study conducted by Peters used semi-structured interviews in order to examine child soldiers in Sierra Leone. The researcher lived with his subjects and engaged in activities such as soccer and likewise used a non-quantitative ethnographic research. He conducted interviews in more quiet periods and in areas where the conflict was ongoing, as well as after it had ended.[48] This approach provided more details and rich data and as Peters pointed out qualitative data should preferably be gauged

[45] Smeulers and Haveman, above note 3, at 90.

[46] P. Verwimp, 'An Economic Profile of Peasant Perpetrators of Genocide: Micro Level Evidence from Rwanda', (2004) 77 *Journal of Development Economics* 297.

[47] S. Schensul, and M. LeCompte, *Essential Ethnographic Methods: Observations, Interviews, and Questionnaires* (AltaMira Press, 1999).

[48] Smeulers, above note 24, at 289.

against quantitative representative findings if these are available.[49] Peters further noted several pitfalls associated with this type of fieldwork, questioning whether the researcher can be certain that the subjects are telling the truth. Quantitative gauging may safeguard against such risks, with a possible option being the technique of triangulation, whereby the sincerity of an informant, even if ultimately prosecuted, is guaranteed by offering him or her complete anonymity using repeat interviewing and covering topics from different angles.[50]

Qualitative research methods offer the advantage of paying closer attention to dynamic social contexts through the medium of interviews. One challenge is that the findings from qualitative work tend to be less generalizable because they are context specific. In addition, qualitative work may be viewed as untrustworthy because it reflects the normative predispositions of the observer or of the people interviewed by the researcher.[51] The difficulties in collecting empirical data in terms of accessing people in order to conduct interviews,[52] and the emotive nature of international crimes, have been suggested as the main obstacles in conducting primary research and ultimately relying on qualitative data. Ideological constraints on international crimes research relate to preconceptions rooted in the demonization of international crimes, whereby those committing mass atrocities may be viewed as not being worthy to be heard, under the assumption that they will be disposed to lie and so the argument goes that it is preferable to hear what the government and its representatives, such as the police, have to say. This position is no doubt questioned in that interviews give a voice to real actors, allowing them to speak freely from their own experiences and convey their conceptions in their own words.[53] The perpetrators of international crimes may differ in their motives and the roles they play in a particular case. Qualitative research methods may assist in creating a typology of perpetrators, which is a pre-requisite to administering justice fairly and imposing fair sentences that match the blameworthiness of the individual.[54] There are

[49] K. Peters, *Footprints to Reintegration: Armed Conflict, Youth and the Rural Crisis in Sierra Leone* (Wageningen University Press, 2006).

[50] Ibid.

[51] G. Shaffer and T. Ginsburg, 'The Empirical Turn in International Legal Scholarship', (2012) 106 *American Journal of International Law* 3.

[52] Kleinman and Copp, above note 22.

[53] S. Kvale and S. Brinkmann, *Interviews: Learning the Craft of Qualitative Research Interviewing* (Sage, 2009).

[54] Smeulers and Haveman, above note 3, at 233.

several high profile examples whereby perpetrators such as heads of state, leaders and other notable figures, admitted their guilt and repented their crimes, such as the leader of the Bosnian Serbs, Biljana Plavsic, with such cases being seen as the benchmark for reconciliation offered by international tribunals. In other cases, such as that of Radovan Karadzic, it is possible for the criminal justice process to reveal hidden political agendas and the roles of states in brokering peace deals behind the scenes.[55]

Not surprisingly, in most cases it will be difficult to obtain perpetrator surveys. An alternative may be to rely on research conducted on other persons who have already been prosecuted or arrested and who are largely representative of the object's characteristics (e.g., members of the same ethnic or other group, similar affiliations, similar age, possibly rank and status). What will obviously be lacking in such comparative analyses are the particular character traits of each perpetrator, but since one's study is general rather than specific – that is, the aim is not to undertake a psychological analysis – but to assess broader patterns of criminality through the eyes of perpetrators, this is a method that provides some potential. Such a sample, however, has inherent limitations, with size and representativeness being key issues, given that it will not take into consideration those that have yet to be apprehended or those who have escaped. Moreover, it is probably rather optimistic to think that somebody who has been prosecuted will actually speak about the atrocities he or she has committed. It comes as no surprise that no self-report surveys for rape have been obtained in Rwanda as yet. With an estimated 200,000[56] to 800,000[57] surviving perpetrators, and given that the conflict has fizzled out on the territory of Rwanda, at least, self-reporting surveys may be possible – at least for assessing the incidence of rape and other sexual offences – in the form of a tailored format among particular groups. It goes without saying that one-size-fits-all surveys are redundant in field research of this nature and just because contact with a particular group fails to produce any visible results, it does not mean that adaptation of one's approach and questions to a neighbouring group is also destined to fail. There have been several, admittedly few, cases at the

[55] *ICTY Prosecutor* v. *Karadzic*, Trial Chamber Decision on the Accused's Holbrooke Agreement Motion (8 July 2009), paras. 1–19, 33–7.

[56] S. Straus, 'How Many Perpetrators were there in the Rwandan Genocide? An Estimate', (2004) 6 *Journal of Genocide Research* 85.

[57] R. H. Haveman, 'Justice for Gacaca', in A. Smeulers and R. Haveman (eds.), *Supranational Criminology: Towards a Criminology of International Crimes*, (Intersentia, 2008) at 357–98.

ICTY where the perpetrators were eager to provide a full account of atrocities and their participation therein, principally as a result of a severe sense of guilt and a desire for closure. The case of Erdemović, who confessed in minute detail his role in the Srebrenica massacre, is emblematic of the potential offered by perpetrator surveys.[58]

Conducting qualitative research on perpetrators might be particularly relevant in the context of empirical transitional justice where the perpetrators' perception of international justice, particularly before international tribunals, contributes to a better understanding of international criminal justice's pursuit of deterrence and non-recurrence of crimes.[59] The opposite is also true, namely that as international trials progress the initial potency of the perpetrator's voice becomes increasingly muted as the relevant civilian population become aware of the facts and the atrocities.[60] This was evident in the context of the former Yugoslavia where the initial overwhelming support for the war and the perception of the perpetrators as heroes gave way to an indifference which even culminated in the surrender of the war's architect, Slobodan Milosevic.

A recent study of perpetrators' perception as to the legitimacy of international criminal justice demonstrated that in-depth interviews may contribute to our understanding of the impact of transitional justice mechanisms.[61] The study used a discourse analysis to interpret the interviews, which used questions centred on the perception of the perpetrators as to their own responsibility for the crimes committed and equally their perception of the trials. The interviews revealed that the respondents perceived themselves as compelled to react to external forces and revealed that the interviewees' perception of the crimes resonates with uncertainty and chaos, lack of agency and acting within the group, raising challenges to the current assumption about elite participation and the individual's power and control in genocide and mass violence that

[58] This case is best known for the applicability of the defence of duress (as a general or partial defence). *ICTY Prosecutor* v. *Erdemović*, Appeals Chamber Judgment (7 October 1997).

[59] M. Rauschenbach, *Ways of Knowing Atrocities*, available at: http://oxfordtransitionaljustice.wordpress.com/2013/07/13/roundtable-discussion-of-the-esrc-project-ways-of-knowing-atrocity-with-dr-mina-rauschenbach-2/.

[60] This gives rise to the communicative effect of law to its wider stakeholder audience. See I. Bantekas, 'The Communication by States of International Law to its Direct Stakeholders', (2010) 3 *Colombian Yearbook of International Law* 123.

[61] Rauschenbach, above note 59.

underpins international prosecutions. The study followed a qualitative approach in order to demonstrate how the method is set in researching the impact of transitional justice practices. It applied an iterative approach by which the researcher goes back and forth between his own interpretation and the accounts of the respondents in order to develop a holistic and coherent narrative of the interviews. The methodological problems encountered in conducting qualitative research were highlighted by the researcher, including the ethical considerations related to the research impact on the respondents.[62] However, the respondents' anonymity was crucial to building a trust-based relationship by stating the objectives of the project from the outset. In fact, it has been demonstrated that quantitative research has been more tailored and suitable for the study of international crimes.

It may be said that the goals anticipated from perpetrator surveys may equally be achieved by reference to quasi-judicial processes, such as truth commissions. In fact, the practice of truth commissions during the phase of transitional justice highlights the need to make the most of the perpetrators' desire to return to normality – at least for the majority of them – without necessarily equating truth commissions with impunity. It is precisely because of the independence of truth commissions from relevant criminal justice processes that the evidence submitted therein may subsequently be used for assessing patterns of criminal behaviour; ultimately, in order to prosecute those not falling within the broader umbrella of amnesties. It has also been shown that truth commissions provide a forum for political discourse because of the absence of a hierarchy (i.e., judges and prosecutors versus defendants) or compulsion; as a result, high-ranking individuals may feel that such commissions are a much better platform within which to communicate a political/personal message as opposed to a courtroom where the daily routine of testimony and cross-examination exhausts the civilian audience, which stops paying attention after a while. This is probably what drove a prominent Sierra Leonian politician, already under trial before the Sierra Leone Special Court, to give evidence to the country's truth commission, even though this evidence was potentially damning to his criminal trial.[63]

[62] Ibid.

[63] See *SLSC Prosecutor* v. *Norman*, Decision on Appeal by the TRC and Chief Norman against the Decision of Bankole J, delivered on 30 October 2003, to Deny the TRC's Request to Hold a Public Hearing with Chief Norman (28 November 2003), para. 41.

Conclusion

The purpose of this chapter was not to provide an in-depth analysis of how one should conduct an analysis of a particular case involving one or more international crimes; rather, the expectation was that the reader, especially those with few or no insights into social science research methods, would come to realize that non-legal methods have a crucial role to play in our understanding of the context of criminal conduct, particularly criminal conduct committed on a mass scale, while at the same it should become clear that said research methods can assist us in the phases of prosecution as well as in transitional justice. As a result, this author considered it prudent to present a sample of a variety of research methods that are commonly used by criminologists and other social sciences in respect of ordinary crime with a view to demonstrating how these may be applied to international crimes. The idea was to introduce these methods and their potential to the large body of lawyers working in the broader field of international criminal justice. Most defence counsel before international criminal tribunals, especially those appointed for the first time, are confronted with a multiplicity of criminal conduct and perpetrators as well as with an abundance of data, some from NGOs, others from more official sources, without a clear understanding of how such data may be used for the benefit of their clients. The same is equally true for those lawyers working on behalf of the prosecution and to a large extent all have to rely on social scientists to provide clues and directions. The situation is compounded further when no data exist and where there is a need to construct solid patterns of criminality and/or assess why mass conduct occurred one way and not another. There is no substitute for imagination in this work and this chapter has not even begun to touch upon the myriad combinations and possibilities that are open to observation. It must also be highlighted that a study is only as good as its depth, accuracy and the manner by which it eliminates inherent limitations, including ethical, substantial and procedural limitations.

Finally, it should be noted, as the author has hopefully made it clear throughout, that the research methods and ideas presented in this chapter are not only useful to professionals prosecuting or defending persons before domestic and international criminal tribunals. Rather, it is important that researchers engaged in the academic study of international crimes and international criminal law realize the significance of primary research. Whereas a good understanding of the law is important, its application without a solid understanding of context, the perceptions of victims and perpetrators, the numbers of dead, wounded or otherwise victimized and what these patterns actually demonstrate only paints part of the story.

3

Understanding and responding to state crime: a criminological perspective

KRISTIAN LASSLETT

Introduction

In 2005 the *British Journal of Criminology* published a special issue on state crime, the first by a criminological journal. In the introduction, Green and Ward condemn criminology's disproportionate focus on street crime: 'Considering the contribution of state agencies to the world's homicide rates and the scale of their economic crimes, the space devoted to state crime in the literature of our discipline remains pitifully small.'[1] Nevertheless, they acknowledge, 'criminologists are beginning – but only beginning – to remedy this omission'.[2]

Since 2005 criminologists have continued to expand the disciplinary space devoted to state crime. This is evidenced by a growing number of state crime research networks, such as the International State Crime Consortium and Supranational Criminology; while 2010 saw the launch of the International State Crime Initiative, a criminological research centre devoted to state crime and resistance.[3] State crime researchers have also organised the field's first scholarly journal *State Crime*, which has proven an important focal point for debates sparked by the increasing range of monographs, textbooks, edited collections and articles authored on the subject. These collective efforts have prompted an eclectic range of state crime doctoral projects, which preludes the emergence of a muscular new generation of scholars. In short, state crime studies is approaching maturity.

However, the emergence of state crime studies should not be viewed as a mere quantitative addition to the interdisciplinary terrain. Rather, it brings a range of concerns and tools that offer a distinct vantage point for engaging with state crime, which compliment allied disciplines such as law, psychology, anthropology and political science. With that in mind,

[1] P. Green and T. Ward, 'Introduction', (2005) 45 *British Journal of Criminology* 431, at 432.
[2] Ibid. [3] See www.statecrime.org (accessed 4 December 2013).

this chapter will critically engage with some of the debates and interventions that have helped forge this unique approach. We will begin by surveying the conceptual frameworks criminologists employ to define state crime. It will be argued that approaches rooted in international law are being challenged by process-driven understandings of state crime, which view criminality as a quality that attaches to certain state practices through censure from below. Complimenting this process-driven approach is the field's growing interest in movements of resistance that emerge in response to criminal state practices. It will be suggested that the latter line of inquiry offers an important opportunity to consider the concrete social realities that prompt civil society actors to appropriate different normative frameworks, and establish them as a standard of conduct which states must either observe or face sanctions.

Having framed state crime as a historical form of social stigma that is strategically attached to certain state actions by resistance movements, we will then proceed to look at the contrasting theoretical methods criminologists use to conceptually articulate this complex social exchange. In particular, a number of integrated theories will be critically reviewed, and then juxtaposed with a Marxist strand of state crime scholarship.

It will be concluded that state crime studies is increasingly being defined by a theoretical and empirical focus that centres upon two intimately connected processes. On the one hand state crime scholars are closely examining the way in which civil society organises and operationalises standards of conduct for the state, while on the other they are tracing and conceptualising the particular determinations that motivate state actors to exceed these boundaries and deflect stigmatising labels. This dialectical concern with deviant state practice and censure organised from below, it will be suggested, is most reflective of the distinctive contribution being forged by state crime studies scholars.

What is state crime?

State crime scholars have over the past twenty years explored a range of methods for defining the field's subject matter. Ward recently underlined the significance of this task: 'Definitions of crime or deviance are important, not because they precisely demarcate the boundaries of a discipline, but because of the questions that they prompt us to ask.'[4]

[4] T. Ward, 'State Crime and the Sociology of Human Rights', (2013) 5 *Revista Crítica Penal y Poder* 77, at 77.

In one key respect there is little disagreement; state crime refers to organisational practices undertaken in pursuit of state goals and interests.[5] However, views diverge when it comes to determining the conceptual basis upon which to deem state practices, 'criminal'. Two distinct strands of thought have emerged. One strand employs a criteria-based approach, while the other opts for a process-driven framework. An overview of each conceptual method will be given, before an argument is made in favour of a process-driven approach.

Criteria-based definitions are distinguished by a search for normative standards that distinguish *criminal* state practices from the undesirable or harmful. The background to this search is a discipline – criminology – which has historically proven sceptical of interventions that waiver from state-sanctioned definitions of crime. As Tappan famously said of white-collar crime:

> [It] invites individual systems of private values to run riot in an area (economic ethics) where gross variation exists among criminologists as well as others. The rebel may enjoy a veritable orgy of delight in damning as criminal almost anyone he pleases . . . Vague, omnibus concepts defining crime are a blight upon either a legal system or a system of sociology that strives to be objective.[6]

To counteract such criticisms, criminologists have cautiously searched for a normative standard upon which to define state crime that is defensible from a disciplinary perspective but untied to state-sanctioned definitions.[7]

One of the most provocative and influential formulations was developed by Julia and Herman Schwendinger during the 1970s.[8] The Schwendingers' approach is distinguished by the clear link they make between ethics and practice. To that end, the Schwendingers argue truly egalitarian social systems generate an environment where all individuals are able to actualise –

[5] See D. O. Friedrichs, 'State Crime or Governmental Crime: Making Sense of the Conceptual Confusion', in J. I. Ross (ed.), *Controlling State Crime* (London: Transaction Publishers, 2000) 53–79.

[6] P. Tappan, 'Who is the Criminal?', (1946) 12 *American Sociological Review* 96, at 99.

[7] As is commonly remarked in the literature, states are reluctant to define their own conduct as criminal. Also, as organisations with a specific range of interests in a socially fractured environment, there is no justifiable basis upon which to treat state-sanctioned norms as neutrally derived. See D. Kauzlarich, R. C. Kramer and B. Smith, 'Toward the Study of Governmental Crime: Nuclear Weapons, Foreign Intervention, and International Law', (1992) 16 *Humanity and Society* 543; H. Schwendinger and J. Schwendinger, 'Defenders of Order or Guardians of Human Rights', in I. Taylor, P. Walton and J. Young (eds.), *Critical Criminology* (London: Routledge and Kegan Paul, 1975) 113–46.

[8] Schwendinger and Schwendinger, above note 7.

in the fullest sense possible – their inherent potential. For such emancipatory social systems to be secured, the Schwendingers suggest human rights norms must be upheld and valorised. Accordingly, they declare:

> All persons must be guaranteed the fundamental prerequisites for well-being, including food, shelter, clothing, medical services, challenging work and recreational experiences, as well as security from predatory individuals or repressive and imperialistic social elites. These material requirements, basic services and enjoyable relationships are not to be regarded as rewards or privileges. They are rights![9]

With this in mind, the Schwendingers suggest that the label crime should be reserved for practices which violate 'basic rights', whose 'fulfilment is absolutely essential to the realization of a great number of values'.[10] For example, 'a danger to one's health or life itself endangers all other claims. A dead man can hardly realize *any* of his human potentialities.'[11]

This broad appeal to human rights has had a significant impact upon scholars working in the process-driven tradition; however, the Schwendingers' influence on criteria-based approaches has waned. In a particularly pointed critique, Cohen chides their 'moral crusade', referring to it as 'sixties rhetoric'.[12] Cohen instead argues for a stricter application of human rights standards, one that is limited to '"gross" violations of human rights – genocide, mass political killings, state terrorism, torture, disappearances'.[13]

Given the disagreement prompted by these divergent approaches, some state crime scholars have looked to international law for firmer ground. In this respect, Kauzlarich, Kramer and Smith offer one of the earliest articulations of this more doctrinal approach. They explain:

> One . . . fruitful avenue to consider in the search for an effective way to translate emancipatory values into a set of specific standards to classify behaviour as criminal for scientific purposes is in the area of international law. Many emancipatory values, peoples' rights and human rights have received legal expression through various international treaties and agreements . . . We propose that the general principles and substantive content of various forms of international law constitutes the specific standards that we use to classify the socially injurious actions of state and government agencies as crime for the purpose of criminological study.[14]

[9] Ibid., at 133–4. [10] Ibid., at 136. [11] Ibid., at 136–7.
[12] S. Cohen, 'Human Rights and Crimes of the State: The Culture of Denial', (1993) 26 *Australian and New Zealand Journal of Criminology* 97, at 98.
[13] Ibid. [14] Kauzlarich, Kramer and Smith, above note 7, at 547–8.

This general approach has been adopted and further refined in more recent interventions. For example, Mullins and Rothe argue 'that the use of international law – customary law, treaties, charters, international humanitarian law, and international human rights law – constitutes the strongest foundation for defining state crime as this framework includes standards such as human rights, social and economic harms, as well as providing a solid legalistic foundation'.[15]

Although approaches rooted in international law may offer a codified foundation upon which to define state crime, they nonetheless share a common methodological basis with broader appeals to human rights. In essence both approaches articulate a particular normative standard – whether rooted in principle or law; state crimes are then said to be organisational practices which contravene these standards. Clearly, while this method identifies breaches of international law or indeed human rights norms as a platform for the concept of state crimes, an emerging tract of state crime scholarship, nonetheless, argues that something more is needed if certain state practices are to obtain the social quality of being criminal. In particular, an active property must be present, a social exchange that stigmatises certain state practices through acts of censure and sanction.

This alternative, process-driven approach finds its roots in a dialectical tradition of scholarship which views the social properties of actions, institutions and people as potentialities that only become actualised through particular forms of structured social exchange. Ilyenkov explains 'each individual separately taken thing comprises its own essence potentially, only as an element of some concrete system of interacting things, rather than in the form of an actually given general feature'.[16] Indeed, in his famous *Theses on Feuerbach*, Marx critiques those analyses that freeze reality – removing its practical content – and then attempt to abstract properties from this static social image. 'The chief defect of all hitherto existing materialism', Marx argues, 'is that the thing, reality, sensuousness, is conceived only in the form of the *object or of contemplation*, but not as *sensuous human activity, practice*'.[17]

[15] C. W. Mullins and D. L. Rothe, *Blood, Power and Bedlam: Violations of International Criminal Law in Post-Colonial Africa* (New York, NY: Peter Lang, 2008) at 8.

[16] E. V. Ilyenkov, *The Dialectics of the Abstract and the Concrete in Marx's Capital* (Moscow: Progress Publishers, 1982) at 130.

[17] K. Marx, *Theses on Feuerbach* (1845) available online at www.marxists.org/archive/marx/works/1845/theses/theses.htm (accessed 28 November 2013).

In contrast to this approach, Marx's dialectical materialism argues for forms of analysis that conceive objects as dynamic historical phenomena, immersed within a socially mediated process of becoming. For example, what gives human beings their historical characteristics, from a dialectical point of view, are the everyday practices constitutive of social life – practices that are prompted by the broader social relationships around which material reproduction is organised – that actualise human potential in precise ways. 'To be a slave, to be a citizen', Marx argues, 'are social characteristics, relations between human beings A and B. Human being A, as such, is not a slave. He is a slave in and through society.'[18]

Once examined from a dialectical perspective, the criteria-based approaches outlined above appear to define state crime in a one-sided fashion. In particular, they focus on state crime's normative dimension – treating it as an object 'of contemplation' – while the practical exchanges which actualise the potentially criminal character of certain state activities are not given weight.[19] Process-based approaches, on the other hand, include a *practical* moment in their definition.

A compelling formulation rooted in this tradition was presented by Green and Ward in an influential paper, 'State Crime, Human Rights and the Limits of Criminology'.[20] Here, Green and Ward argue that state crime has both a subjective and objective moment, which they articulate through the inter-related concepts of deviancy and legitimacy. For Green and Ward, deviancy denotes a form of judgement wherein an audience determines that certain behaviour violates fundamental norms governing social metabolism, and are thus disposed to censure the behaviour and apply certain sanctions.[21] However, in an innovative twist that breaks with criminology's bias towards official judgements administered by the state, Green and Ward argue:

> Deviancy labels and informal sanctions can . . . be applied 'from below' to state action that is perceived as illegitimate; for example . . . in Turkey, those audiences 'from below' include the Kurdish population in the southeast of Turkey; the 'Saturday Mothers' who gather in Istanbul every

[18] K. Marx, *Grundrisse* (Middlesex: Penguin Books, 1973) at 265.

[19] A failure to consider the active side of state crime, borrowing from Ward, can lead to critical questions being omitted from our inquiry. See Ward, above note 4.

[20] P. Green and T. Ward, 'State Crime, Human Rights and the Limits of Criminology', (2000) 27 *Social Justice* 101.

[21] See P. Green and T. Ward, *State Crime* (London: Pluto Press, 2004).

> week to protest the disappearances of their children, and other relatives and human rights groups, trade unions, Bar Associations, journalists, and other media workers whose activities centre on exposing state crime and corruption.[22]

In support of the approach developed by Green and Ward, Grewcock goes so far as to argue, 'without an explicit engagement with civil society and a social audience prepared to condemn particular state behaviours as deviant, sociological conceptions of state crime are rendered virtually meaningless'.[23] Civil society here denotes a fluid social space outside the formal boundaries of the state and economy where consent to the existing order is both organised *and* challenged.

The subjective dimension of Green and Ward's framework has elicited criticism from Rothe. Rothe argues 'this approach is far too vague concerning what constitutes a social audience and which audience may legitimately label behaviour a crime'.[24] This critique echoes Tappan's concern that criminology should avoid overly nebulous definitions of crime. However, in their defence, it must be noted that Green and Ward's approach is grounded in a very different ontological tradition to the one observed by the latter authors. As a result, Green and Ward cannot offer, in advance, the certainty criteria-based scholars' desire. Dialectically speaking, who censures and sanctions, and how they prosecute these stigmatising acts, is an empirical question that can only be answered through social inquiry. Accordingly, what constitutes a social audience and which audience may legitimately label behaviour a crime are questions that can only be answered through examining concrete historical struggles of resistance that have organised censure, and applied sanctions, with some success.

The second dimension of Green and Ward's approach is grounded in the category 'legitimacy'. They observe:

> In any situation where the state's claim to legitimacy is accorded some degree of consent – and exactly what this 'consent' amounts to may be a very difficult question – there is likely to be some tacit understanding of the limits of legitimate conduct (which may be more or less closely related to legal norms), departure from which will attract some kind of censure or sanctions.[25]

[22] Green and Ward, above note 20, at 105.

[23] M. Grewcock, 'Public Criminology, Victim Agency and Researching State Crime', (2012) 1 *State Crime* 109, at 112.

[24] D. L. Rothe, *State Criminality: The Crime of All Crimes* (Plymouth: Lexington Books, 2009) at 6.

[25] Green and Ward, above note 20, at 108.

These limits are set, Green and Ward argue, by established values, norms, and beliefs which make claims to state power justified and 'expressive of consent'.[26] Accordingly, 'a state practice is illegitimate if it departs from the state's own rules or is unjustifiable in terms of the values that the rules purport to serve'.[27] With that in mind, Green and Ward suggest – echoing the argument of the Schwendingers, to whom they are intellectually indebted – that the legitimacy of most contemporary states is premised on a 'real or nominal commitment to human rights'.[28] Of course, this is not a prescriptive statement; Green and Ward leave open the possibility that other normative frameworks may govern state legitimacy in certain circumstances.

Synthesising their core concepts – deviancy, legitimacy and human rights – Green and Ward conclude that state practices obtain the quality of being criminal when they are both objectively illegitimate *and* are subjected to forms of censure and sanction organised by a significant social audience. However, this distinction between state crime's objective and subjective moment is best seen dialectically. The character and strength of norms which legitimise claims to state power are fluid properties whose content and limits are determined through a historical process of social struggle. Accordingly, the objective standards by which states are judged today are the product of yesterday's popular resistance. In this sense movements of resistance are critical to understanding state crime's objective and subjective moment; that is, they expand and strengthen the normative limits upon which claims to state power rest, and are the conduits that activate condemnation when these limits are exceeded.

The latter dialectical argument seems to sit comfortably with Green and Ward's subsequent work. Indeed, in a more recent intervention Green and Ward observe: 'Civil society is both the most important counterweight to state crime and one of the most important sources of the norms that define state crime.'[29] However, they add an important caveat: namely, civil society is not a space free of contradiction: 'It [civil society] is both a complement to state power, educating and disciplining responsible citizens within a hegemonic order, and a potential source of opposition, capable of educating and disciplining the state itself.'[30] Accordingly, the challenge becomes one of understanding the critical fault-lines upon which hegemony and resistance are organised, and the

26 Ibid. 27 Ibid., at 109. 28 Ibid.

29 P. Green and T. Ward, 'Civil Society, Resistance and State Crime', in E. Stanley and J. McCulloch (eds.), *State Crime and Resistance* (Abingdon: Routledge, 2013) at 28.

30 Ibid., at 37–8.

intersecting role played by norms, censure and sanction in the strategies of different social coalitions.

A concrete example of this social dynamic may be found in Grewcock's research on asylum seekers, which illuminates in rich detail a prolonged struggle over the social status of Australia's border control policies. Lying behind this struggle is the Australian government's increasingly punitive response to so-called 'unauthorised maritime arrivals'. Indeed, over the past twenty years asylum seekers arriving in Australia by boat have been imprisoned, brutalised and their access to the courts restricted by the state. In response, asylum seekers have waged a campaign of resistance designed to censure the Australian state's illegitimate actions, with a well-established set of rules governing the rights of refugees acting as a normative foundation. Grewcock observes:

> Self-activity in the form of group protests; escapes; the making of banners; desperate pleas to media outlets and supporters on the outside; hunger strikes and the stitching of lips have all generated debate in the wider community and provided a focus for opposition to government policy.[31]

In order to dull the censuring power of asylum seekers, the Australian government has limited their contact with researchers, the media and activists. Additionally, protesting detainees have been subjected to a range of disciplinary measures, including 'the deployment of special response teams ... the use of tear gas, water cannons and other forceful dispersal techniques; the use of isolation blocks and solitary confinement; and the transfer of non-compliant and troublesome detainees into the prison system or across the detention centre complex'.[32] These efforts have been complemented by a moral panic engineered, in part, by incendiary narratives deployed by the major political parties in Australia, and a Murdoch-dominated media landscape. In these narratives asylum seekers are commonly referred to as 'queue jumpers' and 'illegals' that threaten to flood Australia in an 'unstoppable wave'.[33] McKay, Thomas and Blood claim:

> The moral panic and social anxiety or risk associated with the arrival of asylum seekers by boat ... [is] reinforced [in media accounts] by emphasising the 'illegality' of the method of arrival ... [and by news] reports

[31] Grewcock, above note 23, at 115.

[32] M. Grewcock, *Border Crimes: Australia's 'War' on Illicit Migrants* (Annandale: Federation Press, 2010) at 236

[33] F. H. McKay, S. L. Thomas and R. W. Blood, '"Any One of These Boat People Could Be a Terrorist for all we Know!" Media Representations and Public Perceptions of "Boat People" Arrivals in Australia', (2011) 12 *Journalism* 607, at 616 and 619.

> focused on issues of economic gain for the asylum seekers, and exploitation of Australians, rather than the humanitarian issues that may have caused individuals to flee their home countries.[34]

Grewcock helps contextualise this social narrative by pointing to the particular role nationalism plays in securing the hegemony of capitalist states: 'nationalism demands loyalty in the name of identity, which is reinforced through state enforced notions of citizenship that disguises class inequality and social difference'.[35] In Australia 'exclusion' lies at 'the heart of this ideology, whether expressed through a belief in the inevitable extinction of the indigenous population or as policies directed at keeping out those seen to be of inferior or culturally incompatible status'.[36]

Asylum seekers and their civil society supporters are clearly immersed in a complex normative struggle over the character of their actions *and* the subsequent reaction of the Australian state, which is woven into a broader narrative of nationalism essential to the organisation of hegemony in Australia. Inverting the stigmatising process – which has historically been directed at asylum seekers – through protests, human rights interventions and other forms of resistance, has become a critical strategic technology for asylum seekers and their supporters. It is used to carve out an emancipatory space in which asylum seekers can defend their interests and counteract the brutal treatment meted out to them by the Australian state.

All of which illustrates a critical point, state practices are not intrinsically criminal, nor are they necessarily criminal because they violate international law; rather, state practices become criminal when civil society is able to establish, and then enforce, fundamental rules of conduct. There is nothing absolute here, criminality attaches to certain state actions on different scales and intensities, depending on the strength of established norms and the capacity of civil society to censure the offending conduct. Accordingly, serious attention must be given to the particular determinations that influence the shape of civil society and its capacity to enforce normative limits. To that end, the dialectical relation between local, national and international civil society is an important area in need of further exploration. Consideration must also be given to the way in which local and national movements of censure articulate their condemnation at an international level, and the role

[34] Ibid., at 622. [35] Grewcock, above note 32, at 76. [36] Ibid., at 77.

human rights organs and vehicles of international criminal justice play in either facilitating, co-opting or indeed silencing popular condemnation of illegitimate state conduct.

It is critical, in this respect, to keep in mind civil society is both a 'complement to state power', and 'a potential source of opposition'.[37] Comparing the struggles, norms and sanctions applied by civil society at a local and national level with the focus and strategic struggles waged by key organs of international justice is one potential methodology for exploring the power terrain of international civil society and in whose interests it is slanted. Also there is a need to look at the mechanisms that currently exist for translating national forms of censure into international condemnation and, vice versa, focusing on how these mechanisms strengthen or limit struggles from below.

Of course, this is not a matter of mere 'academic' concern, there is a practical need to understand how, on the one hand, censure can be co-opted and restrained by international civil society in order to minimise criticisms of hegemonic state-powers, and how, on the other hand, international civil society can amplify and strengthen popular condemnation in order to enhance the accountability of all states, regardless of their stature.[38] Here, particular attention should be given to the specific discourses, organisational frameworks and social configurations that mediate this exchange and the potential which exists for enhancing and extending the space reserved for forms of censure and sanction that stigmatise illegitimate state practices without prejudice to the state's position in the international order, or the identity of those resisting from below.

Of course, these critical social processes constitutive of state crime cannot be divorced from wider social conflicts and their economic, political and ideological fault-lines; indeed, the enforcement of certain normative limits always possesses specific concrete meanings and uses for social groups at a national and international level, which must be understood if we are to illuminate the practical dimensions of state criminality. This latter point has been powerfully brought to the fore by a new tract of state crime scholarship which focuses on the struggles of resistance state violence and corruption inspire, a literature to which we will now turn.

[37] Green and Ward, above note 29, at 37–8.

[38] R. Falk, 'Severe State Crime and Double Standards', *State Crime* (forthcoming 2015).

State crime and resistance

Prompted by a 2010 workshop at Victoria University organised by Elizabeth Stanley, criminologists are increasingly examining the way individuals, organisations and communities – at a local, national and international level – resist state criminality. Stanley and McCulloch explain: 'The failure of state crime scholars to include resistance as a core aspect of the study of state crime may lead to feelings of despair, disinterest or impotence among students and other audience, and flowing from this, states of mind that facilitate passivity, even in the face of irrefutable knowledge about state crime.'[39] They add, 'a failure to engage with resistance is also a failure to acknowledge history "from below"'.[40]

This argument has resonated with state crime scholars. Accordingly, over the past three years the field has witnessed a growing number of interventions that seek to define, map and theorise how different communities of resistance emerge and articulate opposition. In one respect there is broad agreement that resistance 'is best regarded in terms of a continuum, ranging from very passive forms to very active ones'.[41] Indeed, Stanley and McCulloch observe: 'resistance ranges from the small, silent and personal through to the multitudinous, spectacular and momentous. The scope of activities that might be defined as resistance is broad. It may be violent or non-violent, passive or active, hidden or open, verbal or physical, spontaneous or strategic, local or global, and frequently a combination of some or all.'[42]

To help distinguish key features of resistance, Stanley and McCulloch develop a number of important concepts. They identify 'four essential elements of resistance: opposition, intention, communication and transformation'.[43] Accordingly, in Stanley and McCulloch's view, for phenomena to be classed as resistance they must consist of acts motivated by some form of conscious opposition to predatory events, regimes or social systems – that is, 'morally and politically meaningful acts' –

[39] E. Stanley and J. McCulloch, 'Resistance to State Crime', in E. Stanley and J. McCulloch (eds.), *State Crime and Resistance*, (Abingdon: Routledge, 2013) at 2. See also E. Stanley and J. McCulloch, 'State Crime and Resistance' (2011) available online at http://statecrime.org/online_article/state-crime-and-resistance/ (accessed 28 November 2013).

[40] Ibid.

[41] D. O. Friedrichs, 'On Resisting State Crime: Conceptual and Contextual Issues', (2009) 36 *Social Justice* 4, at 7–8.

[42] Stanley and McCulloch (2013), above note 39, at 4.

[43] Ibid., at 4–5.

which are designed to communicate disapproval to a wider social audience, and bring about some form of emancipatory transformation.[44]

Resistance, in this sense, captures something more general than what is pinpointed by Green and Ward above; it denotes moments where specific constellations of state power are challenged and reconfigured. Green and Ward's framework, on the other hand, is oriented towards understanding the conditions under which those engaged in resistance – i.e., challenging specific organisations of state power – strategically participate in processes that centre upon rules of conduct and censure, and how this particular social exchange impacts on states and the communities they victimise. Accordingly, it might be said that Green and Ward's approach alerts us to the particular forms of social exchange that inscribe state actions with the quality of being criminal, while Stanley and McCulloch's resistance framework helps situate these exchanges within broader moments of social transformation. The question then arises as to what conditions particular struggles of resistance attempt to enforce rules of conduct and how this intersects with their broader social aspirations.

In order to demonstrate the complex determinations at play here, it is helpful to look at a concrete example. One which I have particular knowledge of[45] involves a struggle of resistance that emerged on Bougainville, a South Pacific island which forms part of Papua New Guinea's (PNG) easternmost province, during 1988.[46] The struggle was

[44] Ibid., at 5. It was recently pointed out to me by David McKeever that this approach parallels formulations of resistance developed in the political sciences (personal communication, 2013). For example, Meszerics writes: 'In sum, an action to count as resistance, it needs to have some negative impact on the regime, which is discernible to observers; the perpetrator must have political motivation beyond a simple striving for power. It also must involve a conscious disregard for the rules of the regime and the belief that its legitimacy is questionable. With some simplification we can see these requirements as the necessary and sufficient conditions for the notion of resistance.' See T. Meszerics, 'Independence before All Else: Hungarian Anti-Communist Resistance in the East European Context, 1945–1956', (2007) 41 *East European Quarterly* 39, at 42.

[45] I have spent ten years researching this conflict through interviews with senior state-corporate officials, combatants and civil society organisations, complemented by archival work.

[46] See K. Lasslett, 'Winning Hearts and Mines: The Bougainville Crisis 1988–1990', in R. Jackson, E. Murphy and S. Poynting (eds.), *Contemporary State Terrorism: Theory and Practice* (London: Routledge, 2010) at 141–62; K. Lasslett, 'State Crime by Proxy: Australia and the Bougainville Conflict', (2012) 52 *British Journal of Criminology* 705; K. Lasslett, 'Power, Struggle and State Crime: Researching through Resistance', (2012) 1 *State Crime* 126; K. Lasslett, *State Crime on the Margins of Empire* (London: Pluto Press, 2014).

triggered by social conflict surrounding a large copper and gold mine – owned by Rio Tinto – which had been operating on the island since 1972. The mine's operation rapidly accelerated a process of social differentiation within, and between, village communities, which had been originally prompted by the uneven emergence of capitalist agriculture. This accelerated dynamic heightened tensions between a nascent rural bourgeoisie and poorer rural households, all of whom were bound together through strong kinship ties and evolving forms of ethnic identity. Exacerbating matters were the mine's deleterious environmental effects and the growing power of economic migrants from the PNG mainland.

In 1988 these tensions erupted in a muscular political campaign spearheaded by a new generation of landowner leaders in the mine area who had peacefully dislodged from power an older elite linked to Rio Tinto.[47] This new leadership rejected the reorganisation of tribal communities along capitalist lines and criticised the instrumental role provincial and national leaders had played in this process. The secretary of the landowners' representative association, Francis Ona, proclaimed:

> We were forced to become passive observers of our own exploitation, first by the racist colonial administration and after independence by the black political leaders in white men's coats . . . We are the 'sacrificial lamb' for the few capitalists whose hunger for wealth is quenchless and unceasing.[48]

In opposition to this exploitative system, resistance leaders proposed a federated structure of tribes committed to upholding tradition and pursuing a development model where both environment, and balance between clan-mates, would be preserved. The mine's closure was viewed as a condition precedent towards this transformation. Accordingly, throughout 1988 landowners staged protests and sit-ins to prosecute the latter aim. When that failed they opted for industrial sabotage.

The latter tactic elicited a militarised response from the PNG state, which was under pressure from Rio Tinto and the Australian government to assert its authority. Villages around the mine site were burnt and residents imprisoned in makeshift detention camps. These provocative acts led landowner resistance to take an armed form, organised through the Bougainville Revolutionary Army (BRA) and its political wing, the Bougainville Interim Government (BIG). Given that the assaults on

[47] Land remains customarily owned in PNG, an arrangement that gives tribal communities important forms of economic and political power.
[48] Francis Ona, Speech, 29 November 1989.

landowning communities were sanctioned by the national government, the BRA viewed secession as the only remaining path through which the movement's social objectives could be achieved. The BRA's call for independence in 1989 garnered widespread support from communities across the island that had witnessed or heard about government atrocities. To break the independence movement, the PNG state launched a wave of brutal attacks on mine area villages in a bid to demonstrate the military arsenal that would be unleashed on a province-wide scale were resistance to continue. Civilian targets were mortared and subjected to aerial bombardment. Men and women were frequently tortured and executed, some were simply disappeared while others were dumped in public areas for all to see.

Facing fierce BRA resistance, in 1990 the PNG state placed a military blockade around the island which stopped the supply of humanitarian aid.[49] It was felt that the strengthening of BRA/BIG hegemony could be prevented by increasing the hardships faced by village communities – thus provoking opposition to the resistance struggle – and then militarising local opposition. Helping PNG to prosecute these measures was the Australian government, which covertly sent defence force officers to the island, and implemented a large package of military support.

At this crucial stage in the conflict – i.e., during 1990 – the BRA/BIG needed undisturbed civic space in which to organise consent on a wider scale for their political programme. The blockade, and the emergence of loyalist paramilitary forces, in conjunction with growing law and order problems, significantly constricted this space by heightening fear, distrust, economic decline and war-weariness. In a planning document dated April 1990, PNG's Department of Defence broadly registered these effects and thus emphasised the importance of maintaining the blockade and further militarising tensions on the island.[50]

Upon these fault-lines an international peace movement emerged in opposition to the violence. It was a loose coalition of community groups,

[49] Evans, who visited Bougainville in March 1991, reported: 'Bougainvillean doctors who have remained on Bougainville throughout the conflict estimate that over 3,000 people have died as a direct consequence of the blockade and that many thousands more are suffering unnecessarily because of a lack of medicines, soaps, detergents and dressings.' L. Evans, 'The Health and Social Situation on Bougainville', in D. Denoon and M. Spriggs (eds.), *The Bougainville Crisis: 1991 Update* (Bathurst: Crawford House Press, 1992) at 45–6.

[50] Defence Intelligence Branch, *An Intelligence Resume for Contingency Planning for North Solomons Province* (Port Moresby: Author, 1990).

NGOs, trade unions, churches and activist organisations that spanned PNG, Australia and New Zealand.[51] At its core were activists who on the one hand backed Bougainville's right to self-determination, and on the other opposed the deviant practices being employed to suppress independence aspirations on the island. This movement was strengthened by the involvement of the UN Special Rapporteur on Extrajudicial, Summary or Arbitrary Executions, Amnesty International, Médecins Sans Frontières and the Red Cross, who scrutinised the conflict's human rights and humanitarian dimensions.

Through a range of interventions that included speaking tours, human rights reports, protests, campaigns of civil disobedience, UN appearances and media exposure, this loose-knit coalition of actors put a spotlight on the deviant organisational practices being employed on Bougainville. Given that the BRA/BIG had frequently criticised the PNG government on human rights grounds, the BRA/BIG backed these actions.[52] Indeed, the reinforcement of human rights norms, particularly those centring upon self-determination, had the potential to open up the civic space needed for the BRA/BIG to normalise social conditions on the island, and organise consent for their political campaign. Given the social and geopolitical ends this campaign championed, the PNG and Australian governments on the other hand wanted to see this civic space starved of further oxygen, and the BRA/BIG isolated and marginalised from their popular support base. Accordingly, the PNG and Australian governments could not afford to have their sorties or blockade stigmatised on a wide scale, or indeed restrained through the popular enforcement of certain normative limits. A range of tactics were, therefore, employed to suppress the flow of information from Bougainville and to undermine reports and interventions organised by activists and human rights organisations.

This prompts two conclusions that help fuse together the approaches articulated by Stanley and McCulloch and Green and Ward. First, the particular forms of social exchange which imprint criminality on state practices must be situated within broader movements of resistance.[53] Indeed, the censure of the PNG state, and its foreign benefactors, derived

[51] Lasslett, 'Power, Struggle and State Crime: Researching through Resistance', above note 46.

[52] Though it should be noted that their activities were also subjected to criticism by this international peace movement.

[53] This should not overshadow the cathartic significance of such exchanges for victims.

its concrete significance from the precise aspirations and interests this action bulwarked, or in the case of the state and mining company, blocked. Which leads on to the second point: although ostensibly a normative act, the designation of certain practices as criminal cannot be divorced from the class-laden contexts in which normative judgement occurs. In the case of Bougainville, stigmatising certain military practices employed by the PNG state became a mechanism that enhanced the capacity of the BRA/BIG to transform the arrangement of class power on the island – which had been dominated by mining capital and an increasingly parasitic state – and to resist the imperial posturing of Australia.[54] Equally, PNG and Australia's vociferous condemnation of the peace movement and its interventions acutely reflected the class arrangements these states were committed to upholding.

In conclusion, it may be said that once synthesised, deviancy, legitimacy and resistance offer an orienting framework which illuminates the exchanges and processes that state criminality emerges out of and from which it obtains precise historical meanings. Researching and articulating the rich social content of these determinations constitutes one of the most critical and unique footings upon which criminology can intervene. However, that said, the clarity of this contribution is invariably linked to the theoretical frameworks being brought to bear on state crime. In this respect, two divergent approaches have emerged.

Understanding state crime: a review of the theoretical landscape

As we have just observed, a theoretical literature on resistance is only beginning to emerge; accordingly, to date state crime scholars have largely directed their theoretical efforts towards understanding the forces which prompt states to employ illegitimate practices. Although significant points of contention exist, there is general agreement that a robust theoretical framework must be able to capture the role played by state officials, organisational structures and the broader social arrangements in which states exist. However, differences emerge when it comes to the scientific method employed to explore these complex realities. Arguably, the most popular theoretical current to date is the integrated approach to state crime theory, which has produced the 'Integrated Theoretical Model

[54] We should also be open to the possibility that attempts to sanction certain state actions are, in some cases, mechanisms for subduing, limiting or indeed marginalising more radical strains of resistance.

of State-Corporate Crime',[55] and the 'Integrated Theory of International Criminal Law Violations'.[56] Diverging from the integrated models is a tract of state crime scholarship influenced by Marxism. To begin, the integrated approach will be reviewed, before the contrasting Marxist tradition is plotted.

A series of important papers delivered by Kramer and Michalowski during the 1990s proved the catalyst for integrated approaches. Having contributed both to a maturing literature on corporate crime and a nascent literature on state crime, Kramer and Michalowski query in these papers the merit of studying state and corporate crime in isolation.[57] They ground their stance in a specific understanding of capitalism. In particular, Kramer and Michalowski argue that the social relations through which capitalism functions blend the practices, interests and institutional arrangements constitutive of states and corporations in complicated and sometimes contradictory ways.[58] As states and corporations are interdependent, Kramer and Michalowski suggest their offending behaviour can rarely be understood in isolation. With this important argument in mind, they set about developing a theoretical model that helps explain what Kramer and Michalowski label state-corporate crime.

A key conceptual innovation informing the model's structure was articulated in a 1991 paper. In this paper Kramer and Michalowski argue that state-corporate crime is brought about by 'a coincidence of pressure for goal attainment, availability and perceived attractiveness of illegitimate means, and an absence of effective social control'.[59] Reflecting this key

[55] R. C. Kramer and R. J. Michalowski, 'State-Corporate Crime', prepared for the American Society of Criminology Meeting, 7–12 November 1990, Baltimore, Maryland, revised September 1991; R. C. Kramer, 'From White-Collar to State-Corporate Crime', Conference Paper, North Central Sociological Association, 22 March 1990, Louisville, Kentucky; R. C. Kramer, R. J. Michalowski and D. Kauzlarich, 'The Origins and Development of the Concepts and Theory of State-Corporate Crime', (2002) 48 *Crime & Delinquency* 263; R. C. Kramer and R. J. Michalowski, 'The Original Formulation', in R. J. Michalowski and R. C. Kramer (eds.), *State-Corporate Crime: Wrongdoing at the Intersection of Business & Government* (London: Rutgers University Press, 2006).

[56] C. W. Mullins and D. L. Rothe, *Blood, Power and Bedlam: Violations of International Criminal Law in Post-Colonial Africa* (New York, NY: Peter Lang, 2008); Rothe, above note 24; D. L. Rothe, 'Criminological Theory and State Crime: How Far Can It Go?', (2013) 5 *Revista Crítica Penal y Poder* 25.

[57] See Kramer and Michalowski, 'State-Corporate Crime' above note 55; Kramer, Michalowski and Kauzlarich, above note 55; Kramer and Michalowski, 'The Original Formulation', above note 55.

[58] Ibid. [59] See Kramer and Michalowski 'State-Corporate Crime', above note 55.

insight, the integrated model features a horizontal axis ordered according to certain 'catalysts of action', in particular 'motivation', 'opportunity' and 'control'.[60] On the model's vertical axis are the three social levels at which these catalysts operate, specifically the 'interactional', 'organisational' and 'institutional environment'.[61] Kramer and Michalowski connect these levels in a holistic manner – the political economy of a particular society is reified in the organisational structures of its commanding institutions, while the resulting institutional cultures and dynamics constitute the social landscape in which agents actualise their potential through practice, all of which is conceived dialectically. Indeed, Kramer argues that these 'three levels of social experience . . . constitute the dialectical totality of human life – the individual, the institutional, and the societal'.[62]

To help unite the levels of analysis and catalysts for action, Kramer and Michalowski forward the following hypothesis:

> Political economies, organizations, and individuals may place greater or less emphasis on the attainment of rationalized goals as the engine for social action. Thus a highly goal-oriented individual, working in an organization that evaluates performance strongly on goal attainment by its workers, in a society whose cultural and institutional framework emphasizes goal attainment above all else, will be more susceptible to pursuing deviant organizational strategies . . . [Secondly] organizational deviance is more likely in a society where legitimate means are scarce relative to goals. The likelihood of deviance increases for those organizations . . . where the allocation of means by the internal structure is inadequate . . . Finally, the operationality of social control at all three levels will serve both as an important restraint on organizational deviance and as a critical element in constructing symbolic frameworks that will operate at the societal, organization, and personal levels as time passes.[63]

What Kramer and Michalowski have in effect created here is a model that delineates the key causes of state-corporate crime, which are then unified through a set of theoretical propositions. The resulting framework acts both as a vehicle for explanation and a guide to resistance.

For a period the Kramer and Michalowski model was the only one available to state crime scholars working in an integrated tradition.

[60] Kramer and Michalowski, 'The Original Formulation', above note 55. [61] Ibid.

[62] R. C. Kramer, 'The Space Shuttle Challenger Explosion', in K. Schlegel and D. Weisburd (eds.), *White Collar Crime Reconsidered* (Boston, MA: North East University Press, 1992) at 216–7.

[63] Kramer and Michalowski, 'The Original Formulation', above note 55, at 24–6.

However, over the past eight years Mullins and Rothe have developed a new integrated framework, which they call an 'Integrated Theory of International Criminal Law Violations'. According to Mullins and Rothe their framework is designed to explain 'state offending as well as that of active paramilitaries and/or militias'.[64] To that end they borrow heavily from Kramer and Michalowski's model, with two important distinctions – Mullins and Rothe add an extra layer to the horizontal and vertical axes. With respect to the former, 'control' is split into 'constraints' and 'controls', in an attempt to distinguish the constraining properties of civil society from the control effected by criminal justice institutions at a domestic and international level. Mullins and Rothe explain:

> Constraints are those social control elements that stand to make a potential crime riskier or less profitable; offenders must navigate around them to neutralize their influence ... Controls are a stronger form of constraint that has the ability to stave off or prevent entirely the criminal action or to address such violations as an after-the-fact control.[65]

On the vertical axis an international layer is added. 'Most organizational criminology', Mullins and Rothe argue, 'has ignored the social forces and incipient social structures occurring within the international realm in favour of focusing on a state itself'.[66] The inclusion of an international level in their model is designed to address this lacuna.

While the two integrated theories outlined above differ in certain respects, they share a common scientific method. Rothe explains: 'the job ... of an integrationist is to provide an underlying framework (and set of assumptions) that makes sense of empirical reality'.[67] The integrationist achieves this by articulating the intricate causal chains which produce state crime events. This involves both delineating catalysts and conceptualising the logics which unify them across numerous social levels. These causative constellations – once conceptualised – are then said to stand behind a diverse range of state and state-corporate crime events.

An instance of this explanatory method may be found in the work of Rothe. Employing Merton's strain theory to unify a series of catalysts, she argues:

> Strain occurs when attempts to achieve culturally emphasised goals and expectations are unattainable, either due to blocked goals or means.

[64] Mullins and Rothe, above note 56, at 9. [65] Ibid., at 12–13. [66] Ibid., at 9.
[67] Rothe, above note 24, at 99.

> Individuals then may respond [in] several ways to this strain: conformity, innovation, ritualism, and rebellion. In the case of criminality, the blocked goals lead to strain and the response is that of an innovator.[68]

For example, Rothe observes:

> through years of political turmoil and marginalization, many militia groups enact alternative means to accomplish political capital, including coups and/or insurgencies that are directly related to the atrocities this theory aims to explain (e.g., LRA [Lord's Resistance Army] in Uganda or the Darfur insurgency that sparked the Sudanese government's harsh military response and collusion with the Janjaweed).[69]

Rothe's argument echoes a theoretical proposition that was first introduced by Gross. Employing 'a variation of Mertonian theory', Gross suggests that *all* organisations are 'inherently criminogenic' due to the fact they are constructed for the specific purpose of achieving goals in competitive social environments.[70] To that end, he argues: 'some organizations seek profits, others seek survival, still others seek to fulfil government-imposed quotas, others seek to service a body of professionals who run them, some seek to win wars, and some seek to serve a clientele. Whatever the goal might be, it is the emphasis on them that creates the trouble.'[71] Gross adds: 'nothing we have said gives any special comfort to those who identify crime with the pursuit of profit and who might see in our remark an argument against capitalistic forms of organization. The problem with organizations is goals – whatever the goals happen to be.'[72]

If we compare the arguments of Gross and Rothe, a common scientific methodology may be observed. The social mechanisms of blocked goals, goal emphasis, the absence of legitimate means and competitive environments help *explain* the criminal actions of organisations in a range of contexts. These social mechanisms are, therefore, determinate social forces, while corporate crime in the USA, Soviet corruption and the violation of international criminal law by militias, are all concrete manifestations of their criminogenic potential.

[68] Ibid., at 95. [69] Ibid., at 104.

[70] E. Gross, 'Organizational Crime: A Theoretical Perspective', (1978) 1 *Studies in Symbolic Interaction* 55, at 56–7.

[71] E. Gross, 'Organizations as Criminal Actors', in P. Wilson and J. Braithwaite (eds.), *Two Faces of Deviance: Crimes of the Powerless and Powerful*, (Brisbane: University of Queensland Press, 1978) at 209.

[72] Gross, above note 70, at 72.

State crime scholars working in Marxist traditions have pointed to certain limitations associated with this approach.[73] Indeed, as I have suggested elsewhere,[74] Marx himself persuasively argued that the above scientific method tends to diminish theory's explanatory power. In *The Holy Family*, Marx and Engels use the following analogy to evidence their point:

> If from real apples, pears, strawberries and almonds I form the general idea '*Fruit*', if I go further and *imagine* that my abstract idea '*Fruit*', derived from real fruit, is an entity existing outside me, is indeed the true essence of the pear, the apple, etc.; then, in the *language of speculative* philosophy I am declaring that '*Fruit*' is the *substance* of the pear, the apple, the almond, etc. I am saying, therefore, that to be a pear is not essential to the pear, that to be an apple is not essential to the apple; that what is essential to these things is not their real existence, perceptible to the senses, but the essence that I have abstracted from them and then foisted on them, the essence of my idea – '*Fruit*'. I therefore declare apples, pears, almonds, etc., to be mere forms of existence, *modi*, of '*Fruit*'. My finite understanding supported by my senses does of course *distinguish* an apple from a pear and a pear from an almond, but my speculative reason declares these sensuous differences inessential and irrelevant. It sees in the apple *the same* as in the pear, and in the pear the same as in the almond, namely '*Fruit*'. Particular real fruits are no more than semblances whose true essence is 'the Substance' – '*Fruit*'.[75]

Applying this critique to the integrated theories, it can be argued that the respective authors have, in effect, extracted an abstract essence from empirical reality, and 'then foisted on' state crime case studies the 'essence' of their 'idea', in order to explain organisational deviance. The rich empirical variation featured in these cases become 'no more than semblances' of a 'true essence', which is captured in the integrated theoretical models.

From a Marxist perspective this approach fails to provide the important conceptual bridge needed to transcend descriptive accounts – with their significant limitations – and reach more concrete understandings

[73] See K. Lasslett, 'Scientific Method and the Crimes of the Powerful', (2010) 18 *Critical Criminology* 211; S. Tombs, 'State-Corporate Symbiosis in the Production of Crime and Harm', (2012) 1 *State Crime* 170.

[74] Lasslett, above note 73.

[75] K. Marx and F. Engels, *The Holy Family or Critique of Critical Critique* (London: Lawrence and Wishart, 1957) at 78.

that illuminate elusive social processes which exist but are not readily amenable to sense-perception. Indeed, Marx and Engels argue:

> By this method one attains no particular *wealth of definition*. The mineralogist whose whole science was limited to the statement that all minerals are really 'the Mineral' would be a mineralogist only in *his imagination*. For every mineral the speculative mineralogist says 'the Mineral', and his science is reduced to repeating this word as many times as there are real minerals.[76]

None of this is to suggest that the integrated theories are without value. They distil down and articulate specific features of the social terrain which have proven especially important to the enactment of state crime. Accordingly, Green and Ward rightly argue that the integrated models are 'useful heuristic' devices which pinpoint criminogenic factors that require close empirical scrutiny.[77] However, if we are to enrich the data collected through empirical inquiry a 'wealth of definition' is needed, which can orient consciousness to the sinuous reality that stands behind state crime events.

This need has prompted an alternative paradigm of state crime theory informed by Marxism.[78] At the heart of this paradigm is a desire to transcend the reified appearances capitalism generates – captured in descriptive accounts – looking instead at its more elusive 'relations and processes', with an eye for the contradictions latent within them.[79] To that end, Tombs and Whyte have pointed to the enduring theoretical relevance of Marx's *Capital*:

> The labour theory of value and the theory of surplus value, the necessarily antagonistic relationship between classes, the inherent tendency of capitalism to expand, destructively, whilst at the same time reproducing the contradictions upon which it is founded, all seem to be crucial tools for understanding and engaging with the trajectories of the world.[80]

[76] Ibid., at 79.

[77] P. Green and T. Ward, 'State Crime: A Dialectical View', in M. Maguire, R. Morgan and R. Reiner (eds.), *The Oxford Handbook of Criminology* (5th edn, Oxford: Oxford University Press, 2012) at 724.

[78] Green and Ward, above note 21; Grewcock, above note 32; Lasslett, *State Crimes on the Margins of Empire*, above note 46; P. Marfleet, 'Mubarak's Egypt – Nexus of Criminality', (2013) 2 *State Crime* 112; F. Pearce, *Crimes of the Powerful: Marxism, Crime and Deviance* (London: Pluto Press, 1976); S. Tombs and D. Whyte, *Safety Crimes* (Cullompton: Willan Publishing, 2007).

[79] Tombs, above note 73, at 175.

[80] S. Tombs and D. Whyte, 'Unmasking the Crimes of the Powerful', (2002) 11 *Critical Criminology* 217, at 222.

Of course, Marx's theoretical work on the capitalist mode of production remained famously unfinished at the time of his death. Accordingly, significant theoretical challenges were inherited by his students. One particular problem confronting state crime scholars is the absence of Marxist categories which define the schema of state power that develops under capitalism and its peculiar impact upon the processes around which the extraction of surplus value is organised.

Then there is the issue of capitalism's uneven development. Although capitalist social relations function on a world-scale, they are operationalised in spatially divergent ways, according to the particular socio-cultural arrangements encountered within regions, the concrete outcomes of social struggle and the overarching global dynamic of the capitalist system. Accordingly, state crime scholarship requires a range of mediating concepts that orient consciousness to the complex relationship between the universal and the particular. Here interdisciplinary dialogue will play an important role, particularly with those theorists working in development studies, anthropology and international relations.

To date, Marxist state crime scholars have produced a number of theoretically informed accounts of state crime including, for example, Marfleet's history of Egyptian state criminality,[81] Green's analysis of state-mediated disasters in Turkey,[82] Tombs and Whyte's work on safety crimes in the United Kingdom,[83] and Grewcock's interventions on border crimes in Australia,[84] to name just a few. Marxist state crime scholars have also produced a range of theoretical innovations. For example, in order to make sense of 'extraordinary renditions', Poynting has employed a Marxist theory of empire to help define the internationally integrated characteristics of state power;[85] Whyte has employed Bourdieu's work on *habitus* and *doxa* to think about the pre-normative assumptions which inform state-corporate elites;[86] while I have drawn upon Marx's *Capital* to consider the criminogenic potentialities latent in mining capital, and the historical conditions which prompt their actualisation.[87] Unifying these

[81] Marfleet, above note 78.

[82] P. Green, 'Disaster by Design: Corruption, Construction and Catastrophe', (2005) 45 *British Journal of Criminology* 528.

[83] Tombs and Whyte, *Safety Crimes*, above note 78.

[84] Grewcock, above note 32.

[85] S. Poynting, 'Empire Crime, Rendition and Guantánamo Bay: The Case of David Hicks', *State Crime* (forthcoming 2015).

[86] D. Whyte, 'Between Crime and *Doxa*: Researching the Worlds of State-Corporate Elites', (2012) 1 *State Crime* 88.

[87] Lasslett, *State Crime on the Margins of Empire*, above note 46.

interventions is a commitment to enriched definitions of the realities that stand behind particular articulations of state crime and resistance, definitions which can help guide specific social movements engaged in emancipatory forms of censure and transformation.

Conclusion

Over two and a half decades a small but growing community of criminologists have established state crime studies as a field of critical inquiry. The importance of this sub-disciplinary focus has been confirmed with startling power over the past five years. Indeed, we have witnessed epoch defining uprisings in the Middle East and North Africa that have censured criminal despots and sparked transformative change. Investigative organs such as Wikileaks have shone disinfecting light on the inner sanctums of state power. At the same time the Occupy movement has brought into focus the corrosive link that exists between governments and the finance industry. Indeed, following a period of history that saw the freedom of states and corporations expand exponentially – facilitating a range of harmful practices – social movements are attempting to reel in excesses of power by championing and operationalising a greater range of normative restraints. State crime studies is well positioned not only to understand these social exchanges, but also to inform them.

To that end, state crime studies has not, and cannot, confine itself to the academy.[88] Its subject matter demands that scholars immerse themselves within different local, national and international currents of resistance, both in order to research state crime and to remedy it.[89] Accordingly, state crime studies has the ability to tell us about how state crime is enacted and, rather critically, experienced and resisted. The insights and conclusions this generates has and will continue to be the most distinctive mark of state crime studies, which shall make it valuable both as a field, alongside others, and as a partner in emancipatory forms of social change.

[88] See Grewcock, above note 23; R. C. Kramer, R. Michalowski and W. J. Chambliss, 'Epilogue: Toward a Public Criminology of State Crime', in W. J. Chambliss, R. Michalowski and R. C. Kramer (eds.), *State Crime in the Global Age* (Cullompton: Willan Publishing, 2010) at 247–61.

[89] Lasslett, 'Power, Struggle and State Crime: Researching through Resistance', above note 46.

4

Investigating complex crime

JONATHAN RUSCH

Introduction

In principle, any type of crime can be successfully investigated. The question in any criminal investigation is simply what investigative methods and techniques are lawful as means of gathering evidence, available to investigators and appropriate to acquire the type of evidence needed to prove elements of the crime. That question, however, is deceptively simple, as all three of those criteria need to be met for successful investigation of the crime in question. While there is a wider array of investigative methods and techniques than ever before – ranging from traditional interviewing and interrogation to computer forensic analysis – many countries deem certain methods, such as physical coercion, unacceptable on moral and legal grounds. Even those methods deemed lawful may be unavailable to investigators in a particular jurisdiction who lack the financial resources to acquire them or the training to apply them effectively. And certain methods, though lawful, may be unsuited to acquiring a specific kind of evidence needed to prove the criminal intent of a particular criminal, or his knowledge and active participation in the crime or crimes in question.

Moreover, each of those criteria comes into sharper relief when we acknowledge that certain types of crime are notably more complex than others. The methods that work well in investigating a simple homicide may be insufficient or ineffective to investigate the operations of a multinational heroin-distribution network that relies on threatened or actual violence to discipline the network's members and to intimidate the communities in which the heroin is sold.[1]

It would be too much to say, as one US court opined, that in transnational criminal law enforcement ordinary tasks such as collecting

[1] See, e.g., J. Beittel, Congressional Research Service, *Mexico's Drug Trafficking Organizations: Source and Scope of the Violence* (April 15, 2013) available at www.fas.org/sgp/crs/row/R41576.pdf, at 1–2.

evidence "are transformed into hurdles that are difficult, or impossible, to pass."[2] Nonetheless, experience has shown that as crimes become more complex due to multi-jurisdictional operations or other factors, police or investigative agencies need to use a wider array of investigative methods and techniques if they are to have a realistic hope of successfully investigating those crimes.

This chapter will first describe the leading characteristics of complex crime. It will then identify and examine the principal investigative methods and techniques that law enforcement agencies use to investigate complex crime. Because there are many varieties of criminal operations that could be considered "complex," this chapter will employ examples from a number of those operations – with particular reference to drug trafficking organizations (DTOs), organized crime groups, mass-marketing[3] fraud and other economic crime networks, and genocide – to explain the relevance and value of each of those methods and techniques. In keeping with the central theme of this book, these crimes possess a transnational character and are therefore rightly described as transnational crimes.

Characteristics of complex crime

In order to define the scope of this chapter accurately, it is first necessary to explain what is meant by the term "complex" crime. After all, even a single homicide by an individual may involve elaborate efforts by the killer to remove or destroy evidence or to create false trails for the police to pursue. On the other hand, crime is not necessarily made complex merely because criminals operate in groups. Groups of two or more criminals routinely engaged in crimes, such as assault, theft or armed robbery, are not inherently complex.

[2] *In re Hijazi*, 589 F3d 401, 403 (7th Cir 2009).

[3] The term "mass-marketing" is derived from the US Sentencing Commission's sentencing guideline pertaining to fraud, which defines the term to mean "a plan, program, promotion, or campaign that is conducted through solicitation by telephone, mail, the Internet, or other means to induce a large number of persons to (i) purchase goods or services; (ii) participate in a contest or sweepstakes; or (iii) invest for financial profit." US Sentencing Commission, United States Sentencing Commission Guidelines Manual Application Note 4(A) (2013), at 90. The term "mass-marketing fraud" has since been adopted by a growing number of law enforcement agencies in multiple countries to refer to fraud schemes that use telemarketing, mass mailing, the Internet, or other mass-communication means to contact and communicate with prospective victims. See, e.g., International Mass-Marketing Fraud Working Group, *Mass-Marketing Fraud: A Threat Assessment* (June 2010).

Existing criminological typologies are not necessarily helpful in this regard. The standard criminological approach of classifying offenders into typologies does not satisfactorily address the reality that some forms of crime may be more successful because offenders work together in ways that reflect longer-term patterns of offending behavior.[4] For these reasons, this chapter will define "complex crime" with reference to the following list of characteristics, although not all criminal groups or organizations will necessarily exhibit all of these characteristics:

(1) *Groups committing the same types of crime over an extended period.* Certain aggregations of criminals have long-term continuity and are organized with the purpose of conducting the same type of crime over an extended period. DTOs routinely conduct the same kind of production, transport, and distribution of drugs over many years, although some have taken over or expanded into new drug trafficking.[5] Mass-marketing fraud schemes are organized to commit fraud against large numbers of people on a continuing basis, even if the specific fraudulent offerings to the public change over time.[6] Organized crime groups, whether hierarchical or less formally structured,[7] are also likely to exhibit substantial continuity[8] and to conduct the same types of profitable crime over time, ranging from traditional local-level activities such as extortion[9] to transnational operations such as cybercrime, human trafficking, drug trafficking and money laundering.[10] And, by definition, genocide

[4] See B. Francis, K. Soothill and R. Fligelstone, "Identifying Patterns and Pathways of Offending Behaviour", (2004) 1 *European Journal of Criminology* 47.

[5] See Beittel, above note 1, at 8.

[6] See, e.g., *United States* v. *Whitehill*, 532 F3d 746, 749 (8th Cir) cert denied, 129 S Ct 610 (2008) (telemarketing fraud scheme changed from fraudulent charitable solicitation to fraudulent offering of credit cards).

[7] See United Nations Office on Drugs and Crime, *Results of a Pilot Survey of Forty Selected Organized Criminal Groups in Sixteen Countries* (September 2002) at 33–44.

[8] See S. Lupo, *History of the Mafia* (Columbia University Press, 2009) at 23.

[9] See, e.g., *United States* v. *Pica*, 692 F3d 79, 81–5 (2d Cir 2012), cert denied, 133 S Ct 1582 (2013); *United States* v. *Gotti*, 459 F3d 296, 307–8, 311–15 (2d Cir 2006), cert denied sub nom *Ciccone* v. *United States*, 127 S Ct 3001 (2007).

[10] See, e.g., Europol, *Threat Assessment: Italian Organized Crime* (June 2013) at 14–15 (numerous activities including corruption, counterfeiting of products and currency, drug trafficking, extortion, human trafficking, money laundering, trafficking in waste); United Nations Office on Drugs and Crime, *Transnational Organized Crime in Eastern Africa: A Threat Assessment* (September 2013) at 3 (heroin trafficking, ivory trafficking, migrant smuggling, and piracy); United Nations Office on Drugs and Crime, *Transnational Organized Crime in East Asia and the Pacific: A Threat Assessment* (April 2013) at iii–x (counterfeit goods, fraudulent medicines, human smuggling for sexual exploitation, migrant smuggling, trafficking in opiates and methamphetamines); United Nations

involves a sustained effort by a government or other groups to eradicate a particular ethnically or racially defined segment of society.

(2) *Geographic and functional dispersion of operations.* A second critical characteristic of complex crime is the organization of a criminal operation whose operational components are dispersed both geographically and functionally. Narcotics-distribution operations are one widely recognized type of criminal activity in which there is broad transjurisdictional and functional dispersion of its components.[11] But economic crime operations are known to have broad functional and geographic dispersion as well.

For example, one of the largest mass-marketing-fraud schemes prosecuted in recent years involved a far-flung operation in which the leader of the scheme, Kyle Kimoto, was based in St. George, Utah, but established a network of US outbound call centers in Utah, Kansas, Oregon, Idaho, Arizona, Virginia, and Florida, as well as Caribbean outbound call centers in Grenada, St Lucia, and St Vincent, an outbound call center in Toronto, Canada, and outbound call centers in India.[12] Other mass-marketing fraud schemes, although less multinational than Kimoto's operation, have routinely set up operations in multiple intra-national or international jurisdictions[13] or outsourced operations to third-party telemarketers,[14] but avoided soliciting prospective victims in those jurisdictions to avoid face-to-face disputes with victims or investigation by local law enforcement.[15]

Cybercrime and identity crime are additional areas of economic crime in which specific functions and participants therein may be scattered across multiple countries. A recent US federal prosecution brought to light evidence that an organization known as Carder.su operated a worldwide online marketplace for stolen personal and financial data. Members of carder.su:

Office on Drugs and Crime, *Transnational Organized Crime in West Africa: A Threat Assessment* (February 2013) at 3–5 (cocaine and methamphetamine trafficking, firearms trafficking, fraudulent medicines, migrant smuggling, piracy).

11 See National Drug Intelligence Center, US Department of Justice, *National Drug Threat Assessment 2011* (August 2011) at 7–11; Beittel, above note 1, at 6, 8.

12 See US Attorney's Office for the Southern District of Illinois, US Department of Justice, Press Release (September 8, 2008) at 1–2.

13 See, e.g., *United States* v. *Whitehill*, 532 F3d 746, 750 (8th Cir) cert denied, 129 S Ct 610 (2008) (telemarketing fraud scheme established offices in three US states and solicited customers throughout the US).

14 See, e.g., *United States* v. *Lyons*, 472 F3d 1055, 1060 (9th Cir), cert denied sub nom *Sanchez* v. *United States*, 550 US 937 (2007).

15 See, e.g., *United States* v. *Duliga*, 204 F3d 97, 98–9 (3d Cir) cert denied, 530 US 1222 (2000) (telemarketing scheme placed fraudulent advertisements in newspapers across the country, but not locally).

> were involved in large-scale trafficking of compromised credit card account data and counterfeit identifications and credit cards, as well as money laundering, narcotics trafficking, and various types of computer crime. The organization operated an internet web portal called a forum, where members could purchase the illicitly obtained data and share knowledge of various fraud schemes. A second forum was also created to vet incoming new members. The forums were generally hosted within the former Soviet Union and the upper echelon of the organization resides within the former Soviet Union. It was estimated that in July 2011, there were over 5,500 members of the organization.
>
> It was determined that members of the organization had different roles, including moderators who directed other members in carrying out activities; reviewers who examined and tested products, services, and contraband; vendors who advertised and sold products, services and contraband; and members.[16]

Organized crime groups in various regions of the world have also expanded and dispersed their operations across multiple countries and even continents. Among Italian organized crime groups, for example, Cosa Nostra's operations can be found in several countries in North America, South America and Africa; 'Ndrangheta's operations are found in Australia and countries in Europe, North America and South America; the Camorra's operations are found in Europe, the USA, and Latin America; and Apulian organized crime operations are mainly in Europe.[17]

As for genocide, genocidal groups necessarily conduct their activities across multiple regions within a single nation, or even across national boundaries (e.g., the Holocaust).

(3) *Targeting of multiple victims.* Another frequent characteristic of complex crime is the targeting of multiple victims. DTOs, of course, seek to sell their drugs to tens of millions of illegal drug users in the USA and other countries. Mass-marketing fraud schemes, for their part, may seek to target anywhere from a few victims, who are targeted for losses of tens or hundreds of thousands of dollars, to tens or hundreds of thousands of victims, who are targeted for far smaller losses of a few hundred dollars each. The Kimoto scheme described above, which fraudulently guaranteed consumers a Visa or MasterCard charge card but charged a one-time fee of $159.95 and failed to provide a genuine credit card,[18] made more than

[16] US Attorney's Office, District of Nevada, US Department of Justice, Press Release (December 6, 2013).

[17] See Europol, above note 10, at 3.

[18] See *United States* v. *Kimoto*, 588 F3d 464, 469 (7th Cir 2009), cert denied, 130 S Ct 2079 (2010).

12 million calls to US consumers and victimized more than 300,000 consumers throughout the USA out of approximately $43 million.[19] Other mass-marketing schemes have often resulted in victimizing thousands of consumers,[20] or targeted fewer victims who were believed to be vulnerable or susceptible, seeking substantial amounts of funds from each of those victims.[21] Genocidal organizations, of course, target vast numbers of victims for killing.[22]

(4) *Use of false or fraudulent statements and withholding of material information in furtherance of crime.* While it is common for criminals to use false names and information in conducting criminal activities, operators of mass-marketing fraud and other economic crimes are highly dependent on providing prospective victims with false information, or withholding complete and accurate information regarding their true identities, professional credentials and experience, and the value of the goods or services the victim has been promised. For example, in the Kimoto credit card telemarketing scheme discussed above, telemarketers would make false and fraudulent statements guaranteeing that the victim would receive a MasterCard, but those conversations with the telemarketers were not recorded; in contrast, the scheme recorded the "verification" portion of the call with the victim, in which the "verifier" would obtain the victim's bank account data in order to debit the victim's account.[23] More recently, in an Israeli-based telemarketing fraud scheme prosecuted in the USA, certain participants in the scheme falsely claimed to be employees of a nonexistent law firm or Internal Revenue Service (IRS) officials to persuade prospective victims that they had won a lottery prize and needed to pay bogus taxes and fees before the prize could be paid.[24]

(5) *Counter-intelligence and counter-surveillance measures and measures to obstruct investigations.* In the USA and other countries, criminal

[19] See US Attorney's Office for the Southern District of Illinois, above note 12, at 1.

[20] See, e.g., *United States* v. *Arcand*, 234 Fed Appx 490, 491 (9th Cir 2007) (unpublished opinion); *United States* v. *Morris*, 2007 WL 684006 (9th Cir) (unpublished opinion), cert denied, 128 S Ct 550 (2007).

[21] See, e.g., *United States* v. *Johnson*, 297 F3d 845, 854 (9th Cir 2002) cert denied, 123 S Ct 1376 and 1647 (2003) (scheme targeted the elderly and took in more than $10 million through about 1,300 sales to more than 300 individuals).

[22] See, e.g., "Numbers", in International Federation of Human Rights Leagues and Human Rights Watch, *Leave None to Tell the Story: Genocide in Rwanda* (1999) (at least 500,000 killed in 1994 Rwandan genocide).

[23] See *United States* v. *Kimoto*, above note 18, at 469.

[24] See *United States* v. *Getto*, 729 F3d 221, 225 (2d Cir 2013).

organizations are known to use various methods to gather information about pending investigations, evidence that law enforcement agencies are gathering and persons who may be cooperating with law enforcement. Organized crime groups are well aware of law enforcement surveillance directed at them,[25] and may take aggressive measures to develop counter-intelligence. For example, the underboss of the Lucchese Cosa Nostra family in New York kept two New York Police Department detectives on a monthly $4,000 retainer "in exchange for their using their law-enforcement positions to collect all the information they could about investigations on any of the five [New York] Organized Crime Families, including the identities of informants, the location of wiretaps, and any imminent arrests, and passing that information to [a Lucchese family associate and the underboss]."[26] On a number of occasions, the detectives did provide information to a Lucchese associate about known or suspected informants and the underboss had those informants killed. In one case, when the informant had been recording incriminating conversations, one of the detectives, "while officially and ostensibly investigating [the informant's] murder, removed the incriminating tapes from [the informant's] apartment and gave them to [the Lucchese family associate and underboss]."[27] In addition, when the detectives learned that the Lucchese family boss and underboss, among others, were about to be arrested, they informed the associate, who alerted the underboss, and both the boss and the underboss fled. During the underboss's flight, he continued to receive sensitive law enforcement information from the detectives, via the associate.[28]

Organized-crime families have also been known to take counter-surveillance measures such as evasive driving maneuvers to identify possible law enforcement "tails,"[29] or talking elliptically or in code to make it more difficult for law enforcement to perceive or understand their interactions.[30] In one case, a de facto boss of the DeCavalcante Cosa Nostra family reportedly bought microcassette recorders so that he could record exculpatory information.[31]

[25] See, e.g., G. B. Smith, *Made Men* (Berkley Books, 2003) at 268–70.

[26] *United States* v. *Caracappa*, 614 F3d 30, 36 (2d Cir), cert denied, 131 S Ct 675 (2010). See also J. Breslin, *The Good Rat* (Ecco, 2008) at 9, 138–41.

[27] *United States* v *Caracappa*, above note 26, at 37.

[28] Ibid.

[29] See M. Russell and P. W. Picciarelli, *Undercover Cop* (Thomas Dunne Books, 2013) at 63; J. Garcia and M. Levin, *Making Jack Falcone* (Touchstone, 2008) at 208.

[30] See, e.g., Smith, above note 25, at 98; *United States* v. *Gotti*, above note 9, at 307.

[31] Smith, above note 25, at 272–3.

Domestic DTOs are known to conduct counter-intelligence activities.[32] They also use a variety of measures to preclude undercover agents or police officers from physical access to retail drug sales and to conduct counter-surveillance operations. For example, drug dealers operating in apartment complexes "may use security designed to screen potential customers. Security may include countersurveillance, electronic detection devices, prescreening interviews, frisk searches, and use of pager sales to known customers."[33] More recently, the leader of a violent DTO in New York had leased vehicles for transporting narcotics, including one that "was outfitted with countersurveillance devices, including rotating license plates and high intensity rear halogen lights to blind pursuers."[34]

Counter-surveillance measures have been seen in criminal enterprises beyond DTOs. For non-drug criminal activities where criminals need to communicate with one another without using permanently assigned landlines, criminals may use "throwaway" cell phones or prepaid calling cards,[35] so that police cannot trace calls back to the scheme over an extended period of time. One telemarketing fraud scheme required its telemarketers, before each individual solicitation, to dial *671 so that the person called could not trace the call back to the scheme's base of operations.[36] Members of the carder.su organization described above "were required to successfully complete a number of security features designed to protect the organization from infiltration by law enforcement or members of rival criminal organizations."[37]

Finally, in the aftermath of genocide there are known instances of groups complicit in killing that take measures to restrict or limit discovery of information. At the end of World War II, the Nazis

[32] See Office of National Drug Control Policy, *National Drug Control Strategy 2010* (2010) at 3.

[33] R. Sampson, *Drug Dealing in Privately Owned Apartment Complexes* (US Department of Justice, 2001) at 4–5.

[34] US Attorney's Office, Southern District of New York, Press Release (October 11, 2005), available at www.justice.gov/usao/nys/pressreleases/October05/williamsxaviersentencingpr.pdf.

[35] See Statement of Todd Hinnen, Deputy Assistant Attorney General, National Security Division, US Department of Justice before the Subcommittee on the Constitution, Civil Rights and Civil Liberties, Committee on the Judiciary, US House of Representatives (September 22, 2009), available at www.justice.gov/ola/testimony/111-1/2009-09-22-nsd-hinnen-patriot-act.pdf.

[36] See *United States* v. *Johnson*, above note 21, at 853.

[37] US Attorney's Office, District of Nevada, US Department of Justice, Press Release (December 6, 2013).

destroyed some of the historical record of their war crimes, though millions of documents were preserved by Allied forces.[38] In 1994, the Rwandan Patriotic Front, even though it reportedly ended the genocide by "defeating the civilian and military authorities responsible for the killing campaign,"[39] sought not only to limit access by journalists and aid workers to "approved" areas, but "to limit investigations that might produce evidence of abuses by their soldiers."[40]

Criminal enterprises may also take steps to destroy documents that they believe law enforcement may acquire to further their investigations. Some mass-marketing schemes have been known to engage in destruction of incriminating documents,[41] and at least one mass-marketing fraud operator persuaded a federal agent to leak information about the federal investigation of the operator.[42] In another area of economic crime, tax evasion, UBS AG, Switzerland's largest bank, entered into a deferred prosecution agreement with the US Department of Justice in 2009 concerning UBS's efforts to provide banking services to certain US customers with accounts not disclosed to the IRS. According to the information filed in connection with the Deferred Prosecution Agreement (DPA), "UBS managers and employees used encrypted laptops and other counter-surveillance techniques to help prevent the detection of their marketing efforts and the identities and offshore assets of their U.S. clients."[43]

(6) *Threatened or actual violence.* Both DTOs and organized-crime groups are known to use threatened or actual violence with regularity. Violence serves as a means of maintaining discipline within the enterprises' ranks, intimidating competitor organizations and government officials, and dissuading the general public from providing information to the authorities. Mass-marketing fraud schemes, though less prone to actual violence, have often resorted to similar threats against their victims, competitors and in-group members. The International Mass-Marketing Fraud Working Group reported in 2010 that law-enforcement intelligence reveals that

[38] See, e.g., *Combating Holocaust Denial: Evidence of the Holocaust presented at Nuremberg*, in US Holocaust Memorial Museum, *Holocaust Encyclopedia* (last updated June 10, 2013).

[39] See "Rwandan Patriotic Front", in International Federation of Human Rights Leagues and Human Rights Watch, *Leave None to Tell the Story: Genocide in Rwanda* (1999).

[40] Ibid. [41] See *United States* v. *Whitehill*, above note 6, at 750.

[42] See *Yarton* v. *United States*, 1996 WL 335371 (9th Cir 1996) (unpublished opinion).

[43] Office of Public Affairs, US Dept of Justice, Press Release (February 18, 2009), available at www.justice.gov/opa/pr/2009/February/09-tax-136.html (accessed December 17, 2013).

some fraud groups employ threats and coercive tactics against uncooperative victims, rival groups and their own group members. Victims have reported that persons posing as law enforcement or government officials have threatened arrest, imprisonment or the seizure of bank accounts and assets should they fail to comply with fraudsters' demands. Within the USA, victims of an online extortion scheme have received emails containing pictures of dead bodies and threatening bodily harm:

> Recent law enforcement intelligence suggests that use of mass-marketing related intra- and inter-group violence is on the rise in some places. Open-source and law enforcement reporting indicate that competing gangs in Jamaica are using murder and other violent tactics to steal victim leads lists and lottery fraud proceeds. In the United States, the operators of a New York-based stock boiler room affiliated with two Italian organized crime families admitted to controlling and disciplining employees with threats and actual violence, including beatings, stabbings, and kidnappings.[44]

Genocide, again by definition, involves the systematic use of violence and threats of violence.[45]

Investigative methods and techniques

Given the various factors described above, it should not be surprising that investigation of complex crime typically requires the use of multiple investigative methods and techniques to amass the necessary evidence. What follows in this section is a discussion of the most prevalent methods and techniques used in complex crime investigation, beginning with the more customary investigative procedures.

(1) *Interviews of witnesses.* It is commonplace in law enforcement that "[t]he police interview is one of the most important investigative tools that law enforcement has close at hand."[46] Certainly, the police interview

[44] International Mass-Marketing Working Group, *Mass-Marketing Fraud* (June 2010) at 23 (footnotes omitted).

[45] See Convention on the Prevention and Punishment of the Crime of Genocide (1948), Article 2 (defining genocide). For example, after the 1975–79 Cambodian genocide, a former commandant of a torture and execution center in Phnom Penh stated that "the Khmer Rouge were all about elimination. Human rights didn't exist." R. Panh and C. Bataille, *The Elimination: A Survivor of the Khmer Rouge Confronts his Past and the Commandant of the Killing Fields* (Other Press, 2013) at 73.

[46] U. Holmberg, *Police Interviews with Victims and Suspects of Violent and Sexual Crimes*, unpublished doctoral dissertation, (Stockholm University (2004)) at i.

is "an important tool in gathering descriptions from those who have any knowledge of the criminal act."[47] Yet interviews may prove to be of comparatively limited value in conducting investigations of complex crime. The more widely dispersed the criminal enterprise's operations, the less likely it is that any single third-party witness, other than a key insider, can provide investigators with significant evidence. Crime victims may not even know the true location, let alone the true identities, of the criminals behind the scheme. And when the crimes involve organizations known or believed to use violence, ranging from DTOs and organized crime to genocide, innocent bystanders and even participants in the crime may be unavailable in the investigating jurisdiction[48] or highly reluctant to provide evidence. Interviews, then, are likely to be a necessity – but only one step toward – in the successful investigation of complex crime.

(2) *Surveillance*. Although not used by all police services around the world,[49] physical surveillance by law enforcement authorities can be a useful technique in investigating complex crime. When various individuals enter and leave the same physical location, or interact with others in that location, over a period of time, physical surveillance can amass evidence with respect to which individuals may be working with each other on criminal activities, which were present on specific dates in the same location, and which specific criminal acts may have been committed.[50]

Organized crime cases have used physical surveillance evidence to prove direct involvement of organized crime associates in illegal gambling operations,[51] interactions between organized crime family members and associates in making "tribute" payments to family bosses[52] and

[47] Ibid., at 1.

[48] See, e.g., International Federation of Human Rights Leagues and Human Rights Watch, *Leave None to Tell the Story: Genocide in Rwanda* (1999) (in 1994 Rwandan genocide, tens of thousands of people fled to neighboring countries).

[49] See A. L. Knoesen, *The Use of Physical Surveillance in Forensic Investigation*, in the unpublished MA thesis, University of South Africa (2012) at iv (general detectives in South African Police Service do not generally use physical surveillance as a technique during their investigations).

[50] See, e.g., *United States* v. *Medina*, 728 F3d 701, 702 (7th Cir 2013) (telephone and physical surveillance confirmed negotiation and delivery of kilo of cocaine between co-conspirators); *United States* v. *Anaya*, 727 F3d 1043, 1048 (10th Cir 2013) (officers witnessed DTO members dropping off and picking up many vehicles from defendant's residence and defendant meeting with known drug dealers).

[51] *United States* v. *Gotti*, above note 9, at 317. [52] See ibid., at 310–11.

resolving interfamily disputes,[53] and even communications between family leaders in approving and carrying out murders of organized crime leaders and others.[54] In public spaces, video surveillance, which police have been increasingly using in recent years,[55] can supplement or stand in for physical surveillance, such as the use of cameras to record drug transactions.[56] As indicated above, however, leaders of a criminal enterprise engaged in complex crime are likely to be watchful for indicia of physical surveillance, and therefore may use counter-surveillance measures or reduce or minimize their public interactions with other criminals.

(3) *Acquisition of documentary and physical evidence.* Criminal investigators also find substantial value in documentary evidence that establishes the duration, size, operating methods, and participants in a criminal enterprise, as well as evidence of specific transactions or acts that may constitute prosecutable crimes. In one organized crime case, telephone records were instrumental, along with other evidence, in proving the involvement of the acting boss and a captain of the Colombo Cosa Nostra family in directing the murder of the family's acting underboss stemming from a struggle of power within the family.[57] In another organized crime case, documents with gambling records and betting figures seized from the residences of three Gambino Cosa Nostra family affiliates were used in the prosecution of multiple family leaders and members.[58]

In prosecutions of mass-marketing fraud schemes, records from third parties and from the scheme's business premises may be highly probative in order to prove the true operations of the scheme as well as to disprove the false and fraudulent statements by the scheme's participants.[59] In one

[53] See *United States* v. *Salerno*, 868 F2d 524, 529, 532 (2d Cir), cert denied, 491 US 907 and 493 US 811 (1989).

[54] See ibid., at 533.

[55] See, e.g., J. Ratcliffe, 'Community-Oriented Policing Service', US Dept of Justice, Video Surveillance of Public Places (2011), available at www.cops.usdoj.gov/Publications/e061120374_POP_Video-Surveillance-508.pdf.

[56] See *United States* v. *Santos-Rivera*, 726 F3d 17, 23 (1st Cir 2013); *United States* v. *Daniels*, 723 F3d 562, 564, 567 (5th Cir 2013), pet for cert filed, No. 13-7658 (US Supreme Court, December 3, 2013).

[57] See *United States* v. *Persico*, 645 F3d 85, 90–91 (2d Cir 2011), cert denied sub nom *DeRoss* v. *United States*, 132 S Ct 593 (2011) and *Persico* v. *United States*, 132 S Ct 1637 (2012).

[58] See *United States* v. *Gotti*, above note 9, at 316–17.

[59] See, e.g., *United States* v. *Mornan*, 413 F3d 372, 374 (3d Cir 2005); *United States* v. *Tarallo*, 380 F3d 1174, 1182 (9th Cir 2004); *United States* v. *Johnson*, above note 21, at 863.

securities fraud scheme, evidence at trial included bank, telephone and business records related to the scheme that showed:

(1) the scheme had handled tens of thousands of short-duration, long-distance telephone calls in a pattern that was consistent with 'boiler room' and 'cold-call' solicitations frequently used in investment schemes;
(2) the omission of the defendant's true positions at the company and their prior criminal convictions from private placement memoranda; and
(3) a false statement by one defendant that he had received degrees from two universities.[60]

The appellate court that reviewed these convictions specifically concluded from this and other evidence "that a rational jury could have found [one defendant's] fraudulent intent beyond a reasonable doubt."[61]

In genocide investigations, the volume and evidentiary value of documentary evidence can vary widely. In 1945, Allied armies captured millions of records documenting Nazi war crimes, and in the 1946 Nuremberg trial, prosecutors submitted approximately 3,000 tons of records.[62] By contrast, some subsequent genocides, which occurred in more rural areas and were less dependent on formal recordkeeping for their operations, have had comparatively few written records that contemporaneously documented genocidal acts.

To obtain access to places in which documentary evidence may be found, investigators will need – absent consent of an authorized person to search the premises or other valid exception – to use some form of compulsory process to compel production of the evidence. In the USA, law enforcement investigators often rely on subpoenas, which may be issued directly by a court or under the authority of a grand jury,[63] or by a

[60] See *United States* v. *Stitsky*, 2013 WL 5645563 (2d Cir 2013) (unpublished opinion) at 4.
[61] Ibid., at 7.
[62] See *Combating Holocaust Denial: Evidence of the Holocaust presented at Nuremberg*, in US Holocaust Memorial Museum, *Holocaust Encyclopedia* (last updated June 10, 2013).
[63] See, e.g., Federal Rule of Criminal Procedure (US), 17. In the US federal criminal justice system, a grand jury is an investigative body, consisting of sixteen to twenty-three lay persons, that is summoned by a federal court to hear evidence of possible crimes and determine whether to return an indictment against one or more persons. See Federal Rule of Criminal Procedure (US), 6(a)(1) and (f). Unlike criminal trials, grand jury proceedings are not adversarial proceedings. Only attorneys for the government, the witness being questioned, an interpreter when needed, and a court reporter or operator of a recording device may be present when the grand jury is in session. See Federal Rule of Criminal Procedure (US), 6(3)(2)(B).

law enforcement or administrative agency. In some circumstances, such as where the recipient of a valid grand jury subpoena has failed to turn over the required documents, a court may issue an order to compel compliance on pain of criminal or civil contempt.[64]

In some cases, where investigators need to obtain and preserve documentary evidence without relying on the good faith of a third party to turn over evidence pursuant to a subpoena, authorities may need to apply for a search warrant from a judicial authority. Certain jurisdictions, such as Canada and the USA, have specific legal proscriptions against unreasonable searches and seizures.[65] Where such legal proscriptions exist, that will typically mean that authorities must obtain prior judicial authorization for a search. That authorization in turn will require evidence sufficient to establish (in the USA) probable cause to believe that a crime has been committed and that relevant evidence is likely to be found at the site to be searched, or (in Canada) reasonable grounds to believe that there is in the site, inter alia, anything that there are reasonable grounds to believe will afford evidence with respect to the commission of an offence.[66]

For certain types of records, such as stored electronic communications (e.g., email and text messages[67]), certain statutory provisions may specifically authorize law enforcement to use various forms of compulsory process to compel production of those records from Internet service providers or other providers of electronic communications services. In the USA, the Stored Communications Act[68] provides for a specific form of court order, as well as search warrants and administrative, grand jury and trial subpoenas, in order to obtain such records, although additional conditions (e.g., prior notice to the email service subscriber) may also apply in specific circumstances.[69]

Where the complex crime in question involves operations in a foreign jurisdiction, the investigators may need to obtain copies of relevant

[64] See Federal Rule of Criminal Procedure (US), 17(g).

[65] See Canadian Charter of Rights and Freedoms, Art. 8, Constitution Act, 1982, Schedule B to the Canada Act 1982 (UK), 1982, c 11; US Constitution, amendment IV. See also *Regina* v. *Vu*, 2013 SCC 60 (Canadian Supreme Court, November 7, 2013) (requiring warrant for search of computers and cell phones).

[66] See, e.g., G Lafrenière, *Police Powers and Drug-Related Offences* (March 6, 2001) report prepared for the Canadian senate special committee on illegal drugs, available at www.parl.gc.ca/content/sen/committee/371/ille/library/powers-e.htm.

[67] See *United States* v. *Daniels*, above note 56, at 567 (text messages between defendants regarding cocaine distribution).

[68] 18 USC §§ 2701–12.

[69] See 18 USC § 2703(a)–(d).

records in that jurisdiction.[70] To do so, the investigating jurisdiction may need to make a Mutual Legal Assistance Treaty (MLAT) request for assistance in obtaining the foreign records, where the requesting and requested jurisdictions have entered into such a MLAT.[71]

Finally, physical evidence – ranging from fingerprints to biological evidence[72] – may be necessary in certain complex crime cases involving violence, to prove the occurrence of specific violent crimes and to establish the presence of a defendant at the scene of the crime. Organized crime prosecutions have involved such evidence as the recovery of a beeper belonging to the defendant at the scene of a double murder of Cosa Nostra family affiliates (and records indicating that the beeper belonged to the defendant),[73] and the discovery of a defendant's palmprint on the handle of a getaway car used for a triple murder of a Cosa Nostra boss and associates.[74] In genocide investigations, investigators have turned to forensic anthropologists to find and exhume bodies and use clothing and other artifacts to identify remains and establish their noncombatant status.[75]

(4) *Testimony of eyewitness or third-party witnesses*. In order to obtain or preserve certain information for a criminal investigation or prosecution, authorities may need to obtain recorded testimony from a witness who was an eyewitness to or a victim of a crime or a third party possessing relevant evidence. In an organized crime murder case, authorities used testimony by the murder victim's wife and daughter to establish not only that the victim was alive on a particular day, but also whom he planned to meet and what one of the defendants said and did immediately after the murder.[76] In another organized crime case, multiple extortion victims agreed to testify about specific defendants' attempted or actual extortion against them.[77] Mass-marketing fraud investigations also use testimony from fraud victims to establish such facts as the false

[70] See, e.g., *United States* v. *Anekwu*, 695 F3d 967, 972 (9th Cir 2012), cert denied, 133 S Ct 2379 (2013).

[71] See *United States* v. *Lyttle*, 2012 WL 284593 (2d Cir 2012) at 3–4 (US MLAT request to Hungary for records relating to transfers of mass-marketing fraud scheme's proceeds).

[72] See, e.g., National Forensic Science Technology Center, *DNA Analyst Training – Types of Evidence*, available at www.nfstc.org/pdi/Subject01/pdi_s01_m01_01.htm.

[73] See *United States* v. *Yannotti*, 541 F 3d 112 (2nd Cir 2008) at 116.

[74] See *United States* v. *Salerno*, above note 53, at 529.

[75] See E. Malkin, "In Effort to Try Dictator, Guatemala Shows New Judicial Might", *New York Times* (March 17, 2013), at Y6.

[76] See *United States* v. *Persico*, above note 57, at 93–4.

[77] See *United States* v. *Gotti*, above note 9, at 311–15.

and fraudulent statements that defendants made to them and the losses they suffered during the course of the scheme.[78] In genocide prosecutions, testimony by survivors and other eyewitnesses are often essential to establish specific acts by specific individuals.

For some types of complex crime, criminal investigators may be needed to summarize certain evidence or to provide expert testimony.[79] In organized crime cases, federal agents and police officers have been used to provide expert testimony about matters as varied as the structure, operations, and practices of organized crime, the positions within organized crime families and illegal bookmaking,[80] and even interpretations of conversations between organized crime family participants.[81] In gang prosecutions, expert law enforcement witnesses have provided similar testimony on "the structure, leadership, operations, and jargon" of a particular gang,[82] and are considered able to "amplify concepts, terms, rules, structure, and history associated with a given gang in a concentrated fashion."[83] In mass-marketing fraud cases, federal agents have given summary testimony about the scope and scale of fraud schemes based on information from cooperating witnesses, law-enforcement representatives, consensual recordings and business records.[84] In US federal courts, federal evidence rules allow law enforcement witnesses to give non-expert and expert testimony,[85] as well as summary testimony.[86]

In the USA, a witness may appear voluntarily or when compelled by subpoena before a grand jury. Because some witnesses may be reluctant to testify if they fear retaliation by the persons whom they implicate, or

[78] See, e.g., *United States* v. *Mornan*, above note 59, at 375 (testimony of twelve claimed victims of fraudulent loan scheme); *United States* v. *Tarallo*, above note 59, at 1182 (victims of investment scheme); *United States* v. *Johnson*, above note 21, at 868 (victims of prize scheme).

[79] See, e.g., *United States* v. *Yannotti*, 541 F3d 112, 116 (2d Cir 2008), cert denied, 129 S Ct 1648 (2009); *United States* v. *Persico*, above note 57, at 90.

[80] See, e.g., *United States* v. *Gotti*, above note 9, at 308, 316–17; *United States* v. *Ardito*, 782 F2d 358, 360 (2d Cir 1986).

[81] See *United States* v. *Locascio*, 6 F3d 924, 937 (2d Cir 1993).

[82] See J. M. Trusty, "Use of Experts in Gang Prosecutions", *United States Attorneys' Bulletin* (November 2012) at 54.

[83] Ibid., at 52.

[84] See, e.g., *United States* v. *Stitsky*, 2013 WL 5645563 (2d Cir 2013) at 4.

[85] See *United States* v. *Díaz-Arias*, 717 F3d 1, 10–15 (1st Cir 2013) (upholding state trooper's voice identification of defendant as lay opinion testimony). See also *United States* v. *Yannotti*, above note 79, at 126 (identifying bases for lay opinion and expert testimony by agents). See, generally, Federal Rules of Evidence (US), 701–2.

[86] See Federal Rule of Evidence (US), 1006.

believe that they may incriminate themselves, US federal statutes provide explicit authority for federal courts to compel testimony under a grant of immunity.[87] Even so, some lay witnesses may be so intimidated that they would prefer to change their testimony or be held in contempt for failure to testify rather than risk harm from retaliation.[88]

(5) *Use of confidential informants and criminal participants.* For some types of complex crime, there is often no substitute for obtaining information or testimony directly from confidential informants or other participants in the crime under investigation. In organized crime investigations, it has become common to use information from confidential informants, some of which may be motivated by money[89] or other considerations such as retaliation against antagonists,[90] and even to use testimony by former leaders, members, and associates of organized crime families, in order to prove criminal interactions between defendants, participation in specific illegal activities, and admissions or other incriminating statements by defendants.[91] DTO investigations have also used confidential informants to link specific individuals to criminal conspiracies[92] and to provide context for surveillance photographs and intercepted phone conversations.[93] Typically, criminal participants provide such testimony at trial because they have already received substantial sentences in other criminal cases and cooperate with the government in the hope of having their sentences reduced.[94] Even economic crime cases may make effective use of criminal participants, as various mass-marketing fraud investigations have convincingly demonstrated.[95]

(6) *Use of undercover agents.* Particularly for criminal groups that are known to threaten or use physical force to ensure silence by its members and outsiders, investigative agencies may find it necessary to move

[87] See 18 USC §§ 6001–3.

[88] See, e.g., *United States* v. *Gotti*, above note 9, at 308 (extortion victim changed testimony from grand jury to trial, pleaded guilty to perjury, and was sentenced to prison).

[89] See, e.g., Attorney General's Guidelines Regarding the Use of FBI Confidential Human Sources (December 13, 2006), at 28.

[90] See Lupo, above note 8, at 251, 253.

[91] See, e.g., *United States* v. *Pica*, above note 9, at 85; *United States* v. *Persico*, above note 57, at 90–3, 95; *United States* v. *Caracappa*, above note 26, at 36–8; *United States* v. *Gotti*, above note 9, at 302; *United States* v. *Salerno*, above note 53, at 533–4.

[92] See, e.g., *United States* v. *Alaniz*, 726 F3d 586, 608 (5th Cir 2013); *United States* v. *Daniels*, above note 56, at 567; *United States* v. *Santos-Rivera*, above note 56, at 23.

[93] See *United States* v. *Daniels*, above note 56, at 576.

[94] See, e.g., Breslin, above note 26, at 11.

[95] See, e.g., *United States* v. *Johnson*, above note 21, at 852, 868–70.

beyond reliance on criminal informants and introduce undercover agents into the group to gather proof of criminal activity. In the USA, since the 1980s the Department of Justice has brought a number of significant prosecutions against organized crime family leaders that stemmed from the use of federal and state undercover agents.[96] One of those agents eventually provided testimony in seventeen criminal trials, "sometimes as a fact witness on the particulars of the crime itself, and sometimes as a witness on the organizational structure of the Mafia and how it operates."[97]

Undercover agents offer several distinct advantages over confidential informants or cooperating witnesses. Unlike confidential informants, whose routine conversations with criminals may not be recorded, undercover law enforcement agents routinely record their conversations with the criminals they are investigating, so that there can be no dispute in later prosecutions about what defendants and co-conspirators said and how they said it.[98] Because they are often infiltrated into a criminal group with the expectation of longer-term interaction with the group's leaders and members, undercover agents can also gather substantial amounts of criminal intelligence,[99] such as who are the current participants and leaders of a criminal group,[100] the relationships between those leaders and underlings, and the details of ongoing criminal activities.[101] In addition, in contrast to criminals, who may have motives such as financial gain or sentence reductions that defendants can attack in open court, undercover agents can be more difficult to cross-examine or to have their motivations called into question.

At the same time, agencies using undercover agents must carefully plan and monitor their use in long-term undercover operations. For example, the longer that an undercover agent actively deals with other criminals, the more suspicious it may be to those criminals if they do not see the undercover agent participate in criminal activities. Accordingly, in the USA the

[96] See, e.g., *United States* v. *Salerno*, above note 53, at 534–5; Russell and Picciarelli, above note 29, at 3, 33 (New Jersey State Police undercover officer who dealt with the Gambino Cosa Nostra family); Garcia and Levin, above note 29, at 5 (FBI undercover agent who dealt with capo and other affiliates of Gambino family); J. Pistone and C. Brandt, *Donnie Brasco: Unfinished Business* (Running Press, 2007), at 37 (FBI undercover agent who dealt with capo and other affiliates of Bonanno Cosa Nostra family).

[97] Pistone and Brandt, above note 96, at 100.

[98] See, e.g., Garcia and Levin, above note 29, at 35.

[99] See Pistone and Brandt, above note 96, at 73.

[100] See Garcia and Levin, above note 29, at 93, 148.

[101] See ibid., at 135, 149.

FBI has set up an elaborate set of guidelines that govern its undercover operations. Among other things, these guidelines specify which FBI officials may approve undercover operations, define, and limit the circumstances in which undercover employees may participate in otherwise illegal activity, and establish extensive procedures to monitor and control undercover operations, including regular meetings of a headquarters-level Criminal Undercover Operations Review Committee.[102]

(7) *Electronic surveillance.* Ultimately, normal investigative procedures – even those including criminal informants and undercover agents – may not be able to gain access to certain critical evidence, such as conversations between higher-level criminal group members.[103] Former undercover agents who infiltrated Cosa Nostra families have noted that because they had not become full "made" members of those families, certain conversations were "off-limits" to them.[104] The only effective way to access such conversations, while preserving accountability and transparency of the process, is to conduct electronic surveillance under careful supervision. Electronic surveillance techniques have often included placement of a microphone or listening device ("bug") in a location where criminals can be expected to discuss their activities freely,[105] and nonconsensual or consensual interception of telephonic or electronic communications ("wiretap").

Wiretap evidence can be highly probative in establishing not only who the leading participants in a criminal enterprise are, but their relative areas of responsibility and their specific criminal actions.[106] For example, one academic study of wiretap evidence from a cocaine trafficking case in New York City was able to identify the structure of the organization, the relative positions of individuals within the organization, and the tasks that those individuals performed by analyzing the content of nearly 600 pages of transcripts of 151 telephone conversations.[107]

[102] See Attorney General's Guidelines on Federal Bureau of Investigation Undercover Operations (May 30, 2002) at 3–18.

[103] See 18 USC § 2518(3)(c).

[104] See Garcia and Levin, above note 29, at 166; Pistone and Brandt, above note 96, at 74.

[105] See, e.g., *United States* v. *Salerno*, above note 53, at 531 (bugging of Lucchese Cosa Nostra family boss's Jaguar automobile).

[106] See, e.g., *United States* v. *Santos-Rivera*, above note 56, at 23 (wiretap recordings of conversations between co-conspirators in cocaine-trafficking organization).

[107] See M. Natarajan, "Understanding the Structure of a Drug Trafficking Organization: A Conversational Analysis", (2000) 11 *Crime Prevention Studies* 273.

Recorded conversations have also played a critical role in numerous organized crime prosecutions, documenting with the defendants' own words their roles in specific criminal acts and knowledge of other criminal matters.[108] These cases, as one appellate court recently explained: "depend heavily on wiretaps. For some of the activities – gambling, drug sales, money lending – there may be no 'victims' to complain. Written records are often minimal. And especially where the organization is large or affiliated with a larger criminal enterprise, co-conspirators may be fearful about turning state's evidence. So surveillance and wiretaps are principal tools of investigation."[109]

One of the organized crime cases that best demonstrated the value of electronic surveillance was the landmark 1980s case that exposed the operations of the Cosa Nostra's ruling body, the "Commission." In that case, recordings proved not only specific charged acts but:[110]

> discussions by defendants and their associates concerning the progress of law enforcement investigations into the Commission's affairs, monitoring of the indictment and arrest of coconspirators, . . . assessments of revelations by the media concerning the Commission, including the highly damaging confessions of former Commission member Joseph Bonanno . . . [,] many comments by the declarants about the history and rules of the Commission . . . [, and] discussions by Commission members or associates about interfamily disputes and how to resolve them.[111]

Such recordings can also strengthen complex crime cases where criminal insiders or undercover agents who testify at trial were parties to or participants in the recorded conversations.[112]

While court-authorized electronic surveillance has been used less frequently in mass-marketing fraud cases, consensual recordings between criminal participants and intended victims have often proved highly valuable. One major undercover operation during the 1990s, "Operation Senior Sentinel," resulted in the arrests of more than 400 fraudulent telemarketers nationwide, based in large part on the making of such

[108] See, e.g., *United States* v. *Persico*, above note 57, at 90; *United States* v. *Gotti*, above note 9, at 304, 306, 309–10, 312.

[109] *United States* v. *Albertelli*, 687 F3d 439, 442–43 (1st Cir), cert denied sub nom *Albertelli* v. *United States*, 133 S Ct 566 (2012), sub nom *Iacaboni* v. *United States*, 133 S Ct 2389 (2013), and sub nom *Gianelli* v. *United States*, 133 S Ct. 2390 (2013).

[110] *United States* v. *Salerno*, above note 53, at 529 (extortion and labor bribery, loansharking, and murder), at 531–2 (extortion in construction industry).

[111] Ibid., at 536. [112] See ibid., at 537.

consensual recordings.[113] More recently, a US investigation into an Israel-based telemarketing fraud scheme led to the Israeli National Police's installation of a clandestine surveillance device in the Israeli boiler room. Based in part on the evidence obtained from the device, multiple defendants were indicted in the USA and one of the defendants was sentenced to 150 months' imprisonment and $8.2 million restitution.[114]

Although the use of electronic surveillance may often be impractical to gather evidence of genocide during the planning or ongoing commission of genocidal acts, there are genocide investigations in which electronic surveillance has been useful to help establish the location of a fugitive defendant and to establish a defendant's complicity. In the investigation by the International Criminal Tribunal for the Former Yugoslavia (ICTY), investigators were able to obtain a contemporaneous recording of a 2005 telephone conversation between a fugitive and his wife that was traced to a jurisdiction in which the defendant ultimately was arrested.[115] More recently, in the ICTY trial of Radovan Karadzic that began in 2009, prosecutors used "transcripts of telephone intercepts in which [Karadzic] threatened the Muslim community with extermination should Bosnia declare independence from Yugoslavia."[116]

In the USA, the key measure that ensures effective oversight of the use of electronic surveillance in criminal cases is Title III of the Omnibus Crime Control and Safe Streets Act of 1968 ("Title III").[117] Title III sets forth a detailed statutory regime that specifically defines the process that law enforcement must use to apply in advance to a court for approval to intercept wire, oral, or electronic communications, the showings that the government must make to justify such surveillance, and the reporting by law enforcement to the approving court on the progress toward achievement of the authorized objective.[118] Failure to comply with these stringent requirements can result in prohibition of the use of the intercepted communications as evidence "in any trial, hearing, or other proceeding in or before any court, grand jury, department, officer, agency, regulatory body, legislative committee, or other authority of the United States, a State, or a political subdivision thereof."[119] Canada has similar detailed

[113] See US Department of Justice, Press Release (December 7, 1995), available at www.justice.gov/opa/pr/Pre_96/December95/609.txt.html.

[114] See *United States* v. *Getto*, above note 24, at 224–6.

[115] See C. Del Ponte and C. Sudetic, *Madam Prosecutor* (Other Press, 2009), at 270–1.

[116] I. Traynor, "Karadzic Predicted Muslim Bloodbath, Bosnian War Crimes Trial Hears", *The Guardian* (October 27, 2009).

[117] 18 USC §§ 2510–22. [118] See ibid., §§ 2516 and 2518. [119] ibid., § 2515.

legal processes for judicial issuance of so-called "Part VI orders" authorizing electronic surveillance.[120]

International cooperation measures

Each of the preceding investigative methods and techniques involves the use of lawful authority under domestic national legal regimes to gather evidence. As a general proposition, criminal investigators from one nation cannot intrude into the territory of another nation to gather evidence without the consent and assistance of the latter nation. Over the past quarter-century, however, a growing array of international and domestic legal measures now enable investigators to seek the assistance of investigators in other nations to obtain evidence of complex crime.

There are two principal types of international instruments to facilitate transnational evidence-gathering. The first is the MLAT, which is generally a bilateral instrument to facilitate cooperation between two signatory nations in criminal and related matters. As of 2012, there were at least fifty-six MLATs between the USA and various foreign jurisdictions. In addition, "on February 1, 2010, 27 U.S.–EU Instruments/Agreements/Protocols entered into force that either supplement existing MLATs or create new mutual legal assistance relationships between the United States and every member of the EU."[121]

The second is the multilateral convention that specifically provides for international cooperation in various types of criminal investigations and prosecutions. Three such instruments are especially relevant to certain types of complex crime. First, the United Nations Convention on Transnational Organized Crime (TOC Convention) contains a broad array of provisions to effect broader international cooperation against transnational organized crime, such as provisions on international cooperation for confiscation of assets, extradition, mutual legal assistance, special investigative techniques, cooperation with law enforcement authorities, and law enforcement cooperation.[122] With regard to the investigative methods and techniques discussed previously, it is noteworthy that the TOC Convention specifically encourages parties to the

[120] See, e.g., *Regina* v. *Pham*, 2009 Can LII 60792 (Ontario Supreme Court, November 4, 2009).

[121] See Bureau of International Narcotics and Law Enforcement Affairs, US Department of State, *International Narcotics Control Strategy Report*, Volume II (March 2012) at 20.

[122] See United Nations Convention Against Transnational Organized Crime, Arts. 13, 16, 18, 20, 26 and 27.

Convention to have their competent authorities use special investigative techniques that include the use of "electronic or other forms of surveillance and undercover operations,"[123] and specifically directs parties to take appropriate measures to encourage current or past participants in organized criminal groups to cooperate with the authorities and provide information for investigative and evidentiary purposes.[124]

Second, the Council of Europe Cybercrime Convention contains a specific commitment by parties thereto to cooperate with each other "to the widest extent possible for the purposes of investigations or proceedings concerning criminal offences related to computer systems and data, or for the collection of evidence in electronic form of a criminal offence."[125] It also contains specific international cooperation provisions on extradition, mutual assistance, preservation and storage of stored computer data, access to stored computer data, and the interception of computer data.[126]

Third, the Convention on Mutual Assistance in Criminal Matters between the Member States of the European Union (2000 EU Convention) also contains specific provisions providing for various forms of international cooperation between European Union Member States on criminal matters in general, such as mutual assistance requests, hearings by video- and tele-conference, controlled deliveries, covert investigations (i.e., undercover investigations), and interception of telecommunications.[127] The European Union can also conclude agreements with non-Member States for mutual assistance in criminal matters, as it did with Japan in 2010.[128]

It is also important to note that two of these international instruments provide specific authority for two or more nations to conduct joint investigations into complex crime. Article 19 of the TOC Convention encouraged parties to "consider concluding bilateral or multilateral agreements or arrangements whereby, in relation to matters that are the subject of investigations, prosecutions or judicial proceedings in one or more States, the competent authorities concerned may establish joint investigative bodies."[129] Article 13 of the 2000 EU Convention

[123] Ibid., Art. 20(1).

[124] See Ibid., Art. 26(1).

[125] Council of Europe Convention on Cybercrime, Art. 23.

[126] See ibid, Arts. 24–5, 27, 29–34.

[127] 2000 European Convention on Mutual Assistance in Criminal Matters between the Member States of the European Union, Arts. 8, 10–12, 14.

[128] See 2010 Agreement between the European Union and Japan on mutual legal assistance in criminal matters, OJ L 39/20.

[129] United Nations Convention against Transnational Organized Crime, Art. 19.

explicitly authorizes the competent authorities of two or more EU Member States to "set up a joint investigation team for a specific purpose and a limited period, which may be extended by mutual consent, to carry out criminal investigations in one or more of the Member States setting up the team."[130] Article 13 contains even more detailed provisions governing the composition and operations of joint investigation teams.

In addition, countries may adopt national legislation designed specifically to assist foreign criminal investigators. The USA, for example, has enacted the Foreign Evidence Request Efficiency Act of 2009 (FEREA),[131] which substantially broadens the range of assistance that the USA may provide in response to foreign requests for assistance in criminal investigations. Even if the USA does not have a pending investigation of its own into a particular matter, it may now assist foreign authorities to gather evidence within the USA through search warrants, warrants for stored electronic communications, judicial orders for pen registers and trap-and-trace devices, and judicial orders requiring the appearance of a person to give testimony or a statement or requiring the production of documents or other things.[132]

Conclusion

Complex crime can often be exceptionally difficult for law enforcement to discover, investigate and prosecute successfully. In order to prove the existence, scope and effects of specific complex crimes, as well as the role of specific participants therein, beyond a reasonable doubt at trial, law enforcement may need to use various combinations of the investigative methods and techniques discussed herein to bring those participants to justice. As this chapter has shown, these investigative methods and techniques, which have a firm foundation in both various domestic laws and international conventions, provide a sound basis for investigation of complex crime by national authorities or international tribunals. Moreover, the utility of a number of these methods and techniques is not limited to drug trafficking, organized crime or economic crime, but can even extend to the pursuit of core international crimes such as genocide and crimes against humanity.

[130] European Convention on Mutual Assistance, Art. 13(1).
[131] Pub L 111–79, 123 Stat 2086 (October 19, 2009).
[132] See 18 USC § 3512(a)(1) and (2).

5

Evidence in cases of mass criminality

DERMOT GROOME

Introduction

The previous chapter enumerated the salient characteristics of investigating complex crimes, characteristics that distinguish these crimes from more conventional crimes and require specialized approaches. This chapter will focus on the complex criminal investigations of alleged violations of international humanitarian and human rights law, their anatomy and the methodology for investigating those most responsible.

Overview of international criminal investigations

Conducting an international criminal investigation is a complex and time-consuming undertaking. It seeks to achieve the same goal as any competent national investigation, that is, to identify and collect all relevant and reliable evidence about an event or series of events. It seeks to do this most often in the setting of ongoing unrest.

One reason international crimes are so complex is that they are most often the product of collective action; the product of a group of people in which individuals make different contributions to the crime.[1] While some in this collective may be the direct perpetrators of crimes and be physically present during their commission, others may be remote perpetrators, participating in ways that are not immediately evident.

The investigation of the actual crime itself (i.e., the victim, the direct perpetrators and the primary crime scene) must be done to the same high standard as crimes investigated by national police services. Often central to an international criminal investigation is the question of whether

[1] For a summary of the collective nature of these crimes see, L. May, *Crimes Against Humanity: A Normative Account* (Cambridge University Press, 2004) at 87–90; and M. A. Drumbl, *Atrocity, Punishment and International Law* (Cambridge University Press, 2007) at 21.

senior military, police or political officials participated in the crime. Exposing this participation requires additional investigations that are very different in nature and scope. The mechanisms of perpetration are usually secretive and unique to particular circumstances of the case. Investigating state officials also requires the careful study of the legal relationships between senior officials, the direct perpetrators and all those who lie in the chain of causality between the two.

International prosecutors also have the burden of establishing the contextual or *chapeau* elements of international crimes in addition to the elements of the specific underlying offences such as murder or rape. For example, establishing that a crime against humanity was committed requires that the underlying crime was part of a widespread or systematic attack against a civilian population. Such investigations require detailed investigations into not only the subject crime but also into the other crimes forming the relevant context and with a nexus to the subject crime.

In addition to these conceptual differences, there are significant operational challenges faced by international investigators. Unlike a domestic investigation where investigators are likely to have immediate access to eye witnesses, international investigators may have to travel great distances to speak with witnesses. Witnesses are most often located in places far from the seat of the relevant court. If they are still in their homes, it is likely a place that is insecure and polarized about the work of international investigators. Very often victims and witnesses will have fled their permanent residences, seeking refuge in countries far away. Locating these witnesses and approaching them in a way that is sensitive to their current situation can be a difficult and time consuming endeavour.

Similar concerns apply to the identification and collection of physical evidence. Crimes scenes are likely to be insecure. Those that can be accessed may have already been tainted by the surrounding conflict or by belligerents seeking to manipulate the findings of prosecutors.

Finally, such investigations occur in unique historical and cultural settings. Before investigators can work effectively they must inform themselves about the historical precursors to the conflict as well as the culture and expectations of the people they will interview. Investigative practices will have to be adapted in a way that respects local cultural sensitivities. Investigators who are unable to speak the local language will need to identify and train interpreters who can be trusted to work on the investigation.

It is often the case that the ability of investigators to work and gather evidence will be improved over the course of an investigation. Evidence that was unavailable at the start of the investigation may become available as time passes and the conflict subsides. Changes in security, the disposition towards the court and the reaction to court proceedings can all prompt the discovery of new evidence. Changes in circumstances may lead to better access to witnesses, crime scenes and archives over the course of a case. Although the prosecutor must always seek the most reliable and probative evidence, this goal must be balanced against the accused's right to know the case against him or her and to prepare a defence.[2]

Anatomy of an international criminal investigation

An international criminal investigation commences when a prosecutor makes the decision to actively identify and collect evidence about an alleged violation of international criminal law.[3] A prosecutor can learn of such events from communications from individuals, governments, non-governmental organizations (NGOs) and the media. In some cases an investigation can be referred by a resolution of the UN Security Council.[4]

[2] During the trial of Slobodan Miloševič, it was a frequent occurrence for previously unknown witnesses to come forward and identify themselves in the ICTY's field offices in response to something they saw in the broadcast of the trial. See also, A. Whiting, 'In International Criminal Prosecutions, Justice Delayed Can be Justice Delivered', (2009) 50 *Harvard International Law Journal* 323. Perhaps the clearest example of this phenomenon was when the Prosecution obtained a video commonly referred to as the Scorpion Video, depicting the murder of six Muslim men and boys by members of a paramilitary unit called the Scorpions after the fall of Srebrenica. Despite concerted efforts to identify and seize video evidence of crimes this tape came into the prosecution's possession when a lawyer representing one of the members of the unit came into the Sarajevo Field Office of the ICTY and turned over the tape on 10 September 2004. See, *Prosecutor* v. *Milošević*, Decision on Application for a Limited Re-opening of the Bosnia and Kosovo Components of the Prosecution Case with Confidential Annex, (13 December 2005) (denying the admission of the Scorpion video).

[3] Article 42(1) of the Rome Statute charges the Office of the Prosecutor (OTP) with the responsibility of receiving and examining information of crimes and initiating investigations when appropriate. Articles 53 to 56 set out some general principles regarding the conduct of investigations. Investigations can be initiated upon the request of a State Party or by a referral from the UN Security Council exercising its Chapter VII authority. OTP can also initiate preliminary investigations on its own initiative pursuant to its authority under Article 15. See also, Regulations of the Office of the Prosecutor, ICC-BD/05-01-09, International Criminal Court, 23 April 2009.

[4] For a summary of the statutory framework of international investigations see, R. Cryer, H. Friman, D. Robinson and E. Wilmshurst, *An Introduction to International Criminal Law and Procedure* (Cambridge University Press, 2007) at 366–68.

The prosecutor must conduct a preliminary assessment of information to determine whether, if the allegations are proved, they constitute a violation of international law and are sufficiently serious to merit investigation. Once a determination has been made that an investigation should be commenced an investigation plan must be developed. Like any other professional inquiry, a criminal investigation benefits from an organized and systematic approach.

An investigation plan in its simplest form sets out the following information:

(1) What are the questions to be answered by the investigation? (For example, was Event A a crime and if so who bears criminal responsibility?)
(2) What information is currently available?
(3) What are the possible crimes?
(4) What are the types of potential physical evidence?
(5) What are the types of potential documentary evidence?
(6) What are the potential investigative scenes (crime scenes) that may contain evidence of the crime?
(7) Who are the potential witnesses?
(8) Has an alleged perpetrator or perpetrator group been identified?
(9) What are the investigative avenues that should be pursued?

At this early stage the investigation plan should be broad and consider that the information presently in possession of the prosecutor is unverified. It should not be relied upon to narrow the focus of the investigation in any way. This is particularly important in cases in which preliminary information includes named perpetrators. Great care should be taken to prevent such early unverified information unduly influencing the investigation.

An investigation plan is an evolving document. As the initial plan is implemented and evidence is collected, that evidence will suggest new avenues of investigation. Reliable evidence will help shape future investigative activities and the investigation plan will develop in a way that responds to this evidence. For example, investigators may process a crime scene in search of a weapon, as described in the initial investigation plan. Upon finding stained clothing at the crime scene the plan should be amended to incorporate this evidence and consider what investigative actions should be taken with respect to it.

Before an investigation arrives at its final conclusions it has undergone a cyclical process in which evidence is gathered, verified, analysed and tentative theories formed, which are in turn tested through additional investigation. Additional new evidence is gathered with an increased focus that is guided by a growing corpus of verified facts. Nascent factual and legal theories may be contradicted, confirmed, or refined by successive trips to the field to interview additional witnesses and collect more evidence.

In broad terms an international criminal investigation consists of four phases.[5] These phases are not rigidly distinct stages, but of different 'mind-sets' that the investigation team undergoes over the course of the investigation.

The first phase of the investigation is the 'casting of the net' phase. Investigators cast a wide 'net' as soon as possible to capture as much evidence as possible. In this phase investigators are trying to collect as much evidence about the event as possible without being too concerned with analysing it. As evidence is gathered investigators must continually inquire whether such evidence indicates the existence of other witnesses or additional evidence. Physical evidence (fingerprints) may contain clues about who might be a witness. Similarly, a witness's account of an event may help identify additional physical evidence.

The second phase relates to 'discovering the case'. Once investigators have gathered most of the physical and testimonial evidence they are aware of they move to the next phase of the investigation. Here, the investigation team starts to analyse the evidence that has been collected. Evidence is assessed for reliability and tentative conclusions are drawn. I intentionally use the phrase 'discovering the case' to emphasize that the early tentative conclusions must emerge from the evidence in a discovery process. This is in opposition to 'creating the case', a process which seeks to impose a preconceived theory of events on the body of evidence by placing undue focus on some evidence while diminishing the clear evidential import of other evidence. Investigators, like all humans, have both biases and an inclination to reaching conclusions quickly. They must make a conscious and deliberate effort to allow the evidence itself to reveal what happened. During this phase it is likely that several theories of events as well as several possible suspects will emerge. The evidence will rarely point to a single conclusion. All possible scenarios and all suspects must be noted and considered at this stage.

[5] For a detailed explanation of the different phases of an investigation, see D. Groome, *Handbook of Human Rights Investigation* (2nd edn, Createspace Independent Publishing Platform, 2011) at 37 ff (hereafter *Handbook of Human Rights Investigation*).

The third phase of an investigation is about 'exploring the case'. During this phase there is a return to a search for evidence. The investigation plan should be amended to identify all of the possible scenarios and suspects identified during the second phase of the investigation. The plan must develop concrete avenues of investigation to gather evidence which will either prove or disprove each possible scenario and implicate or eliminate each suspect.

Each possible scenario must be comprehensively investigated until it is confirmed or eliminated as a possibility. This process continues until there is sufficient credible and reliable evidence to indicate what happened and who is responsible for the crime, all possible theories have been eliminated and the sole remaining theory is supported by evidence that can meet a high standard of proof.

The final phase is about 'building the case'. At this stage the investigation should have gathered sufficient credible and reliable evidence to establish what happened and who is responsible. The focus now turns to the different crimes which may have been committed. Careful analysis must be undertaken to examine the possible crimes, their constituent elements and whether there is sufficient admissible evidence to establish each element beyond a reasonable doubt. Evidential gaps must be identified and additional investigations undertaken to close those gaps.

Overview of evidence in a criminal proceeding

Before discussing the investigation of senior officials it will be helpful to review some of the basic concepts that apply to all criminal investigations, irrespective of where such crimes are prosecuted.

The collection of reliable evidence is the primary objective of any investigation. Unless an investigator is able to discover and collect evidence, he or she cannot uncover the truth regarding the events being investigated. Evidence can be anything that provides information about the incident under investigation. It may include: physical objects; the investigator's observations; the testimony of witnesses and suspects; documents and scientific analysis.

The word 'anything' should be emphasized because evidence comes in many forms from a wide variety of sources. It is often impossible to determine the ultimate probative value a piece of evidence may have early in the investigation. As more evidence is gathered and analysed the significance of each piece becomes more apparent. A seemingly unimportant object becomes relevant when it provides information about the matter being investigated. There is an important distinction between relevancy during the investigative phase of a case and after an indictment has been issued. The concept of relevancy is much broader during the investigative stage of a case. Once an indictment or other charging instrument is drafted relevance will always be controlled by the allegations contained in that document. At the investigative stage, when no conclusions have been reached, an investigator should adopt a broad definition of relevance that considers all evidence that tends to prove or disprove a material fact as important.

One of the most important principles an investigator must adopt in his or her work is that there is always evidence in a case. It is impossible to commit wrongdoing and leave no identifiable trace. The task for the investigator is to identify it, document it and collect it. In some cases, it may be impossible for the investigator to gain access to evidence because of ongoing conflict or a hostile government. If evidence is not presently available, the investigator should still attempt to identify it and exhaust all reasonable efforts to document its existence.

In the case of *Prosecutor* v. *Milan Lukić*, the indictment alleged that the defendants had barricaded and burned dozens of civilians in a house on Pionirska Street in Višegrad. During the defence case, experts asserted that no fire had occurred. When Office of the Prosecutor (OTP) staff originally investigated the crime they were unable to visit the scene because it was too dangerous. As the years passed there was reliable information that efforts had been undertaken to remove any trace of a fire in the concrete structure. In an earlier trial of a co-accused the Trial Chamber found that the eyewitness accounts of survivors were sufficient to establish the occurrence of the fire.[6] During the trial investigators went to the site in response to the defence assertion. Despite the passage of sixteen years they were able to recover charred wood from the door jambs and wall of the house. They also recovered molten copper wire from the walls – wire that melted in the intensity of the fire.[7] Despite earlier efforts to remove evidence of the fire sufficient physical evidence remained to establish the occurrence of the fire.

Direct versus circumstantial evidence

Each piece of evidence proves a fact either directly or indirectly. Evidence that directly proves a fact without the need for drawing an inference is called direct evidence. For example, a woman sees the rain fall on the

[6] *Prosecutor* v. *Mitar Vasiljević*, Judgment (29 November 2002) paras. 50, 125–8.

[7] *Prosecutor* v. *Milan Lukić*, Judgment (20 July 2009) paras. 551 ff.

footpath outside her house. Her observation is considered direct evidence that it rained. Indirect evidence is commonly referred to as circumstantial evidence. This evidence does not directly prove a fact, but when considered in light of our universal experience and common sense it indirectly proves a fact. For example, the same woman awakes one morning to see her footpath wet. Using her experience and reasoning she concludes that it rained during the night.

In most cases there will be both direct and circumstantial evidence. Before circumstantial evidence has any real value in a case an investigator must also gather evidence which excludes all other reasonable inferences that can be drawn from the circumstantial evidence. Reconsider the woman who, after observing her wet footpath, concluded that it rained the night before. Her conclusion would be of little value if her neighbour sometimes wet her footpath when watering his lawn. Whenever there is only circumstantial evidence regarding a material fact great care must be taken to check for other reasonable explanations besides the one pointing to a suspect's guilt. These other possibilities must be investigated to determine whether in fact any reliable inference can be drawn from the circumstantial evidence in question.

In the *Lukić* case, described above, the molten copper wire and charred wood are circumstantial evidence that a fire occurred in the Pionirska house. This evidence's full inferential effect is only possible when coupled with other evidence which established that no other significant fire ever occurred in the building.

Three types of evidence: physical, testimonial and documentary

All evidence can be classified into three groups. These groups are physical, testimonial and documentary evidence. Physical evidence refers to any physical object that can provide information about an event. It may include weapons that were used, the condition of the victim's body, or the area where an attack took place. It may include computers containing data, communications equipment, video and audio recordings. Physical evidence includes objects and traces of materials that can only be detected with scientific testing. Because physical evidence is not subject to human perception, exaggeration or deception it is inherently reliable. Physical evidence, if properly preserved, retains its probative value and is not subject to fading over time like a witness's memory.

In recent years there has been a growing phenomenon of using social media to bring attention to information and evidence of possible crimes.

Both sides in the Syrian conflict have regularly placed videos showing alleged crimes on YouTube and Facebook in an effort to bring attention to these crimes. Given the fact that an authenticated video recording of a crime is perhaps some of the best evidence an investigator can obtain, investigators should try to collect this evidence. The problem with such evidence is its authenticity. An unauthenticated video is unlikely to carry much evidential weight, particularly in a conflict in which the participants are seeking to exploit the propaganda value of such videos.

Testimonial evidence is a broad term that includes the statements of all victims, witnesses and suspects. It is different from physical evidence in that testimonial evidence is only as reliable as the witness that provides it. The accuracy of the information depends completely on the honesty, perception and communication skills of the witness.

The last category of evidence, documentary evidence is a combination of physical and testimonial evidence in that although the document itself is a piece of physical evidence, the information contained in the document is testimonial in nature. Some documents are official records that are generated during the normal operations of an organization. As a general rule documents created closely in time to the events they refer to are more reliable and valuable from an evidential point of view than documents created long after the events.

Documents are a very significant and important source of evidence in large international criminal investigations because it is in documents that the details of military, police and government operations are recorded. Documents, if authenticated, provide one of the most reliable and complete sources of information as to what occurred during times of chaos and conflict. As technology permeates more and more of our daily activities, including warfare, investigators must consider whether valuable information ordinarily found in documents has been recorded electronically. Email, databases and digital communications systems may hold important evidence about the matter being investigated.

Frequently, before admitting evidence in a trial and certainly before placing any weight on an exhibit a court will inquire and consider the provenance of the exhibit. If the exhibit is physical evidence, the court will inquire about the circumstances of its collection and where it has been kept before its introduction in court. If the exhibit is a document the court will expect that the party tendering it can demonstrate its authenticity.

Authenticating documentary exhibits can be particularly difficult in the context of international crimes. These crimes occur during times of chaos and conflict and documentary evidence may have been seized under conditions that did not permit the concurrent gathering of evidence to establish authenticity. In many instances, investigators may be given documents by witnesses who are themselves unsure about the documents' provenance. In these instances investigators will often be required to investigate a document's authenticity before it can be relied on in an investigation or used in court.

It is important to recognize that although evidence falls into these three different categories there will be relationships and interaction between each type. Physical evidence will often have greater meaning after the investigator learns from an eyewitness how the object was used. Witnesses can often help an investigator interpret the meaning of documents collected as evidence. Conversely, documents can sometimes be appropriately used to refresh the recollection of witnesses who may no longer have a clear memory of precise dates and details of particular events.

Hearsay evidence

Hearsay is second-hand information. Whenever the person providing the information did not personally witness it, that information is hearsay. To people unfamiliar with investigations or courtroom procedure, relying on hearsay information does not seem to be problematic. In fact, we rely on hearsay information every day. We get most of our information from hearsay sources and depend upon it quite successfully.

While hearsay evidence is generally not admissible in common law jurisdictions, there is no prohibition against hearsay evidence in civil law jurisdictions or in international criminal courts. The rationale for allowing hearsay evidence is that professional judges are able to properly evaluate hearsay and place an appropriate amount of weight on it. While international courts have and are likely to continue to admit hearsay, such evidence will never have the same weight as the direct observations of a witness. The fact that international tribunals may admit hearsay evidence should not encourage complacency or diminish the importance of locating non-hearsay sources of evidence. Hearsay evidence is never as reliable as direct evidence.

Another way of looking at the issue of hearsay is to consider the effect of these 'additional witnesses' coming between the investigator and the eyewitness. In the case of hearsay the investigator (and later the court) must assess the credibility and reliability of the eyewitness (who is not present), but also the in-court witness relaying the information. The court must now assess just how accurately this second witness is reporting the eyewitness's account.

One of the criticisms of investigations conducted by the International Criminal Court (ICC) Prosecutor is that there has been an over reliance on hearsay evidence. In the *Gbagbo* case the prosecution relied heavily on hearsay, including anonymous hearsay, to meet its burden at the confirmation hearing. The Chamber was very critical of this practice and noted the low probative value of such evidence as well as the implications for the right of an accused to know who is providing evidence against him or her.[8] The Chamber also took issue with the prosecution's reliance on hearsay evidence in the form of documentary and summary evidence, such as press articles and NGO reports and stated that unless the prosecution was to conduct additional investigations there was little prospect of the evidence being accepted at trial.[9] The Chamber expressed its 'serious concern' about the quality of the evidence presented during the confirmation hearing.[10]

The *Mbarushimana* Chamber also indicated that the anonymous hearsay evidence contained in Human Rights Watch reports would, as a general rule, be 'given a low probative value'.[11] The *Garda* Chamber followed a similar approach with respect to anonymous evidence and summary hearsay statements that the prosecution tendered in support of its case.[12]

Anonymous hearsay should rarely, if ever, be adduced as proof to sustain the Prosecutor's burden at any stage of a criminal proceeding. It inherently lacks reliability and is very often factually inaccurate. Many international crimes occur in the context of a conflict in which propaganda is a frequently

8 Rome Statute, Art. 67 (rights of the accused).

9 The *Gbagbo* Chamber stated: 'In light of the above considerations, the Chamber notes with serious concern that in this case the Prosecutor relied heavily on NGO reports and press articles with regard to key elements of the case, including the contextual elements of crimes against humanity.' *ICC Prosecutor* v. *Gbagbo*, Decision Adjourning the Hearing on the Confirmation of Charges Pursuant to Article 61(7)(c)(i) of the Rome Statute (3 June 2013) para. 35 (hereafter *Gbagbo* Adjournment Decision).

10 Ibid., para. 35. In addition to the four separate incidents charged by the prosecution, it also relied on forty-one other incidents to establish the contextual or *chapeau* elements of crimes against humanity. The Chamber found that for the majority of these forty-five incidents, the only evidence adduced during the confirmation hearing was anonymous hearsay from NGO reports, UN reports and press articles.

11 *ICC Prosecutor* v. *Callixte Mbarushimana*, Decision on the Confirmation of Charges (6 December 2011) para. 78 (hereafter *Mbarushimana* Confirmation Decision). This is in keeping with law in many national courts, which are reluctant to find probable or reasonable cause based on anonymous information alone. See, e.g., *Illinois* v. *Gates*, 462 U.S. 213 (1983).

12 *ICC Prosecutor* v. *Bahar Idriss Abu Garda*, Decision on the Confirmation of Charges (8 February 2010) para. 52 (hereafter *Garda* Confirmation Decision).

used tool by all sides. In the context of the former Yugoslavia, a great many fantastic and false stories were spread anonymously in an effort to achieve some end.[13] The anonymity of the information makes it impossible for a chamber to assess the credibility and reliability of the information. The ICC Prosecutor's heavy reliance on anonymous hearsay in cases deprives pre-trial chambers of the ability to check the information against other known sources. A chamber that must evaluate evidence that is predominantly anonymous is unable to cross-check the evidence because it is difficult to assess whether seemingly corroborative evidence is truly corroborative, or simply another formulation of the same information from the same original anonymous source. A competent investigation requires more than aggregating several sources of such hearsay and presenting it to the court. Investigators must find the source of the hearsay and conduct their own independent interview and assessment of the witness.

Despite the limited evidential value of hearsay during court proceedings there is an important role for hearsay evidence during an investigation. Hearsay information can lead to eyewitnesses and physical evidence. Very often the first people an investigator will come into contact with are not eyewitnesses but people who spoke to the eyewitnesses. This hearsay information is valuable because it helps to identify possible eyewitnesses and gives the investigator some idea about what information the eyewitness may be able to provide.

Hearsay can also help orient investigators and provide background about the crimes. Many of the investigations at the International Criminal Tribunal for the former Yugoslavia (ICTY) were commenced after a review of reports from the media and non-governmental human rights organizations.[14] The ICTY also had the benefit of the Bassiouni Commission, an ad hoc commission established by the UN Security Council to conduct

[13] One of the more inflammatory reports that was eventually proven to be false was a claim that Serb babies were being fed to the lions in the Sarajevo zoo. The original broadcast by Rada Djokić can be seen on YouTube. Borislav Herak, one of the early infamous perpetrators of crimes in the Sarajevo area, claimed that he was motivated in part by these reports. J. Rodrigue, 'Politics of Rape', *Dallas Morning News* (5 May 1993), at 1A and 26A.

[14] See, e.g., Human Rights Watch, *Looking for Justice: War Crimes in Bosnia-Hercegovina*, Vol. I (1992); Human Rights Watch, *War Crimes in Bosnia-Hercegovina: Bosanski Samac, Six War Criminals Named by Victims* (1994) available at www.hrw.org/legacy/reports/1994/bosnia/; Human Rights Watch, *Yugoslav Government War Crimes in Racak* (1999). See also Amnesty International, Bosnia-Herzegovina: *To Bury My Brothers' Bones* (1996) available at www.amnesty.org/en/library/asset/EUR63/015/1996/en/8a8a95e2-eaf8-11dd-aad1-ed57e7e5470b/eur630151996en.pdf.

preliminary non-judicial investigations into possible crimes during the break-up of Yugoslavia.[15] These different hearsay sources were instrumental in helping the ICTY OTP find its first witnesses.

Exculpatory evidence

As every investigation begins to focus on particular suspects there will be evidence that not only inculpates them but also evidence that is considered exculpatory, requiring its eventual disclosure to the suspect if he or she is charged with a crime. In international criminal law the concept 'exculpatory' is broader than its common usage and not only includes evidence which would exonerate an accused but also evidence that might mitigate guilt, or which might cast doubt on prosecution evidence generally. Article 54(a) of the Rome Statute of the ICC imposes upon the Prosecutor the affirmative duty to investigate incriminating and exonerating circumstances equally.[16]

Experienced investigators will already appreciate the wisdom in thoroughly investigating exculpatory information. The ultimate goal of any competent investigation is to establish the truth and any investigation that ignores an investigative lead that may be contrary to the current view of the evidence is seriously flawed. There can only be confidence in the results of an investigation if all avenues have been properly pursued. An investigation must always be balanced and always cognisant of the presumption of innocence that protects all suspects and all accused.

Confidentiality agreements

Both the ICTY and the International Criminal Tribunal for Rwanda (ICTR) have special provisions to protect the confidentiality of persons or states that provide evidence confidentially.[17] The ICC in Article 69(5) of its Statute also contains such a provision and imposes an obligation on the Court to 'respect

[15] Commission of Experts' Final Report, UN Doc. S/1994/674, 27 May 1994.

[16] Article 54(a) states: 'In order to establish the truth, extend the investigation to cover all facts and evidence relevant to an assessment of whether there is criminal responsibility under this Statute, and, in doing so, investigate incriminating and exonerating circumstances equally.'

[17] Rule 70 of the ICTY Rules of Procedure and Evidence states in relevant part: 'B. If the Prosecutor is in possession of information which has been provided to the Prosecutor on a confidential basis and which has been used solely for the purpose of generating new evidence, that initial information and its origin shall not be disclosed by the Prosecutor without the consent of the person or entity providing the initial information and shall in any event not be given in evidence without prior disclosure to the accused.'

and observe privileges on confidentiality as provided for in the Rules of Procedure and Evidence'. Article 54(3)(e) empowers the prosecution to accept evidence confidentially for the purpose of generating new evidence.[18] Investigators must exercise great caution when agreeing to accept evidence confidentially. Any decision to accept evidence confidentially should be in writing and reflect a uniform policy established by senior staff of the OTP. Serious problems arise when witnesses are given assurances of confidentiality regarding a particular item of evidence which is determined to contain exculpatory information.[19]

This very situation arose in the *Lubanga* case. After the *Lubanga* confirmation hearing the prosecution recognized that some material it had accepted pursuant to a confidentiality agreement required disclosure under Article 67(2).[20] Proceedings came to an abrupt halt when the prosecution was unable to obtain permission to disclose the material. The Trial Chamber found that during the course of its investigations:

> [T]he Prosecution has incorrectly used Article 54(3)(e) [confidentiality agreement] when entering into agreements with information-providers, with the consequence that a significant body of exculpatory evidence which would otherwise have been disclosed to the accused is to be withheld from him, thereby improperly inhibiting the opportunities for the accused to prepare his defence...[21]

The Chamber further found that the prosecution's actions had effectively prevented the Chamber from being able to review the material and determine whether the non-disclosure of the material would constitute a breach of the accused's right to a fair trial.[22] The prosecution's mistake of giving a grant of confidentiality to material that ultimately proved to

[18] Article 54(3)(e) states: 'The Prosecutor may ... agree not to disclose, at any stage of the proceedings, documents or information that the Prosecutor obtains on the condition of confidentiality and solely for the purpose of generating new evidence, unless the provider of the information consents.'

[19] See, e.g., *ICC Prosecutor* v. *Thomas Lubanga Dyilo*, Redacted Decision on Intermediaries (31 May 2010).

[20] Article 67(2) provides in relevant part: '[T]he Prosecutor shall, as soon as practicable, disclose to the defence evidence in the Prosecutor's possession or control which he or she believes shows or tends to show the innocence of the accused, or to mitigate the guilt of the accused, or which may affect the credibility of prosecution evidence.'

[21] *ICC Prosecutor* v. *Thomas Lubanga Dyilo*, Urgent Decision on the Consequences of Non-Disclosure of Exculpatory Materials Covered by Article 54(3)(e) Agreements and the Application to Stay the Prosecution of the Accused, Together with Certain Other Issues Raised at the Status Conference on 10 June 2008 (13 June 2008) para. 92.

[22] Ibid.

be exculpatory nearly resulted in a termination of the ICC's first trial. The trial was only able to continue after the conditions of the original agreement with the provider were re-negotiated.[23]

Evidence which should be excluded

The rules and jurisprudence of most courts, including the ICC, contain provisions dealing with evidence that is tainted by the way in which it was collected.[24] These provisions are intended to protect the proceedings from being impugned by evidence that is patently unreliable, or obtained illegally or in such a manner that admitting it would jeopardise the integrity of the trial itself. Article 69 (7) states:

> Evidence obtained by means of a violation of this Statute or internationally recognised human rights shall not be admissible if:
>
> (a) The violation casts substantial doubt on the reliability of the evidence; or
>
> (b) The admission of the evidence would be antithetical to and would seriously damage the integrity of the proceedings.

This provision vests the court with substantial authority to exclude evidence that falls within Article 69(7). Investigators should be mindful of this and ensure that their conduct as well as the conduct of their subordinates or others acting on their behalf conforms to all applicable laws and internationally recognized norms.

Witnesses

In all cases, most resources will be focused on identifying and interviewing witnesses. For many reasons witnesses are the most critical part of any case. No matter how much physical and documentary evidence is collected, without witnesses to explain its relevance there is unlikely to be a successful prosecution. Interviewing witnesses is also the most important task an investigator will undertake. If done well, witness interviews will yield compelling, truthful testimony about an event. If done poorly, testimonial evidence can be corrupted in a way that is likely to compromise the entire investigation.

[23] *ICC Prosecutor* v. *Thomas Lubanga Dyilo*, Reasons for Oral Decision Lifting the Stay of Proceedings (23 January 2009).

[24] Rule 95 of the ICTY Rules of Procedure and Evidence states: 'No evidence shall be admissible if obtained by methods which cast substantial doubt on its reliability or if its admission is antithetical to, and would seriously damage, the integrity of the proceedings.'

Unlike physical evidence, information provided by witnesses is rarely entirely complete or accurate. All witnesses, most unintentionally, are affected by the frailties of their own perception and recollection. The investigator must be ever mindful of these human imperfections in order to accurately record all of the reliable information a witness may be able to provide. Chapter 6 provides an in-depth account of the psychological dimension of eyewitness testimony.

Categories of witnesses

In international criminal investigations witnesses generally fall into one of four categories depending upon the type of evidence they provide.

(1) Crime base witnesses. Crime base witnesses are those witnesses who are either victims of a crime or witnesses to it. These witnesses are able to describe the conduct of the direct perpetrator as well as the immediate context of the crime. Some of these witnesses may be vulnerable and require special measures to help them provide their evidence in a way that minimizes the risk of re-traumatization.[25]

(2) Insider witnesses. The term 'insider witness' is used to describe witnesses who by virtue of their membership in an organization are able to provide 'inside' information about it. Some insiders may bear some culpability for the crimes and may have to be treated as suspects irrespective of whether they are a target of the investigation.

(3) Suspects. During the course of an investigation it is likely that the investigation team will consider interviewing the targets of the investigation. Suspects have special rights during questioning that must be scrupulously observed.

(4) Expert witnesses. Expert witnesses are witnesses with specific expertise that facilitates a full understanding of other evidence in the case. Experts usually prepare a report of their observations and conclusions that is then tendered in court.

Interviewing witnesses

The techniques for working with each of these categories of witnesses is different and beyond the scope of this chapter. The kind of interview that is conducted will depend upon the type of witness and whether the

[25] Vulnerable witnesses include: children, victims of sexual violence and severely traumatized persons. See *Handbook of Human Rights Investigation*, above note 5, at 198.

witness is cooperative or antagonistic towards investigators. In general terms, all interviews should explore and carefully record the witness' relevant knowledge in a non-suggestive manner that is fair to both the witness and any people who may ultimately be charged with crimes.

Defence counsels practising before the ICC have asserted that the OTP has failed in some instances to conduct witness interviews fairly.[26] In the *Mbarushimana* case the Pre-trial Chamber, in declining to confirm the charges against the accused expressed its concern regarding interview techniques used by prosecution investigators which 'seem[ed] utterly inappropriate when viewed in light of the objective set out in Article 54(1)(a) to establish the truth by "investigating incriminating and exonerating circumstances equally"'.[27] The Chamber was concerned with how the transcripts of investigative interviews repeatedly demonstrated that the investigators conducting the interviews relied heavily on leading questions, belying their theory of events and showing 'resentment, impatience or disappointment' when witnesses did not provide the answer they wanted.[28] The Chamber noted the objectionable practice in the interviews of three witnesses.

The process described by the Chamber indicates that investigators may have been suggesting the prosecution's case theory to witnesses rather than asking neutral questions. Experienced professional investigators know that the type of interview described by the Chamber should be conducted rarely and only under very specific circumstances. If a witness is truly adverse or is being deceptive the investigator may decide to conduct a second interview to follow-up on the initial non-leading interview by confronting the witness with some of the inconsistencies in the first interview or with some of the evidence that contradicts his or her account.

Communicating with witnesses

One of the most difficult challenges in an international investigation is communicating with witnesses who remain in the area where the crimes

[26] See, e.g., *ICC Prosecutor* v. *Bahar Idriss Abu Garda*, Confirmation Hearing (30 October 2009) transcript at 72; *ICC Prosecutor* v. *Uhuru Muigai Kenyatta*, Decision on Defence Application Pursuant to Article 64(4) and Related Requests (26 April 2013) para. 112 (hereafter *Kenyatta* Article 64 Decision).

[27] *Mbarushimana* Confirmation Decision, above note 11 at para. 51. The Chamber went further to state '[T]he Chamber cannot refrain from deprecating such techniques and from highlighting that as a consequence, the probative value of evidence obtained by these means may be significantly weakened.'

[28] The Chamber noted that the conduct of the investigators was 'hardly reconcilable with a professional and impartial technique of witness questioning'. Ibid.

occurred. It is difficult for investigators to work discreetly and witnesses are likely to be concerned with having investigators come to their homes. One way to facilitate contact with witnesses is to establish an official field office in the country where investigations are being conducted. Field offices located in large business districts and accessible to witnesses will facilitate direct communication with them. The ICTY at the height of its work had six field offices in the former Yugoslavia.[29]

Sometimes the security situation may be so poor that field offices are impossible or witnesses are too afraid to come to them. Contacting witnesses directly in such an insecure environment can have significant security implications for them. In some cases contact with a witness will have to be made through an intermediary. An intermediary is an individual or organization that can be trusted to facilitate confidential communication with investigators in a way that does not arouse suspicion and minimizes the security risks a witness may face. In working with intermediaries it is important that their role is limited to facilitating communication.

The use of intermediaries by the ICC Prosecutor has caused considerable debate, in particular over the appropriateness of employing external intermediaries to perform key investigative functions. In *Lubanga*, the prosecution employed people to assist it in identifying and interviewing witnesses. An OTP investigator identified as P-583 gave evidence at trial that the use of intermediaries was the only way to gain access to knowledgeable witnesses given the security situation that existed at the time.[30] The prosecution relied on seven different intermediaries to secure the evidence of approximately half of the witnesses it called at trial.[31]

The integrity of the intermediaries and the role they played in the investigation became a central issue in the case.[32] In its final judgment

[29] These offices were located in: Belgrade, Sarajevo, Zagreb, Banja Luka, Pristina and Skopje. See Report of the International Tribunal for the Prosecution of Persons Responsible for Serious Violations of International Humanitarian Law Committed in the Territory of the Former Yugoslavia since 1991, UN Doc. A/56/352 (17 September 2001) para. 197; Report of the International . . . since 1991, UN Doc. A/59/215 (16 August 2004) paras. 354, 388; Report of the International . . . since 1991, UN Doc. A/60/267 (17 August 2005) paras. 229, 245.

[30] *ICC Prosecutor* v. *Thomas Lubanga Dyilo*, Judgment Pursuant to Article 74 of the Statute (14 March 2012) paras. 167, 181 (hereafter *Lubanga* Judgment). For a detailed description of the investigation and the problems it encountered, see *Lubanga* Judgment, paras. 124–77.

[31] The prosecution informed the Chamber that it had relied on a total of twenty-three individuals and organizations over the course of the investigation. See *ICC Prosecutor* v. *Thomas Lubanga Dyilo*, Redacted Decision on Intermediaries (31 May 2010) para. 3.

[32] *ICC Prosecutor* v. *Thomas Lubanga Dyilo*, Redacted Decision on the 'Defence Application Seeking a Permanent Stay of the Proceedings' (7 March 2011) para. 198.

the Chamber focused on the conduct of four of the seven intermediaries and set out its detailed analysis of each of them. Intermediary 143 (I-143) was a paid intermediary who introduced the prosecution to twenty-one witnesses and another intermediary (P-031). Five of these witnesses were called at trial. The Chamber found that inconsistent statements by witnesses P-007, P-008, P-010 and P-011, as well as evidence that contradicted their testimony, rendered the witnesses unreliable. The Chamber further concluded that 'it is likely that as the common point of contact he [I-143] persuaded, encouraged or assisted some or all of them [the witnesses] to give false testimony'.[33]

Intermediary 316 (I-316) was under contract with the OTP even though the prosecution was aware of his close ties with the Congolese intelligence service.[34] The Chamber noted with particular concern that the OTP employed an intermediary who was employed by the very same government that had originally referred the case to the ICC.[35] The Chamber considered that it was inappropriate for someone who lacked both independence and impartiality essentially to become a member of the prosecution team.[36] The Chamber concluded that I-316 had 'persuaded witnesses to lie'.[37]

P-321 was another paid intermediary who acted on behalf of the OTP for more than a year and introduced investigators to eight witnesses, four of whom testified in the trial. The Chamber found that all four of these witnesses gave materially false evidence and that there was a 'significant possibility' that P-321's improper influence over the witnesses was the cause.[38]

The Chamber concluded that 'the Prosecution should not have delegated its investigative responsibilities to the intermediaries ... notwithstanding the extensive security difficulties it faced'.[39] The Chamber criticized the prosecution's reliance on these intermediaries and that it had permitted them to work with important witnesses essentially unsupervised.[40]

The OTP's use of intermediaries in *Lubanga* went far beyond helping investigators contact potential witnesses. They became paid agents of the OTP, to whom the Prosecutor delegated important investigative functions. While using intermediaries to make initial contact with witnesses is an

33 *Lubanga* Judgment, above note 30, at para. 291.

34 In addition, the Chamber noted that at least one other member of the Congolese intelligence assisted I-316 in his work. Ibid., at para. 368.

35 Ibid., para. 368. 36 Ibid., para. 368. 37 Ibid., para. 374. 38 Ibid., para. 450.

39 Ibid., para. 482. 40 Ibid., para. 482.

acceptable way of working in a hostile environment, their role must be limited to that. The intermediary should not be involved in the selection of witnesses, nor the exchange of substantive information between the witness and investigators.[41] If intermediaries are to be used, the investigator must carefully consider who to use. Knowingly employing an intelligence operative to act as an intermediary, particularly in the setting of the *Lubanga* case, was fraught with danger from the outset. Investigators have the responsibility to control all aspects of the investigation and vigorously protect its integrity.

Assessment and verification of evidence provided by witnesses

As described above witnesses by virtue of human imperfection can provide inaccurate or untruthful information. It is important that investigators take conscious steps designed to test the credibility and reliability of a witness and verify the information the witness provides.[42] During the interview process the investigator should thoroughly explore areas that are likely to reveal the reliability and credibility of a witness as well as whether they harbour a particular bias that may impact their evidence. Similarly, a witness who is genuinely fearful may also provide inaccurate information in an effort to shield themselves and their families from possible retribution. It is common for such witnesses to provide accurate information about what happened but falsely claim that they were unable to see the perpetrators involved.

After an interview investigators should take steps to verify the information provided by a witness. While it may be impossible to verify everything a witness says, sufficient efforts must be undertaken to ensure that information that is central to the investigation is scrutinized and verified. Ultimately, a chamber will consider testimonial evidence in light of its assessment of a witness's credibility and reliability and this additional information may assist a chamber in making this assessment.[43]

[41] In *Lubanga*, it is reasonably possible that paid intermediaries whose job it was to locate witnesses would have considered that payment would cease unless they continued to 'find witnesses'.

[42] Credibility is whether a witness is being honest and telling the 'truth'. Reliability is whether the facts described by a witness are accurate. This is an important distinction in the case of a witness who is honestly mistaken. For example, a witness may be honestly mistaken in their identification of a perpetrator. In such a case, the witness is credible but unreliable.

[43] *Handbook of Human Rights Investigation*, above note 5, at 190–6.

In *Lubanga*, the prosecution did not take the steps necessary to verify key information provided by some of its witnesses. The defence investigators did and were able to obtain school and other records which established that some of the witnesses who claimed to have been child soldiers were too old for this to be true. Given that the age of a victim/witness at the time he or she was inducted into combat was a central issue in the trial, the prosecution had an important responsibility to independently verify the age of these witnesses before advancing their evidence in court.[44]

Similar criticisms were echoed in *Ngudjolo*, another case from the Democratic Republic of the Congo (DRC). Despite the fact that the *Ngudjolo* Chamber recognized that the prosecution faced significant challenges in conducting investigations in the DRC, it chided the prosecution for its failure to investigate the background of key witnesses adequately, in particular their failure to identify reliable information about their age.[45]

Investigations into the conduct of senior officials

The ICC, as well as the international and internationalized domestic courts, focuses on holding those individuals most responsible for violations of international criminal law. These individuals are most often senior political, military and police officials. Although their participation may be knowing and intentional it is often remote from the crime itself. These individuals are unlikely to have direct contact with victims or have detailed involvement in the planning of individual crimes. Over the last two decades international criminal law has developed in a way that articulates several legal frameworks for assessing the individual responsibility of senior officials.[46]

These senior officials often misuse state institutions, domestic legislation and national resources to achieve a criminal purpose. The mechanisms employed in the commission of such crimes are at least

[44] *Lubanga* Judgment, above note 30, para. 482.

[45] *ICC Prosecutor* v. *Mathieu Ngudjolo*, Judgment Pursuant to Article 74 of the Statute (18 December 2012) para. 121 (hereafter *Ngudjolo* Judgment).

[46] For a comprehensive enumeration of the legal frameworks see, H. Olásolo, *The Criminal Responsibility of Senior Political and Military Leaders as Principals to International Crimes* (Hart, 2009).

as complex as the workings of the state government that has been co-opted. International criminal investigations must develop investigative strategies designed to uncover evidence of this criminal use of state institutions.

The investigation of senior officials for international crimes will always involve a multi-level approach. The number of levels will largely depend upon how far the suspect is removed from the physical perpetration of the crime and the complexity of the structures and institutions employed by the perpetrator. A clear distinction should be made between the primary level of direct physical perpetration and other levels which concern conduct that despite being remote nonetheless amounts to a significant contribution to the crime.

The investigation of the primary level requires a thorough investigation of the direct physical perpetrators of the crime. This investigation will mirror the type of comprehensive investigation undertaken by skilled law enforcement personnel in national police services.

This chapter will not go into detail about the specific steps that should be taken other than to reiterate the importance of detailed and comprehensive investigative work at this stage. The fact that the ultimate suspects in an investigation are senior-level officials does not diminish the importance of competent work at this primary level. Compelling evidence connecting a senior official to a crime will not be sufficient for conviction if the crime itself was not competently investigated. The importance of this first vital component of a case cannot be overstated. Every investigative avenue which may yield information regarding this initial link must be thoroughly explored and documented.

There are four categories of people commonly involved in the complex chain required for international crimes.

(1) Direct perpetrator. A direct perpetrator is the person or persons who physically perpetrate a crime.
(2) Intermediate perpetrator. Intermediate perpetrators are those remote perpetrators who are not part of the highest level of perpetrators, yet knowingly participate in the commission of crimes by the direct perpetrators.
(3) Senior remote perpetrator. Senior remote perpetrators are high-level members of military, police and political institutions who exercise their authority to initiate and participate in the crimes committed by the direct perpetrators. Their participation is often through complex institutional channels under their control.

(4) Instrumentalities. The last category of people is those who, in fulfilling their ordinary (lawful) duties, unwittingly form some significant link in the crime's chain of causality. These people are used as instruments by the perpetrators of the crime. A simple example of an instrumentality would be a military truck driver who in the course of making routine deliveries delivers ammunition and weapons that have been designated for use in a campaign of ethnic cleansing. As long as the truck driver has no knowledge about how the weapons and ammunition are to be used and delivers such in the ordinary course of his or her daily work the driver is not a perpetrator but is an 'instrument' being used by the perpetrators of the crime.

Investigating the direct perpetrators of crimes

Against this backdrop we can turn to the types of evidence that will be probative of the perpetrators in each of the categories discussed. There is considerable overlap and evidence will often be probative of more than one category of perpetrator.

International criminal investigations invariably begin with an investigation of the crime itself. One of the most important questions to be answered at this primary level is the identity of the direct perpetrators and what if any group they belong to. This is often a difficult question to answer because such perpetrators often hide their identity from victims. Victims of, and witnesses to, serious crimes may have been too frightened or preoccupied with escaping to remember details that can help identify the perpetrators and the organization they belong to. However, despite the trauma of having survived serious crimes, victims and witnesses often demonstrate a remarkable recollection about their attackers and are able to provide detailed information.[47]

Even if witnesses are unable to identify a perpetrator they may be able to provide information that can assist investigators. Careful analysis of statements made by the perpetrators can reveal, when considered in light of other information, important clues about the group a perpetrator belonged to. Similarly, careful descriptions of uniforms, even absent insignias, when considered along with other evidence can provide

[47] See, e.g., the testimony of Zehra Turjačanin, the sole survivor of a house fire in which approximately sixty people died. *ICTY Prosecutor* v. *Milan Lukić*, Judgment (20 July 2009) paras. 643 ff. (summarizing the evidence Turjačanin gave at transcript at 2310 ff).

information about the perpetrator's organization.[48] In the *Milošević* case several Bosnian witnesses recalled that the perpetrators spoke with an *Ekavian* dialect, a dialect common to a particular region in Serbia.[49]

If investigators are able to gain the cooperation of an insider, he or she may be able to help investigators understand earlier information provided by witnesses such as nick-names, and descriptions of the uniforms and vehicles used by the group. Evidence gathered early in the investigation may become significant with the assistance of an insider who can explain the inner workings of the group.[50]

Investigators gathering evidence at this primary level should, in addition to following standard protocols of investigation (for the specific crime such as murder, rape, etc.), find and collect evidence likely to disclose the participation of any upper-level perpetrators or groups that may have participated in crimes.

Examination of official documents that record the movements of different units and groups in the area where the crime occurred are equally significant. Such records may be found in logistics documents, or logs kept at border posts and checkpoints. Investigators should try to locate and review the daily reports generated by all units that might have been in the area.

During the course of the investigation into crimes committed in Zvornik in 1992 investigators obtained the records for the billeting of paramilitary troops. These records not only identified the paramilitary members by name but also contained the name and stamp of the local official who authorized the expenditure of funds to house and feed the paramilitaries.

[48] Jovan Dulović, a witness in the *Milošević* case provided a detailed description of a paramilitary unit that wore distinctive military garb during the siege of Vukovar. Men in these unique uniforms and black balaclavas would reappear in Bijeljina months later and would ultimately be identified as members of Arkan's Tigers. See, *ICTY Prosecutor* v. *Milošević*, transcript, at 11647 ff.

[49] See *ICTY Prosecutor* v. *Milošević*, Testimony of Safet Avdić (cross examination by Milošević) transcript, at 24122:

Q. But you're talking about citizens of Foca, and there were no JNA units in town, so surely they must be Territorial Defence.

A. There were some people I didn't know by their appearance but only on the basis of their speech. When I walked around Foca, I made the conclusion, in view of the fact that they spoke Ekavian, that they came from the territory of Serbia, whereas the people of Foca all use the Ikavian dialect.

[50] General Alexandar Vašiljević was a senior officer in the intelligence branch of the Yugoslav Army. He provided important and detailed evidence about a number of paramilitary groups including Arkan's Tigers. Intelligence officers under his command gathered a great deal of information about the inner workings of Arkan's Tigers and other groups. See, *ICTY Prosecutor v Milošević*, transcript, at 15759 ff.

Today mobile phones are ubiquitous. Antenna stations and network software collect detailed information about mobile phones even when no phone calls are made or received. If a crime occurs in an area with mobile phone coverage every effort should be made to secure these records.[51]

Some governments may be in possession of aerial imagery taken from satellites as well as manned and unmanned aerial surveillance vehicles. Countries surrounding the conflict have an interest in obtaining reliable information about the fighting to prepare for the possibility that it may impact them. Prosecutors should consider approaching these countries to determine if they possess relevant intelligence and whether they are willing to share it. Aerial imagery that shows large disturbances of earth in the Srebrenica area helped ICTY investigators locate and excavate these graves. Such imagery was an important part of the evidence in cases related to the Srebrenica massacres.[52]

If international observers are present in the conflict area they should be interviewed and their logs reviewed for evidence.[53] If local or international relief workers were present they should be interviewed regarding their observations.

Today, even in the most remote places video cameras are available and are used regularly to record events. Videos, once authenticated, provide some of the most reliable evidence regarding what happened at a particular time. It is becoming increasingly common for direct physical perpetrators of a crime to have recorded the crimes themselves as a trophy or souvenir or perhaps a way to ensure that all participants in the crime remain silent about their deed.[54] Given the high degree of

[51] In the first trial before the Special Tribunal for Lebanon the Prosecution will rely heavily on information about the location and use of mobile phones. Through factual investigations and analysis of telecommunications data the prosecution hopes to use the phenomenon of 'co-location' to establish the identity of the direct perpetrators of the Hariri bombing. See *STL Prosecutor* v. *Salim Jamil Ayyash, et al.*, Prosecution Opening Statement (16 January 2014) transcript, at 18.

[52] See, e.g., *ICTY Prosecutor* v. *Popović, et al.*, Exhibits: P1723 (aerial images of the Orahovac area); P1747 (aerial images of the Petkovci Dam area); and P1763 (aerial images of Kozluk area).

[53] General John Wilson, Chief of the UN military observers in Sarajevo until November 1992 personally observed indiscriminate shelling on a daily basis during June 1992. He was also able to provide evidence about reports he received from his subordinates stationed at observation posts around the city. See, *ICTY Prosecutor* v. *Perišić*, Judgment (6 September 2011) para. 323 (hereafter *Perišić* Judgment).

[54] In the context of the ICTY the most well-known example of this is the Scorpion Video, a video depicting the murder of six men and boys from Srebrenica. See *ICTY Prosecutor* v.

reliability associated with authenticated video-tapes it is important to consider and explore all investigative avenues which may yield the existence of such evidence. Investigators should query whether or not members of the group kept official or unofficial diaries of their activities or whether a video was made of some part of the operation or crime.[55]

If there is information that some of the perpetrators of the crime were injured or killed during operations investigators should consider checking hospital records or obituaries for indications of this. There is usually some public record of the death of police officers and soldiers, even if they were killed during a clandestine operation.[56]

Investigating the remote perpetrators of crimes

Once investigators have reliably identified the direct perpetrators of a crime they should begin to explore who had *de jure* and who had *de facto* control over them. The number and complexity of the mechanisms employed by senior officials to perpetrate crimes will vary greatly depending upon the institutions and the specific means employed. Once a direct perpetrator's organization has been identified the investigation must explore the particular structure of that organization. It is likely that in the course of investigating the crime itself there will be some indication of others who were involved but were not physically present.

On 26 June 1992 the entire Muslim population of Kozluk, a small rural village in eastern Bosnia, was deported en masse. There were over 1,800 men, women and children in the group. They were presented with a deportation order signed by a man with close ties to the Serbian State

Popović, et al., Judgment (10 June 2010) paras. 597–99 (hereafter *Popović* Judgment) (citing the video admitted as exhibit P3249).

55 General Ratko Mladić kept a detailed military diary of his activities including meetings he held with others. This diary has proved to be an important piece of evidence in at least one case. See *ICTY Prosecutor* v. *Tolimir*, Judgment (12 December 2012) paras. 1082, 1168 (hereafter *Tolimir* Judgment).

56 In the *Milošević* case, Dragan Vasiljković, aka Captain Dragan gave evidence about the Captain Dragan Fund, a fund established by him to provide for the families of killed and injured paramilitaries. He produced the files of this fund in court. These files indicated the identity of seriously injured and killed combatants as well as their affiliations with the Serbian Ministry of Interior and several paramilitary groups. See *ICTY Prosecutor* v. *Milošević*, Testimony of Dragan Vasiljković, transcript, at 16541–42 and exhibit P391 (eleven compact discs containing the records of the Captain Dragan Fund. Included in these files were death notices and medical records submitted in support of claims for financial assistance).

Security Service. They were given an hour to pack their belongings and then forced to sign over their property before being boarded on seventeen buses and two trucks with trailers, which took them across Bosnia's border with Serbia. Most of the villagers had never gone very far from their village, let alone outside of Bosnia. Very few had passports.

In Ruma, Serbia, they were transferred to the passenger and cargo cars of a train that had been especially arranged for their transport to the Hungarian border. When they arrived, those without passports were turned back by Hungarian authorities. Within a couple of days these people were issued Serbian passports and then escorted back over the Hungarian border. Removing these victims from their homes, transporting them across Serbia and expelling them into Hungary suggested the intervention of senior officials of Serbia. The two questions posed by the plight of these people were: (1) Who would have the authority to arrange the use of an entire train; and (2) who would have had to provide authorization for over a thousand Serbian passports to be issued to non-citizens on an urgent basis?

Over time these questions were thoroughly explored. This example illustrates how investigating the primary level of the crime revealed other investigative leads indicating the possible involvement of senior government officials in the crime.

Pursuing the investigative leads that arose during the Kozluk investigation required careful analysis of the laws of Serbia to determine who had the authority to facilitate the deportation. This analysis coupled with interviews of some of the people involved generated new investigative leads that were pursued. With each step a clearer picture emerged regarding the people who were involved.

In a case in which the perpetrators (direct and remote) belong to an institution investigators must develop a clear understanding of its organizational structure. Information about the organizational structures may come from several sources including laws and regulations; witnesses (both inside and outside the organization); and internal correspondence indicating the relationship between units within the organization. Figure 5.1 shows the key personnel in the Bosnian Serb Army as well as their operational relationships. This figure was created with the assistance of an insider witness.

Most organizations and institutions will have record keeping systems documenting their employees and activities. Such systems are necessary for the essential tasks of calculating the pay and benefits due to employees. Investigators should understand these systems and examine records likely to contain information about the activities of a suspect. All possibly relevant communications (phone, radio, computer, written

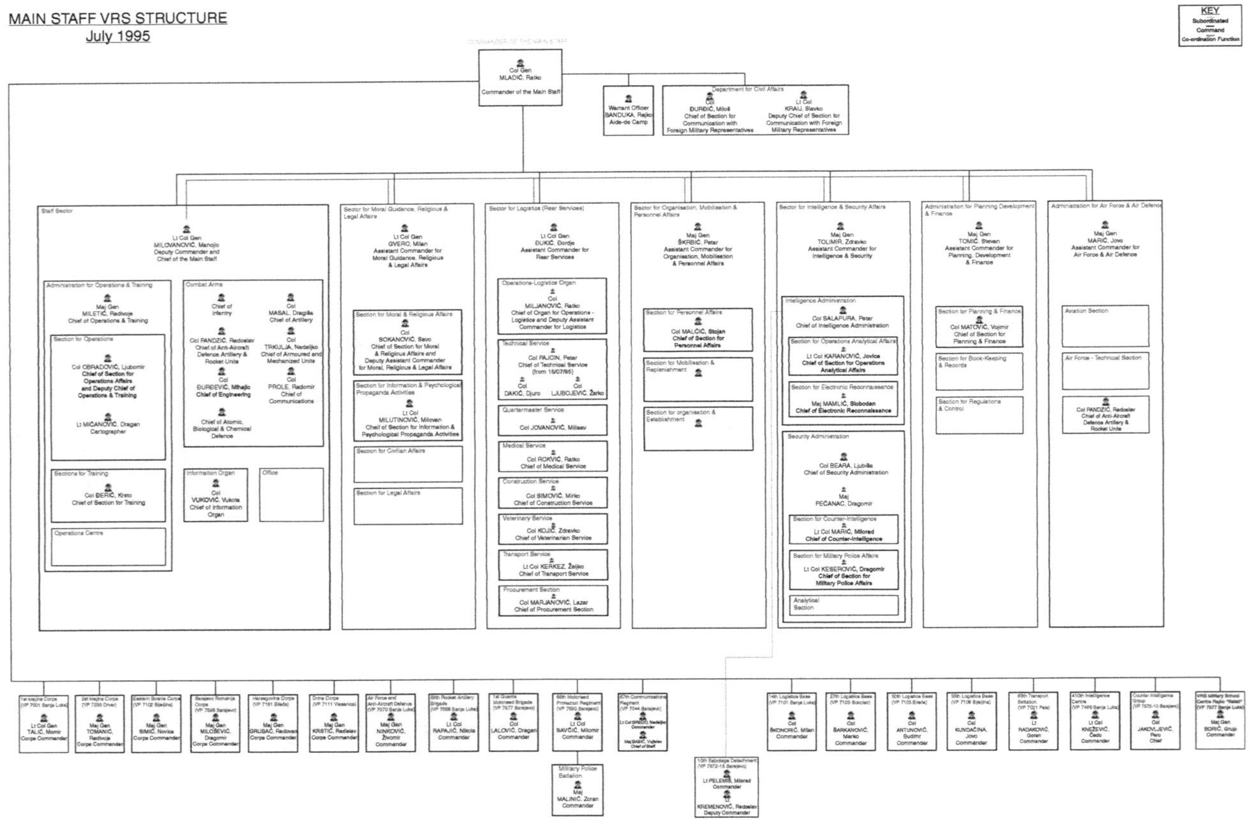

Figure 5.1: Main Staff Organogram drawn by Milovanovic for Tolimir

communications) should be considered and explored. In the *Perišić* case the prosecution tendered personnel documents establishing that officers in the Bosnian Serb Army were in fact being paid by Serbia.[57]

Investigators should consider examining an organization's records of citations and promotions. While it is unlikely that these documents will refer to criminal activity they may help establish a unit's presence in an area where crimes were committed. In the *Milošević* case, the prosecution obtained and tendered a video-tape of an awards ceremony of the State Security Service of Serbia for members of its elite Red Berets unit. During the ceremony awards were given to key members of the unit as well as those who supported its work, including Slobodan Milošević. Franko Simatović, a senior intelligence officer gave a speech in which he enumerated many of the places in the former Yugoslavia where the Red Berets operated.[58] While this speech did not contain explicit admissions of crimes it did contain detailed evidence about the activities of the unit.

Once an investigation has established the identity of the direct perpetrators of a crime and has established their legal and de facto relationship to military, police and political institutions the investigation must then consider which, if any, senior officials should be investigated to determine whether or not they bear responsibility for the crimes committed by the direct perpetrators.

The determination to investigate a particular senior official may be the result of careful legal analysis of a country's laws and regulations which make clear that the official had some authority over and responsibility for the direct perpetrators. In some cases, absent any legal relationship between the senior official and direct and intermediate perpetrators, evidence may establish that the senior official nonetheless may have contributed to the commission of the crime. The investigation must now consider the question of whether such participation constitutes a criminal act.

The investigation at this juncture must focus on three areas:

(1) What was the senior official's participation that furthered the crime?
(2) What did the senior official know about the crime and the impact of his or her participation in the crime?
(3) What authority did the senior official have with respect to the direct and intermediate perpetrators of the crime?

[57] See, e.g., *Perišić* Judgment, above note 53, para. 789 and fn 2190.
[58] See *ICTY Prosecutor* v. *Milošević*, exhibit P390.

At this highest level an investigator must have a clear understanding of the legal and de facto relationship the senior official being investigated had with the intermediary units and direct perpetrators. Once again, evidence of the legal relationship will be found in national laws and regulations. If de facto chains of authority that circumvented legal relationships exist then it will be necessary to identify insider witnesses who can credibly and reliably provide information about this.

Members of the international community who met with the officials under investigation can also provide important evidence in this regard. Their recollection, notes and memos to their government may provide valuable evidence regarding what the suspect knew and what if any authority he or she had over the direct perpetrators of the crime. In the *Milošević* case, Cyrus Vance negotiated a cease fire in Croatia in November 1991. During the negotiations between Tudjman, Milošević and several international interlocutors the topic of paramilitaries arose. At this time Arkan had become notorious for the serious crimes he was perpetrating. Milošević was asked whether he was able to stop the activities of paramilitaries to which he responded that he could. The agreement was signed and for several weeks afterward paramilitary crimes ceased. Unfortunately, the agreement was eventually breached by both sides and crimes by paramilitaries resumed.[59]

The investigation of senior governmental officials should identify and seek to interview international diplomats who had contact with these suspects. Countries that are concerned with reports of international crimes may send diplomats to convey those concerns. These officials can provide detailed information about what senior leaders knew about crimes. In the *Milošević* case Herbert Okun, a special representative of the UN Secretary General, had numerous meetings with Milošević, Radovan Karadžić and other significant actors in the Yugoslav crisis and provided detailed evidence about them.[60]

The investigation should systematically obtain and review all of the public statements by senior-level suspects that may be of relevance. These public statements, when analysed in the context of other evidence, may support inferences about what senior officials knew. Laura Silber, an author and documentary film maker conducted detailed interviews with many of the actors in the Yugoslav crisis for the book and film

[59] See *ICTY Prosecutor* v. *Milošević*, Testimony of Herbert Okun, transcript, at 16925–30, describing exhibit P6.

[60] See e.g., *ICTY Prosecutor* v. *Milošević*, Testimony of Herbert Okun, transcript, at 16880ff and exhibits P396–8.

The Death of Yugoslavia. People like Milošević and Vojislav Šešelj gave lengthy interviews while the war was still ongoing (and before the ICTY was established).

It is likely that senior government officials involved in the perpetration of crimes will have detailed discussions among themselves that are relevant to an investigation. High-level government meetings may have been recorded in some way. While it is unlikely that there will be clear expressions of criminal intent or activity contained in records of these meetings, they can provide reliable information about what officials knew at times relevant to the investigation. In the *Milošević* and *Perišić* cases the prosecution tendered minutes from the Supreme Defence Council of Yugoslavia, the highest governmental body overseeing the Yugoslav Army. These minutes included the verbatim discussions of Supreme Defence Council members, including both Milošević and Perišić.[61]

Investigating the instrumentalities

It is likely that somewhere along the complex causal chain of a crime there are people who were used as instrumentalities. Depending upon how significant a role a particular person played in the chain he or she may be an important and valuable witness. Consider a logistics officer who kept detailed records about the times he was ordered to provide military supplies to a particular unit that was later found to have engaged in criminal activity. This witness, as well as the detailed records he kept, may help establish a link between the person ordering the distribution of the materials and the unit engaged in criminal activity.

These people make attractive witnesses because they are not engaged in criminal conduct themselves and do not have 'blood on their hands' or personal culpability. They do not have the credibility problems that often accompany culpable, or possibly culpable, insiders.

Multi-disciplinary investigation

International criminal investigations regularly require expertise not ordinarily needed in domestic cases. The size, complexity and unique context of international criminal cases often require the assistance of people with specialized expertise.

[61] *Perišić* Judgment, above note 53, para. 765, citing exhibit P709 (stenographic transcript of the 14th Session of the SDC, 11 October 1993). See also *ICTY Prosecutor* v. *Milošević*, Testimony of Zoran Lilić, transcript, at 23935.

Historian

In many cases it is difficult to understand the evidence related to crimes absent some understanding of the broader historical context in which the crimes occurred. Historical evidence can serve to orient judges about the precursors to a conflict as well as long-standing animosities between groups. Knowing the historical context can assist judges in understanding the evidence they receive as well as help them assess whether witnesses may harbour a particular bias when giving their evidence.

In the first trial before the ICTY, the prosecution called Professor James Gow, of Kings College London, as its first witness to help the Trial Chamber understand the historical context of the break-up of Yugoslavia. Robert Donia, a historian from the University of Michigan, has testified as an expert before the ICTY in several cases. Donia has researched and written extensively about the Bosnian Serb Assembly. He was engaged by the OTP to conduct detailed case-specific analyses of the Assembly's minutes. Given the large volume of this material it would have been difficult for investigators and prosecutors to select the relevant passages without the assistance of an expert.

Using someone like Donia with extensive scholarly expertise related to these Assembly sessions to help identify the most relevant portions was an important contribution to the work of the OTP. In the *Milošević* case he examined the Assembly sessions for references to genocide. Perhaps the most well-known is General Ratko Mladić's admonition to the Assembly that the project of demographic redistribution (ethnic cleansing) would likely be considered a genocidal campaign by the international community.[62]

Cultural expert

Each conflict exacts a heavy toll on the cultural heritage and property of the people affected by it. These significant losses are often overshadowed by the magnitude of the loss of life and suffering but nonetheless should be an important consideration in any effort to hold those responsible accountable.

[62] See *ICTY Prosecutor* v. *Milošević*, Testimony of Robert Donia, transcript, at 26516–17. Donia reported that at the 16th Assembly Session Mladić stated: 'People and peoples are not pawns nor are they keys in one's pocket that can be shifted from here to there. . . . We cannot cleanse nor can we have a sieve to sift so that only Serbs would stay, or that Serbs would fall through and the rest leave.. . . I do not know how Mr. Krajišnik and Mr. Karadžić would explain this to the world. People this would be genocide.'

The destruction of cultural and religious property is not only a consequence of conflict but may also be an objective of it in a persecutory or genocidal campaign. Perpetrators may believe that the ethnic group they seek to purge is less likely to return if its religious buildings and cultural property have been destroyed. Investigating and documenting the loss of cultural property is an important aspect of any international criminal investigation.

During the investigation of Milošević for the crimes committed in Bosnia, Andras Riedlmayer, a research librarian from Harvard University with expertise in Islamic cultural property, was asked to undertake a comprehensive survey of the damage to religious and cultural property in Bosnia. He conducted careful research to identify and obtain pre-war photographs of such property and then spent several weeks travelling through the region documenting the damage to that property. He recorded his findings in a comprehensive report which was admitted in the case.[63]

In addition to establishing this injury with evidence, his report made another important contribution to the case. One of the challenges of an international criminal prosecution is the difficulty of accurately reflecting the magnitude and gravity of events in a trial of reasonable length. In the *Milošević* case the prosecution team focused on a few representative municipalities and used evidence of cultural destruction and significant demographic shifts to help demonstrate the overall criminal campaign. Riedlmayer's evidence helped the Chamber to understand the overall nature of the ethnic cleansing campaign without receiving evidence of crimes committed in every municipality in Bosnia. For a more general overview of anthropological research and methodologies relevant to the study of international crimes the reader should consult Chapter 9 of this book.

Demographic expert

If large demographic shifts have occurred as a result of international crimes it is important that judges receive evidence of this. Demographers, using various sources of data, can apply sophisticated statistical analysis to demonstrate demographic shifts and their relationship to other events.

Demographic expert Patrick Ball, executive director of the Human Rights Data Analysis Group, conducts quantitative analysis on issues

[63] See *ICTY Prosecutor* v. *Milošević*, Report of Andras Riedlmayer, P488.

related to international crimes and international human rights violations. He was called as a witness in the *Milošević* case to provide evidence about the significant movements of Kosovar Albanians during a persecutory campaign there in the first half of 1999. During the trial Milošević asserted that significant movements of Kosovar Albanians were not the result of crimes committed by forces under his control but a consequence of the NATO bombardment of Serbia. He mapped killings attributed to Milošević's forces as well as significant population movements. Using statistical analysis he was able to demonstrate a strong correlation between these movements and the crimes of murder. There was no similar correlation between these population shifts and the bombs dropped by NATO aircraft.[64]

The ICTY OTP recognized the importance of this type of evidence and created a demographic unit staffed by full-time personnel. The team's primary responsibility was to assist investigation and trial teams in understanding and using data sources relating to large populations. Analysis of different data sources (e.g., voting, census and death records) yielded important evidence regarding the movement of populations during the war. This analysis also helped establish the death of murder victims in cases where bodies have not been recovered. The head of the demographic unit, Ewa Tabeau, has testified in numerous trials about her work and the conclusions she drew from her study of demographic data. Several Chambers have relied on Ms Tabeau's findings in entering convictions for the crimes of deportation and forcible transfers.[65]

Genocide studies

The *Milošević* prosecution also engaged Ton Zwaan, a professor at the University of Amsterdam, to write an expert report on the aetiology of genocide and other mass crimes. The prosecution considered that the

[64] See *ICTY Prosecutor* v. *Milošević*, P67 ('Ball Report') and P67.1 (corrigendum to Ball Report); Patrick Ball, Wendy Betts, Fritz Scheuren, Jana Dudukovich, and Jana Asher, 'Killings and Refugee Flow in Kosovo March – June 1999' and Testimony of Patrick Ball, transcript, at 19941–78.

[65] *ICTY Prosecutor* v. *Vasiljević*, Judgment (29 November 2002) para. 53 ff.; *ICTY Prosecutor* v. *Stakić*, Judgment (31 July 2003) para. 553 ff.; *ICTY Prosecutor* v. *Simić*, Judgment (17 October 2003) para. 30 ff; *ICTY Prosecutor* v. *Galić*, Judgment (5 December 2003) para. 578 ff; *ICTY Prosecutor* v. *Milošević*, Judgment (12 December 2007) para. 154 ff; *Popović* Judgment, above note 54, para. 625 ff; *Perišić* Judgment, above note 53, paras. 354 and 546 ff; *Tolimir* Judgment, above note 55, para. 50 ff; *ICTY Prosecutor* v. *Stanišić & Župljanin*, Judgment (27 March 2013) Vol. I, para. 19 and Vol. III, para. 57 ff.

Milošević Chamber would be assisted in understanding the prosecution's evidence and its case regarding genocide if it had the benefit of what social scientists considered the aetiology of the crime. As the first paragraph of the report states:

> The primary purpose of this report is to provide tools of analysis by reference to which the reader may understand how genocides and other mass crimes targeting specific groups can occur in human societies. It sets out from a historical and sociological perspective some of the main processes and causative mechanisms which have, in the past, led to the commission of such crimes. The report has been written at the request of the Office of the Prosecutor (OTP) of the International Criminal Tribunal for the former Yugoslavia. It does, however, not deal with the question whether genocide and other mass crimes targeting specific groups took place in the former Yugoslavia.[66]

As the introduction states, Zwaan's expert report was not meant to suggest any particular outcome in the *Milošević* case but to provide the Chamber with the benefit of a sociological perspective of the prerequisites of earlier genocides so that the Chamber could better assess the prosecution's evidence and case.

Social worker/medical worker – impact on victims

One important aspect of international crimes is the significant and often permanent injury suffered by victims. Many victims sustain permanent physical and psychological injuries either as a result of a crime committed against them or by the traumatic loss of a loved one. This issue is further explored in depth in Chapter 12 of this book. Given that only relatively few witnesses will appear in court and testify about such injuries prosecutors have had to look at other ways of establishing the gravity of the collective injury. In some cases this has been done by leading evidence from health professionals who have worked with victims.

In conflicts there tend to be focal points where the injured may go to seek help; very often this is a refugee camp. It is likely that the medical staff and social workers at these camps treat hundreds of victims and are able to make observations about the types of injuries they encounter. Such witnesses are able to provide important information about the impact on victims in a way that does not violate the privacy of

[66] T. Zwaan, *On the Aetiology and Genesis of Genocides and other Mass Crimes Targeting Specific Groups* (November 2003) at 3, available at www.srebrenica-mappinggenocide.com.

individuals, yet helps a court understand the gravity of the injuries sustained by victims.

The *Popović* Chamber, in assessing what sentence was appropriate for several army officers found guilty of committing crimes in Srebrenica, looked to the evidence of a medical professional who had worked with a large number of Srebrenica survivors. The Chamber found that '[t]he sheer scale and cruelty of these crimes and the continuing impact they have had and still have on so many victims and their relatives is overwhelming'.[67]

International criminal investigation – how long should it take?

International criminal investigations are complex and time consuming. It is not always possible to complete an investigation before an accused is brought into custody. The timing and length of investigations is something that has come under increasing scrutiny by judges in the ICC. Judges have been concerned with the continuation of investigations long after the commencement of proceedings. Some defence teams have accused the prosecution of changing their case theory in response to newly acquired witnesses and evidence as the investigation continues.[68] While the Prosecutor must always seek the most reliable evidence and should not close down evidentiary leads once a case proceeds to adjudication, this goal must not undermine the right of the accused to know the charges against him or her and to prepare a defence.

The practice of the ICC OTP to date has demonstrated that it is not uncommon for there to be a relatively short interval of time between the commencement of an investigation and request for an arrest warrant. The OTP's practice of initiating criminal proceedings prior to completing its investigation has resulted in substantial investigations continuing after an arrest warrant was requested and in some cases after the confirmation of the charges. In *Mbarushimana*, the Chamber criticized the prosecution's broad language in the Document Containing the Charges (DCC), which, when specifying the location of crimes used the language 'include

[67] *Popović* Judgment, above note 54, para. 2152 (citing the evidence of Teufika Ibrahimefendić).

[68] See, e.g., *ICC Prosecutor* v. *Francis Muthaura and Uhuru Kenyatta*, Corrigendum to Observations on the Conduct, Extent and Impact of the Prosecution's Investigation and Disclosure on the Defence's Ability to Prepare for Trial with Confidential Annex A, Public Annex B and Public Annex A1 (20 February 2013) (hereafter *Kenyatta* Corrigendum).

but are not limited to. . .'. The Chamber expressed its concern that this was an attempt by the prosecution to keep open the possibility of broadening the case should additional evidence become available later as a result of continued investigations. The Chamber assessed the phrase as meaningless and focused on only those locations specifically set out in the DCC.[69]

The defence in *Kenyatta* recently took issue with the large number of new witnesses that were identified by the prosecution after the confirmation hearing, asserting that they resulted in 'radically altered' allegations.[70] The Chamber in large part rejected this assertion and reaffirmed that the prosecution was not required to rely on the same evidence at trial that it had adduced during the confirmation process. Nevertheless, the Chamber expressed its concern regarding the 'substantial volume of new evidence that was gathered by the Prosecution [after confirmation]'.[71] The Chamber, citing the *Mbarushimana* Appeal Decision, reminded the prosecution that the investigation should be largely completed by the time of the confirmation hearing.[72] The *Kenyatta* Chamber introduced the legal requirement that all investigations that could have reasonably been completed before confirmation must be. The Chamber went further stating that the defence will have remedies available with respect to failures to do this.[73]

ICTY judges have developed criteria to help strike the appropriate balance between newly acquired evidence and the rights of an accused. Whenever the Prosecutor seeks to add evidence after it has filed its

[69] *Mbarushimana* Confirmation Decision, above note 11, paras. 79–83.

[70] *Kenyatta* Corrigendum, above note 68, para. 11 ('The nature of the Prosecution's ongoing and protracted investigation and the manner in which the Prosecution has sought to disclose its evidence have required the Defence to expend considerable investigative resources in order to attempt to deal with an ever-shifting case . . .').

[71] *Kenyatta* Article 64 Decision, above note 26, at para. 112.

[72] Ibid., para. 119 ('The Prosecution should not seek to have the charges against a suspect confirmed before having conducted a full and thorough investigation in order to have a sufficient overview of the evidence available and the theory of the case').

[73] See *Kenyatta* Article 64 Decision, above note 26, para. 121: 'However, the Majority is of the view that the Prosecution should not continue investigating post-confirmation for the purpose of collecting evidence which it could reasonably have been expected to have collected prior to confirmation. If a Trial Chamber finds that this has occurred, it would need to determine the appropriate remedy based on the circumstances of the case.' Although the Chamber does not limit the application of this principle to inculpatory evidence, that is likely what it intended. It would be inconsistent with general principles of justice and fairness for the prosecution's obligations under Article 54 to cease upon the confirmation of charges.

witness and exhibit lists the following criteria will determine their admissibility:

- the relevance and importance of the new evidence;
- whether there is good cause for the late addition of the evidence;
- whether the Prosecutor exercised due diligence in identifying the new evidence; and
- whether allowing the use of the new evidence will result in prejudice to the accused.

Trial Chambers consider and balance these factors to determine whether the interests of justice are best served by either allowing or disallowing the new evidence.[74]

While the concerns addressed by the *Kenyatta* Chamber focused on the procedural unfairness caused by an investigation that continues after confirmation, a failure to investigate a case adequately before commencing a criminal process risks a flawed case that may ultimately have to be withdrawn because of a lack of evidence that is sufficient to meet the prosecution's burden of proof at trial.

This precise situation arose for Kenyatta's co-defendant, Francis Muthaura, for whom charges were also confirmed in January 2012. On 11 March 2013, the OTP filed a notice withdrawing all charges against Muthaura.[75] In the filing the OTP informed the Chamber that having considered all the available evidence 'there is no reasonable prospect of conviction in the case'.[76] When explaining the underlying reasons for the withdrawal, the prosecution pointed to the fact that several witnesses had died, were killed or had become uncooperative. It informed the Chamber that one witness recanted his testimony after receiving bribes from representatives of the accused.

It is difficult to assess the extent to which these problems were foreseeable and could have been overcome by identifying additional witnesses and evidence during the investigation. One clearly troubling aspect of the

[74] See *ICTY Prosecutor* v. *Jovica Stanišić and Franko Simatović*, Decision on Eleventh, Twelfth and Thirteenth Prosecution Motions for Leave to Amend its Rule 65*ter* Exhibit List (10 February 2010); *ICTY Prosecutor* v. *Mićo Stanišić and Stojan Župljanin*, Decision Granting in Part Mićo Stanišić's Motion for Leave to Amend his Rule 65*ter* Exhibit List (19 July 2011); *ICTY Prosecutor* v. *Momčilo Perišić*, Decision on Defence Motion to Amend 65*ter* List and Second Bar Table (1 December 2010).

[75] *ICC Prosecutor* v. *Muthaura*, Prosecution Notification of Withdrawal of the Charges against Francis Kirimi Muthaura (11 March 2013) (hereafter *Muthaura* Notice).

[76] Ibid., at para. 9.

prosecution's submission is that it explains that one of the contributing causes of the collapse of the *Muthaura* case was that the Kenyan government 'failed to assist it in uncovering evidence that would have been crucial'. This suggests that the prosecution may have known at the time of confirmation that it had insufficient evidence for conviction, but proceeded in the hope that such evidence would come into its possession before the start of trial.[77]

More recently, the Prosecutor notified the *Kenyatta* Chamber that it was removing a key witness from its case after learning he had fabricated his evidence. It also asked for a delay in the start of the trial to consider whether it could sustain its burden at trial.[78]

The ICC OTP requested arrest warrants in the Côte d'Ivoire situation only twenty-two days after commencing the investigation.[79] The infirmities of this apparently hurried investigation were the subject of scrutiny by the Pre-trial Chamber considering whether to confirm the charges. After a considerable delay caused in part by a defence application asserting that Mr Gbagbo was unfit to stand trial, confirmation hearings were held in February 2013. The legal standard for confirming charges

[77] *Muthaura* Notice, above note 75, para. 11. The prosecution had acknowledged in a public statement that there were ongoing efforts to undermine its work in Kenya. See Statement by the ICC Prosecutor: ICC Witnesses Undergo Rigorous Tests (17 November 2010). In a related case, Judge Hans-Peter Kaul pointed out the significant risks that are occasioned by such an incremental investigation: '[S]uch an approach, as tempting as it might be for the Prosecutor, would be risky, if not irresponsible: if after the confirmation of the charges it turns out as impossible to gather further evidence to attain the decisive threshold of "beyond reasonable doubt," the case in question may become very difficult or may eventually collapse at trial, and then with many serious consequences, including for the entire Court and the victims who have placed great hopes in this institution.' *ICC Prosecutor* v. *William Samoei Ruto et al.*, Decision on Confirmation of Charges Pursuant to Art. 67(7)(a) and (b) of the Rome Statute (23 January 2012) para. 47 (Kaul, J, dissenting).

[78] See *ICC Prosecutor* v. *Uhuru Muigai Kenyatta*, Notification of the Removal of a Witness from the Prosecution's Witness List and Application for an Adjournment of the Provisional Trial Date (19 December 2013).

[79] In the Côte d'Ivoire situation, the OTP opened its investigation on 3 October 2011 and requested an arrest warrant on 25 October 2011. See *ICC Prosecutor* v. *Laurent Gbagbo*, Warrant of Arrest for Laurent Koudou Gbagbo (23 November 2011) paras. 2, 3. In fairness to the Prosecution there are indications that it was receiving information and conducting preliminary inquiries in the Côte d'Ivoire situation as early as April 2009. See Statement of the Deputy Prosecutor of the International Criminal Court on an Overview of Situations and Cases Before the ICC, 14 April 2009. See also Luis Moreno-Ocampo, ICC Prosecutor's Speech to the Eighth Session of the Assembly of States Parties, 18 November 2009.

against an accused is somewhat elevated from the 'reasonable grounds' standard for an arrest warrant, but still well below the standard of 'proof beyond reasonable doubt' at trial. Article 61(7) of the Rome Statute requires the Pre-trial Chamber to determine 'whether there is sufficient evidence to establish substantial grounds to believe that the person committed each of the crimes charged'.[80] Article 61(7) gives a Pre-trial Chamber three options: (1) to confirm the charges; (2) to decline to confirm the charges; or (3) to adjourn the hearing and request the Prosecutor to provide additional evidence or amend the charges.

The Chamber, having assessed the evidence, came to the view that the prosecution's case was insufficient to meet the 'substantial grounds' test. It reasoned that although the evidence was insufficient it did not 'appear to be so lacking in relevance and probative value that it leaves the Chamber with no choice but to decline to confirm the charges under Article 67(7)(b)'. The Chamber decided that the proper course of action was to adjourn the case and request that the prosecution conduct more detailed investigations.[81] The Chamber could 'not exclude that the Prosecutor might be able to present or collect further evidence and is therefore, out of fairness, prepared to give her a limited amount of additional time to do so'.[82] The Chamber enumerated the evidential avenues the prosecution should investigate further. The Chamber gave the prosecution five months to continue its investigation and present a new DCC.[83]

[80] *Gbagbo* Adjournment Decision, above note 9. The Appeals Chamber has stated that in the application of this standard a 'Pre-Trial Chamber may evaluate ambiguities, inconsistencies and contradictions in the evidence or doubts as to the credibility of witnesses'. *ICC Prosecutor* v. *Callixte Mbarushimana*, Judgment on the Appeal of the Prosecutor Against the Decision of Pre-Trial Chamber I of 16 December 2011 entitled 'Decision on the Confirmation of Charges' (30 May 2012).

[81] The Chamber in applying the gate-keeping threshold of Article 61(7) considered that the Prosecution must have presented its strongest case resulting from a largely completed investigation. Thus, the appropriate course of action was to adjourn the case for additional investigations. *Gbagbo* Adjournment Decision, above note 9, para. 25.

[82] Ibid., para. 37. The Chamber went on to find that giving the Prosecutor this opportunity did not unduly infringe on Gbagbo's right to be tried without due delay.

[83] *Gbagbo* Adjournment Decision, above note 9, para. 23. It is important to note that one member of the Pre-trial Chamber I wrote an articulate and persuasive dissent from the majority's decision. Judge Silvia Fernández de Gurmendi took the view that the majority's decision was based on an erroneous understanding of the applicable evidentiary standard for the confirmation of charges. She went further to take issue with the Chamber's application of the evidentiary standard to the contextual elements of crimes against humanity. Finally, Judge Gurmendi found that the majority's request to the prosecution to deal with specific 'questions' and 'issues' was both irrelevant and inappropriate.

In the Côte d'Ivoire situation there was a legitimate international interest in conducting expedient investigations and securing the arrest of someone believed to be still perpetrating crimes. Using the ICC as a means of interrupting ongoing crimes brings with it the risk that hastily investigated cases will ultimately fail.

Managing the evidence from an investigation

As a final note, the size and complexity of international criminal investigations present significant challenges in managing the evidence that is gathered. In addition to organizing the information in a way that is usable by the prosecution team, the material must be organized in a way that allows the prosecution to discharge its disclosure obligations with respect to this material fully. Given that evidence is being collected before any decision to charge a particular individual has been made it must be organized in a way that allows it to be electronically searched at a later date for potentially exculpatory material should someone eventually be charged. Relevant shortcomings have been an issue in many international trials at every international court.[84]

In the *Kenyatta* case, there was evidence to suggest that, at least in one instance, the prosecution was unaware of all of the evidence generated during the investigation, including clearly exculpatory material. In that case, the credibility of Witness 4, a witness originally deemed of great significance, was undermined when the prosecution disclosed an affidavit containing a contradictory account of his evidence. Due to an oversight, the affidavit, collected during the course of the investigation was not disclosed prior to the confirmation hearing. The defence alleged that the prosecution acted in bad faith and characterized the disclosure breach as a 'clear and systematic failure involving senior Prosecution lawyers with respect to the procedures applied during its investigations'.[85] While the Chamber rejected the defence assertion of bad faith it did express its

[84] See, e.g., *ICTY Prosecutor* v. *Karadžić*, Decision on Accused's Eighty Fifth Disclosure Violation Motion (21 January 2014).

[85] *ICC Prosecutor* v. *Uhuru Muigai Kenyatta*, Public Redacted Version of the Defence Reply to the 'Confidential Redacted Version of the 25 February 2013 Consolidated Prosecution Response to the Defence applications under Article 64 of the Statute to Refer the Confirmation Decision back to the Pre-Trial Chamber' (8 March 2013) para. 29. The Defence asserts that good investigative practice would have required that the statement in question be reviewed: (1) upon receipt; (2) prior to the re-interview; (3) prior to making oral submissions at the confirmation hearing.

'serious concern' with respect to the failure to disclose the affidavit and the 'deficiencies in the Prosecution's internal structure'.[86]

International criminal investigations often involve many investigators and analysts working on different aspects of the investigation. Systems must be put in place to ensure that the evidence gathered is organized and referenced in a way that allows the investigative team to access all relevant information related to individual witnesses and individual accused easily.

[86] *Kenyatta* Article 64 Decision, above note 26, paras. 94–5.

6

Eyewitness psychology in the context of international criminal law

ANDREW SMITH, RODERICK LINDSAY AND BRIAN CUTLER

The accounts of eyewitnesses have proven integral in some international criminal proceedings (e.g., *Prosecutor* v. *Kayishema and Ruzindana*).[1] Even in war crimes, crimes against humanity and genocide, the identity of perpetrators may be in question. Granted the individuals who carry out these massacres are often those in power and thus known by many in the communities in which they reside; however, mistaken identifications may still occur and establishing who participated in a specific act may prove difficult. Given that the accused persons are generally known to international criminal tribunals the role of the eyewitness differs from that of domestic cases. In domestic cases law enforcement personnel will present the suspect – or a photograph of the suspect – to the eyewitness in an identification procedure (i.e., a lineup or a showup) to see if the eyewitness recognizes the suspect. Due to the fact that eyewitnesses often know the alleged perpetrators in international criminal tribunals, such tests of recognition memory would prove unnecessary.[2] Indeed, when an eyewitness knows the perpetrator, an identification by the eyewitness would not be informative. Rather, when the alleged perpetrator is known, evaluating the veridicality of eyewitnesses is based on considering witnessing conditions, post-event information and any other variables that may have influenced the eyewitness's memory of the alleged perpetrator.

This chapter was supported by a doctoral fellowship awarded to Andrew M. Smith from the Social Science and Humanities Research Council of Canada.

1 *ICTR Prosecutor* v. *Kayishema and Ruzindana* Trial judgment (May 21, 1999).

2 They may prove useful to the extent that they provide confirmatory evidence that law enforcement personnel have the person the eyewitness was referring to, but such identification procedures are not tests of recognition memory. See our discussion on the utility of in-court identification procedures.

To illustrate the importance of eyewitness memory in some international criminal tribunals, we begin this chapter with a review of the case against Clément Kayishema and Obed Ruzindana before the International Criminal Tribunal for Rwanda (ICTR).[3] We use evidence from this case throughout the chapter to highlight factors that ought to be considered when eyewitnesses implicate individuals known to them. Following our review of the case against Kayishema and Ruzindana we review eyewitness psychology and its cognitive and social psychological foundations. Next, we provide a brief history of eyewitness psychology and its methodology. We then review how witnessing conditions impact the likely accuracy of eyewitnesses. Afterwards, we consider how post-event information might influence the memories of eyewitnesses. Finally, we conclude our chapter with a review of the best practices for interviewing eyewitnesses.

The facts in *Prosecutor* v. *Kayishema and Ruzindana*[4]

On April 6, 1994 an airplane carrying Rwandan president Juvenal Habyarimana crashed while approaching Kigali airport in Rwanda.[5] Immediately after the death of Habyarimana, Hutu extremists began executing a genocide operation against the minority Tutsi population of Rwanda.[6] As of 1994 the Tutsi population made up approximately 15 percent of the 7.2 million people living in Rwanda.[7] Between April 6, 1994 and mid-July 1994 more than 500,000 Rwandan persons were killed.[8] Individuals seeking Tutsis were able to concentrate their efforts on specific locations, because Tutsis seeking refuge returned to perceived safe places where they had been safe during past attacks.[9] To make

3 *ICTR Prosecutor* v. *Kayishema and Ruzindana*, above note 1.

4 By no means do we intend to suggest that Kayishema and Ruzindana are innocent of the crimes for which they were convicted. Rather, we highlight this case because it includes several identifications and thus many opportunities to discuss factors that affect the reliability of eyewitnesses. Our decision to use this case was based on the second author's (R.C.L. Lindsay's) familiarity with the case as he assisted the prosecution with understanding the eyewitness evidence, thus highlighting a role that eyewitness experts may play in international criminal tribunals.

5 *ICTR Prosecutor* v. *Kayishema and Ruzindana*, above note 1, at para. 13.

6 Report by Human Rights Watch (1995), available at www.hrw.org/reports/1995/WR95/AFRICA-08.htm#P397_139563.

7 Ibid. 8 Ibid.

9 *ICTR Prosecutor* v. *Kayishema and Ruzindana*, above note 1.

matters worse, policy that required all citizens to carry identity cards designating their statuses as Hutu, Tutsi, Twa, or "naturalized" made it easy for those seeking Tutsis to identify their targets.[10] In recognition of the violations of humanitarian law committed in Rwanda the United Nations Security Council created the ICTR.[11] In total, seventy-five cases were tried in the ICTR.[12]

The Republic of Rwanda is divided into eleven prefectures, which are further divided into communes.[13] Kayishema and Ruzindana were found guilty of genocide for their parts in the massacres that took place in the prefecture of Kibuye in the communes of Gitesi, Gishyita and Gisovu.[14] Clément Kayishema was appointed to the position of Prefect of Kibuye on July 3, 1992.[15] The Prefect is the highest local representative of government and has control over government agencies within the respective prefecture.[16] As Prefect, Kayishema was accountable for the maintenance of peace, public order and security of persons and goods within the Kibuye prefecture.[17] In fulfilling his duties as Prefect, Kayishema had control over armed forces (e.g., *Gendarmerie Nationale*).[18] In 1994, Obed Ruzindana was a trader in Kigali.[19]

Clément Kayishema was charged for his participation in four massacres in the prefecture of Kibuye, while Obed Ruzindana was charged for his participation in one of the massacres in which he acted in concert with Kayishema.[20] By April 17, 1994 thousands of people had sought refuge at the Catholic Church and Home St Jean Complex in Kibuye town, Gitesi commune.[21] Many of those who sought refuge at "the Complex" did so under the instruction of Kayishema.[22] After people gathered at the Complex, persons under Kayishema's control surrounded and attacked the Complex.[23] Thousands were killed and many were injured in this attack.[24]

The second massacre for which Kayishema was charged was at the stadium in Kibuye town, Gitesi commune.[25] By April 18, 1994 thousands of persons had sought refuge at the stadium.[26] Many of those who sought refuge at the stadium did so under the direction of Kayishema.[27]

10 Ibid., at para. 14.
11 Report by the United Nations International Criminal Tribunal for Rwanda, available at www.unictr.org/AboutICTR/GeneralInformation/tabid/101/Default.aspx.
12 Report by the ICTR, available at www.unictr.org/Cases/tabid/204/Default.aspx.
13 *ICTR Prosecutor* v. *Kayishema and Ruzindana*, above note 1, at para. 2.
14 Ibid. 15 Ibid., at para. 23. 16 Ibid., at para. 7. 17 Ibid., at para. 9. 18 Ibid.
19 Ibid., at para. 24. 20 Ibid. 21 Ibid., at para. 25. 22 Ibid., at para. 26.
23 Ibid. 24 Ibid., at para. 29. 25 Ibid. 26 Ibid. 27 Ibid.

After people gathered at the stadium, persons under Kayishema's control surrounded and attacked the stadium for two days.[28] Thousands were killed and numerous people were injured during the attacks.[29]

The third massacre for which Kayishema was charged was at the church in Mubuga, Gishyita commune.[30] After persons began seeking refuge at the church, Kayishema visited it on many occasions and on April 10 brought gendarmes under his control to keep the persons inside from leaving.[31] Beginning on April 14, 1994, those under Kayishema's control began attacking those inside the church – the attacks continued for several days.[32] The attacks resulted in thousands of injuries and casualties.[33]

Finally, the fourth massacre for which Kayishema was charged, and the only massacre for which Ruzindana was charged, took place in Bisesero area, which spans the communes of Gishyita and Gisovu.[34] Thousands of Tutsis sought refuge in the area of Bisesero between the dates of April 9, 1994 and June 30, 1994.[35] Throughout this time period Kayishema and Ruzindana brought members of the *Gendarmerie Nationale* and others to the Bisesero region to attack the individuals seeking refuge there.[36] Thousands were killed during these attacks.[37]

In addition to bringing individuals to these massacre sites to attack Tutsis, both Kayishema and Ruzindana personally attacked Tutsis on numerous occasions.[38] Kayishema was found guilty of four counts of genocide and Ruzindana was found guilty of one count of genocide.[39] Several eyewitnesses proffered testimony implicating Kayishema and Ruzindana in the massacres described above.[40] The Court concluded that twelve eyewitnesses reliably identified Kayishema as having participated in one or more of the massacres and that fourteen eyewitnesses reliably identified Ruzindana.[41] Throughout the remainder of this chapter we discuss the relevant identification evidence. Before proceeding to discuss the eyewitness evidence, however, we briefly review eyewitness psychology, its foundations in cognitive and social psychology and its most common research methods.

[28] Ibid. [29] Ibid. [30] Ibid., at para. 39. [31] Ibid., at para. 40.
[32] Ibid., at para. 41. [33] Ibid., at para. 42. [34] Ibid. [35] Ibid., at para. 46.
[36] Ibid., at para. 47. [37] Ibid., at para. 48. [38] Ibid. [39] Ibid. [40] Ibid.
[41] Ibid., at para. 461.

Eyewitness psychology

Eyewitness psychology is the study of factors that influence eyewitness memory and decision-making for persons and events. Eyewitness psychology is an applied science in which scientists conduct research (often experiments) with an end goal of informing the legal system of how some given factor increases or decreases the reliability of eyewitness identification or recall. Eyewitness psychologists are generally interested in factors affecting the recognition and recall abilities of eyewitnesses and variables that can postdict the accuracy of eyewitnesses (e.g., confidence, response latency). To test recognition memory for persons, eyewitness psychologists and law enforcement personnel often use lineups. In a lineup the eyewitness is presented with the suspect embedded amongst fillers (i.e., known innocents) and is asked if the perpetrator is present. If the perpetrator is present the correct response is to identify the perpetrator. The eyewitness can err by identifying a filler or by rejecting the lineup. If the perpetrator is absent the correct response is to reject the lineup. The eyewitness can err by identifying a filler or the innocent suspect.

Tasks of recall require individuals to describe some previously seen person or event. Psychologists and law enforcement personnel test recall memory whenever they ask eyewitnesses for descriptions of perpetrators and events. The eyewitness's goal in description tasks is to describe the perpetrator and event as accurately and completely as possible. Eyewitnesses may err by describing false details (i.e., errors of commission) or by omitting true details.

Cognitive and social psychological underpinnings

Memory can be described as having four stages – perception, encoding, storage and retrieval. In order to encode to-be-remembered information accurately, one must perceive and attend to that information in the first place. Perception is largely an automatic process by which one acknowledges and interprets sensory information in the environment. Encoding refers to the process by which an individual inputs to-be-remembered information into memory. During storage, individuals store memory information for later use. During the retrieval stage of memory an individual retrieves information from his or her memory store through tasks of recognition or recall.

Sensory information is not perceived in an unmediated and objective fashion. The initial perception of information is a constructive process;

one's experiences, current goals, plans and motivations all shape what information is perceived and how that information is perceived.[42] Errors in perception may result from failure to attend to critical information or from misconstructions of reality. Other stages of memory are also susceptible to error. Individuals may fail to transfer information from short-term to long-term information (analogous to forgetting someone's name a minute after she introduced herself to you). Memories in storage may degrade with the passage of time. Moreover, information available at retrieval or even the act of retrieval itself can change one's memory trace or lead to forgetting.[43] Memory is not like a DVD that one can playback over and over again without change;[44] where perception is a constructive process, remembering is a reconstructive process.[45] That is, each time one retrieves a memory, that memory is shaped by the experiences and information one has obtained since the memory was stored as well as by the retrieval context.

In criminal trials securing a conviction often relies on the discovery and analysis of physical trace evidence such as fingerprints, footprints, or blood splatters. Yet, trace evidence is often imperfect and its ability to assist law enforcement personnel is limited. Psychologists often refer to the memory for an event or object as a memory trace. These traces are also physical in the sense that some neurological evidence for a remembered event or object exists in the brain; however, investigators cannot directly observe them.[46] Like physical trace evidence, memory traces are also imperfect. Memory traces are strong and accurate to the extent that eyewitnesses consciously perceive those stimuli of interest, accurately encode them, transfer the information from short-term to long-term

[42] For a review, see Z. Kunda, *Social Cognition: Making Sense of People* (Cambridge, MA: MIT Press, 1999).

[43] K. Nader, "Memory Traces Unbound", (2003) 26 *Trends in Neuroscience* 65.

[44] E. F. Loftus and G. R. Loftus, "On the Performance of Stored Information in the Human Brain", (1980) 35 *American Psychologist* 409.

[45] F. C. Bartlett *Remembering: A Study in Experimental Psychology* (Cambridge University Press, 1932).

[46] G. L. Wells, "Scientific Study of Witness Memory: Implications for Public and Legal Policy", (1995) 1 *Psychology, Public Policy and Law* 726, at 726 ("Past events tend to leave traces, and the process of reconstructing events from the past is aided by various types of *trace* evidence. These traces can be physical, such as a footprint, a blood stain, or a fingerprint. An event can also leave traces of a somewhat different variety, namely memory traces. Although these traces can also be said to have a physical property, in the sense that there exists a biological residue for the event somewhere in the brain, they cannot be observed directly by crime investigators or triers of fact." [emphasis added])

memory, and rehearse the information during storage. Moreover, the ability to access a memory trace for a specific event is also dependent on the strength of the retrieval cues.

According to the encoding specificity principle, remembering is a product of the interaction between encoding and retrieval conditions.[47] The effectiveness of a cue at retrieval is determined by how that cue was encoded. To the extent that the retrieval cue is specific to the encoding conditions, retrieval will be strong (i.e., one will be able to access the memory trace). Thus, one can generally expect individuals to perform better in recognition than recall tasks because the presentation of the target is a powerful retrieval cue specific to the encoding conditions. In tasks of recall, contextual cues may aid retrieval, but such cues generally will not be as powerful as the cues conveyed by the target itself.[48]

Eyewitness memory is a form of episodic memory. Episodic memory is one of two forms of declarative memory, the other being semantic. Where semantic memory is the store necessary for the use of language, episodic memory is the store for separate episodes and events and the temporal relations among them.[49] When one perceives an event, that event may be encoded into the episodic store and the event is always stored along with memories of events already existing in the episodic store.[50] Indeed, episodes are not stored in isolation, similar episodes are stored together and when a sufficient number of episodes exist a schema is formed. Schemas are abstract knowledge structures that assist individuals in making sense of information. As new information is perceived and attended to, that incoming information is interpreted in the context of stored knowledge. When information is incomplete or ambiguous, information stored in schemas allows one to fill in gaps. The development of schemas results in a poor memory for the details of a specific episode, yet it is this organization of episodes that makes long-term memory possible at all.[51] Organizing past episodes in this manner

[47] E. Tulving and D. M. Thomson, "Encoding Specificity and Retrieval Processes in Episodic Memory", (1973) 80 *Psychological Review* 352.

[48] S. M. Smith, "Environmental Context – Dependent Memory", in G. M. Davies and D. M. Thomson (eds.), *Memory in Context: Context in Memory* (Oxford: Wiley, 1988) at 231–44.

[49] E. Tulving, "Episodic and Semantic Memory", in E. Tulving and W. Donaldson (eds.), *Organization of Memory* (New York, NY: Academic Press, 1972) at 385–6.

[50] Ibid.

[51] R. C. Schank and R. P. Abelson, *Scripts, Plans, Goals, and Understanding: An Inquiry into Human Knowledge Structures* (Hillsdale, NJ: Lawrence Erlbaum Associates, 1977).

increases the efficiency of retrieval; without such "economization," memory may not be possible at all.[52]

Without the ability to schematically process incoming information, individuals would be overwhelmed by the vast amount of information they encounter on a daily basis. Incoming information may be processed in either a bottom-up or top-down manner.[53] Bottom-up processing is a relatively data-driven or objective interpretation of information – when one processes information in a bottom-up manner only the data itself influences processing. When one processes information in a top-down manner, one is influenced by the context, specific goals, motivations and desired outcomes – that is, the individual goes beyond the data itself. Bottom-up processing is a relatively objective process, while top-down processing is a relatively subjective process.[54] In practice, no process is completely bottom-up or top-down in nature; indeed, bottom-up and top-down processes comprise two extremes of a dual-process model. Implicit in dual-process models is acknowledgment that there are several degrees of processing that fall between the two endpoints, but solely referencing the end points provides pragmatic value.[55] Thus, when we refer to top-down or bottom-up processing we are speaking in a relative and not an absolute manner.

A concrete example will help us elucidate the difference between bottom-up and top-down processing. Dror, Péron, Hind and Charlton presented participants with several pairs of fingerprints and asked them to determine for each whether the fingerprints were a match or a non-match.[56] In 25 percent of trials fingerprints were an unambiguous match, in another 25 percent fingerprints were an unambiguous non-match, whereas in the remaining trials the pairs were ambiguous (i.e., it was impossible to determine if the fingerprints matched). Before each trial, participants either received no information, a low emotional background

[52] Ibid.

[53] See D. G. Bobrow and D. A. Norman, "Some Principles of Memory Schemata", in D. G. Bobrow and A. Collins (eds.), *Representation and Understanding: Studies in Cognitive Science* (New York, NY: Academic Press, 1975) at 131–49.

[54] R. E. Petty and D. T. Wegener, "The Elaboration Likelihood Model: Current Status and Controversies", in S. Chaiken and Y. Trope (eds.), *Dual-Process Theories in Social Psychology* (New York, NY: Guilford Press, 1999) at 41–72.

[55] See S. Chaiken and Y. Trope, *Dual-Process Theories in Social Psychology* (New York, NY: Guilford Press, 1999).

[56] I. E. Dror, A. E. Péron, S. Lynn Hind, and D. Charlton, "When Emotions get the Better of Us: The Effects of Contextual top-down Processing on Matching Fingerprints", (2005) 19 *Applied Cognitive Psychology* 799.

story and pictures, a high emotional background story and pictures, or a high emotional background story, pictures and subliminal messages.[57] When information was ambiguous, contextual information increased the likelihood that participants would say that a given pair of fingerprints matched; however, top-down information was not able to overcome the bottom-up information when pairs were unambiguous matches or non-matches.[58] Thus, contextual information biased the manner in which gaps in knowledge were filled but was not powerful enough to overcome clear bottom-up information.

In the Dror et al. study, participants were biased by contextual information provided by the experimenters when the stimuli were ambiguous. When participants have stored information in the form of schemas, these schemas may bias how they interpret incoming data. Data will tend to be interpreted in a manner consistent with existing schemas. Consider, for example, a script. A script is a schema formed for routine events. If we told you that an individual cried, how you interpreted this information would be influenced by the context of the tears. If you were told that the individual cried at a wedding, you might infer that the person displayed tears of joy; however, if we told you that the individual cried at a funeral, you would likely infer that the person displayed tears of sorrow.[59] Based on stored information from past episodes the context of the observed event influences how you process the information. Schematic processing is an important issue when considering why eyewitnesses make identifications – especially when conditions are less than optimal – and we discuss it in detail throughout this chapter. Before discussing the identifications of Kayishema and Ruzindana, we briefly review the research methods used by eyewitness psychologists so that readers can gain an understanding of how we know what we know.

Research methods

To investigate tasks of recognition or tasks of recall, eyewitness researchers rely primarily on the laboratory experiment. Experiments offer

[57] Dror et al. above note 56, at 803–4. (For subliminal messages, Dror et al. presented participants with "…'guilty' and 'same' messages … to try and induce them to find a match to convict the suspect." Subliminal messages are presented for such a short period of time [e.g., generally between 250 ms and 400 ms] that it is very unlikely that participants would be able to consciously perceive them.)

[58] Dror et al., above note 56.

[59] Kunda, above note 42.

unique advantages over other methods, including archival analyses or field studies. Unlike archival analyses or field studies, ground truth is known in laboratory experiments. In the laboratory, experimenters can manipulate the presence of the perpetrator at recognition in their experiments allowing them to examine how given procedures affect both perpetrator and innocent suspect identifications. It is important to examine not only the ability of persons to identify perpetrators, but the ability to reject innocent suspects so eyewitness psychologists will include both perpetrator present and absent conditions in their experiments. Equally, for tasks of recall, laboratory experiments allow researchers to compare different interviewing procedures to determine how each affects omission and commission errors. Moreover, laboratory experiments permit researchers to expose many participants to the same conditions, manipulating the variables of interest while holding all else constant. These properties of the laboratory experiment facilitate causal conclusions.

After a sufficient number of studies exist on some topic, researchers may meta-analyse the results. Meta-analysis is a statistical tool in which effect sizes from two or more studies are combined.[60] Individual studies on a given topic sometimes lead researchers to different conclusions due to differences in procedure, chance, or some other moderating factor. By statistically combining effect sizes from multiple studies, researchers can quell some of the equivocality that follows when studies on the same topic produce divergent results. Meta-analysis assists in the identification of moderator variables that might cause divergent findings. Moreover, because meta-analysis pools together effect sizes from single studies it is based on a larger sample size and thus offers a more powerful test of the hypothesis.

Applicability of eyewitness psychology to instances in which perpetrators are known

Over thirty-five years ago Gary Wells distinguished between two types of variables: system and estimator variables.[61] System variables are those variables that law enforcement personnel have control over. For example, law enforcement personnel have some control over the protocol used to interview an eyewitness. Estimator variables are those variables that law

[60] R. Rosenthal and M. R. DiMatteo, "Meta-Analysis: Recent Developments in Quantitative Methods for Literature Reviews", (2001) 52 *Annual Review of Psychology* 59.

[61] G. L. Wells, "Applied Eyewitness-Testimony Research: System Variables and Estimator Variables", (1978) 36 *Journal of Personality and Social Psychology* 1546.

enforcement personnel have no control over. For example, law enforcement personnel cannot control the viewing conditions at the time the eyewitness views the event and can only estimate later how these conditions may have affected the eyewitness's ability to encode information about the perpetrator and event. Wells reasoned that eyewitness psychologists could best assist the legal system by developing best-practice procedures for lineups (i.e., through researching system variables).[62] This reasoning was based on the realization that the legal system is concerned with performance of a *given* individual in a given situation, while psychological science provides information about the *average* individual in a given situation. Thus, by designing best-practice lineup procedures for law enforcement personnel, eyewitness psychologists could prevent mistaken eyewitness identifications as opposed to providing evidence of the likely accuracy of an eyewitness in court. This distinction has had considerable impact on the field of eyewitness psychology. Since its publication, identification procedures have been the primary focus of eyewitness psychologists.

As mentioned above, in crimes such as genocide eyewitnesses often know perpetrators. Accordingly, identification procedures do not test the eyewitness's memory for the perpetrator – they merely confirm that the individual in police custody is the person to whom the eyewitness referred when providing the police with a description of the perpetrator. If the eyewitness says person A committed crime X and person A is in a lineup, the eyewitness will identify person A because the eyewitness knows who person A is, not necessarily because person A was the individual the eyewitness saw committing crime X. This is very different from crimes in which the eyewitness does not know the perpetrator. When the eyewitness does not know the perpetrator and is presented with a lineup, the eyewitness must compare lineup members to his or her memory of the perpetrator at the scene of the crime. When the perpetrator is known to the eyewitness, however, there is no need to compare lineup members to the person from the scene of the crime. The eyewitness merely remembers who the known individual is that the eyewitness believes committed the crime and identifies that individual. All that needs to be remembered at the time of encoding is "Uncle Joe" committed the crime, which is a much simpler task than remembering what an unknown individual looked like. Errors in the identification of persons we know may still occur, but these are more likely to be errors at the

[62] Ibid.

perception stage (the witness thought he saw this person whom he knows but actually saw someone else) rather than errors brought about through retrieval methods such as suggestive lineups.

Two potential causes of such perceptual errors are source monitoring errors and change blindness. Source monitoring refers to the ability to determine where acquired information comes from (e.g., memories, knowledge, beliefs).[63] Unconscious transference is one example of a source monitoring error in the eyewitness context.[64] Unconscious transference refers to the mistaken identification of an innocent person who is familiar from a different context.[65] Unconscious transference results from the eyewitness's inability to correctly recall the source of his or her memory for the innocent suspect. In particular, research demonstrates that bystanders to crimes and innocent suspects seen in mugshots are prone to being identified as the perpetrator in later identification procedures.[66]

Change blindness refers to the tendency for changes to a scene to go unnoticed.[67] Although change blindness and source monitoring errors are distinct phenomena, source monitoring errors can occur as a result of change blindness.[68] Over a series of studies, Davis et al. showed participants vignettes of supermarket thefts.[69] Participants viewed an innocent person walking down the liquor aisle.[70] The innocent person walked behind a display and the perpetrator stepped out from behind the display – in a manner that would suggest continuity between the path of the innocent suspect and the perpetrator – before stealing a bottle of liquor.[71] Large proportions of participants failed to notice the change between the innocent participant and the perpetrator and large proportions of participants mistakenly identified the innocent person as the perpetrator.[72] Furthermore, those who failed to notice the change were more likely to mistakenly identify the innocent person than were those who noticed the change.[73] Distraction

[63] M. K. Johnson, S. Hashtroudi, and S. D. Lindsay, "Source Monitoring", (1993) 114 *Psychological Bulletin* 3, at 3 ("*Source monitoring* refers to the set of processes involved in making attributions about the origins of memories, knowledge, and beliefs.").

[64] D. Davis, E. F. Loftus, S. Vanous, and M. Cucciare, "Unconscious Transference can be an Instance of Change Blindness", (2008) 22 *Applied Cognitive Psychology* 605.

[65] Davis et al., above note 64, at 606.

[66] K. A. Deffenbacher, B. H. Bornstein, and S. D. Penrod, "Mugshot Exposure Effects: Retroactive Interference, Mugshot Commitment, Source Confusion, and Unconscious Transference", (2006) 30 *Law and Human Behavior* 287.

[67] See, for example, D. J. Simons and D. T. Levin, "Failure to Detect Changes to People during a Real-World Interaction", (1998) 5 *Psychological Bulletin and Review* 644.

[68] Davis et al,. above note 64. [69] Davis et al., above note 64.

[70] Ibid. [71] Ibid. [72] Ibid. [73] Ibid.

further decreased the likelihood that participants would notice the change,[74] presumably increasing the probability of later mistaken identification.

Though identification procedures are less useful in instances in which the eyewitness knows the perpetrator, there is still plenty of room for errors in identification. Accordingly, eyewitness psychology may prove valuable in educating the legal system of factors that may affect the accuracy of perception, encoding, storage and retrieval. In the remainder of this chapter we examine the identifications of Kayishema and Ruzindana and analyse the factors surrounding each.

In-court identifications

All prosecution survivor eyewitnesses identified Kayishema and Ruzindana in court.[75] The majority of these eyewitnesses knew Kayishema and Ruzindana prior to the attacks.[76] The court concluded that this prior familiarity with Kayishema and Ruzindana enhanced the reliability of the identifications. Indeed, knowing the accused prior to the attacks would help the eyewitnesses identify those individuals at the scene of the crime; however, as discussed above, identification procedures are not tests of recognition memory when perpetrators are known. If the eyewitness implicates someone by name and that suspect is presented to the eyewitness in an identification procedure, the eyewitness will obviously identify that individual. The identification procedure does not confirm that the person known by the witness was in fact the person at the scene of the crime. Errors at the perception stage could lead a witness to mistakenly conclude that the person observed is the person known.

When the eyewitness knows the alleged perpetrator the eyewitness will have multiple memories for the suspect and investigators cannot discern from which memory the eyewitness recognizes the suspect. Most likely, the eyewitness would not recognize a known individual from any one occasion, but would have a general memory for the alleged perpetrator – we might refer to this as a schema for that specific person. In our discussion of schematic processing we discussed how schemas form from the economizing of similar episodes. Recognition of known persons may result from a similar pattern. Once an individual has a sufficient number of encounters with a target individual, that person may form a general

[74] Ibid.
[75] *ICTR Prosecutor* v. *Kayishema and Ruzindana*, above note 1, at paras. 455–6.
[76] Ibid.

memory for the target. Like other schemata, such economization is likely to result in poor memory for the details of a given episode.

The use of in-court identification is subject to several limitations as a memory test for eyewitnesses who do not know the alleged perpetrator. The problem with in-court identification procedures is that they are inherently suggestive. By virtue of the fact that an individual is sitting in the defendant's box, even the dullest of eyewitnesses can infer that this individual is believed to have committed the crime for which they are in court. The absence of fillers in the in-court identification makes it difficult for a witness to demonstrate a memory error. Accordingly, the problem with in-court identifications is that they introduce confounding variables. That is, it is not readily discernible whether an identification of the defendant is due to the eyewitness's memory of the perpetrator or an inference made by the eyewitness. Although there is no research we are aware of regarding an examination of in-court identifications, we make some inferences from research examining showup procedures.

As in an in-court identification procedure, showups entail the presentation of a single person – the suspect – to the eyewitness. If the eyewitness recognizes the suspect as the perpetrator, the eyewitness should identify the person as such; otherwise, the eyewitness should reject the suspect. Moreover, like in-court identifications, showups are inherently suggestive. By virtue of the fact that only one individual is included in the identification procedure the eyewitness knows who law enforcement personnel suspect committed the crime. Thus, eyewitnesses with weak memories for the perpetrator may be tempted to guess or infer that the suspect is the perpetrator. One can expect this effect to be exacerbated in the context of in-court identifications. Showups generally occur in the field shortly after a crime has occurred.[77] Given this context, there is likely a fair amount of uncertainty surrounding the suspects' culpability. An in-field identification might be considered exploratory – law enforcement personnel conduct a showup because they locate an individual in proximity to the crime in both time and space. In-dock identification procedures are more confirmatory. The suspect has been charged and is on trial by this point and law enforcement personnel and the prosecution are likely confident that the accused is the culprit. The purpose of the in-dock identification is to provide confirmation to the judge or jury that the defendant is the perpetrator.

[77] B. W. Behrman and S. L. Davey, "Eyewitness Identifications in Actual Criminal Cases: An Archival Analysis", (2001) 25 *Law and Human Behavior* 475.

Logic aside, research comparing showups and lineups indicates that showups are equally likely to lead to target identification but put innocent suspects at greater risk of mistaken identification than lineups.[78] Although participants were more likely to choose from target-absent lineups than target-absent showups, showups lead to more innocent suspect identifications. Given that lineups include multiple individuals, whereas showups only include a single individual, incorrect identifications from lineups are dispersed over all members (suspect + fillers) whereas all showup choices are suspect choices. Furthermore, when an eyewitness identifies a suspect from a showup, judges and jurors are left with the impossible task of determining how much of the identification was attributable to the eyewitness's memory for the perpetrator and how much of the identification was attributable to guessing, deduction, or influence by the investigator, all of which are viable explanations for the identification. In-Court identification procedures present judges and jurors with this same problem. It is impossible for judges or jurors to determine how much of an in-court identification is attributable to the eyewitness's memory for the perpetrator or to guessing, deduction or influence.

Event characteristics

Several characteristics surrounding events can limit the abilities of eyewitnesses to accurately perceive and encode information about perpetrators and events. Environmental conditions such as distance and lighting that can prevent eyewitnesses from clearly viewing perpetrators can limit the abilities of eyewitnesses to accurately perceive and encode information about perpetrators. In addition to environmental factors, extreme stress may limit individuals from attending to, perceiving and encoding relevant information. In the remainder of this section we review the relevant research on each of these factors and examine how these factors may have impacted several of the identifications of Kayishema and Ruzindana.

Distance and lighting

Eyewitnesses who implicated Kayishema and Ruzindana claimed to have seen these men from various distances ranging from a few feet away to

[78] N. Steblay, J. Dysart, S. Fulero, and R. C. Lindsay, "Eyewitness Accuracy Rates in Police Showup and Lineup Presentations: A Meta-Analytic Comparison", (2003) 27 *Law and Human Behavior* 523.

over a kilometer away. For example, on one hand, Witness II claims to have witnessed the attackers arrive at Muyira Hill on May 14. Witness II was within a "stone's throw away" as they led the attackers and saw both Kayishema and Ruzindana shoot at the Tutsis.[79] On the other hand, Witness FF claimed to observe the events from an area that was later determined to be approximately 1.5 km away.[80] The remaining distances from which eyewitnesses observed Kayishema, Ruzindana, and the events that took place fell somewhere in between these two extremes. The attacks in the case took place during daytime hours and thus it was assumed that lighting conditions were relatively good.[81] Nevertheless, lighting conditions are not always optimal and the effects of lack of lighting are similar to those of increased distance and so we discuss distance and lighting simultaneously. Evaluating the reliability of the identifications of Kayishema and Ruzindana requires one to decide the maximum distance (or minimal lighting) from which one would consider an identification to be reliable.

It is common sense that it is more difficult to identify someone from further away than it is from up close. But, why is it the case that it is more difficult to identify individuals as the distance between the observer and the observed is increased? As a face is moved further away from the observer the image of the face becomes progressively coarser and features of that face are lost to the observer.[82] Loftus and Harley presented participants with photographs of celebrities – known individuals – and found that 75 percent of identifications made from distances no greater than 34 ft. (10 m) were correct compared to a 25 percent correct identification rate from distances of 77 ft. (24 m) or greater.[83]

De Jong, Wagenaar, Wolters, and Verstijnen examined how recognition accuracy varies with distance and illumination.[84] De Jong et al. used a large matrix by factorially combining seven different distances (10–131 ft. or 3–40 m) and nine different illumination levels (0.3–3000 lux; i.e., qualitatively: night with full moon to daylight clouded weather).[85] Only

[79] *ICTR Prosecutor* v. *Kayishema and Ruzindana*, above note 1, at para. 419.
[80] Ibid., at para. 426. [81] Ibid., at para. 458.
[82] G. R. Loftus and E. M. Harley, "Why is it Easier to Identify Someone Close than Far Away?", (2005) 12 *Psychonomic Bulletin & Review* 43.
[83] Ibid., at 63.
[84] M. De Jong, W. A. Wagenaar, G. Wolters, and I. M. Verstijnen, "Familiar Face Recognition as a Function of Distance and Illumination: A Practical Tool for Use in the Courtroom", (2005) 11 *Psychology, Crime and Law* 87.
[85] Ibid., at 93.

forty-eight of the sixty-three cells were examined because the remaining fifteen conditions – combinations of the least illuminated and furthest distances – were too difficult. Photographs of forty-eight celebrities were used and each was associated with a lookalike. The authors created two stimulus conditions whereby one half of the participants saw twenty-four celebrities and twenty-four lookalikes of the unseen celebrities and the remaining participants saw the remaining forty-eight photographs. Thus, the authors were able to examine both correct and incorrect recognitions. Each participant viewed one photograph in each of the forty-eight cells. At the presentation of each photograph, participants were asked if the person looked familiar and if so, who they thought it was.

In order to assess the reliability of identifications across forty-eight conditions, De Jong et al. calculated the diagnosticity for each cell. Diagnosticity is commonly used by eyewitness researchers and represents how many times more likely it is that an identified suspect is guilty than innocent.[86] Diagnosticity is a likelihood ratio and as such is computed by dividing the proportion of correct identifications by the proportion of incorrect identifications.[87] De Jong et al. reasoned that in order for an identification condition to be considered reliable, it should produce a diagnosticity value of at least fifteen.[88] Thus, the authors considered identification conditions to be reliable if they produced fifteen or more correct identifications for each incorrect identification.[89] Based on the authors' criteria for reliability they concluded that so long as lighting conditions were reasonable (i.e., 30 lux: qualitatively "a badly illuminated room") identifications were reliable for distances of up to 49 ft. (15 m). When lighting conditions were between 3 (i.e., "urban area with bad street lights") and 10 lux (i.e., "urban area with bright street lights") identifications were considered questionable up to 49 ft. (15 m). All other conditions – identifications in excess of 66 ft. (20 m) or lighting of 2 lux

[86] See G. L. Wells and R. C. Lindsay, "On Estimating the Diagnosticity of Eyewitness Nonidentifications", (1980) 88 *Psychological Bulletin* 776, at 779.

[87] Ibid. [88] De Jong et al., above note 84, at 95.

[89] De Jong et al.'s (2005) decision to consider only those conditions that produce diagnosticity values of fifteen or greater as reliable is, of course, based on subjective opinion. Determining the optimal ratio of correct identifications to incorrect identifications is a delicate problem. We do not propose to know this optimal ratio and nor do we advocate strictly adopting a ratio of 15:1. Many legal scholars have advocated that it is better for *x* number of men to go free than to convict a single innocent, but the thrust of such arguments, in our opinion, is to stress the importance of not convicting the innocent rather than to provide a precise ratio.

or less (i.e., "urban area with no street lights") – were considered unreliable. Based on these findings, De Jong et al. concluded that only identifications made from distances of 15 m (49 ft.) or less under lighting conditions of at least 15 lux should be considered reliable.[90]

De Jong et al. reached the conclusion that identifications should not be considered reliable if they are from distances greater than 49 ft. (15 m), finding that identification decisions were considerably more likely to be accurate when assessed from less than 39 ft. (12 m) as opposed to 66 ft. (20 m).[91] Others have failed to find a precise distance at which identifications are no longer reliable.[92] Lindsay et al. presented participants with unknown persons at distances between 13 ft. (4 m) and 164 ft. (50 m). In addition to examining identification accuracy, Lindsay et al. examined other important research questions, including distance estimation and description accuracy.[93] Participants were asked to answer questions about the target while facing the location in which the target had been standing (perceptual judgment condition), even if unable to see the location in which the target had been standing (immediate judgment condition), or through an email the experimenter sent one day later (delayed judgment condition). After answering a series of questions regarding the distance of the target and providing a description of the target, participants were presented with a six-person simultaneous lineup. Half of the lineups were target-present while the remaining were target-absent.[94]

The degree to which participants erred in predicting the distance of the target was greatest in the delayed judgment condition.[95] As distance increased, errors in distance perception tended to be underestimates and participants provided greater range estimates of perceived distances.[96] When the target was present, participants were more likely to respond "not sure" as distance increased; however, when the target was absent, participants' use of the "not sure" response did not vary as a

[90] De Jong et al., above note 84, at 95 ("a reliable diagnostic value of 15 is reached at distances of no more than 15 m (49 ft.), and illumination levels of at least 15 lux."). This recommendation echoes that made by W. A. Wagenaar and J. H. van der Schrier, "Face Recognition as a Function of Distance and Illumination: A Practical Tool for Use in the Courtroom", (1996) 2 *Psychology, Crime & Law* 321, who examined the effects of lighting and distance on recognition of unknown faces.

[91] De Jong et al., above note 84.

[92] R. C. Lindsay, C. Semmler, N. Weber, N. Brewer, and M. R. Lindsay, "How Variations in Distance Affect Eyewitness Reports and Identification Accuracy", (2008) 32 *Law and Human Behavior* 526.

[93] Ibid. [94] Lindsay et al., above note 92, at 528–9. [95] Ibid., at 529.

[96] Ibid.

function of distance.[97] Thus, instead of responding "not sure" more frequently as distances increased and became more difficult to encode features of the target, participants guessed, as reflected by a suspect-to-filler shift from short (< 15 m) to long (> 15 m) distances.[98] Accordingly, the likelihood that the suspect was guilty given identification decreased from 7.66 to 4.20.[99]

Finally, Lindsay et al. examined whether either perceived or actual distance was predictive of identification accuracy. Before controlling for actual distance, perceived distance predicted accuracy for choosers (i.e., those who made a positive identification); however, after controlling for actual distance, perceived distance no longer predicted accuracy (odds correct versus incorrect = 1:1), but actual distance was a significant predictor of accuracy.[100] Thus, perceived distance is predictive of accuracy to the extent that those who witness an event from shorter distances provide shorter point estimates of distance to the target and are more likely to make accurate identification decisions than witnesses who view the target from further distances. Estimates of distance may be useful to the courts to the extent that those viewing a crime from short distances are likely to be more accurate as opposed to those viewing a crime from long distances; however, the courts must exercise caution as errors in self-reported estimates of distance to the target were common, and at times, extreme. Furthermore, given that the actual distance is a better predictor of accuracy than is perceived distance, when possible, the courts should measure the actual distance and consider this when evaluating the probability of eyewitness accuracy.

Some of the eyewitnesses testified to have witnessed Kayishema, Ruzindana, or both participating in the massacres that took place in the Kibuye prefecture from distances from which it would not be possible to discern the identity of an individual. For example, Witness FF claimed to have observed the events at Muyira Hill from a distance that was later determined to be 1.5 km away.[101] Witness JJ testified to have witnessed Kayishema participate in the events at Muyira Hill on May 13 from 300 meters (984 ft.) away, but later claimed that he was 120 meters (394 ft.) away.[102]

[97] Ibid., at 531. [98] Ibid.
[99] Diagnosticity ratios are an unweighted average of the three perception conditions.
[100] Lindsay et al., above note 92, at 533.
[101] *ICTR Prosecutor* v. *Kayishema and Ruzindana*, above note 1, at para. 420.
[102] Ibid.

These eyewitnesses claimed to have witnessed Kayishema from distances beyond which it is possible to accurately encode the facial details necessary for recognition. So, if these eyewitnesses were beyond the distance from which they could recognize Kayishema, why then did they claim to have recognized him? We cannot pinpoint the precise reason why a given eyewitness made a given identification, but we can point out some potential explanations as to why these eyewitnesses may have identified Kayishema in circumstances in which it would not otherwise be possible.

The first potential explanation is that the eyewitnesses overestimated how far they were from Kayishema. It is unlikely, however, that these eyewitnesses would have overestimated the distance to the extent that they would have been able to accurately identify Kayishema from the distance they did observe him from. Loftus and Harley found that only 25 percent of identifications from beyond 77 ft. (24 m) were accurate[103] – even if Witness JJ had overestimated by nearly 600 ft. and was only 400 ft. away from the target, it would still be very unlikely that JJ could have accurately encoded the facial features necessary to recognize Kayishema. That is analogous to sitting directly behind the goal posts at one end of Old Trafford and recognizing someone sitting directly behind the goal posts at the other end.[104] Moreover, Wiest, and Bell found that in more than forty-five studies, on average, participants underestimated distance by 15 percent and that increased retention intervals further compromised the reliability of distance estimates.[105] Unfortunately, very large overestimates can occur. Lindsay et al. anecdotally reported a participant in their research who saw a target at 50 m (164 ft.) but estimated the distance as 800 m (2,625 ft.). Regardless, it seems very unlikely that the eyewitnesses did recognize Kayishema on these occasions but overestimated the distance from which they viewed him.

Another possible explanation is that Witnesses FF and JJ saw what they expected to see. Given that neither witness could possibly have recognized Kayishema from the distances they claimed to have seen him, top-down processing might explain why these two eyewitnesses reported seeing Kayishema. Consider the relevant context. The Tutsis were hiding out

[103] Loftus and Harley, above note 82, at 63.

[104] See Loftus and Harley, above note 82, at 44, for a similar analogy in reference to Yankee Stadium.

[105] W. M. Wiest and B. Bell, "Steven's Exponent for Psychophysical Scaling of Perceived, Remembered, and Inferred Distance", (1985) 3 *Psychological Bulletin* 457, at 460.

together as they sought refuge from their assailants. Many of these individuals had witnessed massacres at other locations and may well have seen Kayishema and Ruzindana at other massacre sites. Indeed, Witness FF testified that he had seen Kayishema, Ruzindana and other assailants participating in the massacre that took place at Bisesero Hill from a distance of 33 ft. (10 m) on May 11, two days prior to the events that took place at Muyira Hill.[106] Thus, at the time FF claimed to have viewed Kayishema participating in the massacre at Muyira Hill, he was aware that Kayishema was leading the massacres taking place in the Kibuye prefecture. To our knowledge, JJ had not seen Kayishema participating in the massacres until the attack at Muyira Hill on May 13; however, Tutsis sought refuge together and presumably they had conversations about the attacks and attackers. Thus, it is quite plausible that JJ had heard from other eyewitnesses that Kayishema was leading the attacks prior to the events that took place at Muyira Hill on May 13.

Based on the knowledge that Kayishema led the attacks at Bisesero Hill, Witnesses FF and JJ may have viewed the leader at Muyira Hill and "seen" Kayishema as a result of gap-filling. It may be the case that Kayishema was leading the attacks at Muyira Hill and indeed other evidence suggests that this was the case; however, it would not have been possible for FF or JJ to see Kayishema from their respective distances and thus, "recognition" may be attributable to top-down processing. Top-down processing may have allowed FF and JJ to accurately "see" Kayishema, or the leader of the attacks at Muyira Hill may have been someone else, but FF and JJ "saw" Kayishema, because that is who they expected to see fulfilling the role of leader in the attacks.

Indeed, Loftus and Harley demonstrated that priming can facilitate the recognition of known persons.[107] Loftus and Harley presented participants with photographs of celebrities that were degraded to the extent that they were unrecognizable – the photographs were made to appear as they would if an individual were 512 ft. (156 m) away. The photographs became progressively clearer until the celebrity portrayed in the photograph appeared as though he or she reached a distance of 16 ft. (5 m). Before the recognition task participants were given a list of the names of sixteen celebrities and were told that eight of these celebrities would appear in the recognition task.[108] Indeed, eight of the sixteen celebrities whom the participants saw in the

[106] *ICTR Prosecutor* v. *Kayishema and Ruzindana*, above note 1, at para. 414.
[107] Loftus and Harley, above note 82, Experiment 2.
[108] Loftus and Harley, above note 82, at 57.

recognition task were named on the list provided before the recognition and participants were able to recognize these primed celebrities (by naming them) at a rate of about 25 percent faster than unprimed celebrities.[109] Thus, in this experiment, top-down processing facilitated the recognition of celebrities, allowing them to be recognized from further distances than their unprimed counterparts. This reflects the constructive component of perception. Although Loftus and Harley did not examine incorrect recognition, it is reasonable to infer that, similar to the findings of Dror et al.,[110] priming would also increase the likelihood of mistaken identification.

There is at least one other potential explanation for why Witnesses FF and JJ identified Kayishema even though he was at a distance from which neither of the eyewitnesses could perceive him. It is possible that neither witness recognized Kayishema at the time of recognition but afterwards came to believe that the individual leading the attacks was Kayishema. Such a process may have occurred as a result of information acquired after the event, or the eyewitnesses may have supplanted information acquired before the event (e.g., knowledge that Kayishema was leading the attacks) into their memories of the event. We discuss research on post-event information below.

Emotions and stress

Perhaps no topic on eyewitness memory elicits more questions from members of the legal community as the way in which emotion or stress experienced by an eyewitness during a crime impacts on his or her memory of the event and the identity of the perpetrator. Common sense suggests that one could not possibly forget a traumatic event. Everyone has experienced emotional and stressful events in their lives and individuals often have vivid memories of such events; thus, the emotion and stress experienced by an eyewitness is often viewed as informative in court. Popular assumption seems to suggest that one should be less skeptical of eyewitnesses subjected to highly emotional and stressful events.

Research does suggest that emotional memories are more vivid than unemotional memories; however, the degree of vividness does not necessarily imply a higher degree of accuracy.[111] Consider research conducted by

[109] Ibid. [110] Dror et al., above note 56.

[111] D. Reisberg and F. Heuer, "The Influence of Emotion on Memory in Forensic Settings", in M. P. Toglia, J. D. Read, D. F. Ross, and R. C. Lindsay, (eds.), *The Handbook of Eyewitness Psychology*, (Hillsdale, NJ: Lawrence Erlbaum, 2007), Vol. I, at 81–110; see also R. Brown and J. Kulik, "Flashbulb Memories", (1977) 5 *Cognition* 73.

Crombag, Wagenaar, and Van Koppen, in which the authors questioned participants about an Israeli cargo plane that crashed in the suburbs of Amsterdam.[112] At 6:28 p.m. on October 4, 1992 a Boeing 747 from Israel crashed into an eleven-storey apartment building in Bijlmemeer, a southern suburb of Amsterdam. Part of the building collapsed and a fire broke out immediately. Four crew members and thirty-nine people in the building were killed in the accident. The accident received considerable media attention. There were very few witnesses to the crash and there was no TV footage; therefore, what individuals knew about the crash itself was based on hearsay or inference.[113]

In August of 1993, Crombag, Wagenaar, and Van Koppen questioned 193 people about the crash.[114] Participants were first provided with a reminder of the crash and subsequently told that the experimenters wanted to test memory in respect of the disaster. Participants were asked: "Did you see the televised footage depicting the moment the plane hit the apartment building?"[115] Thus, participants were provided with false information that video footage of the plane crash existed. Fifty-five percent ($n = 107$) of respondents confirmed that they had seen film of the plane crash.[116] In a second experiment, 66 percent of the participants claimed to have seen the film of the plane crash.[117] Moreover, the majority of the participants who reported seeing the crash also confabulated, indicating when the fire started and the angle of the plane when it hit the building.[118] This study provided strong support that participants can misremember the facts of highly emotional events for which their memories are likely to be vivid. Thus, no matter how vivid a memory, accuracy cannot be taken for granted.

Although vivid memories do not always translate into accurate memories, as events become more emotional memories become more vivid and research does suggest that the gist for highly emotional events is remembered more accurately as compared to emotionally neutral events.[119] Such findings are consistent with Easterbrook's hypothesis that as emotion increases one's field of attention narrows, resulting in a better memory in regard to central details in exchange for a worse memory for peripheral details.[120] One example of arousal narrowing attention in the

[112] H. F. Crombag, W. A. Wagenaar, and P. J. van Koppen, "Crashing Memories and the Problem of 'Source Monitoring'", (1996) 10 *Applied Cognitive Psychology* 95.
[113] Crombag, Wagenaar, and Van Koppen, above note 112, at 97–8.
[114] Ibid., at 98. [115] Ibid., at 99. [116] Ibid. [117] Ibid., at 101. [118] Ibid.
[119] Reisberg and Heuer, above note 111.
[120] J. A. Easterbrook, "The Effect of Emotion on Cue Utilization and the Organization of Behavior", (1959) 66 *Psychological Review* 183.

eyewitness literature is the weapon focus effect. The weapon focus effect refers to the phenomenon whereby in the presence of a weapon eyewitnesses to a crime will carefully attend to the weapon to the exclusion of other relevant cues (e.g., the perpetrator's face). In the absence of a weapon, eyewitnesses make more accurate lineup decisions and provide more accurate descriptions of perpetrators; furthermore, as arousal increases so does the magnitude of the weapon focus effect.[121] Thus, the weapon focus effect is but one example of increased arousal leading individuals to attend to some details (e.g., the weapon) more than others (e.g., the perpetrator's face). In other situations it is likely that the perpetrator's face may constitute a central detail and in such instances one would expect emotion to increase the accuracy of identification.

To this point, we have considered the effects of emotion without mention of how emotion interacts with stress. Both chronic and acute stress can have devastating effects on memory.[122] Deffenbacher et al. meta-analysed thirty-four studies examining the effects of high stress on eyewitness memory.[123] High stress was found to reduce the number of target identifications but had no effect on innocent suspect identifications.[124] Likewise, high stress reduced the proportion of details that were accurately recalled.[125] Consistent with the findings of Steblay,[126] studies using staged crimes produced larger effect sizes than those making use of less realistic stimuli.[127] Thus, the conditions that one would expect to evoke more stress in participants produced larger effect sizes.

Without doubt, those eyewitnesses who testified as to the roles played by Kayishema and Ruzindana were under a considerable degree of stress from April 1994 through July 1994. Not only were the eyewitnesses who testified against Kayishema and Ruzindana under chronic stress during that time period – in addition to a likely lack of food, water and other

[121] N. M. Steblay, "A Meta-Analytic Review of the Weapon Focus Effect", (1992) 16 *Law and Human Behavior* 413, at 419: "The increase in arousal was inferred from changes in the methods used to investigate the weapon focus effect. Low arousal studies included those in which a weapon was present, but no crime occurred, studies in which participants viewed a weapon and the occurrence of a crime on a video or series of slides were considered moderately arousing, and studies in which actors enacted a real life event were considered highly arousing."

[122] Reisberg and Heuer, above note 111.

[123] K. A. Deffenbacher, B. H. Bornstein, S. D. Penrod, and E. K. McGorty, "A Meta-Analytic Review of the Effects of High Stress on Eyewitness Memory", (2004) 28 *Law and Human Behavior* 687.

[124] Deffenbacher et al., above note 123, at 695. [125] Ibid., at 698.

[126] Steblay, above note 121. [127] Deffenbacher et al., above note 123, at 699.

necessities – but the eyewitnesses were also under acute stress during the attacks, when they would have had opportunities to observe the perpetrators. The research reviewed above suggests that the compounding of stress and emotion serves to decrease the reliability of identification. As a result, contrary to popular assumption one should be more sceptical of eyewitnesses that have experienced highly emotional and stressful events.

Post-event information

Memories are not video recordings of events that one can playback over and over again without change.[128] As time passes from the occurrence of an event, one's memory trace of that event will begin to decay and details may be lost. Likewise, when the initial witnessing conditions are less than optimal (e.g., large distances between eyewitness and target) the initial trace will be weaker or less complete than it might otherwise be. When the memory trace is weak, individuals are increasingly susceptible to post-event information. Information acquired post-event may be incorporated into memory in the service of gap-filling. In the 1970s Loftus and her colleagues demonstrated how subtle changes in language can influence memory of an event[129] and developed the misleading post-event information paradigm.[130] For example, the authors presented the participants with slides of car accidents.[131] After viewing the slides, participants were asked to indicate how fast the cars were travelling when they smashed, hit, collided, bumped, or contacted. Participants questioned with the verb "smashed" estimated that the vehicles were travelling faster as compared to questions including other verbs in place of "smashed."[132] These results support the notion that people consolidate information obtained through perception of the original event and information obtained after the event. Eyewitnesses attended to the language used to describe the crash after it occurred and used this information when estimating the speed at which the vehicles were travelling.

[128] Loftus and Loftus, above note 44.

[129] E. F. Loftus and J. C. Palmer, "Reconstruction of an Automobile Destruction: An Example of the Interaction between Language and Memory", (1974) 13 *Journal of Verbal Learning and Verbal Behavior* 585.

[130] E. F. Loftus and E. Greene, "Warning: Even Memory for Faces may be Contagious", (1980) 4 *Law and Human Behavior* 323; E. F. Loftus, D. G. Miller, and H. J. Burns, "Semantic Integration of Verbal Information into a Visual Memory", (1978) 4 *Journal of Experimental Psychology: Human Learning and Memory* 19.

[131] Loftus and Palmer, above note 129, Experiment 1.

[132] Ibid.

In the most basic form of the misleading post-event information paradigm, participants witness some event, are subsequently given a questionnaire about the event and are later presented with a final memory test.[133] Critically, for some participants the questionnaire provides only information consistent with the witnessed event, while for others the questionnaire introduces false information. For example, in one early study Loftus, Miller and Burns showed participants a series of slides in which a red car approached a stop sign before turning a corner and hitting a pedestrian.[134] Following the slides participants completed a questionnaire about the accident. The critical item on the questionnaire asked half the participants if another car passed the red car while at the "traffic" sign. For half of the participants the question said "stop sign" whereas for the remaining participants, the "stop sign" was replaced with a "yield sign". Participants were then presented with a forced-choice recognition test in which the slide they had seen (i.e., the red car approaching the stop sign) was paired with a slide in which the stop sign was replaced with a yield sign. Seventy-five percent of participants provided with consistent information correctly identified the slide with the stop sign, whereas only 41 percent of participants provided with misleading information correctly chose the slide with the stop sign.[135] This finding suggests that misleading post-event information affected the memory of eyewitnesses.

Since the original studies by Elizabeth Loftus and colleagues, a considerable amount of research has examined the effects of post-event information on memory. Researchers have established that sources of post-event information can be both internal and external.[136] Post-event information may arise internally through schematic processing or as a result of an inference-making process.[137] That is, after an event individuals may process information in a schematically or inferentially driven manner in order to fill gaps in memory. The conclusions reached by such inferences are a form of post-event information. For example, during our discussion of distance and lighting we mentioned that Witness FF might have

[133] J. S. Neuschatz, J. M. Lampinen, M. P. Toglia, D. G. Payne, and E. Preston Cisneros, "False Memory Research: History, Theory, and Applied Implications", in M. P. Toglia, J. D. Read, D. F. Ross, and R. C. Lindsay (eds.), *The Handbook of Eyewitness Psychology* (Hillsdale, NJ: Lawrence Erlbaum, 2007), Vol. I, at 233–54.

[134] Loftus, Miller, and Burns, above note 130, Experiment 1. [135] Ibid., at 131.

[136] D. Davis and F. Loftus, "Internal and External Sources of Misinformation in Adult Witness Memory", in M. P. Toglia, J. D. Read, D. F. Ross, and R. C. Lindsay (eds.), *The Handbook of Eyewitness Psychology* (Hillsdale, NJ: Lawrence Erlbaum, 2007), Vol. I, at 189–231.

[137] Ibid.

recognized Kayishema at Muyira Hill because he had seen Kayishema two days prior at Bisesero Hill from a distance of only 33 ft. (10 m).[138] If this occurred, we do not know whether FF would have initially perceived the leader of the attack at Muyira Hill to be Kayishema or whether he reached this conclusion sometime later. If he immediately perceived the leader to be Kayishema this would constitute an effect on perception and not a post-event information effect. If FF did not originally perceive the leader to be Kayishema but later thought of what he had seen two days prior and reasoned that the leader must have been Kayishema, this would be an example of an internal source of post-event information.

External sources of post-event information are many and varied. The news media, co-eyewitnesses and investigators are all potential sources of misinformation.[139] In our discussion of stress and emotion we reviewed a study by Crombag, Wagenaar, and Van Koppen in which, it will be recalled, participants were questioned about an Israeli cargo plane that crashed into an apartment building in a suburb of Amsterdam.[140] Recall that in Crombag, Wagenaar, and Van Koppen's two studies 55 and 66 percent of participants reported seeing a video of the crash, respectively, even though no such video ever existed.[141] Crombag, Wagenaar, and Van Koppen attributed these effects to eyewitnesses having imagined the crashes based on the vivid accounts provided by the media.[142] Having imagined the crash and heard vivid media accounts of the crash the experimenter's suggestion that a film existed elicited false memories from many participants. In this instance, participants were tasked with determining whether or not they had actually seen a video of the crash or had just imagined the crash. Those participants who falsely remembered viewing the film committed a source monitoring error, namely a failure in reality monitoring.

In a series of studies, Shaw, Garven, and Wood demonstrated that co-eyewitnesses could affect the reports of eyewitnesses, both directly and indirectly.[143] In their first of three experiments, Shaw, Garven and Wood had participants answer a series of questions about the O. J. Simpson

138 ICTR *Prosecutor* v. *Kayishema and Ruzindana*, above note 1.
139 Davis and Loftus, above note 136.
140 Crombag, Wagenaar, and Van Koppen, above note 112.
141 Crombag, Wagenaar, and Van Koppen, above note 112, at 101.
142 Crombag, Wagenaar, and Van Koppen, above note 112, at 102–3.
143 J. S. Shaw III, S. Garven, and J. M. Wood, "Co-Witness Information can have Immediate Effects on Eyewitness Memory Reports", (1997) 21 *Law and Human Behavior* 503; for a more recent demonstration of the co-eyewitness effect see F. Gabbert, A. Memon, and K.

trial.[144] Next to ten of the fifteen questions were the responses of previous "witnesses" – half of these responses were incorrect and the remaining were correct.[145] This manipulation was an operationalization of real world situations in which interviewers for law enforcement agencies may provide the responses of co-eyewitnesses to "assist" another eyewitness during an interview. Participants were less likely to respond correctly when they were provided with incorrect information (73 percent) than when they were provided with no information (82 percent), but were most likely to respond correctly when they were provided with correct information (88 percent).[146]

In their second and third experiments Shaw, Garven and Wood examined the direct effect of co-witnesses on eyewitness reports.[147] In each of these experiments participants watched a video of a simulated robbery in the presence of a confederate (i.e., an experimenter pretending to be another participant).[148] After the video, the experimenter asked the participant and confederate twelve questions – for half of the questions the participant responded first and for the remaining the confederate responded first – half of the confederate's responses were correct and half were incorrect.[149] Participants were less likely to respond correctly when the confederate answered incorrectly (35 percent) compared to when the participant answered first (58 percent) or when the confederate answered correctly (64 percent).[150] The third experiment replicated this pattern of results.[151] These results demonstrate how co-eyewitnesses can influence the responses of other eyewitnesses both directly, through face-to-face interactions and indirectly through responses conveyed to an interviewer.

The studies by Elizabeth Loftus and colleagues reviewed at the beginning of this section provide an excellent example of how investigators can influence eyewitnesses. Loftus and Palmer illustrate how subtle changes in language can influence the responses of eyewitnesses.[152] Use of the word "smash" in place of "hit" or other synonyms produced greater estimates of the speed travelled when the two automobiles crashed.

Allan, "Memory Conformity: Can Eyewitnesses Influence each Other's Memories for an Event?", (2003) 17 *Applied Cognitive Psychology* 533.

[144] Shaw et al., above note 143, at 507. [145] Ibid., at 508. [146] Ibid., at 509.

[147] Ibid. [148] Ibid. [149] Ibid.

[150] Ibid., at 513 (note that while in the predicted direction the difference between no information [i.e., participant responded first] and correct information did not reach conventional levels of statistical significance).

[151] Ibid., at 144. [152] Loftus and Palmer, above note 129.

Moreover, the Loftus, Miller, and Burns study reviewed above illustrates that providing participants with post-event information (i.e., yield sign versus stop sign) can have a dramatic effect on responses. When interviewing an eyewitness, an investigator may unintentionally convey information to the eyewitness that may or may not be consistent with the eyewitness's memory and may or may not be correct. Similarly, an investigator may ask the eyewitness close-ended questions (e.g., "Was the car red?") as opposed to open-ended questions (e.g., "What color was the car?"), which may produce similar effects (we review proper interviewing techniques in greater detail in the section to follow).

Theoretical debate exists about the mechanisms involved concerning the post-event impact of extraneous information (e.g., Is the original memory trace altered, is a new memory trace created, or does the phenomenon reflect demand characteristics?).[153] Though these different mechanisms are of theoretical import, the applied implications remain the same: accurate and inaccurate information from internal and external sources presented inadvertently or intentionally does influence the content and accuracy of eyewitness reports.

Although it is unlikely that the media influenced those eyewitnesses that testified against Kayishema and Ruzindana in the Rwanda trials, both co-eyewitnesses and investigators may have been sources of post-event information. As already discussed in our review of lighting and distance, Tutsis sought refuge together and likely discussed the events of the day and who was responsible for the attacks. Accordingly, there were likely ample opportunities for these eyewitnesses to receive information from each other or other eyewitnesses who did not testify in the case against Kayishema and Ruzindana. We do not have any information on how eyewitnesses were interviewed by investigators for the Rwanda trials; so, again, we can only discuss hypothetically how these individuals may have provided eyewitnesses with post-event information. Presumably, eyewitnesses were interviewed alone and were not directly exposed to the recollections of other eyewitnesses; however, co-eyewitnesses may have also been able to influence other eyewitnesses by affecting the information provided or questions asked by investigators in subsequent

[153] See D. A. Bekerian and J. M. Bowers, "Eyewitness Testimony: Were we Misled?", (1983) 9 *Journal of Experimental Psychology* 139; see also Loftus and Loftus, above note 44, and M. McCloskey and M. Zaragoza, "Misleading Post-event Information and Memory for Events: Arguments and Evidence against Memory impairment Hypothesis", (1985) 114 *Journal of Experimental Psychology: General* 1.

interviews. In the following section we make suggestions for those individuals interviewing eyewitnesses.

The cognitive interview

Throughout this chapter we have focused largely on factors that legal experts cannot control, such as the conditions when an eyewitness views a perpetrator. In the present section we review something legal experts do have control over – the techniques used to interview eyewitnesses. In doing so we recommend several practices that the empirical literature suggests will increase the reliability of the obtained evidence.

Fisher and Schreiber described the typical interviewing protocols for American and British police.[154] Police interviewers generally put minimal effort into establishing rapport, frequently interrupted eyewitnesses – opting to ask a series of close-ended questions – demonstrated a lack of flexibility, asked leading questions and did little to assist eyewitnesses when trying to recall information.[155] The cognitive interview was designed in an attempt to elicit more information from eyewitnesses (i.e., decrease omission errors) without increasing commission errors.[156] To this end, the cognitive interview seeks to enhance: (1) social dynamics; (2) communication between the interviewer and eyewitness; as well as (3) the memory of the eyewitness.[157] We briefly review each of these objectives.

Social dynamics

Eyewitnesses are often asked to recall emotional events to an interviewer with whom they have little rapport. Moreover, the interviewer is often of higher social status than is the eyewitness; yet, the eyewitness is the expert for the witnessed events.[158] Accordingly, it is essential that the

[154] R. P. Fisher and N. Schreiber, "Interview Protocols for Improving Eyewitness Memory", in M. P. Toglia, J. D. Read, D. F. Ross, and R. C. Lindsay (eds.), *The Handbook of Eyewitness Psychology* (Hillsdale, NJ: Lawrence Erlbaum, 2007), Vol. I, at 54–5.

[155] Ibid.

[156] G. L. Wells, R. S. Malpass, R. C. Lindsay, R. P. Fisher, J. W. Turtle, and S. M. Fulero, "From the Lab to the Police Station: A Successful Application of Eyewitness Research", (2000) 55 *American Psychologist* 581, at 583.

[157] Fisher and Schreiber, above note 154, and Wells et al., above note 156.

[158] Fisher and Schreiber, above note 154, at 54.

interviewer establishes rapport with the eyewitness and encourages active participation. In order to encourage the proper social dynamic and elicit more information from the eyewitness, interviewers should ask open-ended questions, encourage eyewitnesses to report everything they remember and avoid interrupting the eyewitness.[159]

Communication

In order for an eyewitness to provide the information needed by the interviewer – and in the correct grain of detail – the interviewer must communicate these needs to the eyewitness.[160] The interviewer should encourage the eyewitness to report everything he or she remembers even if it is out of chronological order or contradicts previous statements.[161] And, if a statement appears to contradict a previous statement, the interviewer should wait until the end of the interview to rectify the two contradictory statements.[162] Moreover, some information is reported more accurately through nonverbal means (e.g., through diagrams or drawings) – interviewers should be open to using alternatives to verbal communication when it may be helpful (e.g., when describing the spatial relationships among individuals during a crime).[163]

Memory of the eyewitness

Although interviewers cannot change the eyewitnessing conditions for a given eyewitness, they can create retrieval conditions that enhance retrieval. As mentioned, remembering is a result of the interaction between encoding and retrieval conditions – to the extent that overlap between encoding and retrieval conditions is high, retrieval will be strong.[164] Accordingly, interviewers would be wise to have eyewitnesses attempt to mentally reinstate how they felt at the time of the event and, where possible, bring the eyewitness to the scene of the event.[165] Given that individuals possess only limited cognitive resources, interviewers can help eyewitnesses remain focused by removing all distractions (e.g., turn off cell phones, avoid barraging eyewitnesses with questions).[166] Each eyewitness views the crime from a different angle and attends to

[159] Ibid., at 60–1. [160] Wells et al., above note 156, at 583–4.
[161] Fisher and Schreiber, above note 154, at 61. [162] Ibid. [163] Ibid., at 62.
[164] Tulving and Thomson, above note 47.
[165] Fisher and Schreiber, above note 154, at 59. [166] Ibid.

different features of the crime. Accordingly, interviewers should tailor their questions to the eyewitness as opposed to following a generalized checklist.[167] The interviewer may also ask the eyewitness to consider information from many different perspectives (e.g., reverse chronological order). Finally, when eyewitnesses do not know the answer to a question they are encouraged to indicate that they "don't know" as opposed to guessing.[168]

Across many studies the cognitive interview has elicited between 35 and 75 percent more information than typical police interviews without increasing the proportion of commission errors.[169] Moreover, although it cannot undo the effects of misleading post-event information, research suggests that the cognitive interview can better inoculate eyewitnesses against misleading post-event information acquired after the interview.[170] Accordingly, when interviewers use the cognitive interview they can be less concerned that media exposure or contact with other eyewitnesses after the interview will contaminate the memories of eyewitnesses.

We are unaware of the interview protocols used by legal experts in the case of Kayishema and Ruzindana; however, the benefits of adopting the cognitive interview are clear. The cognitive interviewer avoids leading, suggestive and close-ended questions more generally, limiting the likelihood of any influences upon the eyewitness. Contextual reinstatement, tailoring of questions to eyewitnesses as well as the open-ended and fluid nature of the cognitive interview all facilitate eliciting the maximum amount of information from the eyewitness. Furthermore, evidence suggests that the cognitive interview can inoculate eyewitnesses from being influenced by misleading information acquired after the interview. Finally, the cognitive interview does not increase commission errors relative to standard police interviewing protocols. All of these features make the cognitive interview the optimal interviewing technique whether the case is domestic or international and whether the perpetrator is known or not.

Conclusion

In the present chapter we used the identifications of Clément Kayishema and Obed Ruzindana to discuss eyewitness identification in the context

[167] Ibid. [168] Ibid., at 60. [169] Ibid. See also Wells et al., above note 156, at 584.
[170] Fisher and Schreiber, above note 154, at 69.

of international crimes in which eyewitnesses know perpetrators. Kayishema and Ruzindana were convicted for their roles in the genocide that took place in Rwanda during 1994. More than 500,000 Tutsis were killed in the Rwandan genocide. Eyewitness reliability was a central issue at trial, as the prosecution's case against Kayishema and Ruzindana relied, in part, on the testimonies of twenty-six eyewitnesses. Accordingly, this case included several issues legal experts (including judges, prosecutors, investigators and defence attorneys) ought to consider when evaluating the reliability of eyewitness evidence.

Although the majority of those who identified Kayishema and Ruzindana knew them, the potential for error in identification remains plentiful. As we discussed throughout this chapter, both degraded witnessing conditions (e.g., distance) and top-down processing can lead to false perceptions of a known person. Moreover, post-event information can produce false reconstructions of remembered events. Accordingly, information acquired after an event may lead to remembering persons that were not present at the original event. It behooves legal experts to consider each of these factors when evaluating the likely reliability of an eyewitness.

We concluded this chapter with a review of the cognitive interview. Although legal experts cannot control the conditions under which an event is witnessed, they can control retrieval conditions. The cognitive interview provides investigators with a series of techniques designed to increase the amount of information elicited from eyewitnesses without increasing commission errors.

In addition to reviewing many of the factors above in isolation we hope that the additive effects of these factors are also clear. Where more than one witnessing factor becomes less than optimal (e.g., lighting and distance), identifications become less reliable. Likewise, as eyewitness conditions become less optimal, memory traces become weaker or less complete and, in turn, eyewitnesses become more susceptible to schematic processing, post-event information and other processes that decrease the reliability of eyewitnesses. Indeed, when eyewitness conditions are less than optimal, these extra-memorial processes are more active in the service of gap-filling. Thus, while less than optimal viewing conditions decrease the likelihood that an identification is correct, they also increase eyewitness susceptibility to cognitive errors and external sources of influence, making identifications even less reliable.

7

The role of information systems in the prevention and detection of transnational and international crime

DIONYSIOS DEMETIS

Introduction

All around the world criminal activity remains at the forefront of governmental concerns, not only as a problem that distorts the very fabric of society within the confines of national jurisdictions, but also as a problem that cuts across national borders to exhibit a global dimension.[1] The international dimension of criminal activity remains critical and is generally characterized by a complexity that is unique and requires action on many different levels.[2] Criminals set out to mask their illegal activities and deliberately generate complexity as a means of concealment. In doing so, they exploit new developments in technology that assist them in achieving their ends. This criminality exhibits forms of innovation that stretch far beyond traditional criminal activity (e.g., drug and human trafficking) and manages to attach itself within the broader fabric of society by exploiting the very latest developments.[3] This evolution is necessary as criminals seek not only to escape arrest, prosecution and conviction, but also to enjoy the fruits of their criminality (mostly financial gains). Thus, they seek to develop ways of exploiting the various diffuse norms of social interaction (e.g., trust), financial modes of conduct (e.g., cash-based economies), technological and communication developments (e.g., Internet), and thereby minimize the possibility for detection. By limiting the resources that can be made available for prevention (or making them obsolete when

[1] J. Wolfensohn, 'Making the World a Better and Safer Place: The Time for Action Is Now', (2002) 22 *Politics* 118.

[2] S. Mohamed, 'Legal Instruments to Combat Money Laundering in the EU Financial Market', (2002) 6 *Journal of Money Laundering Control* 66.

[3] J Haines and P Johnstone, 'Global Cybercrime: New Toys for Money Launderers', (1998) 2 *Journal of Money Laundering Control* 317.

developing new criminal behaviour), they participate in this co-evolution actively; and this they achieve by generating complexity.

This dynamic is nothing really new, but the central role that technology has acquired in modern societies, particularly in the last decade, requires a more thorough look at how the spectrum of serious criminality changes in light of these developments. A more thorough investigation is also required in order to better understand how technology can be used to facilitate cooperation between different jurisdictions. Here, another important issue is raised: in the fight against serious international crime, such as terrorism, or cross-border tax evasion, nation states have launched a number of initiatives for which citizen data are being stored in a centralized manner; jeopardizing this data can produce tremendous consequences and create adverse conditions leading to yet more crime. For instance, in the UK, two DVDs that contained a full copy of HM Revenue and Customs (HMRC) entire data of child benefits were lost en route to the National Audit Office in an unrecorded and unregistered package. The lost data affected 25 million people in the UK and jeopardized names, addresses, dates of birth of children, along with National Insurance numbers and bank details of their parents. Ultimately, this has exposed an entire generation to identity fraud. Should we treat these failures as singularities or as systemic occurrences for any large-scale centralized data project? The latter possibility seems more plausible due to the complexity behind these projects.[4]

In India, a project is underway to collect biometric data for the entire population with the aim of thwarting tax avoidance and corruption and securing a single identification scheme for the population. The government promotes the project, not only as a means to tackle corruption and tax evasion, but also as a way to provide particular benefits to the population from government funds and also gain access to banking services. While this massive effort seems to display a near complete disregard for the security risks related to the storage of biometric data in centralized databases,[5] it does

[4] After much debate in the House of Commons and the House of Lords, the biometric-enabled identity card scheme for the UK was halted for both financial reasons as well as doubts about the security of the systems and their potential effect to curb criminal activity by getting a firm grip on individual identity. See LSE, 'The Identity Project', Department of Information Systems, London School of Economics, (2005), available at http://csrc.lse.ac.uk/IDcard/default.htm.

[5] A very useful report to look at comes from the Future of Identity in the Information Society (FIDIS), which has examined the relationship between the Public Key Infrastructure and Biometrics. More can be found in the report: M. Gasson, M. Meints and K. Warwick (eds.), 'D3.2: A Study on Pki and Biometrics', (FIDIS, 2005) at 1–138.

demonstrate that technology is at the top of government agendas in an effort to bridge control of identity with financial crime (as well as other transnational crimes). This irresistible fusion between technology and tackling criminality is very important. It is usually predicated upon the assumed thesis of benevolent effects of technological systems, without taking into account the side effects that are created by a new class of antitheses. In such circumstances, technological implementations create unintended uses, violations, misuses and unpredictable behaviour.[6]

Hence, the handling of information through technology-based systems gives rise to a domain that is becoming more and more central to the development of coordinated action in tackling criminal activity at both national and international levels: the domain of Information Systems (IS), in particular, the role they occupy across various subsystems that focus on tackling criminal behaviour.

IS are considered tools that can be harnessed for both preventing and detecting criminal activity; and, indeed, they have found a number of applications at national and international levels. IS are generally recognized as important catalysts for progress and transformation and there may be good reasons why IS are seen as critical in the fight against crime: they organize data in structured ways, while the character of automation embodied in these technologies is perceived as an enabler that allows for rapid data processing and swift communication between stakeholders. It is believed that this combination of automation/communication can prove critical in tackling criminal activity across national borders.

In addition to the communication possibilities opened up by modern technology, advances in data storage have led, and continue to lead, to long-term storage of large datasets.[7] This creates vastly different dynamics in the way data can be manipulated from small-scale technological installations as data sharing magnifies the phenomenon. The mass of data available can be used to infer characteristics for certain types of behavioural patterns, from which general profiles can be created that encapsulate an abstraction of criminal behaviour. By abstracting such behaviour and subsequently applying its characteristics to future data, one is – in theory – able to estimate the probability of an individual

[6] I. Angell, *The New Barbarian Manifesto: How to Survive the Information Age* (London: Kogan Page, 2000); I. Angell, 'As I See It: Enclosing Identity', (2008) 1 *Identity in the Information Society* 23.

[7] C. Apte, B. Liu, E. Pednault and P. Smyth, 'Business Applications of Data Mining', (2002) 45 *Communications of the ACM* 49.

committing a crime. It is worth pointing out that the digital traces of individuals unrelated to particular criminal activity are also parties to this process. Their contribution lies in simply providing more and more data that can be used to infer how 'normal behaviour' can be categorized and clustered according to different age groups and various other demographics. Against the backdrop of this supposed normality, suspicious behaviour can be flagged and then further analysed, as will subsequently be explored with the use of illustrations regarding money laundering. The effectiveness of this process remains to be examined in more detail. At this stage, it is worth pointing out that the role of IS is not only enabling, by supporting solutions for the problem of criminality and augmenting traditional efforts by automating processes or providing further intelligence, but also constraining in ways that are often subtle and interfere with regulatory intentions. Technology creates bottom-up effects that sometimes counteract top-down impositions.[8] Unintended consequences come into play, despite the strict logical paths upon which technological operations are executed.

On the basis of the context briefly discussed above, this chapter investigates how IS exert influence in preventing and detecting criminal activity. *First*, the phenomenon of data growth is analysed, as it is central to the problems that are created when there is an effort to profile suspicious behaviour. Through a series of properties, data require processing, manipulation, categorization and analysis. *Second*, two key concepts are presented that are very important in pondering the greater role of IS. They are at the core of manipulating large datasets, namely *profiling* and *data mining*. These are examined from a non-technical perspective in order to highlight how they are being used as techniques for spotting suspicious behaviour and how data are being used to profile, algorithmically manipulate and distil actionable information for preventing criminal behaviour. *Third*, the majority of the chapter focuses on the domain of money laundering for highlighting the interaction between technology and the detection and prevention of criminal activity. Reference to the anti-*money laundering* (AML) domain is helpful in considering both how technology is being used as an early warning mechanism in order to flag suspicious activity, and how the development of group/individual profiles that simulate money laundering behaviour have important side effects.

[8] D. Demetis, *Technology and Anti-Money Laundering: A Systems Theory and Risk-Based Approach* (Cheltenham: Edward Elgar, 2010).

By extrapolating from the issues identified above a theoretical framework is presented at the end of this chapter that addresses the influence of technology on tackling criminal activity and considers the information dimensions for monitoring criminality. Peripheral, yet important, issues are factored into the considerations of this framework and include how criminal activity can be balanced with civil liberties, as well as the potential for using Privacy Enhancing Technologies (PETs) for (partly-) anonymous data sharing between stakeholders at an international level.

Data growth, databases and the algorithmic construction of criminal behaviour

Current criminal activity is unfolding (in both its cyber and real-world dimensions) and characterizes our information age. Governments, intelligence agencies, police authorities and other organizations or stakeholders have at their disposal an unprecedented amount of data to prevent or detect criminal activity. Making sense of this data is the challenge at hand; and it is no easy task.

Every year we produce a staggering volume of data, equivalent to about 37,000 libraries the size of the US Library of Congress.[9] Most of these data are unstructured from a computational perspective, meaning they are not tied to a specific coherent database structure. We create text-based data in word processing, presentations, numerical data in spreadsheets, communicate by exchanging emails, publish tweets, produce (or become subjects of) audio recordings, digital pictures and full motion video, while at the same time participating in social networks on the Internet and other forms of web-based communication. In equal measure the various industrial actors produce or store their own sets of data, thus giving rise to different industry-specific data categories participating in the growing pool of data. For example, the medical industry creates medical data such as MRI, or the financial sector stores raw transaction datasets created by individual financial transactions, thereby recording the movement of money. More and more data are being created year on year. These data are stored on paper, film, magnetic or optical storage and flow through broadcasts, telephony and the Internet.

Massive as the volume of data may be, they constitute the raw material that is being monitored, used, analysed, categorized and filtered for

[9] P. Lyman and H. Varian, 'How Much Information 2003?' (2003), available at www2.sims.berkeley.edu/research/projects/how-much-info-2003/.

various reasons. To an extreme level, the volume of data becomes the subject of indiscriminate massive monitoring by intelligence agencies (national security agencies). The approach that has been suggested by the US National Security Agency (NSA) director, General Keith B. Alexander, is to 'collect the whole haystack rather than look for a single needle in the haystack; collect it all, tag it, store it . . . and whatever it is you want, you go searching for it'.[10]

Crime detection and prevention are key concerns that have always made use of various forms of data. Therefore, while there could be an obvious information value in this pool of data for crime detection and prevention, it is the set of consequences that emerge from utilizing data that is fascinating to explore. These consequences create severe side effects, not only on data subjects that may be under investigation, but also on 'future suspects' that will be filtered through the exploitation of data. At an ontological level, a much deeper effect percolates, as the dimensions of criminality are being constructed through technology. Legislation may be regulating the top-down imposition by defining the nature of behavioural activities that can be categorized as criminal (and the penalties for engaging in such activities), but technology maintains the infrastructure through which suspicious cases are advanced and given priority over others. Moreover, the sheer complexity of the operations involved at a computational level implies that the full extent of these processes cannot always become visible.

Technology acts in a bottom-up fashion and often in contradistinction to the function of legislation that sets the norms through which criminality is interpreted. By automating complex processes, technology also carves a different space in establishing a systemic role. In turn, these elements mutate into new social forms. They are transformed into new conditions which take the form of an infrastructural reorganization in the shape of electronic information.[11]

Algorithms create the logical platform through which suspicious behaviour is deconstructed and encapsulated. *Machines* provide the technical infrastructure upon which automated operations are undertaken and communicated. And *humans* are called upon to validate or discard the *technologically constructed suspicious behaviour*. The last

[10] E. Nakashima and J. Warrick, 'For NSA Chief, Terrorist Threat Drives Passion to "Collect It All," Observers Say', (2013), available at www.washingtonpost.com/world/national-security/for-nsa-chief-terrorist-threat-drives-passion-to-collect-it-all/2013/07/14/3d26ef80-ea49–11e2-a301-ea5a8116d211_story.html.

[11] J. Kallinikos, *The Consequences of Information: Institutional Implications of Technological Change* (Cheltenham: Edward Elgar 2006).

stage in this process (i.e., human intervention) maintains the illusion that human judgement intervenes to establish a control mechanism for what is being automatically generated. However, this ignores a complex stratum of technical interconnections that yield unpredictable results. Technology acquires a systemic role that functions in an unpredictable manner, not because at the micro-level the results of specific operations cannot be predicted with accuracy, but because at the macro-level the system of technology acquires such a degree of complexity that it is impossible to monitor all the interactions that take place at the level of the system.[12] At the same time, it is impossible to predict how the interactions between different algorithms will affect the platforms that support them, or how their interactions will play out over time.

An illustration, among many others, can be found in the financial markets. In what is known as 'the crash of 2:45', the Dow Jones Industrial Average recorded the biggest one-day point decline in its history (998.5 points) due to automatic computerized traders on the stock market engaging in 'algorithmic trading', where the automated execution of orders without human intervention led to an unpredictable level of withdrawing from the stock market, thereby creating liquidity problems.[13] This incident was meant to illustrate the unpredictable systemic nature of large-scale automated operations, thereby indicating that technology is not subordinate in the causal sense. It gains an autonomous character that goes against social and legal norms, as the processes that support technology feed off each other in unpredictable ways. Such processes tend to create 'positive feedback loops' that have a tendency to destabilize the system from what an observer would consider as a predictable state.[14] Moreover, in the context of dealing with criminality, the embodiment of human working practices into technologically supported processes means that the nature of work in the fight against transnational (and other forms of) criminality has changed drastically, particularly when international collaboration is demanded.

While the communicative role of technology has established a faster and better way to support the communication between authorities in

[12] N. Luhmann, *Social Systems, Writing Science* (Stanford: Stanford University Press, 1995) at iii, 627; N. Luhmann, *Law as a Social System* (Oxford, New York: Oxford University Press, 2004) at viii, 498.

[13] T. Hendershott, C. Jones and A. Menkveld, 'Does Algorithmic Trading Improve Liquidity?'(2001) 11 *Journal of Finance* 1.

[14] N. Glass, 'Chaos, Non-Linear Systems and Day-to-Day Management', (1996) 14 *European Management Journal* 98.

different countries, there is yet another role that technology acquires. This is primarily concerned with the development of techniques for understanding the nature of criminality with a view to developing mechanisms that facilitate the profiling of criminal behaviour. This is usually based upon a series of techniques, such as statistical analyses of datasets with crime-related information, geographic mapping of hotspots where criminal activity takes place, economic or other indicators which may suggest that a rise in criminality is about to occur, and so on. This exercise in figuring out how criminal behaviour presents itself in different contexts is an important one, but the role of technology therein is largely underestimated. Technology is not only applied to delineate certain patterns of criminal activity/behaviour by shifting large volumes of data. Once that process is over, it is assumed that the results achieved have a near-causal developmental link to the processes that gave rise to them. Put simply, it is assumed that this is 'what criminality looks like'. The next step seems to follow almost naturally, but the leap is significant. Once we have what we believe to be the fundamental building blocks of a criminal phenomenon (in how/when it occurs, what we should be looking for to observe as early signs for future criminal behaviour, etc.) then we can apply this 'pattern' (or series thereof) to new data that are either real-time or near real-time data (or within a certain timeframe) and reduce this new volume of data to a few suspicious cases that could be examined more closely.

This process has nothing to do with the search for a unique suspect that has committed a crime (whether at a national level or through international cooperation) or a network of criminals. It is not a process through which criminals are uniquely identified, but it becomes a process where *potential* criminals are singled out for further investigation because they fit a set of abstract characteristics. These characteristics have been deduced, not only by analysing previous criminal cases, but also by using various other data sources. The process of discovering patterns in large datasets is the overall goal of data mining.[15]

The fact that this constitutes some type of 'pre-emptive strike' against criminality is one element to the process: the one that allows us to simulate and prevent. But the much deeper effect is usually side-lined and not considered at all. This is what, in this author's contention, can be described as the *technological construction of criminality*. In a sense, and

[15] S.-O. Tergan and T. Keller, *Knowledge and Information Visualization: Searching for Synergies, Lecture Notes in Computer Science* (Berlin, New York: Springer, 2005).

in the 'eyes of algorithms' where pattern is king, the results of the applications of filters for criminal activity yield outputs that are already considered as highly possible criminal cases. This algorithmic prejudice inflicted upon the subsequent human evaluation must be taken into serious consideration. As we shall see in the paradigm devoted to AML technology, this has had serious side effects that hinder both national and international efforts in combating the phenomenon.

Reliance on technology for supporting processes that tackle criminality is not only to be found in the communicative role of IS. Technology assumes a more important function as it becomes extensively used to conduct profiling at a pre-criminal level, on the basis of data that are stored from previous criminal cases. The institutionalization of these processes creates an iron cage that treats possibility as suspicion.[16] Through a series of self-referential processes more data leads to more profiling and more suspects, but also to an elevated risk of being completely overwhelmed by the white noise that permeates these processes to begin with. In turn, conducting manual checks becomes a painstaking process; ultimately the checks become more costly and counterproductive, staff may become demoralized and prosecution rates remain low. International cooperation is hindered at the national level as technology places increasing demands on cooperation by simplifying communication. Requests on information for suspects need to be prioritized and the technological modes of operation need to transcend the national in support of the international cases that exhibit a greater degree of complexity. But how has technology shaped the international dimension of cooperation against crime?

The role of information and technology-based systems in the internationalization of policing

From a historical perspective, advances in technology were deemed to be 'instrumental in facilitating the internationalization of policing in a form that is independent of law and politics'.[17] The evolution of technology

[16] P. J. Dimaggio and W. W. Powell, 'The Iron Cage Revisited: Institutional Isomorphism and Collective Rationality in Organization Fields', in W. W. Powell and P. J. Dimaggio (eds.), *The New Institutionalism in Organizational Analysis* (Chicago, IL: University of Chicago Press, 1991).

[17] M. Deflem, 'Technology and the Internationalization of Policing: A Comparative-Historical Perspective', (2002) 19 *Justice Quarterly* 453.

has led towards cross-border cooperation because barriers to communication between institutions were rendered obsolete. Structural conditions that had to be satisfied for the control of international crime were met, for example, by establishing interoperability between systems, or by agreeing on common standards such as methodologies for fingerprint measurements. IS pre-dating the information exchanges that were supported by computers (e.g., telegraphic code, radio communications, printed publications) facilitated the early forms of data exchange. However, the evolution in communication, exchange and storage has been phenomenal; and it is all down to the invention of the microchip, which gave rise to what we can nowadays call a 'computer'. This dynamic has also been completely altered by the invention of the Internet, which removes the locale of information and has a substantial impact on data storage and availability.[18]

Of course, another issue that changes the scope of what data becomes available through the Internet, remains the fact that users are willing to put personal information online, including their locations, photographs, personal preferences, education, age, work experience, activities, and a lot more. This information is available immediately through the Internet and constitutes an ever-growing platform of exploration for intelligence purposes, exploration of social networks and extraction of statistics for developing various models that can assist in understanding demographics, socio-economics, political implications and trends that may be considered as proxies to criminality. While it may not be immediately evident how such data can be used to deal with criminality when they are provided wittingly by non-offenders (in most cases), it needs to be made clear that criminals are perceived as 'anomalies' within the broader system. At least from an IS perspective, they may be viewed as exceptions to the normality that non-offenders may exhibit in their digital traces. It is in the distinction and the difference between criminal/non-criminal that data manipulation rests, while both sides to a distinction[19] are necessary in order to examine the phenomenon and gain a deeper understanding of how the 'anomalies' can be algorithmically traced or how technology can assist in collaborative work between nations for this purpose. Needless to say, privacy implications are very important also, even though not the subject matter of this chapter; the potential misuse

[18] J. Kim, 'Phenomenology of Digital-Being', (2001) 24 *Human Studies* 87.

[19] N. Luhmann, *Theories of Distinction: Redescribing the Descriptions of Modernity* (Stanford, CA: Stanford University Press, 2002).

of data[20] can create negative effects and cast serious doubt upon the aggregated operations of both governments and companies, who are bound to suffer from security breaches as no system can be considered fully secure.[21]

Through automation, and propelled by it, data become the irresistible source that must be harnessed in order to lead to action; data become a source of pre-action. The question then becomes slightly different in the context of tackling criminality. How can we 'derive benefits from this increased data availability'?[22] How can the *anti-criminal value of information* be considered, both in light of the technological developments and in the context of the internationalization of policing?

Forensic technologies are also considered under this prism: for example, fingerprints. While the collection of such biometrics constitutes a physical process to begin with, the internationalization of their use in policing has been facilitated by the deconstruction of a specific set of information characteristics that describe the physical biometric. Interoperability in the methodology for measuring fingerprints (i.e., agreement on the unique measurements that will be taken) is necessary in order to develop an infrastructure that will communicate the measurements, or store the metrics in databases so that they can be shared or searched more effectively. For example, in the case of fingerprints, it is not the image itself that is searched, rather the deduced mathematical structure and numerical pattern that has been extracted from the image.[23] From an information science perspective, this becomes an informational subset that needs to be manipulated. Information then acquires another set of properties that become fundamental and absolutely critical in characterizing the information age. The demands that are placed by the increasing volume of information place further strain on the functionality that needs to be powered by technology in order to improve international cooperation. This requires more thorough forms of international cooperation. For example, there needs to be an

[20] C. Arndt, 'The Loss of Privacy and Identity in the 21st Century: Causes and Possible Solutions', (June 2006) *Biometric Technology Today* 3.

[21] G. Dhillon and J. Backhouse, 'Information System Security Management in the New Millennium', (2000) 43 *Communications of the ACM* 125.

[22] A. Gotlieb, C. Dalfen and K. Katz, 'The Transborder Transfer of Information by Communications and Computer Systems: Issues and Approaches to Guiding Principles', (1974) 68 *American Journal of International Law* 227.

[23] U. Uludag and A. K. Jain, 'Attacks on Biometric Systems: A Case Study in Fingerprints', in *Proc. SPIE-EI 2004* (San Jose, CA: 2004).

agreement on information management, such as an agreement on the categories that should be used in the semantic tagging of crimes throughout different countries; otherwise, comparisons become meaningless and inferences regarding the characteristics of crime are rendered unfounded.

Table 7.1 summarizes some of the key communication technologies and developments that have been used in policing and tackling crime; these have further transcended national borders to achieve some degree of cooperation between nations.

By looking at Table 7.1 one can observe a main strand of development: the communications/technological strand that allows for the establishment of communication between different countries, much like the first telegraphic messages exchanged between the UK and the USA, leading to the Internet, which allows for global communications nowadays. But there is another strand with complimentary characteristics that refers mostly to the storage and processing of data, such as the invention of the microchip, leading to the development of both hardware and software: the constituent components of the modern computer. Nowadays, we have even got the application of anti-crime specific software, or tools for supporting the collaborative work between countries aiming to prevent or detect criminal activity.

In Table 7.1, the Internet is considered as the latest major development as a medium for the communication of criminal cases, suspects, etc., between authorities. Moreover, the Internet is used as a communication facilitator for data across national law enforcement agencies (LEAs) that feed data into specific IS with structured databases.

Table 7.1: *Evolution of communication systems in tackling crime*

Time horizon	Information and communication technologies (ICTs) development
1850	Telegraph
1876	Telephone
1900s	Radio communications
1924	Fingerprint measurements
1932	FBI inaugurates forensic laboratory
1940	Radar used in policing
1964	Facsimile
1970s	Modern computers
1980s	The Internet used as a medium for networking/communication and replacing a lot of pre-existing functionality from other ICTs.

When considering the internationalization of policing and the collaboration through which crime can be prevented and detected, the role of the Internet cannot be stressed enough. Even though important security concerns may be raised in the context of providing multiple cross-national user access to crime-related data,[24] particularly when suspect-related data can be modified, the utility from deploying web-based resources for tackling international crime remains extremely important.

The IS of Europol

Looking at how IS are being used at cross-border level it is pertinent to describe briefly the three core IS being used by Europol in order to facilitate the exchange of information: the Europol Information System (EIS), the Secure Information Exchange Network Application (SIENA), as well as the Europol Platform for Experts (EPE).

The first information system, the EIS, constitutes the 'reference system for offences, individuals involved and other related data to support member states, Europol and its cooperation partners in their fight against organized crime, terrorism, and other forms of serious crime'.[25] Europol not only allows LEAs to transmit data into its systems, but also validates and feeds data from third parties into the system, the majority of which is inserted by means of automated data loading systems. As of December 2012, more than 185,000 data objects reside in its database, including 48,000 suspected or convicted criminals, a rise of 17 per cent compared to 2011. About 34 per cent of the data objects relate to drug trafficking, while the major crime areas that are also identified include forgery of money, robbery, illegal immigration and fraud. Member states transmit data on entities that can be cross-matched, such as persons, cars, telephone numbers and firearms. National LEAs both share and compare data with the EIS. The EIS is being used when conducting investigations, thereby acquiring a detection character, but it is also used as a reference tool from which statistics, characteristics and inferences can be drawn, thereby developing profiling tactics through which criminality can be dissected into categories.

The SIENA system supports secure exchange of both operational and strategic information related to crimes and it is an important information

[24] Basel Committee, 'Sharing of Financial Records between Jurisdictions in Connection with the Fight against Terrorist Financing', (Basel Committee on Banking Supervision, 2002).

[25] Europol, 'Information Exchanges', (2013) available at www.europol.europa.eu/content/page/information-exchange-1848.

exchange network in the context of tackling criminality at an international level. This becomes evident when one examines the initiation of criminal cases; only 8 per cent are actually initiated by Europol itself.[26] The majority are initiated by Member States (82 per cent) while the remaining 10 per cent are undertaken by third parties that have cooperation agreements in place with Europol, thus establishing a means of international communication and cooperation in criminal cases. More than 400,000 operational messages were exchanged through the SIENA system between Member States, with more than 15,000 new cases initiated. The majority of information exchanges between states involved cases related to drugs (almost 30 per cent of all new cases), followed by fraud (15 per cent), robbery (11 per cent), money laundering (9 per cent), and illegal immigration (8 per cent).[27] A number of different countries collaborate in the SIENA system and of the total of sixty parties participating, twenty-seven are Member States.

Finally, exploiting the possibilities opened by collaborative tools in the web sphere, Europol has developed a secure environment, the EPE. This is meant to facilitate knowledge sharing between experts from different jurisdictions in a secure platform where similarities, differences and common practices can be discussed and improved. In this information system no personal data are being used; the aim is to enable sharing of suspect data between users on a variety of topics such as kidnapping, child sexual exploitation, counter terrorism, corruption, environmental crime, financial crime, fraud, etc. More than 2,000 users have joined the different expert online communities in the EPE.

The work undertaken by Europol illustrates that the use of technology to facilitate information exchange between different jurisdictions is multi-dimensional. Technology is used for a variety of purposes and establishes links that assist both in preventing and detecting criminal activity. Technology also allows the parties to gain distributed access to the same digital entities: the digital objects that variously characterize suspects for criminal activities. Distributed access through the Internet allows for the internationalization of tackling criminality,[28] while the aggregation of different digital objects into single platforms allows for the emergence of collaboration as a critical factor. While all

[26] Ibid.

[27] Available at www.europol.europa.eu/content/page/europol-information-system-eis-1850.

[28] G. Papanicolaou, *Transnational Policing and Sex Trafficking in Southeast Europe: Policing the Imperialist Chain* (Basingstoke: Palgrave Macmillan, 2011).

these aspects appear to be positive in advancing the internationalization of policing and the fight against transnational crime, there is a dark side to technological implementation. In addition, there are restrictions on how far automation can be allowed to intrude into human decision-making processes, even when these boundaries are constantly pushed forward (and usually making more room for technology along the way).

Profiling data

Demands to cut down on the complexity generated by increased data availability have led to a number of techniques that attempt to reach a subset of these data, so that their manipulation can become more meaningful in a specific context. This seems to come almost naturally, as it is impossible to consume all the data that we have at our disposal in any given situation. As human beings, this restricts us in a most fundamental way. Let us take Google as an example. Behind a highly efficient infrastructure that swiftly ranks search results by using complex algorithms, lies a peculiar form of profiling that becomes dependent on the search engine itself; human profiling, namely profiling by human beings. The top thirty results from a search receive over 90 per cent (!) of search traffic.[29] The capacity and complexity of computational processing in such scenarios becomes vastly undermined while the output of an algorithm is fiercely cut down by what computer scientists may view as a necessary evil: human processing. Therefore, computer profiling and human profiling become structurally coupled and co-dependent. Advanced computations are irrelevant if they are decontextualized and human decision-making restrictions are not considered, unless of course, computers are allowed in the future to *become decision makers* instead of constructing part of the reality for decision makers. But isn't this technological interference already developing influential preconditions upon which humans are called to exercise their judgement?

In *profiling*, the goals are to extrapolate and formulate a set of characteristics (e.g., behavioural) about an individual, a collective entity, or even a general phenomenon (e.g., money laundering); thereafter, this set of characteristics (i.e., the profile) is applied to other entities that are being treated in light of these same characteristics.[30] While in the field of

[29] B. Jansen and A. Spink, 'An Analysis of Web Documents Retrieved and Viewed', in The Fourth International Conference on Internet Computing (Las Vegas, NV: 2003) at 65–9.

[30] H. Hirsh, C. Basu and B. Davison, 'Learning to Personalize', (2000) 43 *Communications of the ACM*, 102.

information science *profiling* is considered a process with a number of distinct stages, it needs to be acknowledged that the profiling process has two key components which must be distinguished and which are central to the extraction of 'anti-criminal value from information'. The first concerns *profile generation*, which is the process of inferring a profile, and involves analysing personal data in search of patterns, sequences and relationships in order to arrive at a set of assumptions, while the second relates to *profile application*, which treats entities in light of this profile. The latter assists in decision making and more specifically in limiting the number of results (or suspects in the context of criminality) so that the remaining subset becomes meaningful to manipulate.

Hence, the need for profiling emerges from the need to cut down on this complexity (or even just volume).

But what implications does this have for individuals? Firstly, the 'use of extensive data profiles by public or private institutions deprives the individual of the capacity to influence decision making',[31] with decisions being made on the basis of individual 'data shadows'. Secondly, excessive reliance on technological infrastructures or sophisticated software for monitoring criminal behaviour may lead to human decision makers abdicating their responsibilities. But the real issue here is to define the essential characteristics of a decision taken by computer software. According to Bygrave: '... a negative answer would say that software cannot actually make a decision because mental action is required ... an affirmative answer would say that the *logical processes of computer software would seem to parallel sufficiently the processes of the human mind to justify treating the former as analogous to the latter*'.[32] The affirmative answer also implies that human activity is always involved, even if he/she is not part of the process as he/she is responsible for programming the software.

The major flaw in the affirmative position is that the collective actions embedded within the technology cannot be monitored due to an emergent complexity. It must be understood that to attribute a singular intentionality to particular artefacts or technologies:

> simplifies the complex texture of technologically embodied functionalities (because the intentions of many groups are mingled in the design and

[31] L. Bygrave, 'Automated Profiling; Minding the Machine: Article 15 of the EC Data Protection Directive and Automated Profiling', (2001) 17 *Computer Law & Security Report* 17.

[32] Ibid. (emphasis added).

> development process) . . . and that technology influences human agency not by imposing a single and mechanical functionality but by *inviting specific courses of action, courses of action that are engraved by the distinctive way by which each technology frames its reference domain.*[33]

In the context of tackling criminality there has been a tremendous increase in the frequency and intensity of profiling practices.[34] An emergent industry has grown out of this, building upon a number of techniques such as data warehousing and data mining. Software that is specifically designed to assist in investigations comes in various forms, with many different companies offering 'solutions' that can be used by both the private and the public sector in order to prevent and detect several types of criminal activity. In most cases the software is custom-made to detect specific activity (such as software for spotting money laundering). In other cases, particularly useful for large-scale criminal operations, software is being used to determine the structure (and hierarchy) of criminal organizations and to create a platform where different individuals can collaborate in this process, contributing with different data objects, allowing for an online distributed collaborative effort. Software has even been used to screen inmates in prison and their interactions with visitors, attempting to prevent further criminality by monitoring and deconstructing the 'support criminal network' of inmates on the outside in order to infer further suspects.

While simple surveillance can be found in police databases throughout the world, where image/voice recognition and real-time video monitoring is taking place in order to locate suspects, a notable shift is taking place in attempting to monitor the social context in which criminals operate. The more open habitat of information availability lends itself as an excuse to such projects. Monitoring includes close business associates and family members, recognizing that there is a network of support through which serious criminality operates and that the very monitoring of such a network could provide new opportunities for preventing further criminal activities. The social networking dimension of preventing and detecting criminal activity is yet another testament of the need to capture the mobility of criminals and their networks and to consider action plans through international efforts. The chapter now turns to the key example

[33] J. Kallinikos, 'Reopening the Black Box of Technology: Artifacts and Human Agency', in Twenty-Third International Conference on Information Systems (2002).

[34] M. Hildebrandt and S. Gutwirth, *Profiling the European Citizen: Cross-Disciplinary Perspectives* (Berlin: Springer, 2008).

of AML in order to discuss these issues, before presenting a theoretical framework for considering the different information dimensions that interact in the operation of technology against criminality.

IS in tackling money laundering and implications for countering the financing of terrorism

The integration of technology in the fight against money laundering is one of the finest examples where data growth, profiling, the technological construction of criminality, and national/international implications can be brought together. The volume of transacting data that needs to be monitored, coupled with the requirements of profiling such a complex behaviour, creates interesting dynamics.

First of all, financial institutions have to cope with a staggering volume of data. For instance, one large financial institution in the UK deals with about 15–20 million transactions per day. Checking those transactions for money laundering-related behaviour over a period of time (typically for a three-month timeframe) becomes a difficult profiling exercise. The vast mass of data creates a unique challenge: the development of profiling queries (i.e., a series of conditional statements) that will be applied to the totality of these data with the aim of identifying suspects for money laundering. In this process there is an attempt to exploit possible relationships between the data and to uncover transacting anomalies or patterns of transacting that would have a high probability of being the traces of launderers. One problem that arises here lies in the construction of the profiling queries themselves: are the relationships uncovered by profiling meaningful? Or is it simply that the relationships are imposed by the profiling queries in the first place?

Regulators generally ignored these issues. Technology was introduced hastily. Financial regulators around the world wanted banks to deploy transaction-monitoring systems so that they could identify potential money launderers and report them to the authorities (e.g., DP22 in the UK[35]). With money laundering tied to serious primary criminal offences

[35] With Discussion Paper 22 (also known as DP22), the Financial Services Authority (now disbanded and organized otherwise) in the UK, kick-started the suggestion that regulated entities should incorporate 'automated monitoring systems' according to the complexity of their business, number of branches, functionality required, IT infrastructure, etc. See more at FSA, 'Reducing Money Laundering Risk – Know Your Customer and Anti-Money Laundering Monitoring', (2004) available at www.fsa.gov.uk/pubs/discussion/dp22.pdf, at 18–21.

(such as drug and human trafficking), the potential that technology could deliver seemed enormous. Hence, financial institutions globally were forced into a swift adoption of AML software. The software industry around AML, profiling, fraud, AML training, compliance, and so on, boomed in the 1990s. However, the unintended consequences were many and diverse, both in the application of the software and their side effects at the domestic level.

An example from a real bank in the European Union area will help clarify the issue at hand. The financial institution under consideration bought an off-the-shelf software platform. Following the installation of the software and after months of customization efforts, the software produced about 2,000 Suspicious Activity Reports (SARs) per day. But while the SARs were coming in the thousands, manual analysis of the reports by money laundering analysts was limited to roughly one hundred SARs per day. The rest were considered white noise, an obstacle to the method of producing real suspicious reports. After the software had supposedly done its job in producing suspects for money laundering, human decision making took over. Money laundering analysts were called to decide which of those technology-generated cases were truly suspicious. The result was a numerical percentage that is known as the True Positive Rate (TPR). Such a number characterizes the effectiveness of every profiling technique. This rate indicates what percentage of the software-generated suspicious reports were considered as actually suspicious following the manual examination of the reports by analysts. For instance, if the software generates 100 suspects for money laundering, following which due diligence and manual analysis of the suspects finds that only one out of 100 is considered to be truly suspicious (based on human judgement), then the TPR would be 1 per cent. In the financial institution under examination this number was approximately 0.02 per cent. Of course, while this percentage of the TPR is extremely disappointing, it is far from unusual. In fact, most financial institutions start off with TPRs at this range and gradually manage to increase them (to about 15–25 per cent) after years of optimizing the queries that simulate how a money laundering suspect would transact. Even so, this means that technology is generating 75 per cent false suspects for money laundering, at a best-case scenario. These cases that are mistakenly considered as suspect cases are known as *false positives*.

Despite all the computational expertise that is on parade and the evolution in constructing supposedly sophisticated algorithms for tracing suspicious transactions for money laundering, the unintended consequences escalate to cause problems at both national and international levels. The fear of financial fines for non-compliance (a recent example is HSBC, which was fined $1.9 billion for non-compliance with money laundering regulations[36]) has led to a reckless use of such technology. Even with some financial institutions increasing the number of their staff members six-fold to cope with the analysis of the technology-generated suspects, the volume of alerts was much greater. This has resulted in a 'hot-potato syndrome': financial institutions would pass on technology-generated suspects to the national authorities (the Financial Intelligence Units (FIU)) and these in turn will often request assistance from other jurisdictions where financial activities are linked to criminality in other countries. Hence, the volume of data and the reckless use of technology have led to an increasing number of computer-generated suspects, passed on to FIU, which are swamped with white noise instead of useful information. This phenomenon has been responsible for the considerable increase in the number of SARs collected at national level. Examples of this increase for the UK and the USA can be viewed in Figures 7.1 and 7.2.

The increased volume of SARs available to the authorities resulted in the quality of information being jeopardized,[37] accompanied by very low prosecution rates. Similarly, the results in asset recovery have been horrendously poor. In the UK, this led in the past to the dismantling of the Asset Recovery Agency (ARA) after it became known that the cost of investigation for confiscating £40 million (out of an estimated £1.5 billion laundered annually)[38] was £400 million. While at the macro-level the

36 A. Viswanatha and B. Wolf, 'HSBC to Pay $1.9 Billion U.S. Fine in Money-Laundering Case', Reuters (2012), available at www.reuters.com/article/2012/12/11/us-hsbc-probe-idUSBRE8BA05M20121211.

37 A severe and direct consequence was experienced as a result of the above practices, mostly referring here to the issue of *over-reporting*. The databases of Financial Intelligence Units (i.e., the organizations responsible for collecting the SARs for money laundering) were filled with white noise. Instead of useful information that could initiate an investigation and even a prosecution of money laundering, the FIUs ended up receiving useless information. In all these processes, technology has played an important role because it gave the tool to the financial institutions to report excessively. It was specifically this problem that led – much later – to the introduction of the risk-based approach in the Third Directive of the European Union. That introduction alone is meant to reduce the compliance-fear experienced by the majority of financial institutions (accompanied with a series of financial fines for non-compliance) and indirectly to maximize the potential for useful submissions of SARs. Nevertheless, despite the intentions, this approach has led to considerable confusion because of the ambiguities intrinsic in the concept of risk itself.

38 BBC, 'Assets Recovery Failing', (2006) available at http://news.bbc.co.uk/2/hi/uk_news/politics/5077846.stm.

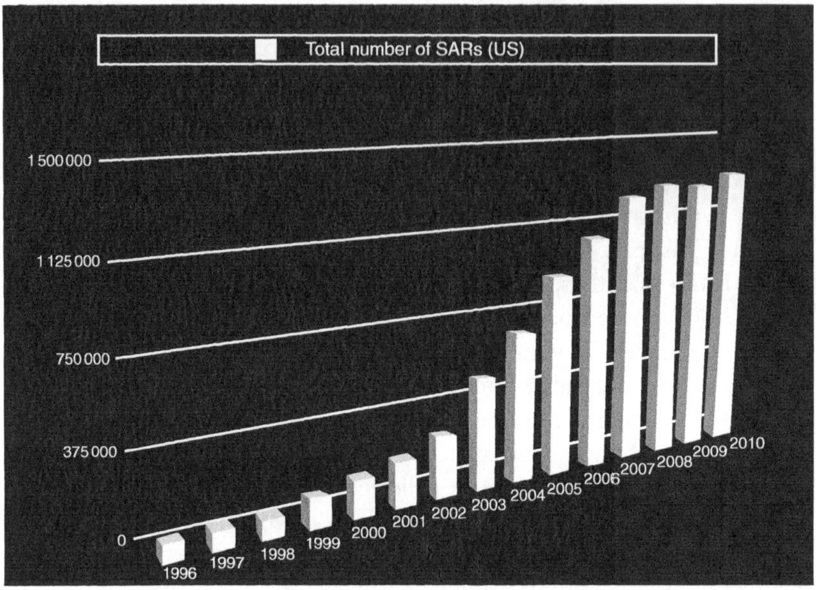

Figures 7.1: Suspicious Activity Reports (SARs) in the USA, 1996–2010

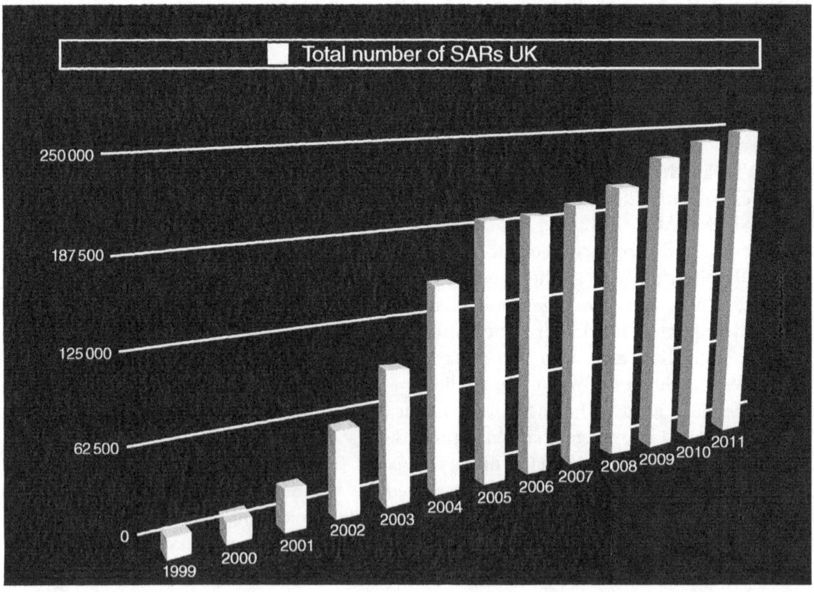

Figure 7.2: Suspicious Activity Reports (SARs) in the UK, 1999–2011

system has become ineffective, at the micro-level the question is why it is so difficult to model money laundering. Why is technology causing so many problems across a wide number of stakeholders in AML (and not just financial institutions)? Furthermore, how should IS be considered in light of an increasing demand to establish international cooperation for tackling criminality while taking security, privacy and civil liberties into consideration?

With IS, data are stored in the databases of financial institutions and other stakeholders. The difficulties in monitoring can be attributed to a number of factors. Firstly, databases degrade and their information value deteriorates due to human error and non-updated information. Secondly, the complexity of the phenomenon cannot be easily encapsulated in a computer model; financial information is a proxy to other types of behaviours (e.g., lifestyle that involves singularities) that are also important but which are not susceptible to a mathematical representation. Thirdly, financial institutions have access to a fragmented view of transacting behaviour, given that customers/suspects may engage in a much broader spectrum of financial transacting through other institutions (and quite often, in other jurisdictions).

Therefore, when a financial institution reports a SAR for money laundering or terrorist financing it identifies a potential suspect (or group of suspects) and sends the identity information to the national authority (i.e., the FIU) along with a record of transactions. The FIU has several options. It can either request additional information from the initial reporting entity (e.g., all transaction data from the account opening), or seek additional information from all other financial institutions for the individual(s) involved. Then it has to wait until it receives a response from the reporting entities and examine whether the collected information constitutes a real money laundering case that can be forwarded for prosecution.

In the totality of a national AML system, the above information workflow can be viewed as both time-consuming and random. Suspicion emerges as an outcome even with only a shadow of the totality of information being available (at national level). Decentralized databases that are scattered in various financial institutions are pieces of the puzzle for identifying suspects for money laundering. A logical next step would seek national access to financial data, with regulators and mostly FIUs demanding some sort of access. This is the situation in Italy where the Italian FIU receives all the raw financial transaction data from all financial institutions in the country. This is done after the transactions are anonymized and the original identity information is kept at the reporting institution. What is sent to the FIU is a proxy-identifier (say an ID number that has been modified). Still, it gives the opportunity to the FIU to store the data in a single database, known as the *Archivio Unico Informatico* and connect with the same identifiers transactions from individuals throughout the country and in different institutions.

Needless to say, an advanced information exchange structure that would support the international effort against money laundering does not exist in this sense. IS that are currently available for the exchange of information between different countries are in use (e.g., through the Egmont Group, Interpol, etc.), but these involve cases on specific suspects. By doing so, they lack in one major aspect: *they do not allow the collective information that is spread out in different countries to be used for the emergence of suspicion itself.* This is where the serious cases of criminality can be found and where organized crime distributes its own information-footprint to avoid detection. In the closing section of this chapter we will see how such a framework can be considered for the exchange of information at an international level for tackling criminality. This constitutes a theoretical contribution that applies to different types of criminal activity, and even though privacy considerations are not examined in detail they are taken into account by introducing layers of civil rights protection mechanisms.

While the use of technology in centralized environments inhibits security risks, it also needs to be pointed out that the transition from more data to both more and useful information is not straightforward. Complexity always finds a way around any system, and as a property of any system, complexity is a transcendental property. It may change form and shape or even philosophical underpinnings, but hardly ever loses its characteristics as complexity. In this manner and when considering technology as an assistant in the tackling of criminality at the international level, we need to recognize that a series of transitions occur. For instance, when there is an effort to monitor money laundering behaviour logical complexity transforms into mathematical complexity, then into algorithmic complexity, followed by profiling complexity and even into visual complexity while data visualization is employed to examine large datasets. From a systems theoretical approach no system can escape the intrinsic complexity of the elements that constitute it.[39]

[39] N. Luhmann, 'Deconstruction as Second-Order Observing', in W. Rasch (ed.), *Theories of Distinction: Redescribing the Descriptions of Modernity* (Stanford, CA: Stanford University Press, 2002) at 94–112.

The aforementioned remarks point towards an important distinction that remains central to the role of technology in all efforts against international and transnational crime. Technology is often viewed outside of its organizational implications and the consequences that are created when an automated function (like that of technology) re-arranges the already-present bureaucracy of organizations. This is only part of the problem. Technology is also viewed as a solution that – when imposed onto the problem domain – will somehow ameliorate the difficulties of spotting criminal behaviour. Such a belief is flawed because it does not consider the contextual use of technology. The integration of technology within an organizational setting has implications that stretch beyond the best of intentions/expectations of computer programmers.

When it comes to any type of technology being embedded within an organizational setting these contingencies give rise to an emergent information system. This interacts with the pre-established basis of other IS and at the same time it constructs part of the organizational reality through which modern institutions attempt to combat criminal activity.

A theoretical framework for the use of IS in tackling criminality

In the development of the theoretical framework that follows there are a number of dimensions that need to be considered before the role of IS can be more specifically laid down. These are presented as distinct dimensions below and reflections on their synthesis are provided at the end of this chapter following the presentation of Figure 7.3. Money laundering is occasionally being used here as an example, without this jeopardizing the generality of the framework.

The goal for outlining this framework is to develop an overview of considerations regarding technology-supported information exchanges for tackling criminality. A number of distinctions and categories are used in order to highlight the different monitoring possibilities. These start with data-specific processes and move onto semantic issues, classifications, as well as possibilities for the exchange of information. Reflections are provided in each dimension in relation to the context in which they are being discussed.

Dimension 1: *types of data*

The type of data being monitored is possibly one of the most interesting starting viewpoints for the purposes of profiling. Generally, five data types can be distinguished: text, number, audio, image and video. Video can be

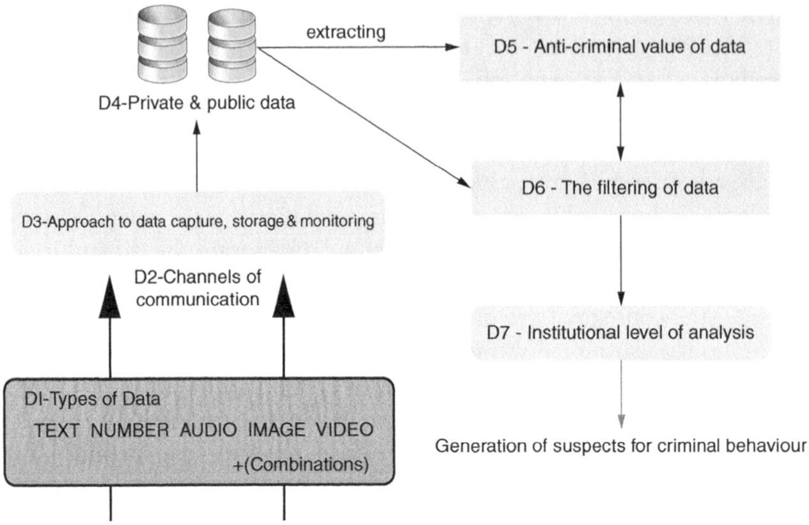

Figure 7.3: A framework for the technological construction of criminality and the generation of suspicion

considered in tandem with the image data-type as it constitutes a consecutive time-sequence of images. In the dimension that we can call 'types of data' there are also possibilities for combinations. For instance, data can include both text and audio. Different combinations yield a different information value, while data manipulation, recognition and analysis become harder as the data represent more media-rich objects (like video).

Dimension 2: *channels of communication*

Supported by cable, satellite or terrestrial technologies, data are communicated between individuals, or between individuals and institutions in all different data types. Basic channels of communication, such as radio, the telephone or the Internet are routinely used to allow for the types of data to be exchanged between users. Depending on the technology used and the medium of exchange (e.g., use of the Internet for exchanging emails) data are stored in different ways or may not be stored at all.

Dimension 3: *approach to data capture, storage and monitoring*

Unless actively monitored for crime prevention purposes, there are data types in certain communication channels that may not be captured or stored at all (e.g., telephone calls). In this scenario their information value is lost immediately. But the transition from analogue to digital, as well as the economies of scale that have made data storage cheap, now means that data are increasingly being captured and stored for longer periods of time. The actual depth and storage of data are difficult to dissect, but recent revelations in the USA about the activities of the National Security Agency point to very ambitious programs whose aim is to collect data indiscriminately. If we exclude the intelligence community that focuses on national security rather than the full spectrum of criminal activity, then data are captured by two distinct approaches that influence the dynamics of profiling in relation to the approach for data monitoring. The first one is a 'collect all' approach that can be considered as more invasive from a privacy perspective. In this case the strategy for the monitoring of data is decided *a posteriori* from its collection. Both public and private data may be collected. The second approach to data collection and monitoring is a 'pre-filter' approach. What data are actually collected is decided on the basis of what is explicitly required in order for particular monitoring processes to be accomplished. For example, if terrorist activity is being monitored on a particular telecommunication channel (e.g., telephone) then keywords that may raise suspicion (e.g., bomb) can isolate certain communications for further analysis. Finally, there are hybrid approaches between the two, of which a good example is Echelon (the international electronic eavesdropping network run by the intelligence communities of the USA, UK, Canada, Australia and New Zealand). While it is not considered to be a real-time tapping network, it captures traffic and then filters it for specific keywords that are semantically considered to be associated with suspicious behaviour. Interceptions are considered to take place through terrestrial radio antennae that intercept satellite transmissions.

Dimension 4: *private or public data*

Data that can be used during a profiling process may include both private and public data. Private data reside in databases that have restricted access to a select number of users. For instance, the raw transaction data stored in the databases of financial institutions are proprietary. Only personnel that are designated to have access to bank transaction data can gain access (excluding security breaches, of course), as well as authorities that demand access in the course of specific investigations. Aggregate collection of such private data by authorities is considered to be more invasive but there are ways to alleviate some concerns.

Anonymization and PETs can be used at that level so that individual identity data become stripped off the data that will be manipulated.[40]

In addition, there exist public data that can be (and usually are) used in profiling. Public data are considered to be available in a format that is accessible to all and is most recently propelled by the use of the Internet and a number of social media in which people participate. But what is surprising about this is that people will willingly share a great deal of information about themselves in order to participate in an online platform. If we take Facebook as an example, then users usually upload information about their hobbies, age, current location, activities, marital status, personal interests and preferences (what they like), what they read, what they share and who they are connected to. While all of this information may not necessarily be in the public domain automatically (depending on the privacy settings of the user) it does demonstrate how users react to having their personal information online.

The value of that public social networking information for countering criminality is notable. In a number of cases, the police have already used such data for monitoring individuals during ongoing investigations. In this way, social networking information has 'anti-criminal value'.[41]

Dimension 5: *the anti-criminal value of data*

Regardless of whether data are stored on known criminals, simple suspects, or non-criminals, data are known to possess an anti-criminal value or dimension. As discussed in relation to Europol IS, there are different ways in which technology can be used. In the case of known criminals, their personal data are stored and shared so that they can be arrested. In the case of suspects, data are shared, corroborated and

[40] See V. Senicar, B. Jerman-Blazic and T. Klobucar, 'Privacy-Enhancing Technologies – Approaches and Development', (2003) 25 *Computer Standards & Interfaces* 147. Privacy mechanisms like PETs include: encryption and steganography (hiding signals inside other signals), blind digital signature, trust centres (TTPs, certification services, etc.), identity protectors (these generate pseudo-identities as needed, convert pseudo-identities into actual identities desired, and combat fraud and misuse of the system), cookie management software, anonymizers, re-mailers, a system called Crowds, Crypto-Heaven, etc. Projects researching and developing PETs are P3P (by W3C), Privacy Incorporated Software Agent (PISA), Roadmap for Advanced Research in Privacy and Identity Management (RAPID), and the EU GUIDES project.

[41] K. Knibbs, 'In the Online Hunt for Criminals, Social Media Is the Ultimate Snitch', (2013) available at www.digitaltrends.com/social-media/the-new-inside-source-for-police-forces-social-networks/.

additional data objects are required to establish criminal acts. But as already discussed in the previous sections there is also an anti-criminal value in the data traces of non-criminals, if only to establish a distinction between criminal/non-criminal for statistical/demographic/socio-economic purposes. It is on the basis of such distinctions that criminal behaviour is supposedly understood: as an anomaly within an otherwise predictable system of norms. Then it is believed that there is some sort of structure in the anomaly itself, a series of behavioural patterns that can be absorbed into algorithmic queries, and that in this process non-criminal data can establish a firmer ground upon which the antithesis can be considered.

Dimension 6: *the filtering of data*

The filtering of data takes place through a 'filter' that constitutes a series of queries that attempt to encapsulate suspicious behaviour. The purpose of the filter is to raise an alarm for specific transactions in respect of a particular crime. The filter contains the algorithmic expressions that attempt to capture suspicious behaviour for different criminal activity (e.g., money laundering, terrorist financing, fraud, identity theft, etc.) and, as it is applied to the data, it also reduces the original population of the data to a supposedly manageable subset. For example, in the context of AML, a financial institution can apply a filter to raw transaction data; the filter describes in algorithmic terms how the potential money launderer would transact and would deliver suspects for further manual analysis. Alternatively, if the analysis were to take place at a national authority (an FIU) that aggregates transactions from all financial institutions, other profiles can be used. The function of the filter is to model (in algorithmic queries) the basic characteristics that can trace a criminal phenomenon by exploring the data. Hence, different filters are required to model different phenomena: money laundering, terrorist financing, imminent terrorist attacks, etc., by exploring both public and private data, different channels of communication, types of data, storage and semantic tagging techniques, etc. Enhancing these profiles for capturing criminal behaviour in more accurate terms is the most critical challenge that institutions face. Of course, this is inhibited by the complexity of the phenomena being studied and their underground activity, as well as the volume of data that is at the heart of the problem (but also the scope for opportunity).

Dimension 7: *the institutional level of analysis*

There are three institutional levels of analysis where technology can participate in order to extract anti-criminal value from data: the local level where institutions have proprietary databases (e.g., banks), the national level (e.g., FIUs) where institutions can demand access (or data) from the local level, and the international level where national institutions typically collaborate by exchanging data on specific cases and advancing shared intelligence (as in the cases of Europol and Interpol). However, the profiling element at the international level is considerably more restricted due to data restrictions and privacy concerns. While this is both understandable and desirable there are ways to include both anonymization and PETs in order to elevate profiling practices towards an international scope. These would target criminal activity that has a truly international dimension and where the silos of nation states restrict a timely response to targeting criminality.

Dimension 8: *time*

While not included in Figure 7.3, time plays a central role throughout any modelling problem. Even though time can be considered as one of the most elusive dimensions, in the context of using technology for combating criminal activities there are some important time-classifications that are relevant. Three different time-horizons can be distinguished: real-time profiling, near-real-time, and batch processing of data. Real-time monitoring is critical in the cases of known criminals that still escape arrest or are monitored for other purposes. For example, the process of embedding terrorist suspects in lists such as the one published by the US Treasury's Office of Foreign Assets Control requires an immediate response if said individuals attempt to carry out any transactions. Financial institutions are required to block their transactions immediately. In respect of decisions that can be delayed enough for human intervention one can move into the category of near-real-time monitoring. Finally, the time horizon can be explored in a more relaxed manner in the context of batch processing. In this scenario, data are examined for anti-criminal information value in certain timeframes where profiles and filters are applied to the data. For instance, in AML transaction-monitoring software this timeframe is typically a three-month window. As some criminal activity like money laundering is spread out over time in particular typologies (e.g., smurfing – or breaking up large amounts of money to be laundered into smaller sums and depositing them just under the reporting thresholds) the time horizon for engaging in profiling is critical. Obviously, the bigger the timeframe to be used the greater the challenge in data manipulation.

Conclusions

Technology occupies an important role in the fight against transnational criminality and there is little doubt that it will continue in an enabling role in communicating data and applying profiling practices. A number of IS influences have been discussed in the context of this chapter and it is important to stress that more theoretical work is necessary in order to delineate part of the complex nexus of effects that technology imposes in the fight against criminal activity. The continuous challenges that are faced in the fight against transnational criminality will require novel considerations and governmental action to apply PETs for curbing the invasive character of data manipulation that proposes a 'collect all' approach.

Similarly, researchers that find themselves at the boundary between technology and the law will need to investigate further the legal implications arising from those technological implementations whose bottom-up approach counteracts existing law. This involves the realization that technology does not always function as a subordinate tool with strictly defined conditions but assumes a systemic role. By doing so it maintains categorical assumptions and distinctions between criminal/non-criminal relations and these are propelled by automation to acquire a more synthetic role. The *technological construction of criminality* (or of criminal reality) as laid down in this chapter denotes precisely this conditioning.

Of course, the challenges that remain in the international dimension of tackling criminality are manifold and will continue to evolve. In this regard, it is important to emphasize again that the technological role of data sharing and collaborative work remains central and needs to be enhanced. But at the same time the emergence of suspicion by profiling through international collaborations constitutes an important step to be explored. The several dimensions discussed above, each entailing a number of other elements, illustrate that the role of technology is critical. While technology allows for the distributed communication of data, the processes that participate in extracting anti-criminal value from said data are more subtle; and it is in this context that fascinating new developments may occur and must be pursued.

8

Using the macro–micro integrated theoretical model to understand the dynamics of collective violence

OLAOLUWA OLUSANYA

Introduction

It is now widely acknowledged that the study of genocide and other forms of collective violence has largely been ignored within the criminological literature.[1] This comes as a surprise given the fact that genocide and crimes against humanity are particularly heinous types of collective violence and therefore one would have expected them to be of interest to criminologists. For instance, genocide occupies a special place as 'the crime of crimes'.[2] It has also been referred to as 'the world's most heinous crime',[3] or 'the worst of all crimes'.[4] At the very least, the lack of consideration of the topic of collective violence (especially genocide and crimes against humanity) is an important lacuna in the criminological literature and one that deserves far closer examination from a criminological and social science perspective.

Nevertheless, in recent years there has been a growing interest in the study of genocide and other complex forms of collective violence. Growing attention is being devoted towards applying criminological theories

1 D. Maier-Katkin, D. Mears and T. Bernard, 'Towards a Criminology of Crimes against Humanity', (2009) 13 *Theoretical Criminology* 227; G. Yacoubian, 'The (In)significance of Genocidal Behavior to the Discipline of Criminology', (2000) 34 *Crime, Law and Social Change* 7; C. Cunneen, 'Postcolonial Perspectives for Criminology', in M. Bosworth, and C. Hoyle, (eds.), *What is Criminology* (Oxford University Press, 2011) at 249–66.

2 *ICTR Prosecutor* v. *Kambanda*, Trial Chamber judgment (4 September 1998); P. Akhavan, 'The Crime of Genocide in the ICTR Jurisprudence', (2005) 3 *Journal of International Criminal Justice* 989; W. Ashby, *Writing History in International Criminal Trials*, (New York, NY: Cambridge University Press, 2011).

3 A. D'Amato, 'On Genocide', (2000) 75 *Naval War College International Law Studies* 119.

4 P. M. Wald, 'Genocide and Crimes against Humanity', (2007) 6 *Washington University Global Studies Law Review* 621.

to these crimes.[5] However, whether traditional criminological theories (for example, Agnew's general strain theory (GST)),[6] Gottfredson and Hirschi's general theory of crime (GTC)[7] and Sutherland's theory of differential association (DA, 1939)), which were designed to explain 'ordinary crimes' at the individual (for example, GST and GTC) or group level (for example, DA; note, however, that there is evidence to suggest that DA emanates from participant self-selection, in other words, birds of a feather flocking together[8]), can reasonably be generalized to genocide and other complex forms of collective violence remains open to doubt.[9] As will be demonstrated in this chapter, owing to their unique characteristics genocide and other complex forms of collective violence can only be explained by a theory that is able to accommodate a large number of variables (including, but not limited to, individual differences, social categories, social relationships, relevant situational variables and cognitive and emotional variables) and which in turn allows for interaction between them. In this regard, significant emphasis will be laid on the suitability and utility of the macro–micro integrated theoretical model (MMITM).[10]

This chapter is divided into three main sections. Section 1 will identify the main elements of collective violence. Section 2 will explain the main features of the MMITM. Lastly, Section 3 will go on to apply the MMITM to collective violence in order to demonstrate how this may work in practice.

[5] O. Olusanya, *Emotions, Decision-making and Mass Atrocities: Through the Lens of the Macro-Micro Integrated Theoretical Model* (Farnham: Ashgate, 2014); O. Olusanya, 'A Macro-Micro Integrated Theoretical Model of Mass Participation in Genocide', (2013) 53 *British Journal of Criminology* 843; J. Hagan and W. Rymond-Richmond, 'The Collective Dynamics of Racial Dehumanization and Genocidal Victimization in Darfur', (2008) 73 *American Sociological Review* 875; A. Brannigan, *Beyond the Banality of Evil: Criminology and Genocide* (Oxford University Press, 2013); A. Brannigan and K. H. Hardwick, 'Genocide and General Theory', in C. L. Britt and M. R. Gottfredson (eds.), *Control Theories of Crime and Delinquency* (New Brunswick, NJ: Transaction Publishing, 2003) at 109–31; A. Smeulers and L. Hoex, 'Studying the Micro-Dynamics of the Rwandan Genocide', (2010) 50 *British Journal of Criminology* 435.

[6] R. Agnew, 'The Contribution of Social-psychological Strain Theory to the Explanation of Crime and Delinquency', in F. Adler and W. S. Laufer (eds.), *The Legacy of Anomie Theory* (New Brunswick, NJ: Transaction Publishers, 1995) at 113–37.

[7] M. R. Gottfredson and T. Hirschi, *A General Theory of Crime* (Stanford, CA: Stanford University Press, 1990).

[8] See A. Walsh and C. Hemmens, *Introduction to Criminology: A Text/Reader* (2nd edn, Thousand Oaks, CA: Sage, 2011) at 145–6.

[9] For a critical review see Olusanya (2014), above note 5.

[10] Ibid.

Identifying the main elements of collective violence

It is logically impossible to discuss collective violence without first defining it or, at least, identifying its main elements. At present, there appears to be a growing synergy between different disciplines (for example, international criminal law, criminology, political science and public health). This disciplinary synergy is leading to a vision of collective violence that locates its thematic focus as situated in a social context, involves complex action and interaction between several actors (many of whom come to see themselves as part of a group with a common purpose), and that is generally characterized by instrumental aggression. By way of illustration, the political science literature has provided the following relevant definition of collective violence:

> The term collective violence means that the infliction of violence must be deliberately carried out by actors who are, or perceive themselves to be, part of a group with a common purpose beyond the immediate act of violence. Individual acts of violence, violent crime and general disorder are thus not included.[11]

In the same vein, the public health literature provides the following definition of collective violence:

> . . .instrumental use of violence by people who identify themselves as members of a group . . . against another group or set of individuals, in order to achieve political, economic or social objectives. Collective violence includes war, terrorism and violent political conflict between or within states, violence perpetrated by states (genocide, torture, systematic abuses of human rights) and organised violent crime such as gang warfare. It may include all categories of violence, be these physical, sexual, psychological, or characterised by neglect or discrimination.[12]

Furthermore, collective violence in international criminal law is defined in the same way as the above definitions. In addition, the legal concept of joint criminal enterprise (JCE) can be used to illustrate this point of view. JCE, despite criticisms as to its sources, structure, and development into a concrete legal principle from legal experts,[13] has become a

[11] M. Brzoska, 'Collective Violence beyond the Standard Definition of Armed Conflict', (2007) *SIPRI Yearbook* 94, at 96.

[12] A. Rutherford, A. B. Zwi, N. J. Grove and A. Butchart, 'Violence: A Glossary', (2007) 61 *Journal of Epidemiology & Community Health* 676, at 677.

[13] See, for example, K. Ambos, 'Joint Criminal Enterprise and Command Responsibility', (2007) 5 *Journal of International Criminal Justice* 159, who notes that it has become a useful tool for prosecuting collective criminality at the international level.

useful tool for prosecuting collective criminality at the international level. Moreover, the following statement by Osiel adds weight to this opinion: 'of the indictments entered since judicial acceptance of this doctrine [JCE] in 2001, nearly 65 percent rely on it. . .'.[14] In addition, in order to establish the existence of a JCE the prosecution must prove the following elements: a plurality of persons, the existence of a common plan, design or purpose which amounts to or involves the commission of a crime and participation of the accused in the common design.[15] The aforementioned elements are clearly indicative of collective violence. Furthermore, it is noteworthy to mention that JCE now appears to lie at the confluence of streams of thought pursued by several different disciplines. JCE is emerging as a useful conceptual framework for multidisciplinary research on collective violence. For instance, Hagan and Rymond-Richmond have developed a criminological approach that 'attempts to match the judicial construction of a "joint criminal enterprise"'.[16] Hagan and Rymond-Richmond made the following relevant statement in this regard:

> We found compelling evidence that collective processes of racial motivation and intent influenced the severity of victimization across settlements, above and beyond this influence at the individual level, and that this collective frame mediated the concentration of attacks on densely settled areas and particular African groups. This evidence documents the kinds of *organized social processes increasingly emphasized in international criminal law and is relevant to a social scientific determination that genocide did occur in Darfur. Specifically, our findings are consistent with a sociological theory of what international law recognizes as 'criminal organization,' 'common purpose,' and 'joint criminal enterprise'*.[17]

Drawing together relevant sources we can make a number of observations regarding collective violence. First, collective violence includes a systematic dimension comprising organized and goal-directed acts of violence. In addition, several cases provide further clarity regarding the

[14] M. Osiel, *Making Sense of Mass Atrocity* (New York, NY: Cambridge University Press, 2009) at 48.

[15] See, for example, C. H. Gibson, 'Testing the Legitimacy of the Joint Criminal Enterprise Doctrine in the ICTY: A Comparison of Individual Liability for Group Conduct in International and Domestic Law', (2007) 18 *Duke J Comp & Int'l L* 521, at 524.

[16] J. Savelsberg, *Crime and Human Rights: Criminology of Atrocities and Genocide* (London: Sage, 2010) at 70.

[17] Hagan and Rymond-Richmond, above note 5, at 895 (emphasis added).

meaning of 'systematic'. For instance, the International Criminal Tribunal for Rwanda (ICTR) Trial Chamber in the *Akayesu* case stated that:

> The concept of 'systematic' may be defined as thoroughly organised and following a regular pattern on the basis of a common policy involving substantial public or private resources. There is no requirement that this policy must be adopted formally as the policy of a state. There must however be some kind of preconceived plan or policy.[18]

Moreover, in the case against *Kunarac, Kovac and Vokovic*, the International Criminal Tribunal for the former Yugoslavia (ICTY) Appeals Chamber pointed out that: 'patterns of crimes that [constitute] the non-accidental repetition of similar criminal conduct on a regular basis are a common expression of [a] systematic occurrence'.[19] Similarly, the ICTY Trial Chamber in *Naletilic and Martinovic* held that: '[t]he element "systematic" requires an organised nature of the acts and the improbability of their random occurrence'.[20] Second, as will be discussed in more detail below, a high level of heterogeneity exists among participants in collective violence (for example, different personality traits).[21] Third, collective violence typically involves a large number of participants. For example, in 1997 an estimated 92,000 genocide suspects were locked up in Rwandan jails, all of whom were suspected of having assumed a greater or larger role in the preceding genocide.[22]

Explaining the main features of the MMITM

The MMITM aims to increase the explanatory power of traditional criminological theories by integrating them into a comprehensive multidisciplinary framework. The MMITM was developed to explain large-scale and complex criminal activities involving heterogeneous social

[18] *ICTR Prosecutor* v. *Akayesu*, Trial Chamber judgment (2 September 1998) para. 580.

[19] *ICTY Prosecutor* v. *Kunarac, Kovac and Vokovic*, Appeals Chamber judgment (2 June 2002) para. 94.

[20] *ICTY Prosecutor* v. *Naletilic and Martinovic*, Trial Chamber judgment (31 March 2003) para. 236.

[21] See, for example, C. R. Browning, *Ordinary Men: Reserve Police Battalion 101 and the Final Solution in Poland* (New York, NY: Harper/Collins, 1985) at 168; M. Mamdani, *When Victims Become Killers: Colonialism, Nativism, and the Genocide in Rwanda* (Princeton, NJ: Princeton University Press, 2001) at 224.

[22] A. M. Danner and J. S. Martinez, 'Guilty Associations: Joint Criminal Enterprise, Command Responsibility and the Development of International Criminal Law', (2005) 93 *California Law Review* 75.

networks characterized by complex webs of relationships between various micro, meso- and macro-level actors, however loosely or tightly organized, for the benefit of those participating in these criminal activities at the expense of others (for example, out-group members).

In addition, several features distinguish the MMITM from other theoretical approaches (such as GST, a GTC and rational choice theory). For instance, in contrast to traditional criminological theories, the MMITM recognizes the fact that emotions are essential for flexible and rational decision making,[23] and, as a result, views emotions as complex, dynamic systems made up of several separate components with different functions: physiological arousal, affect or subjective feelings, cognitive processes and action tendencies. Furthermore, the MMITM postulates that large-scale and complex criminal activities undertaken by a multitude of people will be unsuccessful if they are undertaken without emotions. For example, the emotion of trust[24] has been described as 'the emotional glue that can bond people to an organization'.[25] Moreover, fear has been identified as crucial for effective coordinated large-scale and complex criminal activities such as genocide, as is evident from the following statement:

> Seizing and maintaining control was not just a matter of passing laws and decrees, however; behind these measures was the use of terror. In the spring of 1933, units of the SA, SS, Gestapo, and police sealed off whole areas of towns and cities and combed them house by house (these operations were well planned and often involved hundreds of personnel), searching for anything and anyone considered anti-Nazi, leaving no stone unturned. The raids were accompanied by threats, beatings, and arbitrary

23 A. R. Damasio, *Descartes' Error* (New York, NY: Harcourt, 1994); G. L. Clore and J. R. Huntsinger, 'How Emotions Inform Judgment and Regulate Thought', (2007) 11 *Trends in Cognitive Sciences* 393; A. Bechara, 'The Role of Emotion in Decision-making: Evidence from Neurological Patients with Orbitofrontal Damage', (2004) 55 *Brain and Cognition* 30, at 30; A. Bechara, H. Damasio and A. R. Damasio, 'Emotion, Decision Making and the Orbitofrontal Cortex', (2000) 10 *Cerebral Cortex* 295.

24 R. Plutchik, *Emotions and Life: Perspectives of Psychology, Biology and Evolution* (Washington, DC: American Psychological Association, 2000); R. J. Vallerand, and C. M. Blanchard, 'The Study of Emotion in Sport and Exercise: Historical, Definitional, and Conceptual Perspectives', in Y. L. Hanin (ed.), *Emotion in Sport* (Champaign, IL: Human Kinetics, 2000) at 3–39.

25 W. Bennis, *The End of Leadership: Exemplary Leadership is Impossible without Full Inclusion, Initiative, and Cooperation of Followers* (Boulder, CO: Westview Press, 2006) at 139; L. A. Downey, J. Roberts and C. Stough, 'Workplace Culture Emotional Intelligence and Trust in the Prediction of Workplace Outcomes', (2011) 6 *International Journal of Business Science and Applied Management* 30, at 37.

> arrests. They created an atmosphere of fear and helplessness and the subsequent build-up of the Gestapo surveillance system made resistance very difficult and dangerous.[26]

The above statement demonstrates how the Nazis forced citizens to conform to their ideas and beliefs through fear and intimidation. Moreover, the MMITM seeks to bridge the divide between the individual and the group by merging personal self-interest with group self-interest via emotion-cognition interactions. The MMITM emphasizes, among other things, the importance of interactions between three types of participants in group violence: reluctant executioners, true believers and psychopaths. The MMITM postulates that emotional arousal and affiliation among group members might lead to depersonalization under conditions of high cognitive dissonance and that, as a result, individuals will not only categorize themselves as members of the in-group but will also react emotionally when situations or events affect the in-group. Therefore, individuals may eventually come to see themselves as interchangeable members of the in-group. The end result is relevant group-based emotions (for example, anger) and action tendencies (for example, revenge) toward the out-group (for example, as a righteous response to perceived harm or injustice). In the next section the MMITM will be applied to explain the necessary elements of collective violence

Applying the MMITM to the explanation of collective violence

The previous sections have identified the main elements of collective violence and explained the main features of the MMITM. The present section now aims to bring together the various elements identified above by applying the MMITM to the explanation of collective violence.

A large number of participants

The fact that collective violence involves a large number of participants poses a challenge for traditional criminological theories. Rational choice theory can be used to illustrate this point. Rational choice theory posits that collective criminal enterprises are no more than an aggregate of self-interested individuals. However, this assumption appears logically impossible. Why would rational, self-interested individuals work together

[26] P. Darman, *The Holocaust and Life Under Nazi Occupation* (New York, NY: The Rosen Publishing Group, 2012) at 25.

towards a common purpose? In this regard, Olson argued that 'rational, self-interested individuals will not act to achieve their common or group interests'.[27] In addition, Olson drew attention to the problem of free riding to illustrate his argument. In economics, the free-rider problem refers to a situation where an individual benefits from services (for example occupying land belonging to Tutsis) without paying for the cost relating to accruing the benefit (for example, non-participation in the violence against the Tutsis). In addition, it is well known that very large groups, as opposed simply to individuals, are particularly susceptible to free riding. As stated by Olson: 'the larger the group, the further it will fall short of providing an optimal amount of a collective good. In short, the larger the group, the less it will further its common interests.'[28] In the same light, Hardin (2003) made the following relevant statement:

> When the number of members of a group that would benefit from collective action is small enough, we might expect cooperation that results from extensive interaction, mutual monitoring, and even commitments to each other that trump or block narrowly self-interested actions. But when the group is very large, free riding is often clearly in the interest of most and perhaps all members.[29]

Moreover, in order to appreciate the extent of the challenge posed by the free-rider problem to a rational choice theory of collective violence it is necessary to consider the number of participants that are typically involved in large-scale forms of collective violence, such as genocide and crimes against humanity. In this regard, it should be pointed out that genocide and crimes against humanity are typically committed by tens of thousands of people who are under a mistaken belief that they are under 'attack' by an out-group aggressor and thereby mistakenly use force in 'self-defence' against members of that aggressor group.[30] For instance, Straus estimates the number of Hutu perpetrators of the mass violence against the Rwandan Tutsis at 175,000–210,000.[31] In addition, it

[27] M. Olson, *The Logic of Collective Action* (Cambridge, MA: Harvard University Press, 1965) at 2.

[28] Ibid., at 36.

[29] R. Hardin, 'The Free Rider Problem', in E. N. Zalta (ed.), *The Stanford Encyclopaedia of Philosophy* (Summer 2003 edition), available at http://plato.stanford.edu/archives/sum2003/entries/free rider/.

[30] G. Gahima, *Transitional Justice in Rwanda: Accountability for Atrocity* (London: Routledge, 2012) at 72–3.

[31] S. Straus, 'How Many Perpetrators were there in the Rwandan Genocide? An Estimate', (2004) 6 *Journal of Genocide Research* 85.

is worth mentioning that this is a very conservative estimate due to the fact that several forms of participation are excluded from Straus's definition, as is clearly evident from the following statement:

> Perpetrators thus would be those who directly killed or assaulted civilians and those who participated in groups that killed or assaulted. During the genocide, there were other kinds of participation. Many Rwandans joined state-ordered civilian night patrols. Sometimes the members of these patrols attacked civilians, and if they did they would be 'perpetrators' under my definition. However, if they did not, they would not be. There also was a significant amount of looting during the genocide. If killing accompanied the looting, then looters would be 'perpetrators' under my definition. However, if Rwandans looted property, but did not join attacks where civilians were killed, they would not be perpetrators. The central idea behind this definition is that a perpetrator is someone who materially participated in the murder or attempted murder of a non-combatant.[32]

From the perspective of rational choice theory one would expect that rational individuals will free ride on the contributions of others in the genocidal enterprise. In addition, it is possible to explain the sequence of effects or outcomes that might result from this free-riding behaviour. First, seeing that their contributions (which represent a cost to them; for example, the risk of future prosecution) will not make any real difference to the genocidal enterprise, since a considerable number of others are more than willing to contribute directly, rational individuals will decide to withhold their contributions and simply free ride off the contribution of others. Second, their decision will most likely lead to lower participation rates. Third, if that turns out to be the case, observing that not enough others will continue to contribute to the genocidal enterprise, rational individuals will decide once again to withhold their contribution in order to avoid an unnecessary waste. Therefore, the logical outcome is that collective violence will be impossible to effectuate either way (in other words, when participation rates are high or low) because rational individuals will come to the conclusion that it makes no difference whether they contribute to the genocidal enterprise or not. As stated by Shilling and Mellor: '. . .if every individual acted "rationally", the aggregate outcome would be the collapse of the union and its power'.[33]

[32] Ibid., at 87.

[33] C. Shilling and P. A. Mellor, *The Sociological Ambition: Elementary Forms of Social and Moral Life* (London: Sage, 2001) at 173. This statement, while made in relation to participation in a trade union, nevertheless has implications for understanding collective violence.

In contrast to rational choice theory and its focus on the aggregated effects of individual self-interest, the MMITM posits that social identity is the 'social glue' that binds participants in collective violence together. The MMITM views social identity as a function of the emotional significance placed on a particular group membership and emphasizes the critical role played by emotions in this process. In this regard Tajfel defined social identity as 'the individual's knowledge that he belongs to certain social groups together with some emotional and value significance to him of this group membership'.[34] The MMITM argues that the salience of group membership has a transformative effect on personal self-interests. In other words, it shifts social identity from the self ('my own best interests') to the collective ('our own best interests'), thereby creating a cooperative orientation within the group.[35]

Organized and goal-directed acts of violence

As stated earlier, collective violence includes a systematic element, that is, organized and goal-directed acts of violence. This element rules out acts that are unplanned, reactionary, impulsive and driven by intense emotions.[36] In this regard, it should be pointed out that both

[34] H. Tajfel, 'La catégorisation sociale', in S. Moscovici (ed.), *Introduction à la psychologie sociale* (Paris: Larousse, Vol. 1, 1972) 272, at 292.

[35] C. J. Turner, 'Some Current Issues in Research on Social Identity and Self-Categorization Theories', in N. Ellemers, R. Spears and B. Doojse (eds.), *Social Identity: Context, Commitment, Content* (Oxford: Blackwell, 1999) at 6; M. B. Brewer and R. M. Kramer, 'Choice Behavior in Social Dilemmas: Effects of Social Identity, Group Size, and Decision Framing', (1986) 50 *Journal of Personality and Social Psychology* 543; R. M. Kramer and M. B. Brewer, 'Effects of Group Identity on Resource Use in a Simulated Commons Dilemma', (1984) 46 *Journal of Personality and Social Psychology* 1044; M. van Vugtand and C. M. Hart, 'Social Identity as Social Glue: The Origins of Group Loyalty', (2004) 86 *Journal of Personality and Social Psychology* 585; B. Zdaniuk and J. M. Levine, 'Group Loyalty: Impact of Members' Identification and Contributions', (2001) 37 *Journal of Experimental Social Psychology* 502; K. L. Dion, 'Cohesiveness as a Determinant of Ingroup-Outgroup Bias', (1973) *28 Journal of Personality and Social Psychology* 163; D. T. Miller, J. S. Downs and D. A. Prentice, 'Minimal Conditions for the Creation of a Unit Relationship: The Social Bonds between Birthday Mates', (1998) 28 *European Journal of Social Psychology* 475.

[36] See, for example, E. S. Barratt, 'Measuring and Predicting Aggression within the Context of a Personality Theory', (1991) 3 *Journal of Neuropsychiatry* 35; R. J. Houston, M. S. Stanford, N. R. Villemarette-Pittman, S. M. Conklinand and L. E. Helfritz, 'Neurobiological Correlates and Clinical Implications of Aggressive Subtypes', (2003) 3 *Journal of Forensic Neuropsychology* 67; D. G. Cornell, J. Warren, G. Hawk, E. Stafford, G. Oramand and D. Pine, 'Psychopathy in Instrumental and Reactive Violent Offenders', (1996) 64 *Journal of Consulting and Clinical Psychology* 783; K. A. Dodge and J. D. Coie, 'Social-

GST[37] and the GTC are associated with reactive aggression.[38] Therefore, both have comparatively little explanatory power with respect to collective violence. For instance, Friedrichs and Schwartz made the following relevant statement in relation to the GTC:

> . . .adopting Gottfredson and Hirschi's view pushes us to focus on some forms of crime over others and to exclude vast territories of criminal activities that somehow do not correspond to their theory. Essentially, by definition, low self-control theory would have us think of crime mainly in terms of impulsive, . . . simplistic actions (such as smash and grab thefts and assaults) while largely discouraging our interest in other forms of crime . . . [p. 147] In contrast to Gottfredson and Hirschi's approach, the notion of low self-control is problematic here, because the degree of control by others rather than impulsivity or a focus on immediate benefits seems to be the key factor in compliance or non compliance with organizational efforts to control the behaviour of employees.[39]

Moreover, the fact that '[i]n general strain theory, Agnew uses a frustration-aggression approach to explain all forms of crime not just those involving aggression',[40] is important because 'reactive aggression has its theoretical roots in the frustration-aggression model'.[41] Thus the frustration-aggression model serves as a conceptual bridge between GST and reactive aggression.

The remainder of this section seeks to challenge the existing dichotomy between two forms of collective violence: bureaucratic violence and mob violence. Mob violence, is viewed as fundamentally spontaneous, irrational, random and unorganized. It is widely assumed that 'members of the mob usually experience strong emotions, and [that] the behaviour and reactions of the mob are considered to be fairly irrational'.[42]

Information-Processing Factors in Reactive and Proactive Aggression in Children's Peer Groups', (1987) 53 *Personality and Social Psychology* 1146; S. J. Kingsbury, M. T. Lambert and W. Hendrickse, 'A Two-Factor Model of Aggression', (1997) 60 *Psychiatry* 224.

[37] R. B. Felson, 'A Rational Choice Approach to Violence', in M. A. Zahn, H. H. Brownstein and S. L. Jackson (eds.), *Violence: From Theory to Research* (Newark, NJ: LexisNexis/ Anderson, 2004) at 72.

[38] D. O. Friedrichs and M. D. Schwartz, 'Low Self-Control or High Organizational Control? The Paradoxes of White-Collar Crime', in E. Goode (ed.), *Out of control?* (Stanford, CA: Stanford University Press, 2008) at 147–9.

[39] Ibid., at 148–9. [40] See Agnew, above note 6, and Felson, above note 37, at 72.

[41] D. Connor, *Aggression and Antisocial Behavior in Children and Adolescents: Research and Treatment* (New York, NY: The Guildford Press, 2002) at 15.

[42] See, for example, D. Olweus, 'School Bullying: Development and Some Important Challenges', (2013) 9 *Annual Review of Clinical Psychology* 751, at 753; G. Lindzey (ed.), *Handbook of Social Psychology* (Cambridge, MA: Addison-Wesley, Vol. 1, 1954).

In addition, this view has to some extent permeated research on collective violence. This is evident, for example, in the following statement by Maier-Katkin, Mears and Bernard, which was made in relation to the brutal slaughter of Polish Jews at Jedwabne by their own Polish neighbours:

> [W]hen the original sources of strain and arousal are invisible or invulnerable, it is likely that aggression will be displaced onto visible and vulnerable targets in the immediate environment. In Jedwabne, local Catholic Poles, *guided by the leaders among them, responded to the strain of insecurity and political oppression by targeting the only group to which they could safely direct their anger and aggression—the local Jews.* Notably, if the angry aggression arising under this confluence of circumstances is directed at the cause of strain – at the Nazi invaders of Jedwabne, for example – it would not constitute a crime against humanity, but rather self-defense, resistance or martyrdom.[43]

It appears from the above statement that frustration–aggression–displacement theory was applied to explain the behaviour and reactions of the Polish mob. The problem however, is that there is scant, if any, empirical evidence for the frustration–aggression–displacement theory.[44] Whitley and Kite made the following statement in this regard:

> Another problem is that frustration aggression theory is, at heart, a theory of individual, not group behaviour: the theory cannot explain why individual frustration should result in scapegoating of groups . . . prejudiced people seem to be aggressive against everyone, not just the targets of their prejudices as the theory would predict.[45]

In the same vein Woolf and Hulsizer commented that:

> [C]ontemporary researchers have found that frustrated individuals lash out against any out-group – regardless whether the group is liked or disliked . . . Obviously, other factors besides simply being an out-group influenced the decisions to target . . . Tutsis for extreme levels of persecution and genocide . . .[46]

[43] Maier-Katkin, Mears and Bernard, above note 1, at 247 (emphasis added).

[44] B. Whitley and M. Kite, *The Psychology of Prejudice and Discrimination* (Cengage Learning, 2010) at 348.

[45] Ibid., at 348. See also J. Duckitt, *The Social Psychology of Prejudice* (New York, NY: Praeger Publishers, 1992/94).

[46] L. M. Woolf and M. R. Hulsizer, 'Psychosocial Roots of Genocide: Risk, Prevention, and Intervention', (2005) 7 *Journal of Genocide Research* 101.

Furthermore, in contrast to mob violence, bureaucratic violence is considered to involve organization, coordination and goal direction.[47] In addition, to some extent, the following statement by Osiel captures the dichotomy between bureaucratic violence and mob violence:

> Even so, it would surely be wrong to describe seemingly wanton local grudge fests as irrelevant to the rulers' aims, when rulers know that these very animosities will be unleashed and that their expression can be directed in ways that advance larger regime goals. Here we may have neither a bureaucracy nor a network united by common purpose exactly but something more like 'anomie', almost 'crowd behaviour'. The latter is a concept that – because of its implications of irrationality – sociologists sympathetic to mass movements have spent a century trying to flee. In the archetypal crowd, Durkheim wrote, 'each one is borne along by the rest' into an impassioned, trance-like state of ecstasy, bordering on automatism ... in reality, this conception of the relevant behaviour as crowd-induced automatism, goes much too far in stripping genocide from its social and administrative roots. Even in Rwanda, for instance, where riotous crowds appeared prominent, violence was not random or truly spontaneous, but well organized and directed primarily against members of one ethnic group by those of another. The resulting genocide thus cannot be ascribed to the immediate experience of 'the crowd' itself in liberating normal restraints on destructive passions. Moreover, despite some journalistic reporting of orgiastic frenzy, more thorough accounts have stressed the organized and routinized nature of most work done by Hutu killing teams.[48]

However, Osiel seems to have overlooked one important fact, that is, mob violence can be spontaneous and simultaneously goal-directed. In this regard, is the following observation by Ohlin:

> It is important to realize that in such situations, the intention of each individual regarding the actions of the crowd arises somewhat spontaneously, without prior deliberation, but this does not mean that there is no intention or coordination at all. Spontaneous and intentional coordination should not be confused with no coordination at all.[49]

Ohlin, however, failed to clarify this conceptual paradox, that is, a spontaneous form of JCE or a situation in which the decision to

[47] Z. Bauman, *Modernity and the Holocaust* (Cambridge: Polity, 1989).

[48] See Osiel, above note 14, at 69–70.

[49] J. D. Ohlin, 'Joint Intentions to Commit International Crimes', (2011) Cornell Law Faculty Publications, Paper 169, available at http://scholarship.law.cornell.edu/facpub/169, at 730.

participate in purposeful or goal-directed behaviour appears to have been (at most) coincidental with joining other crowd participants who are perhaps meeting each other for the first time.

Arguably, the MMITM is able to clarify this paradoxical situation. The MMITM makes the following propositions. First, it posits that crowd events heighten social identity salience[50] and that in turn the activation of a social identity is sufficient to result in depersonalization.[51] Second, as a result of depersonalization, members will pay close attention to the facial expressions (angry facial expressions) of fellow group members and will be more likely to mimic their angry facial expressions.[52] Third, afferent facial feedback will influence their internal emotional experience, in other words they will also experience anger.[53] Fourth, this in turn will increase the likelihood of hostile collective action against the out-group. Notably, this is an automatic process.[54] Thus, regardless of where they congregate, as long as they are located in settings in which their social identity becomes salient (for example, in a bureaucratic organization or a crowd), individuals, guided by group norms, will act in an organized and goal-directed manner that is consistent with the aforementioned characteristics.

[50] M. A. Hogg, 'Social Categorization, Depersonalization and Group Behavior', in M. A. Hogg and R. S. Tindale (eds.), *Blackwell Handbook of Social Psychology: Group Processes* (Oxford: Blackwell, 2001) 56, at 63.

[51] J. E. Stets and P. J. Burke, 'Identity Theory and Social Identity Theory', (2000) 63 *Social Psychology Quarterly* 224, at 231.

[52] T. L. Chartrand and J. A. Bargh, 'The Chameleon Effect: The Perception–Behaviour Link and Social Interaction', (1999) 6 *Journal of Personality and Social Psychology* 893; A. Dijksterhuis and J. A. Bargh, 'The Perception–Behavior Expressway: Automatic Effects of Social Perception on Social Behavior', in M. P. Zanna (ed.), *Advances in Experimental Social Psychology* (San Diego, CA: Academic Press, 2001) 1, at 33; M. Yuki, W. W. Maddux and M. Brewer, 'Cross-cultural Differences in Relationship- and Group-based Trust', (2005) 31 *Personality and Social Psychology Bulletin* 48, at 49; R. B. van Baaren, W. W. Maddux, T. L. Chartrand, C. de Bouterand and A. van Knippenberg, 'It Takes Two to Mimic: Behavioral Consequences of Self-Construals', (2003) 84 *Journal of Personality and Social Psychology* 1093.

[53] J. van der Schalk, *Echoing Emotions: Reactions to Emotional Displays in Intergroup Context*, a dissertation submitted in partial fulfilment of the requirements for the degree of Doctor of Philosophy in Psychology, Faculty of Social and Behavioural Sciences, University of Amsterdam (2010), available at http://dare.uva.nl/document/175795, at 62.

[54] Ibid., at 62.

Group heterogeneity

In contrast to criminological theories that seek to homogenize participants in collective violence, for example, Agnew's GST, Gottfredson and Hirschi's GTC and rational choice theory, and consistent with the literature on collective violence,[55] the MMITM postulates that these perpetrators, especially at the outset, represent a highly heterogeneous group with different beliefs, emotions and attitudes towards members of a targeted group. In essence: 'the good the bad and the ugly'. These three disparate sub-groups, despite their differences, at some point in the course of destructive events, appear to work together to achieve a common criminal objective. From this perspective, it becomes important to recognize that collective violence involves associations between individuals following different pathways, and, in addition, it is important to appreciate the fact that participants in collective violence are motivated by a variety of different incentives (for example, positive stimuli such as monetary incentives, opportunities for rape and plunder; or negative stimuli such as group pressure).

Furthermore, the MMITM emphasizes, among other things, the importance of interactions between three types of participants in collective violence: reluctant executioners, true believers and psychopaths. True believers are people whose negative emotions are attributable to an early onset of cognitive, physiological and behavioural synchronization in response to the evaluation of an external stimulus event that is highly relevant to them. The Rwandan Hutu militia, known as the *Interahamwe*, and Sudan's mysterious Arab militia, referred to as the *Janjaweed*, arguably belong to this category. Moreover, true believers are more likely to suffer from antisocial personality disorder (ASPD) emanating from any given combination of different factors, including: genetic predisposition, environmental factors or community risk factors such as poverty, socioeconomic status or unemployment.[56] In addition, the empirical evidence suggests that people with ASPD exhibit traits of impulsivity, high negative emotionality and low conscientiousness, and that such people are biased towards negative or threatening cues.[57] The following statement by Prunier, which was made in relation to the *Interahamwe* in the

[55] See, for example, B. A. Valentino, *Final Solutions: Mass Killing and Genocide in the Twentieth Century* (Ithaca, NY, and London: Cornell University Press, 2004) at 40–1.

[56] For a review of the empirical evidence see Olusanya (2014), above note 5.

[57] Ibid.

context of the Rwandan atrocities, arguably adds weight to the view that ASPD is associated with low socio-economic status:

> In Kigali the Interahamwe ... had tended to recruit mostly among the poor. As soon as they went into action, they drew around them a cloud of even poorer people, a lumpenproletariat of street boys, rag-pickers, car-washers and homeless unemployed. For these people [men] the genocide was the best thing that could ever happen to them. They had the blessings of a form of authority to take revenge on socially powerful people as long as they were on the wrong side of the political fence. They could steal, they could kill with minimum justification, they could rape and they could get drunk for free. This was wonderful. The political aims pursued by the masters of this dark carnival were quite beyond their scope. They just went along, knowing it would not last.[58]

The same is true of the work of Brosché and Rothbart, who emphasized, just like Prunier, the low socio-economic level of livelihood of the *Janjaweed* in the context of the Darfur atrocities, which serves to confirm the association with ASPD:

> Early on in the Darfur crisis, the government converted these loosely affiliated pockets into an organized military group through training, indoctrination, and promises of material reward. The government also sought to exploit the poverty and experiences of marginalization that many Darfuri Arabs endured by enticing their young men to serve in a campaign against their hated non-Arab neighbours. The government even supplied them with uniforms and insignia of the national army. Furthermore, the government released prisoners to fight for the Janjaweed and gave impunity for certain communities that fought alongside the SAF [the Sudan Armed Forces].[59]

On the other hand, 'reluctant perpetrators' are people who demonstrate a low propensity for crime. These are essentially people with strong morals and a strong sense of justice. It is therefore assumed that their strong moral inhibitions will make them more susceptible to experiencing high levels of emotional dissonance arising from a discrepancy between their inner feelings and outward expressions. One would expect them to

[58] G. Prunier, *The Rwanda Crisis: History of a Genocide* (New York, NY: Columbia University Press, 1995) at 231–2; see, also, D. W. Black, *Bad Boys, Bad Men: Confronting Antisocial Personality Disorder (Sociopathy)* (New York, NY: Oxford University Press, 2013); V. Murali and F. Oyebode, 'Poverty, Social Inequality and Mental Health', (2004) 10 *Advances in Psychiatric Treatment* 216.

[59] J. Brosché and D. Rothbart, *Violent Conflict and Peacebuilding: The Continuing Crisis in Darfur* (London: Routledge, 2013) at 15.

undergo a process whereby surface acting develops into deep acting. The end result is that the emotions felt by these individuals will become totally congruent with what the genocidal enterprise requires.

In contrast to true believers and reluctant executioners, psychopathic individuals demonstrate deficits in emotional response. It appears that psychopaths play only a minimal role in mass atrocities. In this regard, it should be pointed out that psychopathy is a personality disorder characterized among other things by a lack of empathy and remorse and that a lack of empathy and remorse increases the propensity for sadistic violence.[60]

There remains, however, a crucial question: why do birds of different feathers flock together? A possible explanation for this unusual phenomenon is that true believers and psychopaths, acting as agents of a genocidal state, may have used coercive methods to force reluctant executioners to take part in collective violence. As a result, reluctant executioners may have experienced a gradual erosion of their moral motivations and behavioural inhibitions. Therefore, reluctant executioners, under such stressful circumstances, may have eventually begun to think, act and feel like other genocidal group members as a result of having incorporated elements of the collective identity (albeit forcibly) into their social identity.[61]

Conclusion

How are disparate groups of people brought together for the duration of a specific, time-limited criminal project? How do we evaluate the fit of each individual in terms of his or her likelihood of following each offending trajectory? How do we trace these distinct offending trajectories? And how is evil unknowingly perpetrated by the 'good', who clearly constitute the majority of perpetrators? The foregoing discussion has demonstrated the usefulness of the MMITM in solving these complex questions. As pointed out earlier, the MMITM was developed to explain large-scale and complex criminal activities involving heterogeneous social networks characterized by complex webs of relationships between

[60] S. E. Holt, J. R. Meloy and S. Strack, 'Sadism and Psychopathy in Violent and Sexually Violent Offenders', (1999) 27 *Journal of the American Academy of Psychiatry and Law* 23; S. Porterand and M. Woodworth, 'Psychopathy and Aggression', in C. J. Patrick (ed.), *Handbook of Psychopathy* (New York, NY: Guilford Press, 2006) 481.

[61] For an in-depth discussion see Olusanya (2014), above note 5.

various micro-, meso-, and macro-level actors, however loosely or tightly organized, for the benefit of those participating in these criminal activities at the expense of others (for example, out-group members). In addition, emotion-cognition interactions constitute an important component of the MMITM. As stated above, in contrast to traditional criminological theories, the MMITM recognizes that emotions are essential for flexible and rational decision making, and views emotions as complex, dynamic, systems made up of several separate components with different functions: physiological arousal, affect or subjective feelings, cognitive processes, and action tendencies. Finally, from the perspective of the MMITM, collective violence, in other words, organized and goal-directed large-scale acts of violence, cannot occur without emotions.

9

The anthropological dimension of international crimes and international criminal justice

ILIAS BANTEKAS

Introduction

The enforcement of norms involves a series of objective actions, in the sense that what is at stake is not the perspective of the judge, the prosecutor, the accused or the victim as to the appropriateness and legitimacy of the relevant law. On the contrary, subjectivity should play no role in the administration of criminal law and the entire criminal justice system operates in such a way as to avoid the infusion of personal biases. This, of course, is welcome because the law is already publicly available and hence any personal views of the judge or the prosecutor would violate the principle against retroactivity. Hence, this chapter attempts to explain why a departure is necessary in order to understand the particular context of societies in conflict and the social interactions inherent therein. For a very long time, international crimes have been assessed solely on the basis of the norms regulating armed conflict and criminal conduct, absent a thorough examination of the social and cultural context within which the relevant actors existed. However, what is different between the perspective of culture and society provided by anthropology as opposed to other social sciences is its particular vantage point; that is, its view of society and culture from the point of view of the direct participants under observation. The anthropologist is interested in the way that his subjects view family, lineage, religion, work, socialisation and everything else that makes them who they are and behave in the way they do. It is therefore no accident that the term *cultural relativism*, which is so prevalent in human rights discourse, originated in anthropology but possessed from the outset a very different meaning.[1] Boas, who first conceived but did

[1] In human rights it is taken to mean that culture ultimately validates the legitimacy and application of particular rights, thereby rejecting the notion that human rights apply to all

not coin the term, was dissatisfied with evolutionist theories of his time, which viewed some civilisations as higher or superior to others. To him cultural relativism was a method of examining cultural variation free from prejudice. Given that prejudice is inherent in all observation of the external world, Boas sought to see the world from the eyes of the informants, or natives (the term is not used pejoratively).[2] It is only when one possesses a good enough understanding of the lives of others that one is legitimised to offer moral judgement against them and, in the case at hand, to apply criminal sanctions in a just and equitable manner.

As the chapter goes on to demonstrate, our understanding of a particular culture prior to the outbreak of hostilities or mass human rights violations serves numerous purposes which for the most part have been outside the radar of contemporary international criminal tribunals and their respective mandates. At a functional level, anthropology may tell us what the affected societies aspire to and what they think about international criminal justice,[3] which in turn should shape – not necessarily dictate – the international community's relevant transitional justice policies.[4] This aside, culture paints a fairly accurate picture as regards hierarchies, membership and affiliation in clans and kinship mechanisms, which in turn helps determine complex liabilities, such as command responsibility and joint criminal enterprise

without distinction; i.e., that human rights are universal. This conception of culture risks justifying violations of human rights, as is the case with the practice of female genital mutilation. See J. Donnelly, 'Cultural Relativism and Universal Human Rights', (1984) 6 *Human Rights Quarterly* 400.

[2] F. Boas, 'Museums of Ethnology and their Classification', (1887) 9 *Science* 589.

[3] See P. Pham and P. Vinck, 'Research Note on Attitudes about Peace and Justice in Northern Uganda', Human Rights Centre at UC Berkeley Report (August 2007) at 2. Of those surveyed in Northern Uganda 29 per cent were in favour of the ICC, 28 per cent preferred Ugandan courts, 20 per cent were in favour of the amnesty commission, while only 3 per cent supported the sole use of traditional justice mechanisms. However, when asked if they favoured peace with amnesty or peace with trials, 80 per cent of the respondents supported peace with amnesty.

[4] Anthropology has been employed extensively by the International Bank for Reconstruction and Development (IBRD) in relation to projects that affect the livelihoods of indigenous peoples. In most recorded cases, however, the IBRD ignores the true wishes of the affected group and is disinclined towards any form of consensual social engineering. In the case of the indigenous Baka/Bakola of Cameroon, for example, the group wished to escape their subservient status to another tribe and acquire land and educate their children. The consultants advised the IBRD to retain the group's traditional nomadic status and simply to provide them with monetary forms of compensation for the impact caused by the project to their traditional livelihood. See T. Griffiths, 'Indigenous Peoples and the World Bank: Experiences with Participation' (Forest Peoples Program, 2005), available at www.forestpeoples.org/sites/fpp/files/publication/2011/08/wbipsandparticipjul05eng.pdf.

(JCE), among others. Moreover, anthropological observation helps us decipher the contextual meaning of concepts that verge between the social and the natural sciences, such as race, ethnicity and gender, by means of their *social construction*. This chapter paves the way for the realisation of the crucial function of anthropology in the investigation of mass crimes and the need for specialist research alongside legal developments.

Why anthropology is relevant to the investigation of international crimes

Anthropology and law seem at first glance to have nothing in common. The first seeks to elucidate collective human behaviour and assess the particular meanings understood by the participants (or *informants* in anthropological parlance), whereas the second is concerned with rules and order. It is evident that, since rules and order are not produced in a void but rather with a view to regulating human relations, it follows that law is a necessary component of culture in the same manner as work, leisure, art, religion and others.[5] Law need not necessarily be formal, as is otherwise the case with legislation that is promulgated under strict constitutional procedures, but it may just as well be informal without the sanction of government. This informal law does not only exist in past and present rural societies in the heartlands of Africa and Asia, but also in the very midst of industrialised Western societies. The so-called *lex mercatoria* and the pursuit of self-regulation by particular industries, as is indeed the very concept of contract and party autonomy thereto, is evidence of man's desire to regulate in certain cases human interaction by means of informal, but no less binding, prescriptions.[6] Besides regulating human relations, both formal and informal law, particularly the latter, provide evidence of social relations, status and social interaction within a given community. By way of illustration, the village chief is typically the judge and the recognised authority in the interpretation of customary law and, as such, is regarded as a revered figure. Equally, the male warriors of the tribe, whose authority to hunt is recognised as a

5 For a general overview, see J. M. Conley and W. M. O'Barr, 'Legal Anthropology comes Home: A Brief History of the Ethnographic Study of Law', (1993) 27 *Loyola of Los Angeles Law Review* 41.

6 According to Teubner, the ultimate validation of *lex mercatoria* rests on the fact that not all legal orders are created by the nation state and, accordingly, that private orders of regulation can create law. G. Teubner, 'Global Bukowina: Legal Pluralism in the World Society', in G. Teubner (ed.), *Global Law without a State* (Dartmouth, 1997) at 15.

customary entitlement, may enjoy first rights to the tribe's game. Social status and the existence of complex roles and rules are also evident in the internal sphere of criminal gangs operating in industrialised settings.[7] In Islamic law, too, the *social* from the *legal* is inseparable in countries strictly adhering to classical *Shariah*. For example, the inferior status ascribed to women in terms of entitlements (e.g., the right to be elected, weight of testimony, etc.) also determines their social status.

The study of social interaction should have been of primary importance to international criminal tribunals, but in practice it has been peripheral if not outright redundant. The Office of the Prosecutor (OTP) in the International Criminal Tribunal for the former Yugoslavia (ICTY) and the International Criminal Tribunal for Rwanda (ICTR) did assess various background aspects to the conflicts in Yugoslavia and Rwanda, but the emphasis was on political and military organisation. The prosecutors and their assistants were naturally lawyers, some of them successful prosecutors in their own jurisdictions, where the nature of crimes was pretty straightforward and background assessments were unnecessary. Hence, no one even considered that perceptions about class, ethnicity, race, symbolism, peace, aggression, and the like, by the natives themselves were of any significance to the work of the tribunals. This is a particularly significant observation given that two of the stated aims of the tribunals were their capacity to record history and promote reconciliation.[8] It is certainly difficult to record the nature of particular discord without a solid understanding of the views and perceptions of the participants in the turmoil. Equally, reconciliation is meaningless unless one is acutely aware of the divisions of the feuding parties as expressed and felt by them alone; although, admittedly, external, unbiased, views are also significant.

[7] See J. D. Vigil, 'Urban Violence and Street Gangs', (2003) 32 *Annual Review of Anthropology* 225; D. Lamm Weisel, *Contemporary Gangs: An Organisational Analysis* (LBF Scholarly Publishing, 2002).

[8] For example, reference to universally accepted anthropological thinking about aggression could have been incorporated in the historical analyses of the Tribunals' judgment. According to this, there is no empirical basis to the contention that aggression is an inborn quality. In fact, the word itself is unknown in the more traditional societies, such as the Chewong in the Malay Peninsula. If anything, humans exhibit a disposition towards solidarity and peace. See S. Howell and R. Willis (eds.), *Societies at Peace* (Routledge, 1989) at 25 ff. Without such an analysis the Tribunal may well, inadvertently or otherwise, give the impression to the entire world that the perpetrator's entire ethnic group is naturally inclined towards violent crime, which cannot surely lead to any sort of reconciliation and explains to a large degree the hostility of the Serbian people towards the ICTY.

The ICTY, in a very cursory manner, opined that Bosnian Muslim identity and culture was traced to 'the long Turkish' occupation[9] and that the three ethnic groups (i.e., Muslim, Serb and Croat) lived largely in separate villages but often intermarried,[10] and that in any event they all considered themselves Slav.[11] It concluded its anthropological analysis by claiming that 'politics began to divide along the lines of ethno-national communities'.[12] This, of course, fails to say anything about the actual identity and culture professed by Bosnians. Culture, by way of illustration, is a complex phenomenon and scholars such as Geertz have viewed it as a web of shared meanings expressed through public communication, not in the sense of sharing the same knowledge and skills but in the sense that persons who in fact share a culture share a common world view that is expressed through common symbols and language.[13] What is this Slavic world view in Bosnia and what metaphors or literal meanings are used to express it? Moreover, if the people of Bosnia had achieved social integration, how was this possible given their conflicting individual/clan tendencies? There are various ways of thinking about this conundrum, so I will mention only two. Barth believed that shared values, expressed through interaction, are the result of strategic and calculating *transactions* between agents driven by a desire to achieve value maximisation.[14] For Bourdieu, in order to assess whether the members of a group share or do not share common values one must distinguish that which is taken for granted by the group and that which is beyond discussion (*doxa*), such as faith in God or unquestionable adherence to a political system, from things that are actively discussed among group members and are not therefore axiomatic (opinion).[15] If we knew precisely what constituted common or disparate *doxic* perceptions among the various groups in Bosnia, pertinent choices would have been severely curtailed and we would also understand by default which *doxic* beliefs may have in time shifted to the realm of opinion. In fact, anthropology has largely dismissed the notion of static ethnic identity

[9] *ICTY Prosecutor* v. *Tadić*, Trial Judgment (7 May 1997), para. 56. In reality, a Turkish nation and distinct Turkish culture were proclaimed in the early 1920s, although the neo-Turkish movement was active at least a decade before. Until then, from the fourteenth to the early twentieth century what the ICTY calls 'Turkish' was in fact distinctly Ottoman, which was quintessentially multicultural, as are all empires.

[10] Ibid., para. 64. [11] Ibid., para. 67. [12] Ibid., para. 83.

[13] C. Geertz, *The Interpretation of Cultures* (Basic Books, 1973).

[14] F. Barth, 'Models of Social Organisation' (Royal Anthropological Institute Occasional Paper No. 23, 1966). These transactions are numerous and are continuously negotiated by the relevant actors.

[15] P. Bourdieu, *Outline of a Theory of Practice* (Cambridge University Press, 1977) at 164–70.

based merely on the enjoyment of a particular culture and belonging to a specific ethnic group.[16] Boundaries between ethnic groups, especially those living in close proximity to one another, are ambiguous and in a state of continuous fluctuation. The characterisation by the ICTY that the Slav population of Bosnia in 1993 identified itself along three ethnic groups with some inter-marriages is at best simplistic, but in reality it was wrong and was not predicated on any scientific data. Anthropologists studying Bosnian society agreed with the general theory that variations among ethnic groups are greater on key indicators than in respect of their systematic differences. They dismissed the conflict(s) as ethnic or that it could be explained by reference to culture and ancient animosities.

> The conflicts were relatively recent and they were not caused in any way by cultural differences. In important respects, the differences between town and country were greater than between, for example, Serbs and Croats sharing the same territory.[17]

As the chapter will subsequently demonstrate, anthropological research is not only important for possessing a clear understanding of the background of conflicts and the motives of the immediate perpetrators and their victims. It provides us, among others, with the necessary tools for deciphering the elements of international crimes, such as 'racial',[18] 'ethnic' and 'religious' in respect of genocide, accessory liability and JCE in respect of 'kinship',[19] and

16 See F. Barth, *Ethnic Groups and Boundaries: The Social Organisation of Culture Difference* (Little, Brown & Co, 1969).

17 T. Hylland Eriksen, *What is Anthropology?* (Pluto Press, 2004) at 158.

18 It is interesting to note that the science of genetics has long disproved the existence of distinct races as such. Nonetheless, race as a social construction remains important because it tells us how people view themselves and others.

19 In *ICTR Prosecutor* v. *Akayesu*, Trial Chamber Judgment (2 September 1998), para. 81, the Trial Chamber did make some mention to kinship, arguing that Rwandan society was comprised of eighteen clans whose distinguishing feature was lineage as opposed to ethnicity. Even so, the Tribunal argued, the demarcation line was blurred and people could pass through each clan. The Trial Chamber then went on to discuss the views and considerations not of the local population about their membership but of their colonisers: ibid., at paras. 82–4. This lacks any sound methodology and when later the Chamber was forced to admit that the Genocide Convention does not encompass conduct against members of one's own ethnic or racial group, it had to turn to particular perceptions of the perpetrators and the victims. This *selective anthropology* is misleading and is utilised only in order to serve a particular conclusion. The vast literature on African kinship would have made it abundantly clear that in weakly integrated African nations the operational level of political power is located at the kinship level of the periphery. As a result, *de facto* power based on kinship is usually much stronger than *de jure* power structures. See L. Holy, *Anthropological Perspectives on Kinship* (Pluto Press, 1996).

'loyalty' and 'clan membership', all of which lose their meaning if subject merely to strict legal characterisations.

At yet another dimension, the labours and methods of anthropology assist us in distinguishing between myth and reality and give us a fundamental idea about *mens rea* and *mens rea*-related defences and excuses. D argues that he killed his mother but in fact it could very well have been a distant cousin, simply because his linguistic tradition uses a single word for all females in his lineage. This is pretty clear to him but not to a foreign judge without any anthropological or linguistic insights into D's culture. The Japanese word *aoi*, for example, encompasses what in Europe we conceive as green, blue and pale (as in a pale demeanour), and the Welsh language had until recently similar colour connotations that departed from those employed by their English neighbours.[20] Later on we shall examine the mythology and symbolism of cannibalism in Sierra Leone and the limitations of language therein, but it is instructive at this point to emphasise that what are otherwise rather straightforward notions, which cannot under any circumstances possess a third (grey) meaning, are in fact diffuse and ambiguous to other cultures. In a landmark study of the 1920s, Rivers examined the Melanesian people of the Solomon Islands. What is particularly striking is the use of the local word *mate* which translates as 'dead' but also 'very sick' and 'very elderly'. Clearly, this is not in accord with our strict distinction between dead and alive. Surely, a person can only be one or the other. Rivers understood this to project a classification, rather than a biological determination, from the point of view of the Melanesians. The very infirm and the very elderly were as good as dead because they could no longer partake in the group's activities and the idea was to draw a dividing line between the *mate* and the *toa* (alive).[21] Under this light, it would have been perfectly acceptable for the Melanesians to eliminate all the *mate* in their midst. However, from the perspective of international criminal justice such an act would not only be reprehensible but would no doubt constitute a crime against humanity. The juristic and ethical problem here is obvious. Is it legitimate to convict someone of conduct undertaken throughout one's lifetime and which constitutes part of his or her culture? I am not here going to entertain a discussion as to whether this

[20] See E. Ardener (ed.), *Social Anthropology and Language* (Tavistock, 1971) at xxiv and xxii.

[21] W. H. R. Rivers, 'The Primitive Conception of Death', (1911–12) 10 *Hibbert Journal* 393, at 406.

anthropological finding is pertinent to excusing the accused from liability (as a defence) or in mitigation of punishment, but the reader certainly understands the implications. I am certainly not defending the contention that an unchecked self-proclaimed cultural relativism is a valid defence to all international crimes.[22] Rather, my desire is to offer a new, or additional, perspective to our understanding and application of international criminal norms through the study of *context*.

Infusing anthropological research methods in international criminal investigations

The principal research method for anthropological research is that of *participant observation* through fieldwork. This requires framing a research question from the outset and identifying a community for observation. Fieldwork is generally constant and in order for someone to undertake a thorough investigation it is evident that significant time periods must be spent living with the observed group, in addition to mastering the group's particular language, if at all possible. It is generally considered that the minimum length of time required is one year. At the end of one's field work, notes and interviews are taken back home and the researcher tries to make sense of them, in light of their particular context, with a view to shedding light on his or her research question. The researcher may, or may not, compare his findings to those offered in respect of other groups, being simply content with the study of the particular group in question.[23]

The problem, of course, for criminal investigations is that tribunals have little time to send out an anthropologist for a year to conduct field research, even if appointed at the same time the prosecutor begins to collect evidence and establish a solid indictment. Experience has shown that this is not an insurmountable problem given that from the time they are established until their first judgment is rendered international

[22] The proponents of such arbitrary cultural relativism have claimed that the recruitment of children in Africa to fight in armed conflicts is largely voluntary and the enlisters do not consider their actions as legally or morally culpable. T. Kelsall, *Culture under Cross-Examination: International Justice and the Special Court for Sierra Leone* (Cambridge University Press, 2009) at 146–70. See, also, from a socio-legal perspective, I. Bantekas, 'Individual Responsibility and the Application of *Ignoratio Juris Non Excusat* in International Law', (2011) 19 *European Journal of Crime, Criminal Law & Criminal Justice* 85.

[23] For an excellent practical guide, see K. O'Reilly, *Ethnographic Methods* (2nd edn, Routledge, 2012).

criminal tribunals usually require a period of at least three years. This is more than sufficient for a group of anthropologists who are expert in the particular group(s) to undertake thorough field work and come up with concrete findings for the tribunal, or commission, as the case may be.[24] The International Criminal Court (ICC) may well require six months to a year before embarking on solid prosecutions. The more serious methodological concern, however, is that the situation before and after the commission of widespread atrocities will in all likelihood be fundamentally different. Several parameters of culture will necessarily change – although this has not been tested – and previous power structures will have been altered by the disappearance of the perpetrators for fear of revenge or prosecution.

Hence, if any form of participant observation is to take place at all in post-conflict societies this must be undertaken with this context in mind and the framing of very specific research agendas. Fortunately, the vast majority of societies have been studied by anthropologists in one form or another. This is to say that there is a significant body of literature on all social groups, but this does not encompass all their cultural traits and social interactions. Hence, the courts, with the assistance of experts, can readily turn to the existing body of knowledge and decide whether more research is necessary to fill particular gaps that are subsequently identified. No doubt, anthropologists should have access to the abundance of material that is collected by the prosecutor and non-governmental organizations (NGOs) in the course of their investigation, or material gathered in the course of providing assistance to victims and witnesses. Much of this may seem irrelevant, either because it is hearsay, repetitive, biased etc., but even so an expert may be able to detect solid patterns that are linked to existing findings and which are not repudiated by the scholarly community. These observations do not, of

[24] In this chapter and throughout the book the idea is that the offences under consideration are prosecuted by domestic or international criminal tribunals. However, it is not unusual for several serious international offences to be handled by truth commissions, whether UN-based or other. The findings in this chapter are pertinent to the work of these commissions even if they are composed solely of people belonging to the same ethnic group as the perpetrators. It should not be assumed that they have a perfect understanding of their culture. We have already discussed Bourdieu's concept of *doxa*. Anthropologists frequently refer to *homeblindedness* as a methodological limitation. This refers to fieldwork undertaken by someone well-versed in the society under examination, which prevents him from gaining deeper insights because he takes things for granted and looks at them through a distorting lens.

course, suggest that the judges must confer their fact-finding and judicial role to anthropologists, but that they must take cognisance of social relationships with which they are unfamiliar in order to serve both the narrow (dispensing of justice) and broad (history-writing, reconciliation) aims of international criminal justice. A necessary disclaimer should, of course, underlie all interaction between judges and anthropologists; namely, 'publication' confirmation bias. This is essentially a distortion in human information processing where reviewers/editors of books and scientific journals accept for publication papers that support their views while ignoring and discrediting those that do not.[25] This phenomenon is more prevalent in the humanities than in legal scholarship because of the tendency to set up doctrinal 'schools' upon which succeeding scholars base their theoretical and empirical work, and hence tribunals should verify the veracity of their information from multiple sources, if available.

Anthropology as a tool for assessing complex liabilities

At a very basic level and in respect of assessing complex liabilities pertinent to international crimes, such as command responsibility, anthropology can assist us to ascertain those elusive *de facto* indicia that are necessary for constructing authority, power and ultimately effective control. It also allows us to understand whether the 'subordinates' that committed the crimes were under sufficient compulsion or control by their superiors, such that justifies the latter's conviction despite the absence of direct fault. Before we go on, however, it is important to make a significant observation that relates to semantics. If anthropology is viewed as a method by which to draw conclusions pertinent to the fault-liability paradigm or complex liabilities, then this method requires an appropriate language in order to communicate concepts and ideas into the sphere of law.[26] Communication is crucial not only because certain words are not translatable from one language to another, as we have already had the chance to explore, but also because wholesale concepts and ideas themselves are alien from one

[25] J. Mahoney, 'Publication Prejudices: An Experimental Study of Confirmatory Bias in the Peer Review System', (1977) 1 *Cognitive Therapy and Research* 161.

[26] See E. Mertz, 'Language, Law and Social Meanings: Linguistic/Anthropological Contributions to the Study of Law', (1992) 26 *Law & Society Review* 413.

culture to another.[27] The so-called Sapir-Whorf hypothesis, elaborated by the respective anthropologists in the 1930s, suggests that language gives rise to fundamental differences in the respective life-worlds which the various groups inhabit. In their case study, the North American native Hopi language was found to contain few nouns but many verbs, which necessarily connoted action and movement. They concluded from this that the Hopi world was predicated around movement and that it was largely disinterested in objects.[28]

A very poignant example, apart from those already provided in previous sections, is necessary in order to better illustrate the point. In the case against Charles Taylor, a prosecution witness named 'ZigZag' Marzah was quite clearly unfamiliar with the Western idiom of remorse and conscience.[29] He also claimed that he was involved in cannibalism of enemy corpses, arguing that this was something expected of all warriors battling on the side of Charles Taylor.[30] Whether or not this statement is true, it certainly stirs a wealth of emotions in the Western psyche and reinforces myths and stereotypes associated with primitive Africa. In fact, anthropological research suggests that cannibalism was historically unknown in human history,[31] or that in any event it was alien in

[27] See M. van Hoecke, *Law as Communication* (Hart, 2002), in which the author's central thesis is that all legal relations are to be understood in terms of dialogue, conversation and communicative processes, rather than as traditional command–obedience structures. Legal anthropologists such as Bohannan argued that Western legal terms and categories should not be employed to study the organisation and order of non-Western societies. He believed that such a methodology prevented a comprehensive understanding of other cultures and argued in favour of using native legal terms whose meaning would become evident within an ethnographic context. P. Bohannan, *Justice and Judgment among the Tiv* (Oxford University Press, 1957). This also leads to the so-called methodological distortion of *ethnocentrism*.

[28] The most contemporary manifestation of the hypothesis is currently known as *linguistic relativity*, which posits that language does have some effect on thought, but this is small as opposed to decisive. See P. Kay and W. Kempton, 'What is the Sapir-Whorf Hypothesis?', (1984) 86 *American Anthropologist* 65.

[29] G. Anders, 'Testifying about Uncivilised Events: Problematic Representations of Africa in the Trial against Charles Taylor', (2011) 24 *Leiden Journal of International Law* 937, at 944–5.

[30] Ibid., at 948–9.

[31] However, for the sake of scientific accuracy it has to be said that a good number of anthropologists reject the claim that cannibalism is just a myth created from prejudice. Works such as that of W. Arens, *The Man-Eating Myth: Anthropology and Anthropophagy* (Oxford University Press, 1980) are reflective of the attitude that rejects cannibalism. More recent forensic research of human bones from an Anasazi pueblo in south-western Colorado reveals that nearly thirty men, women and children were butchered and cooked

contemporary African societies. Anders recalls the *Human Leopards* case investigated by a Special Commission Court set up by British colonial authorities in early twentieth-century Sierra Leone. There, and without any corroborating forensic evidence, the court was convinced that members of a secret society dressing up in leopard skins went about ritual cannibalism. The basic story was described by insider witnesses whose communication with their colonisers must have been agonising, through language that was fraught with significant misunderstanding and symbolism and which was moreover read through two very different socio-cultural perspectives. Anders accurately captures this as follows:

> In Sierra Leone and Liberia, as in many parts of Africa, social relationships and personal development are framed in a rich language of eating and consumption. Initiation into secret societies such as the *poro* is also expressed in an idiom of being eaten or devoured by the bush spirits in order to be reborn as a full member of the community. ... The political sphere, in particular, is conceptualised as a potentially dangerous terrain where powerful people 'eat' each other in order to grow 'big'. This has been famously coined by Bayart as the politics of the belly, who describes the consumption of the State's resources by politicians and bureaucrats. In Sierra Leone, corrupt politicians are referred to as *bobor bele* – literally, guys with a belly eating the State's resources. Therefore, the frequent cannibalism accusations in West Africa must not always be read literally. They should rather be interpreted in terms of a highly symbolic political language and critique of existing injustices [as is the case with Sierra Leone].[32]

To a Western audience it seems implausible that anyone can genuinely confuse symbolism with reality, or, to put it bluntly, confuse actual cannibalism with its metaphors. How can you say one thing and, without intentionally lying, actually mean something completely different? How is it that symbolism can be so easily transformed into action? This is not the time or place to expand fully on these issues but it is widely admitted in the anthropological literature that ideas of witchcraft, spirit possession and shamanistic injunctions had a normative effect on the members of the vast majority of traditional societies.[33] The same is largely true today in the industrialised world with

there around 1100 AD. See T. D. White, *Prehistoric Cannibalism at Mancos 5Mtumr—2346* (Princeton University Press, 1992).

32 Anders, above note 29, at 956.

33 See S. Brandes, *Power and Persuasion: Fiestas and Social Control in Rural Mexico* (University of Pennsylvania Press, 1988); H. M. Bergsma, 'Tiv Proverbs as a Means of Social Control', (1970) 40 *Africa: Journal of the International African Institute* 151.

pious members of religious groups. This is no doubt a form of social control. To illustrate the point I shall offer two case studies from the recent past.

A significant part of the Rwandan genocide was predicated on a myth or symbolism reiterated and spread by the Hutu that the Tutsi were cockroaches and inferior beings. Whereas no Hutu would typically act on this myth unilaterally, it was the seed for future events, when animosity was stirred through artificial means and channels; and an illiterate and highly polarised populace was unable to separate myth from reality. Anthropological research on the Rwandan genocide tends to show that one of the principal cultural metaphors in Rwanda, the 'flow', may shed some light on some of the methods for killing and torturing used by the Hutu. 'Flow' in general represents something healthy, as is the case with our blood stream or the transformation of food into faeces and insemination into childbirth. Blockage of 'flow' is associated with disease and death. The impalement of victims from the anus to the mouth as well as mass killings at check points, in addition to other motives, symbolises the end of 'flow'.[34] To a Western audience it may to some degree explain certain acts of sheer cruelty (although certainly not fully), as well as demonstrate the existence of genocidal patterns amounting to *systematic*.

The second example is very similar, despite the fact that it took place more than fifty years earlier and fuelled the psyche of a much more literate and 'civilised' population. I am referring to Nazi propaganda, well prior to the commencement of World War II in 1939, through a process of dehumanising its enemies, such as Slavs, communists and Jews. In a world where international travel was exceptional and propaganda had crept into every aspect of social life (school, private clubs, censoring of all publications and broadcasts) it did not take long for the Nazi party to cast doubt in the minds of the German population about the humanity of other races and peoples. This dehumanisation was nothing more than myth-creation, as was also the case for the superiority of the Aryans.[35] However, it is well known that such myths occupy a significant place in the collective consciousness of a nation, which is susceptible to manipulation for committing crimes

[34] C. C. Taylor, 'The Cultural Face of Terror in the Rwandan Genocide', in A. L. Hinton (ed.), *Annihilating Difference: The Anthropology of Genocide* (University of California Press, 2002) at 137–78.

[35] D. J. Goldhagan, *Hitler's Willing Executioners: Ordinary Germans and the Holocaust* (Alfred Knopf, 1996).

against class enemies[36] or in order to achieve less 'innocuous' political objectives.[37]

In the context of the ICTR's investigation, legal anthropology necessarily turned out to play a significant part in the reconstruction of liability for genocide, albeit largely unbeknown to the judges. It will be recalled that in its first case, that of Jean Paul Akayesu, the Tribunal was reluctant to apply the exact terms of Article II of the Genocide Convention, which required that the crime could only be committed against members of another ethnic, national, religious or racial group. Forensic evidence demonstrated that the Hutu and the Tutsi were not ethnically or racially distinct; quite the opposite. Their respective 'ethnic' designations had been engineered by their Belgian colonisers and these had subsequently matured into distinctions of class or social status. The Tribunal therefore turned to what it might have perceived as legal anthropology in order to construct a more objective theory of victimhood for the purposes of the Genocide Convention. It held that beyond external characteristics such as race and ethnic origin, membership of a group may also come about by the personal belief of a group's members as to their distinctiveness.[38] Thus far it is at par with the fundamental tenets of social anthropology. However, this personal self-distinction and self-categorisation is sanctioned only if it is perceived as such by the group under consideration itself (informants), not external observers. The Tribunal offered no prior study, nor one commissioned by itself, that would have shown the views of the informants. This demonstrates that international criminal tribunals perceive extra-legal matters as common knowledge, not worthy of further scientific research, upon which a reasonable man is well suited to reach a reasonable conclusion.

This is, no doubt, a convenient mechanism by which to construct group characteristics in an artificial rather than a social science manner.

[36] See C. C. Wang, *Words Kill: Calling for the Destruction of Class Enemies in China, 1949–1953* (Routledge, 2004).

[37] An interesting, highly critical, insight is offered by Chomsky, on the imagery employed in liberal nations to achieve pre-ordained social and political goals by elites. N. Chomsky, *Necessary Illusions: Thought Control in Democratic Societies* (South End Press, 1989).

[38] *ICTR Prosecutor* v. *Akayesu*, Trial Chamber Judgment (2 September 1998), para. 702. In *ICC Prosecutor* v. *Al-Bashir*, Decision on the Prosecution's Application for a Warrant of Arrest against Omar Al-Bashir (4 March 2009), para. 137, an ICC Pre-Trial Chamber claimed that three Sudanese tribal groups living in the same area, namely the Fur, the Masalit and the Zaghawa, constituted distinct ethnic groups because each possessed its own language, tribal customs and traditional links to its lands. Without realising it, the Pre-Trial Chamber made an anthropological observation with legal significance.

Its foundation is hardly scientific but is based on the judges' efforts to fit the groups, and members thereof, under discussion within the terms of the Genocide Convention and other forms of criminal liability. Whether or not the Tribunal's assessment of collective identity would withstand thorough anthropological research is a different issue altogether. It is therefore critical that when foreign judges assess the criminal liability of persons from cultures they know little about the assistance of a team of anthropologists, experts in the peoples in question, be sought. The objective of the experts must be to map the various social interactions and institutions of the pertinent people so as to provide a guide as to what is acceptable in the community, distinguish myth and symbolism from reality and apprise the Tribunal of those cultural factors that may inhibit witnesses and victims from testifying. This will no doubt assist the prosecutor and the defence in asking the right questions and thus save precious judicial time.

Obedience and effective control in social culture: understanding leadership and command in army and rebel outfits

One of the key issues in war crimes trials is the degree to which a subordinate would obey a superior order not as a matter of military compulsion but as a matter of ingrained culture. An assessment of such culture, as well as class or similar social constructs, is important because it signifies the degree to which one may assume effective control in respect of jungle-based armies and militias and thus provide an understanding of the structure of hierarchical systems and their distinct organisation. This is by no means a new theme, given that it has troubled law-makers and courts since complex liabilities, such as command responsibility, were first punctuated on the legal map with the *Yamashita* case.[39] There, it was controversially held that Yamashita retained effective control over Japanese troops that went on the rampage against civilians in Manila, even though he had split the Japanese forces in the Philippines into four distinct groups, with all communication between them having been severed by their adversaries. The Tribunal maintained that the atrocities were so widespread that Yamashita must have known about them and could have prevented them, despite the argument of the accused that he had given strict instructions to the

[39] *Trial of General Tomoyuki Yamashita*, 4 Law Reports of Trials of War Criminals 1.

Manila-based commander to evacuate the island and return to Japan. Clearly, in the absence of any direct orders the Tribunal could not have constructed Yamashita's command liability had it not arbitrarily assumed that he enjoyed effective control of all Japanese forces on the island.

Whatever the actual facts on the ground, a retrospective examination of effective control would no doubt be illumined by reference to anthropological data. Again, it is not my intention to go into any significant detail, but given that the case hung on whether Yamashita's subordinates had in fact disobeyed his orders to evacuate and avoid harming civilians, it is worth investigating Japanese military culture at the time. With the adoption of *Shinto* as the country's official State religion in 1890, an Emperor cult was established whereby the Emperor's divinity was based on his descent from the Goddess *Amaterasu*. This meant that the Emperor's commands, and by implication those of his representatives, were to be obeyed without objection. This unswerving loyalty to the Emperor as the basis of the Japanese State (known as *kokutai*, which may be translated manifold, particularly 'sovereign' or 'national essence') had earlier been institutionalised by the introduction of universal conscription, which resulted in the indoctrination of the country's youth and which continued through subsequent generations.[40] This cultural dimension, coupled undoubtedly with fear and other elements, accounts for the acceptance of brutality within the ranks of the Japanese army and its members' 'loyalty-to-the-death'. As a result, it would have been characteristically untypical and out of all logic for the forces under Yamashita's *de jure* command to disobey their commander's direct orders. By logical implication, no distinction can be made between *de jure* and *de facto* command in respect of the Japanese military organisation during World War II because, even if separated from their commanders, units and subunits would always religiously adhere to their superiors' original orders – unless, of course, there were other available orders. This observation also suggests that in this particular socio-military context the absence of material capacity to prevent or punish is irrelevant in establishing *de*

[40] In fact, *kokutai* was introduced as a fundamental building block in Article 4 of Japan's 1890 Constitution, also known as the Meiji Constitution, on account of the Tenno dynasty which assumed power through the 1868 Meiji restoration, remaining in power until 1945. See G. M. Beckmann, *The Making of the Meiji Constitution: The Oligarchs and the Constitutional Development of Japan, 1868–1891* (University of Kansas Press, 1957).

facto or *de jure* command because the conduct of subordinates is uniform irrespective of the person under command.

In the Rwanda conflict, *de facto* command and control became a central issue because, unlike the military-styled paramilitary groups on the territory of the former Yugoslavia, a significant amount of authority was exercised on the basis of traditional socio-economic structures. Rwandan society, like most of Africa, is tribal and class-based, with authority and privileges typically belonging to the elite in each tribe or clan.[41] As a result, authority and wealth go hand-in-hand, with the elite also being the richest and better educated among the tribe. Until the creation of the ICTR the construction of command responsibility had been applied to regular armies and, at worst, to tightly structured paramilitary units, which, however, resembled regular armies principally because they were formed and run by ex-military personnel, as was the case with indictments before the ICTY. The most complex cases had been those dealt with by subsequent World War II military tribunals in respect of civilians, particularly industrial and political leaders.[42]

The ICTR paid particular attention to these distinct anthropological features in its construction of hierarchies and authority in Rwandan society, although admittedly inadvertently and without the requisite methodological or scientific rigour. In the *Akayesu* case the accused was the burgomaster of Taba commune, a position akin to that of mayor in Western parlance. Whereas Western mayors enjoy no other authority than to enact peripheral by-laws and set the municipality's economic agenda on the basis of municipal taxes and other income, in Rwanda the burgomaster enjoyed far greater authority.[43] His powers were found to be much wider than his *de jure* authority.[44] In fact, he was perceived as the

41 For an excellent anthropological account, see R. Lemarchand, 'Power and Stratification in Rwanda: A Reconsideration', (1996) 6 *Cahiers d'études Africaines* 592.

42 See *Government Commissioner of the General Tribunal of the Military Government for the French Zone of Occupation in Germany* v. *Roechling* 14 Trials of War Criminals before the Nuremberg Military Tribunals (Trials) 1097; *USA* v. *Flick* 6 Trials 1187; and *USA* v. *von Weizsaecker* (*Ministries* case) 14 Trials 308. Once again, although no direct anthropological questions were asked by these tribunals, it was deemed implicit that those to whom powers were delegated by the Nazi regime enjoyed sufficient control over persons committing particular crimes. This was a direct consequence of Nazi culture, which permeated all elements of the Reich's socio-economic *raison d'être*.

43 This is confirmed by the vast literature in respect of weakly integrated nations where the real power lies with powerful individuals in the periphery. See J. Gledhill, *Power and its Disguises: Anthropological Perspectives on Politics* (Pluto Press, 1994).

44 *Akayesu* Trial judgment, above note 38, para. 57.

'father' of the people, whose every order was to be obeyed without question or deviation.[45] Clearly, informal law and power arrangements, whether explicit or implicit, played an important role in ascertaining the enjoyment of effective control over the actions of civilian populations acting as mobs, random groups or under a self-perceived identity. The existence of such effective control is further reinforced by class and education. This African case study exemplifies the Tribunal's desire to construct (or expand) complex liabilities on the basis of anthropological observations in order to reach a just conclusion; in the case at hand to establish the liability of an influential figure urging those under his circle of influence to commit genocide.

The role and origin of *influence* in Sierra Leone's armed groups

We have already made extensive reference to myth and symbolism in the popular culture of Sierra Leonean society. The Sierra Leone Special Court (SLSC) has only indirectly examined the anthropological dimension of the various armed groups and its relevance to our understanding of conduct and hierarchies. With respect to the latter, the jurisprudence of the SLSC has revealed two broad types of military authority. The first is consistent with that found in regular armies and rebel forces, on the basis of a strict or not so strict hierarchical structure. This seems to be the case with the Armed Forces Revolutionary Council (AFRC) and the Revolutionary United Front (RUF). The second type of authority depends less on formal hierarchies and is instead entrenched in symbolism and mythology. This much is true with respect to the *Kamajors* and their Civil Defence Forces (CDF). No doubt, elements of both types of authority are found in all groups in one form or another.

That mythology, mysticism and symbolism played a role in the military organisation of Sierra Leone's factions comes as no surprise, as was revealed earlier in this chapter. This was further facilitated by the fact that, although the country is host to twenty African groups (the largest of which are the *Temne* and *Mende*), it is multi-religious and the war did not start along ethnic or religious lines. Rebel groups and militias were thus ethnically and religiously diverse, a phenomenon already reflected in membership of the country's secret societies, particularly the *poro* and the *bondo*. Exceptionally, the composition of the *Kamajors* was *Mende*-

[45] Ibid., paras. 55, 74.

based, albeit their aim was not necessarily to engage in inter-ethnic rivalries.[46] That the SLSC made a serious effort to explain the mythology and mysticism underlying the organisation of the *Kamajors* is evidence of the fact that social phenomena are of acute relevance in ascribing the attributes of authority in order to construct complex liabilities. It will be recalled that the ICTY largely rejected or, at least, ignored such factors on the assumption that factions on the territory of Bosnia were neatly divided along ethnic/religious lines and, as a result, there was no need to enquire into other shared traits between members of the groups.

I will draw on one element here that is intriguing and which, although rejected by the ICTY, should have found a place in the jurisprudence of the SLSC. I am referring to the power or authority to 'influence' as an indication or evidence of effective control. Indeed, in the *Čelebići* case the accused Delalič was found to be a highly influential figure in the Bosnian army. He would possess authority to sign contracts and release orders in a prisoner-of-war (POW) camp and to liaise with the highest echelons of the Bosnian Muslim authorities; yet, he did not possess formal authority over other subordinates, especially those in the POW camp. The Tribunal did not consider that this highly influential individual, in the absence of any direct subordinates, yielded sufficient control over those running the POW camp such as would have allowed him to intervene in the commission of crimes against the prisoners.[47] This conclusion was drawn at a time when the construction of the complex liability of command responsibility did not warrant open-ended expansion. It was enough for the Tribunal that only persons exercising effective control over subordinates were subject to the doctrine. The Tribunal rightly felt that if everyone yielding influence could also be encompassed the floodgates would be open to convict persons who were not at fault.[48] The key word here is *fault*. If D, a boy-scout leader, has exerted and continues to exert significant influence over a group of boy scouts who are recruited as

[46] K. Dupuy and H. M. Binningsbø, *Power-Sharing and Peace-Building in Sierra Leone* (CSCW Papers, 2007) at 3–4.

[47] *ICTY Prosecutor* v. *Delalić et al.* (*Čelebići* case), Trial Chamber judgment (16 November 1998), paras. 266, 653–6.

[48] This is particularly reflected in its pronouncements in *ICTY Prosecutor* v. *Brdjanin and Talić*, Trial Chamber Judgment (1 September 2004) paras. 276, 281; *ICTY Prosecutor* v. *Naletilić and Martinović*, Trial Chamber Judgment (21 March 2003), para. 68. These judgments certainly influenced the decision of the State Court of Bosnia and Herzegovina in *Prosecutor* v. *Alić*, Trial Chamber Judgment, Case No X-KR-06/294 (11 April 2008) at 46.

minors by a rebel group, it cannot be seriously claimed that he possesses sufficient control over all their future actions, particularly when they are spatially and geographically removed from him. D clearly lacks fault for failing to use his powers of influence to dissuade the youths. However, if D was in proximity to the minors and was an influential figure in the broader echelons of the group, he possesses the material capacity to employ his influence over the minors, even if he does not enjoy effective control by reason of direct subordination. In this latter scenario D is at material fault, although it will depend on the particular circumstances as to whether this fault may substantiate command responsibility or other types of complex liabilities. These particular circumstances are none other than D's material capacity to act.[49] It defies logic and the dictates of justice to assert that a person with the direct capacity to save hundreds of lives by simply averting the would-be perpetrators bears no liability simply because he was not incumbent with a pre-existing duty to act. This is not merely an iteration or transplantation of the duty to save strangers typically associated with civil law jurisdictions. It goes at the very heart of material fault and all that it stands for.

It is not clear whether the SLSC shares this conviction, given that it has not expressly rejected or upheld this thesis.[50] It is certain that the SLSC was unaware of the scholarly literature suggesting that power of influence is possible even in the absence of authority over one's target audience.[51] Imagine if influence and authority are merged into a single entity. Had the Special Court been cognisant of these arguments it might have taken up the proposition that in situations where the power relations and social status between several individuals is chaotic, direct subordination is not necessary in order for the more influential person to establish effective control merely by his or her powers of influence.[52] This chaotic power

[49] This is why Mettraux sides with the judgments of the ICTY to reject influence as establishing *de facto* control. See G. Mettraux, *The Law of Command Responsibility* (Oxford University Press, 2009) at 183 ff.

[50] In *SLSC Prosecutor* v. *Brima, Kanaru and Kanu*, Judgment (20 June 2007), para. 788, the SLSC referred to a number of indicia as evidence of effective control. These may implicitly be read – although one could argue otherwise – as encompassing cases of significant and overpowering influence.

[51] See L. A. Hill, *Exercising Influence without Formal Authority: How New Managers can Build Power and Influence* (Harvard Business Press, 2008); A. R. Cohen and D. L. Bradford, *Influence without Authority* (Wiley, 2005). Hill's motto, a pioneer on this topic, is that: 'all influential managers have power but not all powerful managers have influence'.

[52] *Influence* is probably not the appropriate term here and this certainly explains why the ad hoc tribunals have rejected influence-based effective control out of hand. It should be

gap certainly existed in the context of the military factions engaged in Sierra Leone's bloody wars. The spiritual leader of the *Kamajors*, Kondewa, is an interesting case study. The *Kamajors* were originally organised as a group of *Mende* hunters who responded to the directives of their various chiefs to protect people from the rebels.[53] As a result, its members did not possess the military skills and discipline of a regular or rebel army. They were in need of organisation and guidance in order to become an organised fighting unit.[54] This guidance came both from military as well as spiritual leaders. Kondewa was of the latter kind:

> He was the head of all the CDF initiators initiating the *Kamajors* into the *Kamajor* society in Sierra Leone. His job was to prepare herbs which the *Kamajors* smeared on their bodies to protect them against bullets. Kondewa was not a fighter, he himself never went to the war front or into active combat, but whenever a *Kamajor* was going to war, he would go to Kondewa for advice and blessing. ... The *Kamajors* believed in the mystical powers of the initiators, especially Kondewa, and that the process of the initiation and immunisation would make them bullet-proof. The *Kamajors* looked up to Kondewa and admired the man with such powers. ... Because of the mystical powers Kondewa possessed, he had command over the *Kamajors* from every part of the country.[55]

The Special Court opined that Kondewa's mystical powers did not automatically confer upon him military authority over the recruits and their operations.[56] On the contrary, it was his *de jure* position of High Priest of the CDF that granted him some degree of effective control in certain situations and it was in respect of this that he was found to enjoy effective control.[57]

The SLSC missed a golden opportunity to defy the *Čelebići* myth by expressly stipulating that under certain circumstances the yielding of influence between asymmetric actors can give rise to effective control irrespective of the military, civilian or other context in which it is exercised. If a person can convince another that following a ritual he will be unaffected by his adversaries' weapons, it is absurd to claim that this person does not possess powers akin, if not far superior, to those enjoyed

understood as possessing the material and mental power to compel another to do or abstain from doing something.

53 *SLSC Prosecutor* v. *Fofana and Kondewa*, Judgment (2 August 2007), para. 354.

54 Even so, universal discipline remained problematic because some fighters 'acted on their own without knowledge of central command because their area of operation was so wide'. Ibid., para. 358.

55 Ibid., paras. 344–6.

56 Ibid., para. 806.

57 Ibid., para. 686.

in a superior-subordinate relationship. Such powers of influence are no doubt rare, but in Sierra Leone, where the mystical and the symbolic coincide with the real and the brutal, the anthropological basis of the relevant relationships should have been given much more prominence. Just as the results of one anthropological study cannot be transplanted into another – although some general observations may be possible – in the same manner the findings of the SLSC need not necessarily be accepted as immutable truths applicable in all future conflicts. I am not convinced by the argument that influence can never give rise to effective control-type situations. This position is sustainable, of course, as long as it is proven that the person in question had the material capacity to prevent or punish the crimes committed by those persons over whom he enjoyed significant influence. I can only hope that the jurisprudence will take anthropological evidence into consideration and finally move towards this direction.

Conclusion

As is the case with all the chapters in this book, this chapter is meant to provide a fresh perspective to international criminal justice. The law continues to remain paramount, as does its objectivity, but here the emphasis was placed on understanding the societies where violence occurred, and deciphering the social relations of their people. This is crucial not only for the well-functioning of international criminal tribunals and the correct application of the pertinent law, but also for making the correct policy choices in respect of post-conflict or transitional societies.[58] As far as the latter is concerned, if we are aware of the aspirations of the local population and if it were to be demonstrated that very little, if any, animosity exists between the rival groups, it makes sense to adopt a policy that reinforces a combination of domestic criminal justice and physical reconstruction rather than place all resources and energy upon a single international criminal justice mechanism. Equally, our comprehension of social and cultural relations and the causes behind a conflict provides a tribunal with the necessary tools to

[58] Numerous anthropologists suggest that female genital mutilation (FGM), for example, is best tackled through non-legal means, not only because enforcement institutions are weak but also because the persistence of FGM is based on the lack of empowerment and hostile customary attitudes. See N. Vitalis-Pemunta, *Human Rights and Socio-Legal Resistance against Female Genital Cutting: An Anthropological Perspective* (Verlag, 2011), who studied the FGM practices of the Ejagham in Cameroon.

assess power relations – through kinship and lineage arrangements – and paint a largely accurate picture of the situation. This in turn may well be the first step towards writing a historical record, which is after all a stated objective of international criminal justice. We have shown in this chapter that anthropology assists not only in supplementary criminal justice goals (i.e., reconciliation, reconstruction and history-writing), but also in primary ones, namely the correct application of international norms.

The ICTY and the ICTR were largely disinclined to employ anthropological data, and this is clearly evident from the introductory sections of their first judgments, where they are content to cite only historical and intelligence sources in order to explain the underlying causes of the conflict. As these judgments went on, however, it was clear that the Tribunals lacked concrete definitions to crucial legal questions, namely whether the Tutsi were racially or ethnically diverse from the Hutu, or whether the real power structure in the communes of Rwanda was in practice much different than that on paper. The ICTR ultimately responded to these questions by inadvertently resorting to anthropological research methods and, although the outcome was satisfactory, the process was poor. The same poor results are encountered in the work of the SLSC, which should have learned from the mistakes of its predecessors and infused a serious anthropological dimension into its adjudicative function. Its inability to distinguish between myth, symbolism and reality in respect of the cannibalism described by some of the witnesses and attested to by some of the alleged perpetrators is a serious impediment to the just application of the law. A person may well be convicted for conduct which when described in one language means one thing but when translated means something completely different.

The recommendation of this author is that although anthropology is not a *sine qua non* condition for the application of international criminal justice, it must nonetheless become an integral part of international investigations. When a tribunal is established, or when the ICC takes on a new situation, it is imperative that a team of experts with particular expertise in the region and peoples under investigation be established with a view to bringing forth existing knowledge and in order to conduct new investigations if necessary. The experts' research tools and findings must guide the tribunals but should never substitute or pre-empt sound judicial determination. In this manner, it is hoped that blind justice will also assist the society under consideration, as well as other societies on the brink of conflict, to assess its distortions and ultimately address them from within.

10

Mental health and international crimes

HENRIK ANCKARSÄTER, TOVA BENNET, THOMAS NILSSON AND SUSANNA RADOVIC

Introduction

Ever since its historical beginnings during or after the French Revolution, psychiatric pioneers claimed expertise in the field of crime and punishment. Theirs was a humanistic stance directed against the cruel punishments that were considered 'just' and 'necessary' by their time. Their drive was the Enlightenment world-view, a revolutionary zest for world-improving and some discrete elements of triumphalist medicine. Proudly proclaiming as scientific facts: (1) that madness causes crimes, or alternatively that crimes expose hidden forms of madness ('moral insanity'), or combinations thereof; (2) that psychiatric treatment is superior to punishment from a societal protection perspective; or (3) that there can be no personal responsibility or free will, as the physical laws of nature also apply to the human psyche, 'positive criminology' and forensic psychiatry became established as central societal players with influence over the correctional system. Nineteenth-century Italian criminology pioneer, Cesare Lombroso, argued that criminal behaviour results from physiological anomalies or fragilities, which he thought could be used in criminal, legal and penal policy for predictive and preventive purposes. While influential in the USA, Europe shunned Lombroso's approach at first, but eventually adopted refined variants during the first half of the twentieth century, drawing inspiration from the eugenic policies, racial biology and genetics adopted throughout the Western world during this time.[1]

[1] D. J. Kevles, *In the Name of Eugenics: Genetics and the Uses of Human Heredity* (Berkeley & Los Angeles, CA: University of California Press, 1985); P. A. Lombardo, *A Century of Eugenics in America: from the Indiana Experiment to the Human Genome Era* (Bloomington, IN: Indiana University Press, 2010); G. Broberg and N. Roll-Hansen (eds.), *Eugenics and the Welfare State: Sterilization Policy in Denmark, Sweden, Norway, and Finland* (East Lansing, MI: Michigan State University Press, 1996).

The claims to science made by psychiatrists at the time were not – in any strict sense – backed by empirical evidence, but rather by case histories and various examinations of highly selected series of patients. It would take more than 150 years for the cards to be called. Faced with the 1970s' devastating critique of psychiatry as a power structure rather than a science, it became necessary to present corroborative data.[2]

In the following, we will start by briefly discussing the relationship between mental disorders and violent crimes in general and international crimes in particular. Then we will give a brief presentation of the insanity defence in the context of international crimes and the international criminal court, and move on to discuss whether an insanity defence should be included in international law. We will further consider on what grounds a person should be acquitted due to insanity when it comes to these kinds of crimes and what kind of psychiatric disorders might become relevant in these circumstances. In this context we will focus on personality disorders, mental retardation, psychotic disorders and thought disorders. Finally, we will briefly touch upon the subjects of psychiatric treatment and risk assessments in relation to offenders of international crimes.

Mental disorders and violent crimes

Today, empirical data are indeed at hand to evaluate (preliminarily, as in most applied sciences) the basic assumptions made by forensic psychiatry and positive criminology, principally as a result of systematic meta-analyses of reasonably well-designed and conducted studies.[3] By and large, these evaluations have shown that there is something of value in applying psychiatry, neuroscience and behavioural sciences to criminality, but an overall explanatory model for the causation of crimes or criminal careers, or a working strategy for their prevention, still eludes us.

[2] For example, see T. Szasz, *The Myth of Mental Illness* (New York, NY: Harper & Row Publishers, 1974); R. D. Laing, *The Divided Self: An Existential Study in Sanity and Madness* (Harmondsworth: Penguin, 1960); M. Foucault, *Madness and Civilization* (London: Vintage Books, 1967).

[3] See, for example, S. Fazel and K. Seewald, 'Severe Mental Illness in 33,588 Prisoners Worldwide: Systematic Review and Meta-Regression Analysis', (2012) 200 *British Journal of Psychiatry* 364.

The latest paradigmatic developments in forensic psychiatric research have mostly come from epidemiology.[4] Violent crimes have been shown to have a highly skewed distribution, with a small number of perpetrators (about 1 per cent of the population, generally males with an early onset of aggressive antisocial behaviour combined with substance abuse) responsible for a disproportionate number of offences.[5] This status has been given many names (partially overlapping phenotypical definitions), such as conduct disorder, type-2 alcoholism or antisocial personality disorder. In the background of those exhibiting such disorders, researchers are able to trace childhood-onset hyperactivity, impulsivity and attention problems. Otherwise, a common-language explanation of today's research frontier could be that mental disorders, just like a number of other health issues and social disadvantages, have probabilistic relationships with crimes, increasing the likelihood for criminal behaviour, convictions and relapse. As most of these susceptibility factors are inter-correlated in the population it is not possible to use available empirical studies to decide their specific roles or *how* they interact in a chain of causation (today's statistical methods are almost uniformly linear and identify the most salient factors while obscuring discrete and non-linear effects, even if these latter might have stronger causal roles). Once a pattern of aggressive antisocial behaviour is established it seems to be self-enforcing, just like any other behavioural pattern, which makes it possible to predict future crimes better than chance. The empirical evidence for any further clear 'inner' or 'mental' features to add to the prediction of future criminal behaviour, once previous behaviour and substance abuse have been considered, is scarce. The relation between crimes and proposed crime-related phenotypes (such as psychopathy or

[4] R. Yu, J. R. Geddes and S. Fazel, 'Personality Disorders, Violence, and Antisocial Behavior: A Systematic Review and Meta-regression Analysis', (2012) 26 *Journal of Personality Disorder* 775; K. Witt, R. van Dorn and S. Fazel, 'Risk Factors for Violence in Psychosis: Systematic Review and Meta-Regression Analysis of 110 Studies', (2013) 8 *PLoS One*, available as e55942. doi: 10.1371/journal.pone.0055942; S. Hodgins, M. J. Piatosa and B. Schiffer, 'Violence among People with Schizophrenia: Phenotypes and Neurobiology', (2013) *Current Topics in Behavioral Neuroscience* 1.

[5] O. Falk, M. Wallinius, S. Lundström, T. Frisell, H. Anckarsäter and N. Kerekes, 'The 1% of the Population Accountable for 63% of All Violent Crime Convictions', (2013) *Social Psychiatry and Psychiatric Epidemiology*, available at DOI 10.1007/s00127-013-0783-*y*; S. Fazel, N. Långström, A. Hjern, M. Grann and P. Lichtenstein, 'Schizophrenia, Substance Abuse, and Violent Crime', (2009) 301 *JAMA* 2016; S. Fazel, G. Gulati, L. Linsell, J. R. Geddes and M. Grann, 'Schizophrenia and Violence: Systematic Review and Meta-Analysis', (2009) 6 *PLoS Medicine*, available as: e1000120. doi:10.1371/journal.pmed.1000120; S. Fazel and R. Yu, 'Psychotic Disorders and Repeat Offending: Systematic Review and Meta-Analysis', (2011) 37 *Schizophrenia Bulletin* 800.

'early starter schizophrenics') depends far more on previous behaviours than on any features that would only be recognized by a specialist psychiatrist or psychologist.

There is also an emerging understanding of violence as a public health issue per se, which means that it can be addressed by general (e.g., parental support, child nutrition, education) and specific (e.g., involuntary treatment of adolescent recidivistic offenders with substance abuse) health initiatives.[6] Genetic and neurobiological methods for prediction, treatment and prevention are proposed to offer an alternative to continuing incarceration of increasing numbers of young men, a strategy that has especially spiralled in the USA.[7]

Mental disorders and international crimes

International crimes differ from general violent criminality in several respects of relevance to psychiatry and psychology. They are almost always performed under exceptional (warlike) circumstances and in a social context of multiple perpetrators rather than as a form of individual conduct. They are dependent on societal power structures with clearly identified opposing parts, certainly very much related to particular ideologies, ideas about other people and thought content rather than being driven by personal gain or emotions (even if emotions may, by all means, still play a very important part). In some cases, as when a soldier is required under international law to refuse the execution of illegal orders imposed by a commanding officer, education about the relevant legislation is necessary, as such regulations are probably less known to people than general criminal law. This indicates that this group of offenders may be very different from general violent offenders.

We will leave group dynamics largely out of this chapter, as this is a somewhat alien area to psychiatry, but it may be well to keep in mind that the natural barriers against violence seem to be reduced by the number of people involved in perpetrating a crime. Whereas two normally developed teenagers can commit atrocities by inciting each other in the context of a small group of five to ten persons, individual capacities are no longer of any decisive importance when faced with a situation in which group hatred is explicit.[8]

[6] A. Raine, *The Anatomy of Violence: the Biological Roots of Crime* (New York, NY: Knopf Doubleday Publishing Group, 2013).

[7] Ibid., at 242–302.

[8] P. Zimbardo, *The Lucifer Effect: How Good People Turn Evil* (London: Rider, 2007).

International crimes and criminal responsibility

The most well-known contribution of forensic psychiatry concerns situations whereby mental health experts are called by criminal courts to assess whether an accused defender might not have been criminally sane; that is, aware of what he/she was doing and in control of his/her behaviour at the time of the crime. Different jurisdictions deal with this issue in various ways. In most countries, a psychiatrist may be called as a witness for the defence when the defence argue for a 'not guilty by reason of insanity' verdict. Perhaps the most famous formulation of not being guilty by reason of insanity concerns the so-called M'Naghten rules, which are used in common law systems (including, e.g., England, Canada, India, the USA, Australia, South Africa and Zimbabwe). The M'Naghten rules were formulated after a high profile criminal case in England in 1843. Daniel M'Naghten tried to assassinate the British Prime Minister, Sir Robert Peel, but ended up killing his secretary in the belief that he was the Prime Minister. The defence argued that M'Naghten was insane and therefore not responsible for his actions. M'Naghten was not sentenced to death but was detained at a mental hospital and the case started an intense debate in which, among others, Queen Victoria expressed doubt as to whether M'Naghten should really be regarded as bearing no responsibility on account of his insanity. The dispute eventually led to the formulation of the M'Naghten rules. These state that in order:

> to establish a defence on the ground of insanity, it must be clearly proved that, at the time of the committing of the act, the party accused was labouring under such a defect of reason, from disease of the mind, as not to know the nature and quality of the act he was doing; or, if he did know it, that he did not know that what he was doing was wrong.[9]

American jurisprudence is not uniform on the standards of insanity that must apply in any given case. While some states follow the M'Naghten rules, others use a broader approach introduced by the Model Penal Code.[10] This Code adds a volitional criterion, stating that a person should not be held criminally responsible if he lacked substantial capacity to appreciate the criminality of his conduct or to *perform his conduct to the requirements of the law.*[11]

[9] *Mc'Naghten* case, House of Lords (1843) 8 ER 718.

[10] The Model Penal Code is a statutory text that was developed by the American Law Institute (ALI) in 1962.

[11] Model Penal Code, § 4.01(1).

In some countries, such as the Netherlands, a forensic psychiatric evaluation is court-ordered and does not form a party pleading, although this mission still concerns the question of criminal responsibility. Finally, there are some examples of jurisdictions, such as that of Sweden and a few states in the USA, which do not allow acquittals due to insanity at all. In the Swedish justice system every person that commits a crime by intention is considered responsible for his or her actions, regardless of that person's mental status. A differentiation is then made as to the appropriate choice of sanction, particularly in cases where the criminal code prohibits the courts from sentencing an offender to incarceration if the crime was committed under the influence of a *severe mental disorder* that deprived the offender of the ability to understand or control his or her actions. The available sanction in that case is compulsory psychiatric care.

Paramount for an insanity defence is the presence of a mental condition of some kind. The terms differ from one legislation to another, such as 'disease of the mind' (Model Penal Code), 'mental impairment' (Australia) and 'mental disorder' (Canada). With a few exceptions (e.g., Norway), it is not spelt out in medical terms what constitutes a mental condition for the purposes of the criminal law and particularly criminal liability. It is important to keep in mind that *insanity* under these circumstances does not denote any specific psychiatric condition but is merely a legal concept. Courts in the USA have pondered over a list of diseases that would satisfy the insanity criteria and the range of conditions here has come to vary, from hyperglycaemia to severe organic brain damage.[12] However, it is primarily the presence of psychotic disorders that leads to successful insanity defences.[13]

In the history of international criminal law a mental incapacity defence has seldom been used, but there are some exceptions. A well-known example is the defence unsuccessfully raised by Rudolf Hess in the course of the Nuremberg trial.[14] The principle was also applied in the *Celebici*

[12] M. Scaliotti, 'Defences before the International Criminal Court: Substantive Grounds for Excluding Criminal Responsibility – Part 2', (2002) 2 *International Criminal Law Review* 1; I. Marchuk, *The Fundamental Concept of Crime in International Criminal Law* (Berlin: Springer, 2014), at 253–77.

[13] J. A. Lymburner and R. Roesch, 'The Insanity Defense: Five Years of Research (1993–1997)', (1999) 22 *International Journal of Law and Psychiatry* 1, at 3–4; M. Rice and G. T. Harris, 'The Predictors of Insanity Acquittal', (1990) 13 *International Journal of Law and Psychiatry* 217.

[14] M. Scaliotti, 'Defences before the International Criminal Court: Substantive Grounds for Excluding Criminal Responsibility – Part 1', (2001) 1 *International Criminal Law Review* 111.

case, tried before the International Criminal Tribunal for the former Yugoslavia (ICTY) in 1998.[15] One of the defendants, Esad Landzo, advanced the plea of diminished responsibility in respect of all charges against him.[16] Despite the fact that he did recognize the wrongful nature of his actions he claimed to have been, on account of his abnormality of mind, unable to be in complete control of his actions.[17] A total of five psychiatrists testified during the course of the trial.[18] The Chamber concluded that Landzo did suffer from 'an abnormality of the mind' but that this did not completely prevent him from controlling his actions and, as a result, he was deemed responsible for his actions. The Chamber here referred to English criminal law and stated that diminished responsibility could not be a defence that might lead to acquittal, but only a basis for mitigating one's sentence.[19]

The ICTY Statute does not include an insanity defence as such.[20] It is, however, mentioned in its Rules of Procedure and Evidence (RPE).[21] There, it is stated that the accused shall notify the prosecutor of his intent to offer any special defences, including that of diminished responsibility or lack thereof. The incorporation of diminished responsibility in the RPE was the only guideline available for the Trial Chamber in the *Celebici* trial and the concept was thoroughly discussed in the case of the accused, Landzo. The Chamber established a two-part test of 'diminished responsibility': at the time of the alleged acts the accused must have been suffering from an 'abnormality of the mind' which 'substantially impaired' the ability of the accused to control his or her actions.[22]

[15] *ICTY Prosecutor* v. *Delalic et al.* [*Celebici* case], Trial Chamber judgment (16 November 1998).

[16] Ibid., at paras. 1156–87.

[17] L. F. Sparr, 'Mental Incapacity Defences at the War Crimes Tribunal: Questions and Controversy', (2005) 33 *Journal of the American Academy of Psychiatry and the Law* 59.

[18] More on the psychiatric aspects of the case can be found in L. F. Sparr, 'Personality Disorders and Criminal Law: An International Perspective', (2009) 37 *Journal of the American Academy of Psychiatry and the Law* 168.

[19] The result of the *Celebici* judgment regarding diminished responsibility is further discussed in Scaliotti, above note 12, at 22; Marchuk, above note 12, at 257; J. Tobin, 'The Psychiatric Defence and International Criminal Law', (2007) 23 *Medicine, Conflict and Survival* 111.

[20] Nor does the ICTR.

[21] Rules of Procedure and Evidence of the International Criminal Tribunal for the former Yugoslavia, original version February 1994, Doc. IT/32, 67A(ii)(b).

[22] This is further discussed in P. Krug, 'The Emerging Mental Incapacity Defense in International Criminal Law: Some Initial Questions of Implementation', (2000) 94 *American Journal of International Law* 317.

During the preparatory discussions preceding the Statute of the International Criminal Court (ICC), several aspects of the mental incapacity defence were debated. It started with an initial discussion on whether the Statute should include an exhaustive list of defences at all. The need for flexibility in the face of unforeseeable circumstances was considered an important argument against an exhaustive list and finally outweighed concerns that an open list would give the Court unintended legislative power.[23] The final version of the mental incapacity defence in Article 31 of the ICC Statute states that a person shall not be criminally responsible if, at the time of that person's conduct:

> the person suffers from a mental disease or defect that destroys that person's capacity to appreciate the unlawfulness or nature of his or her conduct, or capacity to control his or her conduct to conform to the requirements of law.[24]

During the preparatory discussions, the formulation 'lacking substantial capacity' was suggested, but instead the more restrictive 'destroy' was decided upon.[25] A 'mental disease or defect' is a wide definition that is consistent with the intention to give emphasis to the effects of the mental state rather than to any specific diagnostic label. The perpetrator's state must be more than a momentary defective mental state.[26]

Diminished capacity is not mentioned in the relevant provision, which is only concerned with full defences, but the list of defences is not meant to be exhaustive.[27] The Court can thus consider other grounds that may arise from any source of law referred to in Article 21 of the Statute, in particular customary international law or general principles of law. Humanitarian law and case law from the ICTY and the International Criminal Tribunal for Rwanda (ICTR) may also serve as important sources for aiding the interpretation of the ICC in the future.[28]

The ICC Statute thus leaves very little room to consider diminished responsibility.[29] In the *Celebici* case, the accused, Landzo, appealed, claiming that diminished responsibility should be considered a full defence, which should naturally culminate in his acquittal. The ICTY Appeal Chamber referred to the ICC Statute and concluded that, since

[23] Scaliotti, above note 14, at 119; Marchuk, above note 12, at 111–72; Tobin, above note 19, at 116–17.

[24] Article 31(1)(a) ICC Statute. [25] Krug, above note 22, at 321.

[26] K. Ambos, 'Defences in International Criminal Law', in B. S. Brown (ed.), *Research Handbook on International Criminal Law* (Cheltenham: Edward Elgar, 2011) at 302.

[27] Ibid., at 299. [28] Ibid., at 299–300. [29] Tobin, above note 19, at 116.

there is no mention of diminished responsibility in the Statute, the ICTY RPE description was not sufficient to determine that diminished responsibility could constitute a special defence and thus only allowed for mitigation of sentence. This conclusion has been perceived as controversial.[30]

Assessing legal insanity in relation to international crimes

The broad definition of the underlying psychiatric condition ('mental disease or defect') in the ICC Statute leaves room for many potentially applicable mental disorders, a circumstance which may be regarded as problematic in this context since it grants the expert witnesses great power to influence the legal proceedings. However, as Peter Krug points out, even though a more specific standard could narrow the role of the expert witnesses it may also fail to recognize the on-going re-definition of mental illness within the psychiatric discipline, as well as the unique nature of each individual's mental state.[31]

The term 'destruction' cannot be found in any definition of criminal insanity used in national jurisprudence and was essentially discredited in the case of *Hadfield* in England in the year 1800. At that time an insanity defence required 'a total deprivation of memory'. It was stated that in order 'to protect a man from punishment, he must be in such a state of prostrated intellect, as not to know his name, nor his condition, nor his relations to others'.[32] James Hadfield was charged with treason as a result of having fired a gun at King George III in a theatre, but ultimately failed to harm him. His defence counsel, Thomas Erskine, proposed a different test by which to assess his client's mental state. Following serious injuries to his head, inflicted at the Battle of Tourcoing in 1794, Hadfield was suffering from delusions. He believed himself to be on a mission to save the world, which not only resulted in an attempt to kill the King, but also his eight-month-old son a few days earlier. Erskine argued that Hadfield would not have attacked the King had he not been suffering from these delusions. As a result he was acquitted even though he could not adequately be described as suffering from a total deprivation of memory.

The question of how to interpret the requirements of an insanity clause is debated and the absence of clear guidelines in this context is

[30] Ibid., at 116. [31] Krug, above note 22, at 324.

[32] D. N. Robinson, *Wild Beasts and Idle Humours: The Insanity Defence from Antiquity to the Present*, (Cambridge, MA: Harvard University Press, 1996) at 145.

striking. To start with, there should be a link between the disorder and the loss of ability to understand and control one's actions. In the ICC it is formulated in terms of the defect or disease destroying the capacity. Other examples of formulations in national laws are that the lack of understanding should be a 'result of' (M'Naghten), 'product of' (Durham/New Hampshire test), or 'a consequence of' (Australia) the disorder. These wordings indicate a causal relation between the disorder and the lack of understanding.

So what is actually meant when we say that a person does not appreciate the nature or unlawfulness of his or her actions? The issue has been debated by scholars from different fields. The ICC formulation potentially makes the interpretation simpler, since the capacity to understand and control one's actions, respectively, should be destroyed in order for someone to be considered legally insane. While formulations in terms of 'impairment' or 'seriously diminish' give room for discussions about whether it is sufficient that certain aspects of the cognitive and volitional capacities are impaired or whether the impairment rather should be a global lowering of these abilities, 'destroy' is more straightforward. The ICC formulation can but be understood as that the capacities should be missing altogether (which poses some other problems, as explained below).

Military and political leaders

The primary targets for international law are individuals who have been leaders and organizers of the type of criminality that is defined and described in this book (and in the docket of all international criminal tribunals), namely persons who have been capable, over a significant amount of time, of influencing, organizing and, when applicable, leading political developments in directions that include destructive and aggressive actions. Although it is not assumed that they actually carried out the prohibited conduct, even if they were in some sense complicit, they were nevertheless responsible from the outset for conduct attributed to subordinates. Individuals able to influence others to such a degree in the perpetration of violent behaviour must necessarily possess several abilities such as leadership, talent and effective communication in order to convey their ideas and convince others. The capacity to uphold these kinds of roles is hardly consistent with the presence of any form of serious mental disorder that would qualify as the mental foundation of legal insanity in any national jurisdiction. This is probably one of the strongest reasons explaining why the various forms of insanity defences have seldom been applied to leaders in the history of international criminal proceedings. This stance is further supported by available data. By way of illustration, all the Nuremberg defendants underwent a thorough psychiatric and psychological examination which showed that almost everyone was well functioning and gifted with IQs clearly above what was then considered normal.[33] This seems to apply not only to the high-ranking leadership but also to those of the rank-and-file that participated in Nazi war crimes and other atrocities. The authors of *The Quest for the Nazi Personality* conclude that the origins of Nazi Germany should not be sought in clinical psychological assessments of personalities, but rather in the context of social, socio-psychological, political and cultural circumstances.[34]

Personality disorders

The ICC is not, however, explicitly reserved for trying top-level military and civilian leaders. There are data demonstrating that soldiers committing war crimes may show a different psychiatric picture from that exhibited by their leaders. Goreta and Covic published a study that surveyed forensic psychiatric evaluations of 120 persons prosecuted for crimes directly or indirectly relating to the war in Croatia between 1991 and 1995.[35] They found that as many as 59 per cent of the subjects had been convicted of one or several crimes before taking part in the Croatian war. For 20 per cent of the subjects, data were found to indicate correctional measures in reaction to criminal behaviour during adolescence. Almost one fourth of the subjects had been in contact with psychiatric services before the war. The most common reason for both psychiatric in-patient and out-patient treatment concerned problems associated with personality disorders and alcohol abuse. The subjects also belonged to a younger age-group. These data (however limited) thus show that offenders of international crimes share the same risk factors as persistent violent offenders who commit crimes in civilian life, namely, a young age, previous criminal behaviour (with an early onset) and drug abuse.

[33] E. A. Zillmer, M. Harrower, B. Ritzler and R. P. Archer, *The Quest for the Nazi Personality: A Psychological Investigation of Nazi War Criminals* (London: Routledge, 1995).

[34] Ibid. (especially the chapter entitled 'The myth of the Nazi personality'), at 173–94.

[35] M. Goreta and I. Peko Covic, 'Forensic Psychiatric Evaluations of Perpetrators of Crimes committed During the War in Croatia (1991–1995)', (2004) 27 *International Journal of Law and Psychiatry* 207.

In the psychiatric evaluations performed in connection with the relevant trials, the most common diagnosis was some kind of personality disorder (52 per cent), with antisocial personality disorder being by far the most common. Other diagnostic categories included (albeit much less common) neurotic disorders (10 per cent), alcohol dependence (7.5 per cent), mild mental retardation (5.8 per cent), etc. Acute alcohol intoxication at the time of the crimes was diagnosed in 69 persons (58 per cent). A diagnosis of post-traumatic stress disorder was made in respect of nine subjects.

The defendants were prosecuted in accordance with the Croatian Criminal Code.[36] This code included at the time a graded insanity clause, distinguishing between three categories, namely, the unaccountable who should not be punished at all, those with an essentially diminished accountability (and who should receive milder sanctions) and, finally, those with diminished (but not *essentially diminished*) accountability. Most of the subjects in this study fit the category of 'diminished but not essentially diminished accountability', primarily based on factors caused by circumstances of war, such as reactions to frustrating situations, sleep deprivation or drunkenness, and not on any psychiatric conditions per se. One-third of the subjects were assessed as having an 'essentially diminished accountability'. Disorders 'in the structure and dynamics of a perpetrator's personality' had the greatest weight, along with antisocial behaviour, while acute alcoholism was also a major factor. A diagnosis of post-traumatic stress disorder was only a major factor in three cases. In sum, the assessments of diminished accountability were based on personality disorders in addition to intoxication. None of the subjects was considered (completely) unaccountable.

It seems quite obvious that none of these subjects would have been assessed as not responsible due to mental insanity had the ICC criteria been applied instead. A lesson to be drawn from this, however, is that any army wishing to protect its integrity has to screen persons with histories of severe antisocial behaviours and substance abuse. The second lesson may be that responsibility for uncontrolled substance abuse in an armed force may be sought higher in the chain of command.

Mental retardation

Mental retardation and severe developmental aberrations could be of such a severe nature that they are tantamount to legal insanity, according to some legal standards, and a severe mental retardation may even be said to

[36] Osnovni krivie`ni zakon Republike Hrvatske, Narodne novine No. 31/93.

have *destroyed* a person's capacity to appreciate the nature and unlawfulness of his or her actions. Dementias or organic psycho-syndromes may exert similar influences on mental capacities. A thorough psychiatric evaluation including psychological testing will reveal the existence of this type of mental problem and it is reasonably easy to establish how deep and extensive these problems are. Individuals suffering from considerable mental retardation and/or developmental aberrations have, however, a small chance of being enrolled in politics or the armed forces in the first place. These individuals would hence most probably not even be considered for prosecution in international courts, with the exception of the specific situation of civil war where paramilitary groups could have used weak and retarded individuals to commit crimes. There is, however, a grey zone corresponding to marginal or mild mental retardation (IQ of about 70–80 or 50–70, respectively), that cannot be said to destroy a person's ability to understand and control his or her actions, but may have to be considered as a factor for mitigating punishment according to established practices.

Psychotic disorders

Several studies have showed that the psychiatric diagnosis most strongly correlated with successful insanity pleas in national jurisdictions worldwide concerns a variety of psychotic disorders.[37] Again, it does not seem probable that individuals who have been leaders and organizers of crimes falling under international jurisdictions can suffer from the most common forms of psychoses, which include some degree of disorganization, disorientation or confusion (the only type of psychosis that is regularly found in combination with lucidity and orientation is paranoia, which may take on the forms of a pure disorder of thought content). However, under prolonged stress, all humans eventually lose their mental faculties and become psychotic (this is often referred to as a reaction to stress in relation to a lowering of the psychosis threshold), even if the resilience (i.e., the individual's threshold) varies widely from one person to another and is also dependent on general health. Sleep deprivation, hunger, thirst, pain and inflammation are external factors that greatly influence the individual's resilience. Combatants in war situations are exposed to extreme forms of stress and are thus under the risk of

[37] Lymburner and Roesch, above note 13; Rice and Harris, above note 13.

developing mental break-downs, especially in heightened and pressed situations with aggressive outbursts as a result.[38] Affected persons could, under such circumstances, run amok and kill prisoners of war, civilians, officers or even their comrades by mere chance encounter; a type of incident that has been seen in almost every war during the last century. This is a situation demanding some degree of psychiatric assessment in the case of international crimes, since the crimes committed could have been carried out in a mental state comparable with legal insanity, even if this is notoriously difficult to ascertain in retrospect, particularly in the absence of adequate documentation.

Thought disorders

To many people, it may seem that there is something severely 'deranged' about a person who firmly believes that it is justified to commit the kind of atrocities that took place during, for example, the Second World War, in Rwanda, or in the war in the former Yugoslavia. Even if the leaders were intelligent and organized enough to be neither mentally retarded nor psychotic, their values and world-views seem utterly wrong from a moral perspective, but also as compared to historical conduct, actual human interactions or what most people believe. Could there still be something wrong with these persons from a psychiatric point of view that has implications for their criminal responsibility? The classic disorder of thought content is paranoia (ranging from paranoid ideation to paranoid disorder and paranoid schizophrenia). Paranoia literally means 'besides knowledge', and refers to ideas that no longer conform to reality, from odd and aberrant thinking, often linked to suspiciousness, to a personality disorder characterized by consistent suspiciousness, extreme jealousy or schizotypal – that is, magic – thinking, to a psychosis where the afflicted is deeply convinced of something that is in clear contrast to all evidence about reality and, finally, to a schizophrenic disorder that generally includes bizarre delusions that could not happen in the universe as we know it, such as having one's thoughts controlled by the CIA through a chip inserted in one's brain.[39] Paranoid schizophrenia also carries other symptoms of the most severe psychotic conditions, such as

[38] D. G. Dutton, *The Psychology of Genocide, Massacres, and Extreme Violence* (Westport, CT: Praeger, 2007) at 68–72 and 114–22.

[39] H. I. Kaplan and B. J. Sadock (eds.), *Comprehensive Textbook of Psychiatry*, Vol. 1 (6th edn, Williams & Wilkins, 1995) at 1032.

hallucinations, catatonia or impaired lucidity/orientation. Just as all psychoses, paranoid states may give rise to secondary mood swings, medical disorders or psychoactive substances. It should be stressed that paranoia exists as a spectrum ranging from the slightly odd to the outright bizarre, and often involves ideas that may be of relevance to international crimes, such as race, gender and sexual orientation.

In autism spectrum disorders (such as Asperger's syndrome), thought content is affected in a different way than in paranoia, even if the two may overlap. People on the autism spectrum often assume ego-centrical and idiosyncratic perspectives and have fixations on interests that may be ideas. Generally, autism, like paranoia, is thought to decrease the possibility of successful social interaction, but may confer 'charisma' to individuals operating in strictly hierarchical organizations. The social disability in autism specifically hampers reciprocal interaction, but may not be evident in command interaction. Indeed, ranking is often a preoccupation of people on the autism spectrum, who often think of other humans in terms of hierarchies. There is also a blurred line between autism spectrum disorders and psychotic disorders, meaning that the peculiar patterns of thinking encountered in autism may take on psychotic features.[40]

In mass criminal activity, group dynamics are probably of the largest interest. However, paranoid thoughts about other groups of people are known to play a toxic role when disseminated. It is now established that persons with thought content disorders can produce hate ideology that may subsequently gain tremendous force once set in action, far beyond what the initial ideologue could imagine. For example, it is known that harsh condemnations of homosexuality by religious leaders can increase the risk of attacks against homosexuals in the community, even if there was no violent or even discriminatory intent. In even more dangerous environments, such as ethnic or religious conflicts, absurd thinking can easily become accepted. Hateful ideologies that fuel armed conflicts tend to be the norm rather than the exception and, even if they take the shape of paranoid ideations, it is uncertain whether they could be viewed as 'true' paranoid ideas. They are shared by many and regarded as true conceptions of the object under consideration as well as about the conflict itself. Individuals embracing such well-spread ideas, which are

[40] L. Mazzone, L. Ruta and L. Reale, 'Psychiatric Comorbidities in Asperger Syndrome and High Functioning Autism: Diagnostic Challenges', (2012) 11 *Annals of General Psychiatry* 16.

often built on fear and prejudices, could not be said to be in a paranoid state motivating a legal insanity defence.

In extreme cases the difference between paranoid delusions and a mere personality variant may be the presence of others who share the same thought content, as exemplified by the well-known case of anti-Islam Norwegian terrorist Anders Breivik. His extremely complicated and contradictory psychiatric expert evaluations partly came down to the doctors' knowledge about Internet extremism (the first evaluation, which resulted in a diagnosis of schizophrenia, lost its credibility in the face of testimonies on the existence of similar subcultural ideations on the Web to those fostered by Breivik, and a new evaluation had to be performed, which resulted in an appraisal of Breivik's ideas as non-delusional).[41] The core definitions of delusion have been contested on all points, both by psychiatrists and philosophers. According to the American Psychiatric Association's DSM-IV, a delusion is:

> a false personal belief based on incorrect inference about external reality that is firmly sustained despite what almost everyone else believes and despite what constitutes incontrovertible and obvious proof or evidence to the contrary. The belief is not one ordinarily accepted by other members of the person's culture or subculture (i.e., it is not an article of religious faith). When a false belief involves a value judgment, it is regarded as a delusion only when the judgment is so extreme as to defy credibility.[42]

Yet, as many scholars have argued, delusional beliefs do not necessarily have to be false (a person can suffer from 'morbid jealousy' and at the same time actually be cheated on by his or her partner). A delusion does not have to be about external reality, but could be about the self. Furthermore, people in general tend to hold on to convictions (especially of a religious and moral nature) despite obvious proofs to the contrary. Finally, many delusions have a religious content.[43] Convictions of an ideological character held by participants in a war may be seen on a continuum ranging from political or religious convictions held by almost

[41] See Anders Behring Breivik Psychiatric Report 2012–04–10, available at https://sites.google.com/site/breivikreport/documents/anders-breivik-psychiatric-report-2012-04-10.

[42] American Psychiatric Association (APA), *Diagnostic and Statistical Manual of Mental Disorders* (4th edn, Washington, DC: APA, 2000) at 765.

[43] M. Spitzer, 'On Defining Delusions', (1990) 31 *Comprehensive Psychiatry* 377; A. S. David, 'On the Impossibility of Defining Delusions', (1999) 6 *Philosophy, Psychiatry and Psychology* 17; M. R. Broome, L. Bortolotti and M. Mamel, 'Moral Responsibility and Mental Illness: A Case Study', (2010) 19 *Cambridge Quarterly of Healthcare Ethics* 179.

everyone participating (in the war), through idiosyncratic perceptions of self and others via fixed or over-valued ideas, to full-blown delusions. These facts suggest that the question as to whether an accused should be acquitted on grounds of criminal insanity must preferably not be dependent on his or her ideas being shared by others (or not), but instead be assessed by the presence or absence of other psychotic symptoms. Therefore, assessments of paranoid thought content should categorically be excluded as a defence in the absence of other clear symptoms of psychosis, such as disorganization, disorientation or diminished lucidity of the thought process.

The relevance of legal insanity to international crimes

There are several reasons suggesting that a mental capacity defence might be especially problematic in the context of international criminal law, not only from a psychiatric perspective, but also from a legal viewpoint. The ICC Statute constitutes a merger of conceptually different legal systems, where insanity and mental incapacity are concepts that have been interpreted quite differently in the various jurisdictions.[44] An insanity defence also implies incorporation of methods and concepts from the field of psychiatry, which could lead to additional issues of a substantive, procedural and evidentiary nature.[45] As Ambos has pointed out, responsibility may also be excluded by lack of intent if the mental defect is so serious as to exclude the actor's awareness or ability to act at all.[46] However, the highly restricted formulation of insanity raises the question as to whether there exists a mental state that is susceptible to acquittal on the ground that the subject lacks mental capacity, but which would not also constitute a lack of intent. John Tobin maintains that since a destruction of mental capacities must be regarded as rare, the standard in the ICC Statute seems impossible to use in legal practice. He recommends an interpretation that entails a partial destruction of mental capacities, which, in his opinion, would lead to a more compassionate understanding of the defendant.[47]

Moreover, it has been questioned whether an incorporation of an insanity defence in international law is meaningful in the first place. It might be argued (see above) that it is doubtful that anyone suffering from a serious mental illness would ever be prosecuted before the ICC in the

[44] Tobin, above note 19, at 112–13. [45] Krug, above note 22, at 319.
[46] Ambos, above note 26, at 303. [47] Tobin, above note 19, at 121.

first place, given that the ICC's main concern (also in view of the great costs of the procedures), is the prosecution of political and military leaders for crimes which require a high level of organization.[48] Scaliotti offers a similar view by finding it implausible that crimes involving extensive planning and preparation, and which are principally committed by top-level military and civilian leaders, are consistent with a mental state of insanity.[49] However, he does go on to point out that relevant case law on war crimes demonstrates that, aside from superior orders, insanity is one of the main pleas invoked by defendants.[50]

Tobin takes a different view and emphasizes that it is the ideological tendency to view offenders of mass murder and genocide as 'less than human' which entails denying their human strengths, qualities and weaknesses. This extends to denying that they could be victims of any mental illness. He believes that the true reasons for the absence of an insanity defence in the statutes of the ICTY and ICTR (and the restricted formulation in the ICC Statute) should be sought in the aforementioned denial of victimhood, combined with a fear that insanity-based acquittals may be perceived as a deception of the court by the defendant.[51] He stresses the importance of preventing the principle of retribution from subverting the defendants' right to justice.

Fitness to stand trial

In the practice of international criminal tribunals there are few examples where a defendant's fitness to stand trial has been assessed, one notable exception being the trial of Rudolf Hess before the Nuremberg Tribunal,[52] albeit this claim has also been raised in the context of the ICTY.[53]

The ICTY discussed this claim in the case of Paul Strugar,[54] where the Trial Chamber stated that in order to exercise 'his expressed and implied rights' the defendant had to have the capacity to plead, understand the nature of the charges, understand details of evidence, instruct counsel, understand the nature of proceedings, and testify. The standard was specified as a minimum standard of overall capacity below which an accused cannot be tried without unfairness and injustice. It does not

[48] Marchuk, above note 12, at 277.
[49] Scaliotti, above note 12, at 26.
[50] Scaliotti, above note 14, at 44.
[51] Tobin, above note 19, at 112.
[52] Scaliotti, above note 12, at 18.
[53] Krug, above note 22, at 321, note 29.
[54] *ICTY Prosecutor* v. *Pavle Strugar*, Trial Chamber judgment (31 January 2005), paras. 510–11.

matter if the unfitness is due to a mental or physical illness, and the burden of proof lies with the defendant.[55]

Unfitness to stand trial is not mentioned in the ICC Statute, but the ICC RPE[56] include, on recommendation from Amnesty International,[57] a rule allowing the court to order a medical examination of the defendant[58] and a rule stating that the Trial Chamber should adjourn the proceedings when it is satisfied that the accused is unfit to stand trial.[59]

Risk assessments

Forensic psychiatric expertise is also often used in making estimations of criminal recidivism and, naturally, also in order to treat offenders with mental health problems, either in special hospitals or in the prison system, with the primary goal of restitution of health, but also with a secondary goal, more or less clearly stated, of reducing the risk of criminal recidivism in the interests of the patient and society alike. Offenders with mental health problems also include individuals who have committed the type of crimes that fall under the rubric of international crimes. The question of criminal recidivism is often raised when an offender is seeking probation, or when he or she is considered for discharge after a period of treatment. In these situations, risk assessments are often carried out focusing on the risk for relapsing into new, violent criminality. Nowadays, risk assessment tools are regularly used. These may be specific for the type of violence assessed (e.g., sexual, spousal or general violence). Risk assessment could also come into question when an offender is deemed legally insane since the level of dangerousness has consequences for the type of mental care the affected person should receive. There are, however, no evidence-based instruments or methods for risk assessments focusing on the risk for international crimes, and it is almost impossible to imagine how the risk arising from such persons should be assessed since it is so tightly interwoven with the specific situation in which crime is committed. Assessments of individual risk levels for crimes of this type seem

55 Tobin, above note 19, at 118–19.

56 ICC Rules of Procedure and Evidence ICC-ASP/1/3 (Part II-A) 09.09.2002, available at www.icc-cpi.int/.

57 Amnesty International, *The International Criminal Court: Drafting Effective Rules of Procedure and Evidence concerning Trial, Appeal and Review* (1999) (AI Index: IOR 40/12/99).

58 ICC Rules of Procedure and Evidence, Art. 135.

59 Tobin, above note 19, at 118.

meaningless, since such assessments can only be done after the war or conflict has ended, and then the recidivism risk will depend on geopolitics (such as neo-Nazis recruiting liberated war criminals) rather than on any individual mental factors.

Psychiatric treatment

In the study of Croatian war crimes, the sanctions recommended for the offenders consisted of involuntary treatment of substance dependence in penal institutions; which seems reasonable enough given the rather severe impact alcohol intake had on the perpetration of the crimes.[60] Intoxication affects the brain and the mental faculties in ways that weaken or destroy the ability to inhibit and control behaviour, which may lead to destructive actions. The drug defence in international crime is, however, disputed since many have objected that it is not reasonable that voluntary intake of alcohol and/or drugs should be used as a ground for excluding or diminishing criminal responsibility.[61] Alcohol and drugs have been used in many war situations to inhibit empathy, dampen the moral conscience and enhance aggression among combatants.[62] The situation would be different where it was demonstrated that low-ranking combatants were given intoxicants by their commanding officers or responsible medical officers with the goal of making them more likely to commit violations.

The question of criminal sanctions might be discussed in isolation from the question of responsibility. Even if the ICC does not excuse any offender, it is still worth considering if the offenders might be in need of some kind of psychiatric treatment. A potential problem with international criminal law is that there is no established system, normative or procedural, connected to international prosecutions for handling defendants acquitted or deemed to be unfit to stand trial.[63] Scaliotti emphasizes that there should be no other sanction than complete acquittal, since the defendant may well pose no threat either to himself or to

[60] Goreta and Peko Covic, above note 35.

[61] W. A. Schabas, *An Introduction to the International Criminal Court* (Cambridge University Press, 2004) at 110–14.

[62] P. R. Kan, *Drug Intoxicated Irregular Fighters: Complications, Dangers, and Responses* (Carlisle, PA: Strategic Studies Institute, 2008); C. Browning, *Ordinary Men: Reserve Police Battalion 101 and the Final Solution in Poland* (New York, NY: Harper Collins, 1998).

[63] Krug, above note 22, at 333–4; Tobin, above note 19, at 121–2.

anyone else.[64] Krug, on the other hand, stresses that the absence of a system for involuntary forensic psychiatric treatment on the basis of dangerousness threatens both the credibility of international prosecution as well as the culture of legality.[65] Tobin suggests that the defendant in such a case should be referred to an ICC-built psychiatric institution, which, in his opinion, may lead to the ICC being more comfortable with accepting an insanity defence.[66] In our view, there is no need for a special psychiatric clinic for those deemed unaccountable in the ICC. The compulsory psychiatric treatment might preferably take place in existing psychiatric institutions, according to logic similar to how offenders of international crimes come to serve their prison sentences. In cases where a defendant is not judged as legally insane, but still assessed to be in need of psychiatric treatment, his or her sanctions may very well also be served in countries with state-of-the-art medical treatment available to persons serving sentences in their correctional systems. A more pressing problem is the apparent absence of legal provisions for admitting a defendant who is acquitted due to legal insanity in the ICC to compulsory psychiatric treatment.

Concluding remarks

It is reasonable to assume that psychiatric or medical assessments are reliable to rate consciousness, lucidity and orientation, but once thought content is on the table, insecurity will reign, even for the best professionals. It is impossible to base a judgement of thought content just on a transcription of the subject's ideas. Theoretically, a psychotic idea should not be widely shared, so idiosyncrasy is a core point. At the same time, it is obvious that ideas generally held in cultures could be deemed 'unhealthy' to a single individual who holds them just for himself. Bizarre delusions are in a class of their own, but due to their unacceptability for other persons they should be expected to be less common in international crimes or group crimes. Unfortunately, the most common ideations behind these crimes will be the most difficult to assess from the standpoint of contemporary psychiatry.

A clinical assessment often focuses on accompanying symptoms. Odd and unusually intense ideas encountered in a person with a mood disorder, catatonia, obsessive-compulsive rituals, or even with just

[64] Scaliotti, above note 12, at 27.
[65] Krug, above note 22, at 334.
[66] Tobin, above note 19, at 122.

stereotypical movements, will be considered pathological much more quickly. Clinicians also make their assessments in view of treatability, which further complicates the specific evaluations of thought content. It does not seem reasonable that legal responsibility should be linked to whether some ideations may change after long-term administration of antipsychotic drugs. It therefore seems reasonable that the evaluation of psychotic thought content should be based on the lucidity of the thought process rather than on the content of ideas.

When evaluating expert evidence it is necessary to be clear about what is said based on which type of knowledge. Scientific data should not be naïvely translated in such a way as to fit into a legal vocabulary. The first step in a correct medico legal exchange – of paramount importance, if often overlooked – is to respect the respective fields of expertise between the lawyer and the medical doctor. The latter may have a shallow appreciation of what constitutes a crime and how legal responsibility should be assessed, but otherwise possess a limitless confidence in the possibility of scientific explanations concerning human actions.

Additional methodological issues need to be briefly stressed. Science aims at establishing knowledge that is generalizable and predictive of the future. However, when interpreting group data on individuals, confidence intervals broaden[67] and it is always wise to keep in mind that 'the future ain't what it used to be', especially when it comes to the now commonly performed risk assessments. In addition, even if scientists sometimes advocate a deterministic world-view that seems to diminish or even 'destroy' individual responsibility,[68] this is not a scientifically tested model but rather a theory about the world and humans based on radical materialism,[69] nor is it necessarily relevant for jurisprudence.[70]

Keeping these methodological and theoretical problems in mind there may still be a need for psychiatric expertise in international law. It is improbable that perpetrators of international crimes form a homogenous

[67] D. J. Cooke and C. Michie, 'Limitations of Diagnostic Precision and Predictive Utility in the Individual Case: A Challenge for Forensic Practice', (2010) 34 *Law and Human Behavior* 259.

[68] A. R. Cashmore, 'The Lucretian Swerve: The Biological basis of Human Behavior and the Criminal Justice System', (2010) 107 *Proceedings of the National Academy of Sciences* 4499.

[69] H. Anckarsäter, 'Has Biology Disproved Free Will and Moral Responsibility?', (2010) 107 *Proc. Natl. Acad. Sci* 28.

[70] S. J. Morse, 'The Non-Problem of Free Will in Forensic Psychiatry and Psychology', (2007) 25 *Behavioral Sciences and the Law* 203.

group as regards their motives or indeed their psychological make-ups (profiles). Crimes committed during war by young soldiers who kill civilians on a drinking spree probably cannot be explained in the same way as the criminal conduct attributed to a group of soldiers violating international humanitarian law in furtherance of a superior order. The same is true in respect of senior officers making the relevant orders and issuing commands to subordinates. It seems unconvincing that a person enjoying command authority (including those yielding political power), who is capable of performing complex daily tasks, may be considered (severely) mentally disordered in a way that would render him or her legally insane.

It is equally unsustainable that soldiers able to understand superior orders and work together in a group are insane in the legal sense (e.g., acutely psychotic). However, there may be exceptions to this rule that justify the inclusion of an insanity clause in international criminal law (treaties or domestic legislation). One cannot completely rule out *a priori* the possibility of a person developing some form of acute psychosis during wartime, in such a way that at least severely damages that person's ability to assess reality in the correct manner. Even though an insanity defence may be rarely applicable in the international context, it is an important statement of justice and legality.

The highly restricted description (in terms of destroyed capacities) of legal insanity in the ICC Statute might be viewed as advantageous since psychiatric expertise will probably be used only in court proceedings involving severe mental disorders. Defendants exhibiting deviant ideations without other clear symptoms of psychosis will most likely not be advised to use an insanity defence, which, in turn, will limit discussions among experts about which ideations should be considered deviant enough to qualify as grounds for insanity. At the same time, the wide definition of mental incapacity (disease or defect), in combination with the extensive possibilities for presenting evidence, potentially reinforces the status of expert witnesses in international criminal proceedings. Furthermore, as Krug points out, experts can be expected to play a central role not only in the factual inquiry, but also by influencing the prospective shaping of the normative content of the mental incapacity defence.[71] On the other hand, the international setting might enlarge the conflict between a variety of expert opinions, as these may be derived from different scientific traditions or make use of several diagnostic systems, which in turn will allow the courts more space for legal determinations of insanity.

[71] Krug, above note 22.

Ideas of how offenders should be treated by the criminal justice system depend on underlying assumptions of guilt, responsibility and the purpose of criminal sanctions. The majority of jurisdictions rest on a variety of underlying principles, namely retribution, deterrence, rehabilitation, as well as societal protection. The function of the justice system is to punish those who break the law and the sanction should be in proportion to the criminal offence. Another function of criminal sanctions is societal protection against crimes, and deterrence can contribute to general prevention. But treatment is an integral part of individual prevention. In the Croatian cases described above, a large proportion of the sentenced offenders received mandatory substance abuse treatment as a sanction. It seems reasonable to assume that many perpetrators of international crimes would benefit from psychiatric treatment of some kind. It seems rational, therefore, that such treatment is provided by the countries entrusted with their incarceration.

11

Understanding collective violence: the communicative and performative qualities of violence in acts of belonging

JEFFREY STEVENSON MURER

This chapter explores the motivations for joining violent groups across a range of circumstances. In particular, the chapter will explore the similarities in the role of violence as a marker of identity within groups as diverse as street gangs and ethnic communities. Frequently, membership in violent groups is explained in terms of individual material gain or the attainment of individual fame, in very rationalist and individualistic terms.[1] These violent encounters or employments of violence by young people are often defined as being interpersonal in nature; that is, the motivation to use or not use violence is held by a single individual expressing individual agency in making a choice whether or not to deploy violence.[2] This focus on individual choice and motivation has likewise been extended to studies of terrorism and rationalist interpretations for the motivation to participate in civil wars or other armed conflicts.[3] Indeed, many of these studies treat joining these violent groups and the deployment of violent acts as being anti-social, as if the choice to engage in violence is one wholly against social norms or social values.[4] However, much can be gained by seeing these groups in completely the opposite

J. S. Murer was the Principal Investigator of the European Student of Youth Mobilisation from April 2008 to November 2011. This project was supported by the British Council through its InterCultural Navigators Programme. Some of the research from the ESYM is presented here.

1 L. Richardson, *What Terrorists Want: Understanding the Enemy/Containing the Threat* (Random House, 2006).

2 D. Gottfredson and E. Bauer, 'Interventions to Prevent Youth Violence', in *Handbook of Injury and Violence Prevention* (World Health Organisation, 2006).

3 See P. Collier and A. Hoeffler, *Greed and Grievance in Civil Wars* (World Bank, 2000); J. Horgan, *The Psychology of Terrorism* (Routledge, 2005).

4 J. H. Hitchcock, 'Adolescent Gang Participation: Psychological Perspectives', (2001) 16 *Journal of Police and Criminal Psychology* 33.

light: gangs, communal factions, militias, even terrorist organisations can be seen as highly social environments, especially for those who feel that they have limited opportunities for social capital accumulation or mobility within the larger society, or indeed have even been expelled from a mainstream social mobility milieu altogether. Within such social milieus violence is but one form of social action among a whole range of social acts;[5] or, to put it more succinctly, in such circumstances violence itself is a social act. This chapter will examine the performative qualities of violence and the role that violence plays in the experience of belonging in large groups and in collective identity formation.

The first part of the chapter will explore the communicative aspect of violence and its role in the processes of collective identity formation. The second section examines the relationships between the performances of collective identity and the accumulation of social capital. The third section explores these processes more deeply by analysing the importance of subject positions and the judgement or evaluation of identity performances through a new proposal of a violence triangle. The fourth section explores how violence can be held as a group value and examines this proposition in light of some of the findings from the European Study of Youth Mobilisation (ESYM).[6] The chapter concludes by suggesting that if we understand the social meaning of violence in a given set of circumstances it may be possible to replace violence with a less harmful social practice.

The discourse of violence: symbolic dimensions

Violence is not senseless. Rather violence is a set of actions, whether verbal or physical, personal or institutional, that is performed or imagined by social beings under specific historical conditions for concrete reasons. Collective narratives are constructed to explain and make sense of acts of violence made in a group's name. Such narratives carry these acts of violence into the collective imaginary, weaving them into the very identity fabric of the group. Violence, therefore, is not devoid of meaning. It also does not just happen; rather, it is done and is 'not

[5] T. K. Beck, 'The Eye of the Beholder: Violence as a Social Process', (2011) 5 *International Journal of Conflict and Violence* 345, at 346–7.

[6] British Council, *Listening to Radicals: Attitudes and Motivations of Young People Engaged in Political and Social Movements Outside of the Mainstream in Central and Nordic Europe* (British Council, 2011).

something that people do in general, but is always done to something or someone in particular'[7] even if the target was not the one intended. Moreover, violence comes in many forms, beginning with the physical and the interpersonal, but also ranging to the collective and communal, the structural and the symbolic. As such, violence is a realm of social interaction. Further, it is legitimated; or, to use David Riches' definition of violence, it is an act of harm deemed legitimate by the perpetrator and some witnesses.[8] More than that, Riches suggests that violence is a form of communication that is accessible, easily perceived and easily understood.[9] It is an act based in legitimacy by the perpetrator and some witnesses and will form the basis of making sense of the outcomes in a similar framework of legitimacy. Teresa Koloma Beck points out that the anthropologically inspired Berlin school, led by Georg Elwert, began to investigate the interactions between violence and other social acts and the formation of larger social structures 'at a time when dominant discourses emphasised the barbaric and irrational character of contemporary violence'.[10] The social component was important for Elwert, for, as Bettina Schmidt and Ingo Schröder write, while 'violence without a witness will still leave people dead, it is socially meaningless'.[11] For the likes of Elwert, Schmidt and Schröder, dismissing violence as simply 'bad' or, worse, something so repugnant as to not be studied, is to miss a whole realm of everyday sociability and interaction defining many communities. Georg Simmel engaged in a similar investigation nearly one hundred years before Elwert, as he was one of the first to look beyond violence as some 'unregulated primordial aggressiveness in the depths of mankind'[12] and to see it as a realm of interaction, set in a particular context, often to serve specific ends. In a piece from 1903, he argued that enmities and conflict play multiple roles both within and across groups: 'enmities [do] not merely prevent gradual disappearance of the boundaries within a society –and for this reason these enmities may be consciously promoted as [the] guarantee of the existing social constitution – but more than this the enmities are directly productive

[7] V. Bufacchi, *Violence and Social Justice* (Palgrave-Macmillan, 2007) at 33.

[8] D. Riches, 'The Phenomenon of Violence', in D Riches (ed.), *The Anthropology of Violence* (Basil-Blackwell, 1986) at 8.

[9] Ibid., at 11. [10] Beck, above note 5, at 346.

[11] B. Schmidt and I. Schröder, 'Introduction: Violent Imaginaries and Violent Practices', in B. Schmidt and I. Schröder (eds.), *Anthropology of Violence and Conflict* (Routledge, 2001) at 6.

[12] Ibid., at 1.

sociologically'.[13] In this Simmel saw violence as a synchronic event of social relations between individuals and a collective that served specific functions at both an inter-group and intra-group level. The violence both shapes and is shaped by those inter- and intra-group relationships.

Although often difficult to see, conflict and its frequent partner violence can serve many roles, some of which may be productive, perhaps even constructive. One role that violence often does serve is to delimit the boundaries of large group identities. Determining who is a target of violence and who is not; who is to be protected and who is to be made vulnerable; who is to be trusted and who is not to be trusted are questions that inform the often split-second decisions by which individuals determine who is within their own large group constellation, who is outside it and, therefore, who is a threat. To explore the role of violence within identity formation it is first necessary to examine some of the processes of collective identity formation.

One of us?

Identity derives from *identidem*, the contraction of the Latin expression of *idem et idem*, literally 'same and same' and it is in this perspective of identification that we come to see something as the same or similar. Yet, in making that assessment there is a parallel, if unspoken, assessment of difference. How much two things are alike depends on how much difference can be tolerated and similarity still asserted. In many regards the assessment of similarity is relational, not absolute; what might be intolerable in one circumstance may be the basis of unity in another. For everyone, one of the first acts of self-identification is recognising the distinction between the infant-self and a distinct and separate parent.[14] We recognise the distinction of our bodies, our own desires and needs and those of our parents and other family members and their friends. This first move of recognising what Lacan phrases as the distinction between 'I' and 'Not-I' becomes extended to other social groupings: family/not-family; neighbourhood/not-neighbourhood; nation/not-nation. These social groupings become the constellations of collective identity to which each

[13] G. Simmel, 'The Sociology of Conflict: I', (1903) 9 *American Journal of Sociology* 492.

[14] For Melanie Klein one of the most important moments for an infant is the recognition of the child that it is distinct from its mother. See M. Klein (1935), 'A Contribution to the Psychogenesis of Manic Depressive States', in J. Mitchell (ed.), *The Selected Melanie Klein* (London: Penguin Books, 1986) at116.

individual belongs: race, gender, class, sexual orientation, religion, ethno-linguistic group and relevant intersections between these. Each of us enjoys countless collective identities, some spatially oriented as in the example of a neighbourhood or housing estate, others are voluntary associations such as football clubs or political organisation, but the attachment, emotional investment or cathexis is no less strong. Moreover, the sum total of these collective identities and social groupings is one way by which each of us comes to define ourselves individually. We derive a sense of self-worth and value through our affiliations; or, as Daniel Druckman put it: '[m]embership in a clan, religious group, or ethnic group, becomes part of the individual's self-identity and critical to a sense of self-worth'.[15] As some of these identifications become attenuated and perhaps slip away altogether, we change, and yet that previous identification still marks us, whether as someone from the working class who now has found new riches and needs to negotiate the new social spaces and expectations that come with wealth, or as someone who once passionately rooted for one football team, became disillusioned and now roots for another. We hold fast to those identities that continue to provide us with a sense of self-worth and perhaps sever ties with, or no longer identify with, those that do not. Each of us can carry multiple perspectives and life experiences and our identities reflect that; our identities change, as identities are fluid, and our past identities inform our present and future ones.

This flexible and fluid system of belonging has perils, however. On the one hand, just as we remake our individual selves, groups, too, are constantly being made and remade.[16] Groups are the totality of the individuals who identify with them and so as individuals come and go, join and fall away, are born and die, these groups change. In a social sense we can think of collective identity as a process of dual ascription, each aspect being equally important. Firstly, individuals ascribe themselves to a particular group – self-ascription – and, secondly, the group makes a determination as to whether the individual belongs to the group or not –ascription by the collective.[17] That determination is often based on the assessment of a

[15] D. Druckman, 'Nationalism, Patriotism, and Group Loyalty: A Social Psychological Perspective', (1994) 38 *Mershon International Studies Review* 49.

[16] F. Dalal, 'The Paradox of Belonging', (2009) 14 *Psychoanalysis, Culture and Society* 75.

[17] J. S. Murer, 'Ethnic Conflict: An Overview of Analyzing and Framing Communal Conflicts from Comparative Perspectives', (2012) 24 *Terrorism and Political Violence* 566; S. Wallman, 'The Boundaries of Race: Processes of Ethnicity in England', (1978) 13 *Man* 206, in D. Hastings and T. M. Wilson, *Borders: Frontiers of Identity, Nation and State* (Berg, 2001) 22–3.

performance associated with the group. Individual members of groups enact their identity in such a way that others will recognise these enactments. They may include wearing certain articles of clothing, as say certain patterns of textiles or certain colours associated with one clan or another. In this way clothing becomes a text of identity, wherein what one *chooses* to wear comes to be seen as a performance of ascribed and desired identity. 'Dress plays the role of social rank, stamping a person as belonging to a certain corporate body and contraposing him to those who do not belong to it.'[18] These acts may also include eating or not eating certain items, as the 'consumption or rejection of particular kinds of food amalgamates people into a community to the degree that it separates them from other people'.[19] Dietary restrictions, enforced or relaxed, represent an act of distinction. Together with its function in social intercourse, literally bringing people together to commune, food also acts as social separation. 'All peoples have been known to have customs forbidding or restricting meals between certain groups of people, e.g. men and women, members of different castes, social classes, religions.'[20] In this way, every community has its own set of values and norms. Those who do not abide by them can expect some kind of social sanction. On the other hand, in order to demonstrate that one does belong, one must make these performances in accordance with expectations. At other times the social demands for strict adherence may wane, rendering the distinction no longer relevant; in such circumstances, as previously separate communities join more closely together, earlier acts of distinction may transform into what is perceived as shared activity. These performances are taught and learned through socialisation and socially discursive processes, practised again and again. Vikki Bell describes this as the embodiment process: '[t]he production of the effect of identity, the effect (and affect) of various modes of affiliation, is an embodiment process' whereby these affective effects shape individual everyday behaviour.[21]

Lois McNay writing about Judith Butler's definition of performativity, particularly as regards the construction and realisation of gender, suggests that it should not be seen as a 'quasi-permanent structure', rather she writes that identity 'should be thought of as a temporal regulation of

[18] B. F. Porshnev, 'Opposition as a Component of Ethnic Self-Consciousness', in L. A. Despres (ed.), *Ethnicity and Resource Competition in Plural Societies* (Mouton Publisher, 1975) at 141.

[19] Ibid., at 141. [20] Ibid., at 141.

[21] V. Bell, 'Performativity and Belonging: An Introduction', in V. Bell (ed.), *Performing and Belonging* (Sage, 1999) at 8.

socio-symbolic norms and practices, where the idea of the performative expresses both the cultural arbitrariness of the "performed" nature of . . . identity, and also its deep inculcation in that every performance serves to re-inscribe [that identity] on the body'.[22] In this way we can think of identity as something that we do. Carl Jung put it nicely stating that: 'not that you are, but that you do is the self. The self appears in deeds and deeds always mean relationships.'[23] As such, these performances are judged and evaluated within the structures of social relations to give them meaning and marking inclusion or exclusion to those relationships. In this way, no one is simply 'of' a group in some essentialist way; rather, each individual must make performances of their identity to be acknowledged as members or non-members. Put another way, Fredrik Barth wrote that the criteria by which 'membership is signalled, and the standards by which members are evaluated and judged are tied [together] in shared symbolic systems'.[24] The symbolic systems set out those criteria upon which performances will be judged. So, some performances might be sartorial in nature, as for example football fans looking to see which jersey someone else might be wearing. Declaring allegiance to one football team or another is performed through the shared symbolic systems of jerseys, hats and scarves. Similarly, rival gang members might wear blue or red, as both sides understand the shared significance of wearing one colour or the other. In just such a way Vamik Volkan described how when he was growing up in Cyprus fishermen would all wear sashes; this can be seen as a unifying distinction of Cypriot fishermen from other Mediterranean fishermen. However, Greek Cypriots would wear blue sashes, whereas their Turkish Cypriot counterparts would wear red; and when sitting in cafés the Greek Cypriots would smoke cigarettes from blue packets and the Turkish Cypriots would smoke cigarettes from red, making it possible to see, upon entering the café, who was a Greek Cypriot and who was a Turkish Cypriot.[25] But these acts of distinction

[22] L. McNay, 'Subject, Psyche and Agency: The Work of Judith Butler', in V. Bell (ed.), *Performing and Belonging* (Sage, 1999) at 176.

[23] C. Jung, *Nietzsche's Zarathustra: Notes on the Seminar Given 1934–1939*, (Princeton University Press, 1988) 73.

[24] F. Barth, 'Introduction', in F. Barth (ed.), *Ethnic Groups and Boundaries: The Social Organisation of Cultural Difference* (George Allen and Unwin, 1998 [1969]) at 6.

[25] V. Volkan, 'Individual and Large-Group Identities: Does Working with Borderline Patients Teach Us Anything about International Negotiations?', Working Paper, available at www.vamikvolkan.com/Ind%FDvidual-and-Large-group-Identities%3A-Does-Working-with-Borderline-Patients-Teach-Us-Anything-About-International-Negotiations-.php (accessed 12 February 2014); V. Volkan, *Cyprus War and Adaptation: A Psychoanalytic History of*

could be the choice as to which language one speaks in, or perhaps even the pronunciation of a word, such as the difference between the Croatian manner of saying milk *mlijeko* and the Serbian *mleko*.[26] The significances of these distinctions are themselves relational. What might be the tolerable dialectal variation in the common language of Serbo-Croatian at one time, might be the unacceptable marker of an enemy-other speaking 'another language' in another instance, to be rendered insignificant or unimportant again, on a third occasion. In this way it is not the performances themselves that render difference, but how they are understood in a social context that provides meaning. It is the social construction of a boundary separating one group from another, where both sides understand the significance of that boundary. An English traveller to Scotland notices the different pronunciation north of the border but may not be able to distinguish between a Glaswegian and a Dundonian accent. All three of these accents from the British Isles are different from the broad, flat American accents, yet they are all from the English language. The differences are very real, but it is not the different pronunciations that lead to war. The boundary is fluid and dynamic, changing with context, changing with time. It is the boundary that represents the social significance of separation, not any one performance. As Barth put it: 'it is the boundary that defines a group not the cultural stuff it encloses' and the group's continuity is dependent on the maintenance of that boundary.[27] Groups, whether small street crews or large *ethnies* stretching across multiple countries, are constantly being re-created in acts that construct and maintain the boundary between one group and another. So, while groups are often spoken of in static or fixed term, especially ethnic groups or nationalities associated with particular qualities or activities likewise described in endless or permanent terms, 'they are all nevertheless in some sense not only always "made", but also are continuously in a process of being made'.[28] These social practices that maintain the boundaries are themselves also in parallel processes of dynamic change through interpretation, performance, reinterpretation and transmission.

Two Ethnic Groups in Conflict (University of Virginia Press, 1979); D. Goleman, 'Amid Ethnic Wars, Psychiatrists Seek Roots of Conflicts', (1994) *The New York Times* C13, available at www.nytimes.com/1994/08/02/science/amid-ethnic-wars-psychiatrists-seek-roots-of-conflicts.html?src=pm&pagewanted=2 (accessed 14 February 2014).

[26] V. Volkan, 'Large-group Identity: "Us and Them" Polarizations in the International Arena', (2009) 14 *Psychoanalysis, Culture and Society* 11.

[27] Barth, above note 24, at 15.

[28] Dalal, above note 16, at 75.

One consequence of this ceaseless process of groups making and remaking themselves through the constant redefinition of the border is the recognition that in the act of inclusion there is a parallel act of exclusion. While those included within a group can feel secure in the inclusion in the group, there is an underlying anxiety regarding the possibility of being excluded in another instance. This tension, or what Dalal calls the 'paradox of belonging',[29] represents both the possibility of the boundary shifting in the future such that one may not be included, or that a performance may be judged to be inadequate or defective in such a way as to no longer warrant inclusion. On the one hand, large group identities not only provide self-worth, as described above, but also provide a sense of security along with the sense of belonging. 'People experience levels of security in relation to their own and other's perceptions of their structural position' within the group.[30] This inter-subjective engagement of self-presentation and group reception constitutes this dynamic process of reproducing, retransmitting and interpreting group values, norms, traditions and customs. The internalised self-conceptions of the quality of group performances are only realised in their public presentation. It is in this moment that anxiety often arises regarding the adequacy of the performances. So, on the other hand, the very acts that demonstrate membership and which should provide a sense of security through belonging in a large group, are also the very same acts that are judged and may in the end be the basis for exclusion if the performances are deemed insufficient or defective.

Norbert Elias described these fast moving, shifting sands of identity in his historic essay 'The Civilising Process', in which he suggests it is not enough to study a single element of a group to stand for the whole. Rather, Elias argues that in order to understand a group it is necessary to examine the social relationships between various elements of the group and the shifts within the power relations and balances between these various sub-elements *within* the group. The social structures and social processes 'demand a study of the relationships between the different fundamental strata that are bound together within a social field, and which, with the slower or more rapid shifts of power relationships arising from the specific structure of the field, are for a time reproduced over and

[29] Ibid.

[30] C. Kinvall, 'Globalization and Religious Nationalism: Self, Identity, and the Search for Ontological Security', (2004) 25 *Political Psychology* 749.

over again'.[31] The changes in the social structures do not originate in one class or element or another, but arise in conjunction with the tensions between the different functional groups in a social field. In this way different elements are competing to define the whole. Those who may not agree or refuse to engage in the demanded performances associated with the new definition of the group may then be expelled or, at least, no longer considered members and at most may become the targets of violence. While groups are often analysed in terms of the shifts within the ruling strata, it is also important to examine how other strata accept or do not accept new definitions of identity performance. These performances vary from the reproduction of original myth narratives, to articulating the group's history as a specific sequence of significant moments, to engaging in acts of violence. This dynamism is the contestation of power and status among different strata within a given group. Whether activities said to define the group through ritual performance change, is dependent upon the power of elements within the group to actualise this change, and to persuade, coax, or even coerce others to emulate the change. One way to conceive of this realisation of power is through Pierre Bourdieu's notions of social and cultural capital.

Violent performances and social capital

For Bourdieu, like Elias and Barth, social networks are not given or natural but must be made through the active investment of time, energy, attention and effort to solidify group relations in such a way as to render them as a resource for all the members. Social networks and social groups are created through the efforts and energy put into them and the sum total of that effort and energy becomes a resource for the entire group. A given group's strength can be measured in the quality of the solidarity of the group and, likewise, the solidarity of the group becomes one of its strengths. Bourdieu wrote that 'the profits which accrue from membership in a group are the basis of the solidarity which makes them possible'.[32] In this way we can think of social spaces

[31] N. Elias, 'The Civilizing Process', in J. Goudsblom and S. Mennell (eds.), *The Norbert Elias Reader* (Wiley-Blackwell, 1997) at 65.

[32] P. Bourdieu, 'The Forms of Capital', in J. G. Richards (ed.), *Handbook of Theory and Research for the Sociology of Education* (Greenwood, 1985) at 249; A. Portes, 'Social Capital: Its Origins and Application in Modern Sociology', (1998) 24 *Annual Review of Sociology* 1, at 3.

as being constructed of different types of resources, power being one of them. Bourdieu refers to these social spaces as 'social fields', which are 'areas of structured socially-patterned activity of "practice"'.[33] These social fields are organised around everyday practices, assumptions, expectations, protocols, characteristic behaviours and, most of all, self-sustaining values. Bourdieu refers to the totality of these practices in a given field as 'habitus'. Richard Terdiman suggests that for Bourdieu 'a field is like a magnet exerting a force on all those that come within its range, but those who experience these "pulls" are generally not aware of its source'.[34] The field is both the rules of the game and the environment in which the game is played, and those playing the game socially hold the rules collectively. Bourdieu does uphold the possibility of becoming socially conscious and reflexive about one's own position within a given field, and even to move between fields. Developing what Erving Goffman called 'a sense of one's place' is the social mastery of the social field, both its 'objective side' of structures and institutions and its 'subjective side' of social prohibitions, taboos, mores, morals and values. 'The sense of one's place, as a sense of what one can or cannot "permit oneself" implies a tacit acceptance of one's place, a sense of limits or a sense of distances to be marked, kept, respected or expected.'[35] We can think of this 'sense of one's place' as a sense of position within the group and an assessment of the relative power or capital possessed or accrued by a given actor within that field. Each field or sub-field corresponds to a particular arrangement of forms of capital, whereby a social field can be described as the multi-dimensional space of positions where actors are distributed according to the overall amount of capital or power each possesses, according to the arrangement and priorities of the composition or combination of the various forms of capital. For Bourdieu, each social field is distinguished by the composition of four forms of power or capital: economic, cultural, social and symbolic, the last being the ability to render the other forms fungible such that accumulations in one form can be transformed into another. While Bourdieu emphasises the potential fungibility of the forms, each possesses its own dynamics and expectations;

33 R. Terdiman, 'Translator's Introduction to P Bourdieu, The Force of Law: Toward a Sociology of the Juridical Field', (1986) 38 *The Hastings Law Journal* 805.

34 Ibid., at 806.

35 P. Bourdieu, 'The Social Space and the Genesis of Groups', (1985) 14 *Theory and Society* 723, at 728.

'and relative to economic exchange they are characterised by less transparency and uncertainty'.[36] For example, social capital obligations and debts are repaid in forms different to the way in which they were acquired. Social capital transactions are not quid pro quo and are often characterised by the uncertain time horizons associated with generalised reciprocity.[37]

The mastery of group expectations regarding the ability to engage in the most appropriate behaviour valorised by the group in any given situation becomes the means of accumulating social and cultural capital. However, the field in which a given actor is concerned might be very local indeed. So, while norms and expectations of a larger group may be violated, the violations themselves may constitute acquiescence to another set of values and norms, a more local *habitus*.[38] In this regard, some actors may in fact accumulate social capital by violating norms of a larger group, as they are abiding by local expectations. If social capital can be seen as an embodied state of power, the ability to set expectation and norms – to contribute to the establishment of *habitus*, realised in practice – is a formidable social force. *Habitus* is that which governs and dictates practice, made and remade through practice, but is largely invisible or unnoticed within the social field it governs. This is symbolic power. 'It is the power to make groups by making the "common

[36] Portes, above note 32, at 4.

[37] A cinematic example of such a transaction occurs in the opening scenes of Francis Ford Coppola's *The Godfather*, when the character of Vito Corleone says to Bonasera: 'You were afraid to be in my debt...' After Bonasera agrees to call Corleone 'Godfather', they enter into a social relationship of power, and of debt and obligation. Bonasera acquires a debt by asking for an action, to which Corleone says: 'Some day, and that day may never come, I will call upon you to do a service for me, but until that day accept this [agreement for action] as a gift on my daughter's wedding day.' Here we can see the complexity of social capital, where reciprocity is completely unspecified as an undefined 'service'; the time horizon is likewise opaque as reciprocity may come 'some day', and moreover, the principle of reciprocity itself is denied as 'that day may never come' and at present the social act that otherwise would be accrued as a debt is to be regarded as a gift. The very act of subordination in Bonasera's calling Corleone 'Godfather' creates Corleone's social capital.

[38] Robert Putnam, who offers his own definition of social capital, sees its accumulation in largely normative terms. Accumulating social capital is good. But in so professing, Putnam does not associate 'bad' behaviours with social capital accumulation. He equates social capital with civic engagement, and those communities without what he sees as proper civic engagements, such as the areas of Calabria and Sicily in Italy where the so-called Mafia are active, as *incivisme*, or uncivil, suggesting that these are not sites of social capital accumulation. See R. Putnam, 'The Prosperous Community: Social Capital and Public Life', (1993) 13 *American Prospect* 35, at 36.

sense", the explicit consensus of the whole group.'[39] Since status is afforded to those who best embody the values of the group, those that exhibit, embody and transmit the attributes of 'common sense' will gain more status. If performing acts of violence is 'common sense' in certain situations for actors in a given social field, then those who anticipate the context in which violence is expected, and become well versed in the nuances of the expected manner of such performance, will ultimately accumulate social capital. The symbolic struggle over the production of 'common sense' is the struggle to impose what is seen as the legitimate vision of the social world.

One can easily imagine a small neo-Nazi group somewhere in Europe. For this group, expressing anti-Semitism and anti-Roma sentiments becomes a way of demonstrating membership in the group and reproducing group values. Further, those who are 'better' at making these expressions, accrue greater amounts of social capital. So, while these expressions would be seen as anti-social in most European contexts, within the group the expressions are the means to accumulate social capital. The greatest expression of social power would be to set forth the criteria and perhaps determine the content by which others in the group will judge identity performances. Choosing the texts, and perhaps writing the slogans to be repeated by the group, would be demonstrative of this symbolic power.

Bourdieu wrote of this symbolic power as the power to construct reality, to establish a gnoseological order, realising Foucault's or Durkheim's idea of 'knowledge power'. For Durkheim, this knowledge power represented a logical conformity, creating within a group a 'homogenous conception of time, space, number, and causes'.[40] These unifying perspectives make possible a consensus of how the world is and how it works; and it is with this common sense of the world that a social order is produced. This common perspective is present as a universal interest at least to the whole group, if not to the entire world. Paradoxically, this 'united' vision itself becomes the basis for distinction, as those who do not share this common sense world view are seen as defective and must be excluded from at least the group, if not the world. This becomes one of the means of de-humanising the other, by which those who do not conform to this 'common sense' of the world may be deemed not to be worthy of it, and therefore become legitimate targets for violence. Thus, the dominant elements within a group, through the articulation of a

[39] Bourdieu, above note 35, at 729.
[40] P. Bourdieu, 'Symbolic Power', (1979) 4 *Critique of Anthropology* 77, at 79.

common culture or a fictitious integration of the group as a whole, are able to neutralise any alternative perspective from those within the group with less status by asserting the legitimacy of the established order, through the establishment of distinctions and the legitimation of those distinctions. 'The dominant culture produces its specific ideological effect by concealing its function of division (or the creation of hierarchies) under its function of communication; the culture unites, separates and legitimates distinction by defining all culture in terms of their distance from the dominant culture.'[41] One of the most important advantages that accompanies this ability to divide the world through the act of describing the world – imposing distinctions through the articulation of definitions – is that the acceptance or the normalisation of these distinctions becomes the source of legitimation and status of those that articulate the definitions. Just as Judith Butler describes the enactment of gender definitions as the 'forced reiteration of norms', these embodiments are the realisation of the power of the 'compulsory and constraining idea that impels and sustains [this] identity'.[42] That is, each submission to the discursive power of the norm becomes not only a validation of that power but is itself a realisation of the power and the means of its reproduction and retransmission. Bourdieu observed this in one of his earlier works when he wrote that 'the power of words and commands, the power of words to give order and bring order, lies in the belief in the legitimacy of the words and the person who utters them, a belief which words themselves cannot produce'.[43] It is in this elementary power to name that we can see the fundamental power of distinction: the power to exclude and to render that exclusion as 'common sense' and the power to declare that it has always been thus.

Violence in the formation of identity is not reactionary in the way that it is most often thought of, negatively, but is defensive and constructive. The violence of exclusion can be world making and can shape and reshape identities through the construction of 'a world of rules, rights, regimes, and people in imagined communities'.[44] Building on the work of Julia Kristeva, I have written elsewhere that vulnerable group identities

[41] Ibid., at 80.

[42] J. Butler, *Bodies That Matter: On the Discursive Limits of Sex* (Routledge, 1993) at 94.

[43] P. Bourdieu, 'Le langage autorisé. Note sur les conditions sociales de l'efficacité du discours ritual', (1975) 5–6 *Actes de la Recherche en Sciences Sociales* 183–90, in P. Bourdieu, 'Symbolic Power' (1979) 4 *Critique of Anthropology* 83.

[44] G. Bowman, 'The Violence in Identity', in B. Schmidt and I. Schröder (eds.), *Anthropology of Violence and Conflict* (Routledge, 2001) at 42.

can be made secure through the violent expulsion of 'untrustworthy' elements, redefining the collective whole, denying the relationship to the destabilising elements and using violence against those expelled as a unifying performative act, joining together the newly reimagined collective self in a common understanding of distinction: this distinction has always been thus.[45] The boundary between those included in the newly redefined self, and those expelled into the status of being other, is characterised by profound violence, for the boundary is a rigid prohibition preventing the once unified self and other, included and excluded, from merging into one another. These acts of violence signal to each side of the boundary the position of the actor, the performance of which will be judged, potentially by others on both sides of the border, to confirm the status of belonging.

Violence triangles

The popular conception of violence is of an act of harm between two people: a perpetrator and a victim. This depiction as a singular, instantaneous act between two people empties violence of all its contexts: history, spatiality, normativity and sociability. Slavoj Žižek suggests in the introduction to his volume on violence that the 'overpowering horror' of violent acts creates an empathy with the 'victim' that makes it difficult to explore the motivations and justifications of the 'perpetrator'.[46] However, David Riches provided a new perspective, long anticipating Žižek's criticism regarding the 'sympathy' for a 'victim' and the antipathy expressed toward a 'perpetrator'. Riches suggested that one think of the perpetrator as a 'performer' of violent acts and that these performances are directed toward a 'target' rather than a victim. This is a rather important shift, as in many situations the targets of violence are often the perpetrators of violence themselves, whether they be mutual combatants in a formally declared military conflict or members of rival street gangs. Further, Riches suggested that there is a third perspective to the social practices of violence, that of a witness.[47] Vittorio Bufacchi found Riches' formulation of this

[45] J. S. Murer, 'Constructing the Enemy-other: Anxiety, Trauma and Mourning in the Narratives of Political Conflict', (2009) 14 *Psychoanalysis, Culture and Society* 109; J. S. Murer, 'Institutionalizing Enemies: The Consequences of Reifying Projection in Post-Conflict Environments', (2010) 15 *Psychoanalysis, Culture and Society* 1.

[46] S. Žižek, *Violence: Six Sideways Reflections* (Routledge, 2009) at 3.

[47] Riches, above note 8, at 8.

triadic relationship to be too relativistic, whereby the legitimacy of a given performance of violence depends on the relative perspective of the performer, target or witness. He wanted to provide a more impartial perspective, suggesting that reconceptualization of the 'witness' to be a 'spectator that is able to provide an impartial perspective and an objective assessment of the perpetration of violence'.[48] I would like to offer a different alternative, one that realigns the violence triangle more closely to the one envisioned by Michel Foucault, who saw the three points of intersection as the 'sovereign, the victim and the audience'.[49] Riches and Bufacchi's triangles both centre on a primary relationship similar to the common dyadic approach to violence, where the witness or the spectator appear as separate, or perhaps neutral, third-parties who observe an act of violence and adjudicate its legitimacy post hoc. I would like to suggest a triangle of performer, target and audience, in which the primary relationship is between the performer and the audience. The performer is not merely concerned with whether the audience will see the act of violence as legitimate or not, but rather the audience is making a determination as to whether the act conforms to the collective norms and values as embodied in social capital.

One can easily imagine a scenario in which a young man walking down the street with other members of his street crew, the Blues, encounters a person symbolically signalling membership in a rival gang, the Reds. In the violent imaginary of the Blues street crew, there is no question of the moral superiority of the position of the Blues and the polarised relationship between 'Us' and 'Them'. There is no ambiguity as to the legitimacy of the use of violence against the 'threatening-rival-enemy'. In this encounter with the rival-other, our young man's primary social concern is not with the Red, but with his social standing and status among his social-peer Blues. He then pulls a knife and attacks the rival member of the Reds. The relationship between the performer of the violence and the target is largely a structural one, whereas the relationship between the performer and the audience is a social and intersubjective one. In this case, violence is not maladaptive or anti-social, but rather is expected and constitutes the means to obtaining or accruing further social capital. All too often analysts focus too much attention on the use of violence as an instrumental means to some specific end vis-à-vis the target or the victim. But in this example we can see that it is not

[48] V. Bufacchi, above note 7, at 33–4, and 47.
[49] M. Foucault, *Discipline and Punish* (Pantheon, 1977) at 68.

the consequence of the violence that is important; that is, the outcome between the performer of the violent act and the target is relatively unimportant. Rather, it is the act itself that is important to the performer and the audience. It is not necessary to kill or eliminate the other as a consequential act, but rather simply to act against the other. In this environment of permissive violence, or what Norbert Elias called a 'culture of violent solutions',[50] not to participate in violence, or not to abide by the norms of the group regarding the fantasy of what to do when encountering a member of the 'threatening-rival-other' is to expose oneself to the potential of social sanction, isolation, or even to become a target of violence one-self. Conversely, Richard Felson suggests that violence becomes a routine activity, whereby those engaged in a culture of violent solutions seek out conflict, or put themselves in places where they expect a conflict to occur, so that conflicts may occur between like-minded members of various street groups, each of which understands that acts of violence are the stepping stones along the path of obtaining ever greater social capital.[51]

Additionally, with this restructured violence triangle, which focuses on the relationship between performer and audience, it is possible to imagine a scenario in which the target and the audience are from the same group, rather than the performer and audience sharing an identity. Here again, rather than being impartial or 'objective' as explicitly stated in Bufacchi's model, the 'accessible, easily perceivable, easily understood' communication of violence[52] is intended to convey a message beyond the body or the symbolic site of the target and is to be perceived by the audience. This is similar to the communicative aspect of terrorism as described by Schmid and Graaf, where the target is selected by the terrorist-performer for the maximum resonance with the audience.[53] The positions within this triangle are relational, as is suggested in Riches' original formulation. Yet, there is no privileged position somehow outside the conduct of the violence, as suggested by Bufacchi. Additionally, it is possible for a single individual to occupy any of the

[50] J. R. Kurtz and J. Turpin, 'Untangling the Web of Violence', in J. R. Kurtz and J. Turpin (eds.), *The Web of Violence: From Interpersonal to Global* (University of Illinois, 1997) at 209.

[51] S. Zdun, 'Violence in Street Culture: Cross Cultural Comparisons of Youth Groups and Criminal Gangs', (2008) 119 *New Directions for Youth Development* 43.

[52] Riches, above note 8, at 11.

[53] A. P. Schmid and J. de Graaf, *Violence as Communication: Insurgent Terrorism and the Western News Media* (Sage, 1982).

three positions: not simultaneously, but in succession. Teresa Koloma Beck likewise suggests a triangle of performer, target and observed, in which the roles are not fixed but constitute changeable modes of experiencing violence. Beck argues that violence is experienced as a pain that is distinct from pain as a result of fate or hazard, for the pain of violence was inflicted to deliberately enforce the will of one against another.[54] I would agree with Beck and suggest the audience member who experiences the pain of losing a loved one due to violence aimed at a different target indeed experiences a pain distinct from that of mere accident. For the pain was experienced in the environment of violent solutions, even if the target was not itself specifically aimed at, or even a party to, the conflict.

This is not dissimilar to Ivana Maček's triadic model regarding the perception of the violence of armed conflict. Based on her field research conducted in Sarajevo during the siege of the Bosnian war, Maček argues that one's perception of the violence depends on one's subject position, of which she posits that there are three: civilian, soldier or deserter.[55] Maček suggests that often one individual would experience the violence from each of the subject positions, and that the quality of that experience was fundamentally different depending on the subject position. In this regard, members of the same large group who share a collective identity constellation may yet have different subject positions that require intra-group reconciliation to make sense of the violence.

Violence as group value

Elias' 'culture of violent solutions' does not mean that everyone in the group will be violent, nor does it even mean that the most violent members of the group will be violent all of the time; it does, however, mean that a violent imaginary is at the centre of the group's self-conception.[56] This violent imaginary is a shared world view for all the members of the group. Yet, the vast majority of the literature on radicalisation, or political and social mobilisation outside the mainstream,

[54] Beck, above note 5, at 353.

[55] I. Maček, 'Predicament of War: Sarajevo Experiences and Ethics of War', in B. Schmidt and I. Schröder (eds.), *Anthropology of Violence and Conflict* (Routledge, 2001) at 197–223. This article was developed into a full book. See I. Maček, *Sarajevo Under Siege: Anthropology in Wartime* (University of Pennsylvania Press, 2009).

[56] Kurtz and Turpin, above note 50, at 209.

focuses on men. The association of radicalisation or radical politics to violence moves such politics into the sphere of masculinity and masculine performance. However, some of these performances are also performances of belonging, demonstrations of group norms or articulations of group values. In this regard, holding similar views, or expressing similar sentiments to that of the rest of the group becomes the very means of expressing group identity and membership. Even the most outlandish articulation of racial hate and exclusion can be the means of binding a group together. Sini Perho has described such processes while writing about skinhead groups in Finland, but these groups are not exclusively composed of young men or boys, but include girlfriends, sisters, mothers, wives and partners. In such groups 'being racists links young people into a community, giving them a feeling of solidarity and belonging to something'.[57] A shift of the analytic focus on belonging to group performances would suggest that we find similar articulations by all group members regardless of their personal experience; that is, if the collectivity portrays itself as being deprived of resources that other groups have access to, individuals identifying with the group will articulate similar expressions of deprivation, regardless of their individual material circumstance. The identification with deprivation is a group value, and is held strongly, irrespective of personal experience. There is no conflict because the expression is one of belonging to the group, not an account of personal experience. This was found with respect to violence through the ESYM.

From March of 2008 through October 2010 the ESYM interviewed more than 800 young people who saw themselves outside mainstream politics in five cities in Central Europe – Bratislava, Brno, Budapest, Krakow and Warsaw – in addition to holding workshops with more than 250 academics, police practitioners, local authorities, community activists and government representatives from across Nordic Europe to compare their experiences of working with violent youths mobilised from the radical right, radical left and environmental movements, as well as street gangs and religious cults.[58]

ESYM afforded a rare opportunity to explore a comparison of group value articulations by gender, because, unlike most studies that focus on the behaviours associated with men or boys, ESYM had no gender

[57] S. Perho, 'Boys' and Girls' Position in a Racist Milieu', in L. Suurpää and T. Hoikkala (eds.), *Masculinities and Violence in Youth Culture* (Finnish Youth Research Network, 2005) at 49.

[58] See British Council, above note 6.

Table 11.1: *Budapest responses to ESYM questionnaire number 62*

My friends think physical force is necessary at times.		
	Women	Men
Not at all (1)	68	64
2	37	43
3	29	29
4	28	27
5	13	12
6	7	7
Very much (7)	30	27
Total	212	209

criteria. Young men and women who were interviewed were not given instructions or selection criteria for the referral of the next respondent, save that the person referred was someone with whom the interviewee regularly engaged in politics, whether as conversation, debate or action. The surprising consequence was near-gender equality across the study as a whole and across the groups within the study.[59]

Remarkably, throughout the ESYM there is tremendous similarity between the responses of women and men on a whole host of questions. Most striking are the very similar responses regarding political expression and the legitimacy of violence. On aggregate, recognising that not the same number of men and women answered every question, the distribution of women's responses mirrors that of the men. This is perhaps most obvious and interesting in articulations regarding feelings of intimidation, the inability to express oneself adequately, being harassed, or thinking that their friends thought that violence is justified (see Table 11.1).

For example, when each of the 421 participants from Budapest were asked if each as an individual thought that force could be justifiable in local politics, thirty men and twenty-six women responded that they believed 'a great deal so', indicating so by choosing 7 points out of 7. Most of those respondents were supporters of the Hungarian far-right political party, Jobbik, and it was the women who expressed this sentiment more frequently. Nineteen of twenty-five Jobbik women and fifteen of twenty-four

[59] Ibid., at 11.

Table 11.2: *Responses to ESYM questionnaire number 62 for Jobbik and ethnic Jewish activists*

My friends think physical force is necessary at times.								
Group members	Not at all (1)	2	3	4	5	6	Very much (7)	Total
Male Jobbik supporters	0	0	0	0	1	1	22	24
Female Jobbik supporters	0	0	0	1	0	0	24	25
Male ethnic Jewish activists	14	2	1	3	1	0	0	21
Female ethnic Jewish activists	13	1	1	0	2	1	0	18
Total	27	3	2	4	4	2	46	88

Jobbik men individually thought that force could be justified, at the level of 7 out of 7. The remaining fourteen agreed at levels 5 and 6. When asked what they thought the other members in the group thought, twenty-four of the twenty-five women and twenty-two of the twenty-four men from Jobbik thought that the rest of the group also believed that physical force might be necessary. That is, forty-six of the forty-nine Jobbik supporters answered by giving a 7 on a 7-point scale to indicate that they thought 'my friends think force is necessary at times' (see Table 11.2).

Although the obverse might be less convincing, eighteen of the twenty-two ethnic Jewish men and sixteen of the eighteen ethnic Jewish women agreed that force is 'not at all' justifiable. This clustering of responses based on the group can again be seen in Table 11.3, which illustrates the response to the question: 'If a government is not listening force may be justified.' Within the same groups, the responses from men and women again mirrored each other closely, as can be seen in Table 11.1, which shows all the responses from Budapest to the question: 'To what extent do you agree with the statement: "My friends think physical force is necessary at times?"'

When ten combined questions relating to the use of violence and physical force are amalgamated in a scale there is even greater similarity demonstrated between the responses of men and those of women.[60]

[60] The items included in the scale were: (1) If the government will not listen or respond to the people or a specific community physical force may be required to get the

Table 11.3: *Responses to ESYM questionnaire number 64 for Jobbik and ethnic Jewish activists*

If the government will not listen to a community, force may be required to gain attention

Group members	Not at all (1)	2	3	4	5	6	Very much (7)	Total
Male Jobbik supporters	0	0	0	0	0	6	18	24
Female Jobbik supporters	0	0	0	2	0	4	19	25
Male ethnic Jewish activists	18	2	0	2	0	0	0	22
Female ethnic Jewish activists	14	2	0	0	0	0	2	18
Total	32	4	0	4	0	10	39	89

In Figure 11.1 it is possible to see the tight alignment between the male and female positions on the use of violence for all of the groups, save for the radical socialists and the Baptists. The very tight alignment between male and female respondents among Jobbik supporters is well demonstrated by the lines overlapping. In Figure 11.2, it is possible to see a divergence of opinion between men and women from Bratislava and Brno associated with the far-left and the earth defence movements. Opinions begin to converge with the gay/feminist activists and grow more closely together as one moves towards the right end of the political spectrum.

Thirty-nine of the forty-nine Jobbik members expressed that they believed that force was justifiable in local politics by answering 7 on the

government's attention. (2) I think that violence is justifiable at times in local politics. (3) My friends think violence is necessary at times. (4) When the police approach a peaceful demonstration with riot gear on it is justifiable to throw stones at them. (5) Physical force in the act of resisting the police, even when directed against the police is justifiable. (6) The world is becoming a more violent place. (7) People who use violence against the government have reasons to do so. (8) The use of violence by some groups is seen as more legitimate than if used by other groups. (9) My group would be legitimate in resisting against the police if it needed to do so. (10) To what extent do you believe that physical force is justifiable in an effort to change a government or governmental system?

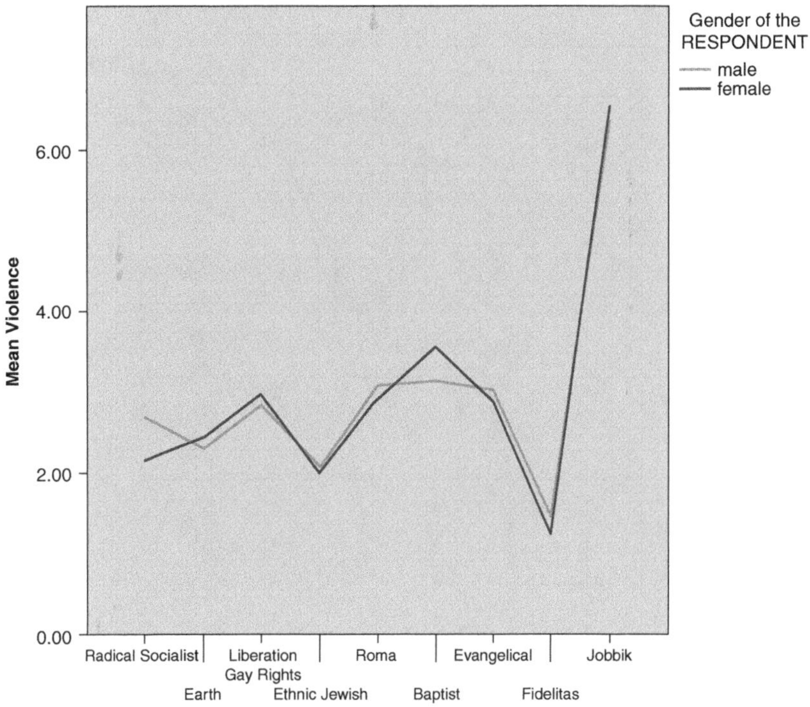

Figure 11.1: Budapest violence scale by gender of respondent

7-point scale, and forty-seven out of forty-nine similarly answered 'very much' by selecting 7 out of 7 to agree that physical force is necessary in resisting the police. Likewise, forty-eight out of forty-nine agreed 'very much' to the proposition that 'the world is becoming a more violent place'. The forty-ninth member agreed at the level of 6 out of 7. Finally, forty-eight out of forty-nine Jobbik members agreed that 'people who use violence against the government have reason to do so'.[61]

The findings of the ESYM have two significant implications. The first is that group values are held collectively. If one does not believe in these values, the dissenting individuals will be asked to leave in one way or another. The second, perhaps more important, implication of the findings is that men and women see violence similarly within the same group. The value is held over the group irrespective of gender.[62] Expressing

[61] In this case the forty-ninth Jobbik member did not provide an answer.

[62] As can be seen in Figure 11.2 there was a divergence among the left-wing activists in Bratislava and Brno.

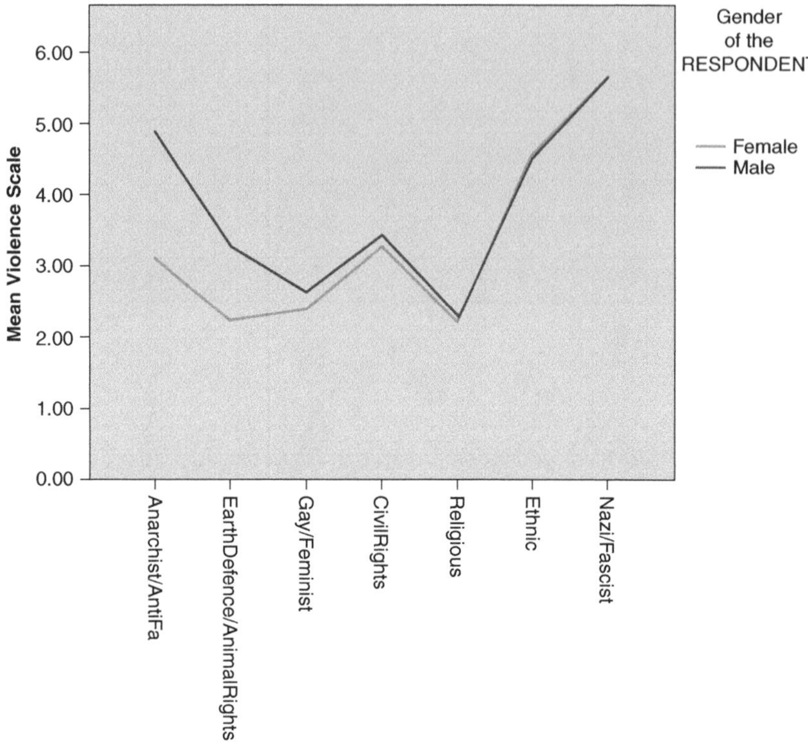

Figure 11.2: Bratislava/Brno violence scale

shared values is one way of performing belonging and identification with a group. This is no less true of tolerating or even expecting or endorsing violence as a group value. Elias' 'culture of violent solutions' is an expression of these shared values.

These 'cultures of violent solutions' can be micro-environments unto themselves. That is, they may be sub-cultures within larger cultural environments that do not value violence in the same fashion. In looking to violent solutions to solve social problems, participants may actually gain status within the group and within the micro 'culture' even if the action conflicts with broader social norms. For example, in a different study a respondent from Glasgow told us that his father encouraged him to carry a knife. He was also encouraged by his father to fight. This was largely an expression of sticking up for himself, to demonstrate his self-esteem and that he was not to be bullied or taken advantage of. He was encouraged to carry a knife because 'all the other fathers carried knives when they were young and are telling their boys now the same story'.[63] On the one hand, the father's advice is rather practical: if everyone carries a knife, perhaps it is best not to be the only one unarmed. On the other hand, it is the reinforcement of the neighbourhood's *habitus*. For those people who find themselves marginalised by the larger mainstream culture the pursuit of social capital within the local micro-cultural groups provides an alternative for achieving social status. Adherence to the group norms affords an opportunity for social capital accumulation and social mobility that would not otherwise be available to those who do poorly under the terms of hegemonic social capital accumulation schemes. In this way, adherence to local practices, even when out of line with dominant or hegemonic practices in the larger society, remains an important means of obtaining social recognition. If violence is regularly reinforced, if it is seen as a valued practice, then it will be the means of obtaining social capital and status within the local group. The exclusion of those who measure status through a counter-hegemonic or local system of disposition from the larger society only goes to reinforce the desirability to remain in the alternate frame.

Belonging before believing: a conclusion

To better understand violence it is necessary to explore what violence does. It is not only an action of destruction but also an action of creation. It joins groups; it creates loyalty. It becomes the realisation and the demonstration of belonging. Recognition and social integration are realised through the acceptance of social group norms.[64] If violence as the means of conflict resolution is valued as a group norm, then committing violence can be seen as the means of developing social capital with a view to increasing social status. This was a theme repeated by many respondents in the ESYM and was articulated well by a self-described Earth liberation activist in Brno, Czech Republic; as regards belonging to his group, he said: 'You are not invisible; you can do something, gain respect – you can be someone.' A respondent to the Violence Report by the Violence Prevention Network expressed a similar sentiment: 'I get

[63] Author interview, St Andrews, Scotland, 14 October 2011.

[64] W. Heitmeyer and A. Reimund, 'Disintegration, Recognition, and Violence: A Theoretical Perspective', in W. Heitmeyer and S. Legge (eds.), *Youth, Violence and Social Disintegration* (Jossey-Bass Publishers, 2008) at 25–38.

noticed when I use violence; I have a feeling of power and superiority.'[65] This is not something to achieve an end, but rather is an experience in and of itself. This is particularly important for young people who feel excluded from other avenues of social status attainment. A former neo-Nazi in Stockholm told his story of being an outsider at school because he had reading difficulties, yet once inside the White Power Movement he could become a leader. He could not do well at school, but he could be violent and be good at being violent. This provided him with a sense of self-worth, which was then reinforced by the group.[66]

These performances of violence can also function as a test of an individual's depth of attachment to the group. A self-described neo-Nazi respondent told the ESYM that 'violence is the initial phase you must go through to become a member, and that you must return to [in order] to be [seen as] active'. Violence therefore can function as a commitment. It is a commitment of the body and it is a commitment to the group. One defends the group as a whole, upholds the values and ethos of the group and, most importantly, individual members feel that they are both recognised and that they can recognise each other. In the context of 'cultures of violent solutions' every challenge demands an aggressive reaction to defend one's reputation. Such challenges demand both the defence of the collective's reputation and the opportunity to make a performance on behalf of the group; the opportunity to do the group proud. It is in this moment that an actor displays his group identity and makes a performance that distinguishes him from the challenger, or a non-aligned bystander. In this way multiple group members can experience a slight or act of disrespect on behalf of another group member. It is not only the direct slight or perceived challenge that demands action; it is the experience of group identity to experience a challenge collectively as a shared experience of group cohesion. 'It is very much, you hit my friend and I hit your friend.'[67] As a radical Earth Liberation activist told the ESYM group: violence provides the 'feeling that someone will stand up for you'. This feeling is particularly important for those who feel otherwise left out or excluded. This violent imaginary unties the group, as the violence is the border between group-self and enemy-other.

[65] See Zdun, above note 51.

[66] Author correspondence and conversations from December 2008 through November 2012.

[67] K. Kintera, J. Bannister and J. Pickering, 'Its Just an Area – Everybody Represents It: Exploring Young People's Territorial Behavior in British Cities', in B. Goldson (ed), *Youth in Crisis?: Gangs, Territoriality and Violence* (Routledge, 2011) at 55–71.

The imagination that someone would stand up for me provides me with a sense of security, which I can reciprocate in my own fantasy of defending someone in the group. However, not participating in the violence that defines the group can expose the one who refuses violence to social isolation or even becoming the target of violence himself.[68]

John Pitts writes that what prompted many of the young people that he has met in the field to join a gang or engage in gang violence was the concern of becoming a target of that violence: 'gang affiliation was prompted, first and foremost by a concern for personal safety'.[69] The lack of an affiliation can be at the root of insecurity, whether that affiliation is with a gang or some other social structure. For those who appear not to be afforded protection by other social organisations, gang affiliation may be an important alternative. But this consideration is as much existential as it is practical and as much about an ontological security of belonging as it is about immediate physical security of being. It is through the consideration of ontological security that we can see how these considerations of gangs link back to considerations for *ethnies* or other status groups.

In cases of ethnic conflict or other conflicts between status groups – clan-based conflicts, or conflicts regarding religious affiliation, race or class – those whose identities are ambiguous may feel the greatest insecurity or anxiety in times of identity conflict. That is, those of mixed parentage, recent arrival, dynamic class mobility, bilingualism, recent religious conversion, those who may appear to have transgressed a boundary, or those with the most vulnerable identities within society, perhaps a name that sounds like the language of the enemy-other or a different skin colour, may be required to perform the most demonstrative confirmation of their loyalty or identity. Anxiety for them comes with the fear that they may not adequately reproduce the group-self ideal, also because, as noted above, this ideal is fluid and not fixed. The arbiters of what constitutes an ideal performance may change or the ideal may change over time. Rather than simply assume the ideal is internalising, it may become necessary for those most vulnerable, or the most insecure, to perform their understanding of the social ideal through a public enactment of identity, which may include the performance of violence. By being willing to engage in violence, the vulnerable individual demonstrates to the larger collectivity his membership in the group-self. By actively distinguishing himself from the enemy-other, the vulnerable

[68] Zdun, above note 51, at 39.

[69] J. Pitts, *Reluctant Gangsters: The Changing Face of Youth Crime* (Routledge, 2008) at 101.

seeks the acknowledgement of the collective for 'defending' the group-self from 'incursions' or defilement by the other. Such perpetrators of violence are 'committing "heroic' acts under the economy of identity' by defending other members of the collective self from the 'violence' of the isolation and anxiety they themselves have felt.[70] Thus, the enactment of violent debasement does two things: first it reinforces one's declared collective identity. That is, the act of distinction, demonstrating that 'I am not the other', is accomplished by my willingness to commit violence against the enemy-other, who I only see as object and not as subject. This also demonstrates the commitment of the individual self to the larger collective self through the exposure both to violence and to the 'enemy-other' in himself. A willingness to commit violence against the other, especially to kill the other, is a willingness to kill the other within, to eliminate any doubt regarding one's status, even if only in imagination, but especially in actuality.[71] This confirmation of membership comes through the performance of exclusion of others. To be recognised as a member of the collective self it may be necessary to violently debase the other.

This performative violence is not instrumental in a material sense, but rather this violence is a demonstration of commitment to a collective identity. In many ways performative violence demonstrates a kind of 'creative violence'. Through this recognition it may be possible to replace the violence with another activity that can also perform this creative, bonding task of providing a sense of belonging and security. Further, an alternative may provide a greater sense of ontological security and well-being, because the requirement to commit repugnant acts of violence engenders its own anxiety: to not perform this violence may result in my being subjected to it. This was certainly the case in the unspeakable violence of the Rwandan genocide, when Hutus were compelled to harm other Hutus who were unwilling to likewise commit violence or were otherwise deemed to have made 'defective' identity performances. Pierre Bourdieu pointed out that the Greek word *katēgoresthai*, from which the verb 'categorize' and the noun 'category' are derived, means to accuse publicly.[72] To determine into which category someone belongs can also be seen as a public accusation. This is power. It is the power to name; the power to demand an identity performance; and it suggests the power to adjudicate the sufficiency of that performance. Walter Benjamin wrote

[70] S. Žižek, 'Love Thy Neighbour? No Thanks!', in C. Lane (ed.), *The Psychoanalysis of Race* (Columbia University Press, 1998) at 156–7.
[71] See Murer, above note 45. [72] Bourdieu, above note 35, at 729.

that defence of a cause, or family life, or civil society 'becomes violent, in the precise meaning of the word, when it enters into moral relations'.[73] He was interested in examining the meaning and importance of violence present in the framework of society (and ultimately in the state), and, while Benjamin's project was very different to what is explored in this chapter, his discarding of a monolithic violence in favour of an analytic framework that not only explores different manifestations of violence but suggests that they are used for different ends, is useful. In order to better understand how to minimise the harmful effects of violence and to ameliorate the conditions that engender such violence, we would likewise do well to follow Benjamin's lead and ask of every particular case, what is being expressed socially through violence? In other words, in order to better understand how people come to join violent groups and engage in violent acts, we must ask what violence is doing in this situation. If we move away from seeing violence as a singular thing, as an object, and see violence as performances, as social acts, we can explore the social work that violence is doing in a given context and a specific moment, and perhaps present an alternative set of acts that can replace the violence. Those who commit violence may not be making an individual decision to be 'bad' or 'evil'; they may be responding to social expectation and norms in a specific environment. They may be performing their identity.

[73] W. Benjamin, *Critique of Violence, Selected Writings; Volume 1, 1913–1926* (The Belknap Press of Harvard University Press, 1996) at 256.

12

Defining victims: a proposed typology for victims of war crimes and their need for reparation

JO-ANNE M. WEMMERS AND AMISSI MANIRABONA

Introduction

Born in the ashes of the Second World War, the field of victimology has grown tremendously in recent years, where we have seen much excellent empirical research done on victims. Much of the research deals with specific types of victimization (e.g., domestic violence, rape), empirical aspects of victimization in general (e.g., victimization surveys) and the consequences of victimization (e.g., post-traumatic stress disorder (PTSD)).[1] However, despite the many empirical studies, relatively little attention has been paid to theoretical aspects of victimology.[2] As Landau and Freeman-Longo point out, the dearth of theoretical work in victimology is surprising given that in a relatively new field problems of definition and boundary-setting would be an important starting point for further studies therein.[3]

Victimologists have not always shied away from theoretical work. Early victimologists, such as Hans von Hentig, Benjamin Mendelsohn, Marvin Wolfgang and Ezzat Fattah, were very active in developing theoretical victimology. Each developed their own typology of victims in order to better understand, explain and hence prevent victimization. By the early 1980s, under the influence of the victims' movement, these typologies lost much of their original popularity, as victimology moved away from

[1] J. Shapland and M. Hall, 'What Do We Know About the Effects of Crime on Victims?', (2007) 14 *International Review of Victimology* 175.

[2] J. M. Wemmers, 'The Meaning of Fairness for Victims', in S. Shoham, P. Knepper and M. Kett (eds.), *International Handbook of Victimology* (Boca Raton: Taylor Francis Group, 2010) at 27–43; see also J. M. Wemmers, C. Chamberland, M. M. Cousineau and S. Guay, 'Victimes et Victimisations: Les Progrès Récents en Victimologie', in M. Cusson and M. Leblanc (eds.), *Traité de la Criminologie* (4th edn, Montréal: Les Presses de l'Université de Montréal, 2010) at 199–224.

[3] S. Landau and R. E. Freeman-Longo, 'Classifying Victims: A Proposed Multidimensional Victimological Typology', (1990) 1 *International Review of Victimology* 267.

criminology and stopped trying to explain crime. As Ezzat Fattah observes, there was a shift 'from victimology of the act to victimology of action' as victimology became increasingly associated with victim support.[4]

The adoption of the Declaration of Basic Principles of Justice for Victims of Crime and Abuse of Power (hereafter the 'Declaration'), by the General Assembly of the United Nations in 1985,[5] marks a shift in our approach to victims and a break with penal victimology, which limits victimology to the study of victims of crime.[6] Article 1 of the Declaration states: 'victims means persons who, individually or collectively, have suffered harm. . .'. Article 2 specifies that the term victim also includes the family of the direct victim and persons who suffered harm in intervening to assist victims in distress or to prevent victimization. Thus, the Declaration provides a broad definition of victims, which extends well beyond the individual, direct victim of crime and includes many different groups of persons.

Much of the early work of victimologists focused on what Mendelsohn referred to as the '*couple-penal*', the penal couple, or the victim and their offender.[7] While this definition of the victim may work from a legal perspective, from a victimological perspective it is far too narrow. The effects of crime and especially serious crimes, such as war crimes, can reach far beyond the direct victims. In this chapter, we will approach the question of victims from the angle of *therapeutic jurisprudence*.[8] We will use social science (victimology) to study the extent to which legal rules and practice (international criminal law) promote the psychological and physical wellbeing of the people they affect.

Because the word 'victim' can mean so many different things we need to define the different categories or types of victims. This will allow us to

[4] E. A. Fattah, 'From Victimology of Act to Victimology of Action and the resulting Impoverishment of the Scholarly Discipline of Victimology', in M. Groenhuijsen, R. Letschert and S. Hazenbroek (eds.), Liber Amicorum *in honour of Professor dr. Jan J. M. Van Dijk* (Nijmegen: Wolf Publishing, 2012) at 85–98.

[5] UN General Assembly, A/RES/40/34, 29 November 1985, 96th Plenary Session.

[6] See J. M. Wemmers, *Introduction à la Victimologie* (Montreal: Les Presses de l'Université de Montréal, 2003) at l.

[7] B. Mendelsohn, 'La Victimologie', (1956) 10 *Revue International de Criminology et de Police Technique* 99; E. A. Fattah, *La Victims est elle Coupable?* (Montreal: Les Presses de l'Université de Montréal, 1971) at 27; see also Wemmers, above note 6, at 36–9.

[8] D. Wexler and B. Winick, *Law in a Therapeutic Key* (Durham, NC: Carolina Academic Press, 1996); E. Erez, M. Kilchling and J. M. Wemmers, *Therapeutic Jurisprudence and Victim Participation in Justice: International Perspectives* (Durham, NC: Carolina Academic Press, 2011).

better understand the possible consequences of crime for the different types of victims, and with this understanding we will be in a better position to address their needs. This approach gives priority to victims and ensures that satisfying their needs is above all other goals, such as political or economic goals. Yet, at the same time we live in a real world where it will not always be possible to meet all victims' needs fully. This is especially true in the case of war crimes, where there may be hundreds of thousands of victims and very few resources available. Unlike previous typologies, which aimed to explain crime, this victim-centred framework allows us to prioritize needs and identify which needs are the most urgent.

After reviewing and discussing existing typologies, we shall present our typology of victims. This typology is victim-focused and the categories are based on the victims' emotional or psychological proximity to the crime. This typology will then be used to analyse the needs of victims of war crimes and, in particular, their need for reparation in the context of the International Criminal Court (ICC).

Early typologies

In 1948, Hans von Hentig, who is now considered to be one of the founding fathers of victimology, published his classical work, *The Criminal and His Victim.*[9] Von Hentig's typology takes into consideration biological, psychological and social factors which make people vulnerable to victimization.[10] His typology consists of thirteen categories, which are divided into two general groups (see Table 12.1).

Mendelsohn, another pioneer in victimology, proposed a very different typology.[11] His object of study was the victim-offender relationship, or, as he called it, the 'penal couple'. A former criminal lawyer, Mendelsohn emphasized that not all victims are innocent and that sometimes the victim is really the offender. His typology centred on victims' degree of responsibility for the crime and consisted of five categories:

(1) the entirely innocent victim;
(2) the victim who is less guilty than the offender;

[9] H. von Hentig, *The Criminal and His Victim* (New Haven, CT: Yale University Press, 1948).

[10] See Landau and Freeman-Longo, above note 3, at 268; See also Wemmers, above note 7 at 36–7.

[11] See Mendelsohn, above note 7, at 106.

Table 12.1: *Von Hentig's typology*

(1) General types (vulnerable due to the biological, demographic or social characteristics)	(a) the young
	(b) the old
	(c) females
	(d) immigrants
	(e) minorities
	(f) the mentally ill
	(g) dull normals
(2) Psychological categories (vulnerable due to their mental state)	(a) the depressed
	(b) the acquisitive
	(c) the wanton
	(d) the lonesome and heartbroken
	(e) the tormented
	(f) persons who find themselves blocked or in an impossible situation

(3) the victim who is as guilty as the offender;
(4) the victim who is more guilty than the offender; and
(5) the guilty victim.

Another approach is to focus on types of victimizations rather than types of victims.

Sellin and Wolfgang (1964) suggest a typology consisting of five categories of victimizations, based mainly on the victim-offender relationship.[12]

(1) Primary victimization: personalized or individual victims.
(2) Secondary victimization: commercial establishments such as department stores. The victim in this case being impersonal, commercial and collective.
(3) Tertiary victimization: a very diffuse victimization that extends to the larger community and includes offences against the public order, social harmony or the administration of government.
(4) Mutual victimization: cases in which the participants engage in mutually consenting acts, such as statutory rape.
(5) No victimization: offences that could not be committed by an adult and are commonly referred to as 'juvenile status offenses', such as running away from home.

[12] J. T. Sellin and M. Wolfgang, *The Measurement of Delinquency*, (New York, NY: John Wiley and Sons, 1964) at 155–6.

Work on typologies continued well into the 1970s when there was a push to expand victimology beyond the limits of criminology. Until that time, as already mentioned, all of the above typologies focused exclusively on crimes. However, not all victimologists believed that the field of victimology should be limited to criminal law.[13] For example, Quinney (1972) suggests that the field of victimology be expanded to include victims of war and victims of abuse of power.[14] This view also gave rise to new typologies of victims. Schafer for example, created a typology which integrated notions already found in earlier typologies, such as vulnerability and the victim-offender relationship and added a new category, namely political victims.[15] The latter were not crime victims but victims of abuse of power. Recognition as victims of abuse of power did not depend on domestic law but on international standards and norms. Schafer's typology contained five categories:

(1) unrelated victims;
(2) provocative victims;
(3) biologically weak victims;
(4) socially weak victims; and
(5) political victims.

However, despite the inclusion of victims of abuse of power, Schafer's typology, like those before it, focused exclusively on direct victims. These typologies fail to include individuals who may not have directly been the object of a crime but feel victimized nonetheless. For example, the family and friends of crime victims who were nowhere near the victim at the time of the crime may also be traumatized and suffer both material and non-material losses following the victimization of their loved one.[16]

A very different typology was provided by Crelinsten (1977).[17] In his work on the dimensions of terrorism, Crelinsten identified different groups of victims affected by terrorist acts. According to Crelinsten, the person who is the object of a terrorist act is typically not the primary

[13] R. Quinney, 'Who is the Victim?', (1972) 10 *Criminology* 314; S. Schafer, *Victimology: The Victim and his Criminal* (Reston, VA: Reston Publishing Company, 1977); R. Elias, 'Transcending our Social Reality of Victimization: Toward a Victimology of Human Rights', (1985) 10 *Victimology* 6.

[14] See Quinney, above note 13, at 323.

[15] See Schafer, above note 13, at 47.

[16] M. P. Armour, 'Experiences of Co-victims of Homicide: Implications for Research and Practice', (2002) 3 *Trauma, Violence and Abuse* 109.

[17] R. Crelinsten, *Dimensions of Victimization in the Context of Terroristic Acts* (Montreal: International Centre for Comparative Criminology, Université de Montréal, 1977).

victim.[18] For example, in the events of 9/11 the people who were actually in the Twin Towers of the World Trade Center at the time of the attacks were to some extent arbitrary. The real target, or in the words of Crelinsten, the *primary victim*, was the American or capitalist financial establishment. The direct victims (i.e., the people in the Twin Towers) were, according to Crelinsten, *secondary victims*. In addition to these groups of victims, Crelinsten adds *indirect victims*, which he divides into two subgroups: (1) relatives and friends of the direct victims; and (2) the general public who are terrorized by the events. His fourth group is *tertiary victims*, which Crelinsten defines as those who are victimized in reaction to the terrorist act.[19] For example, the airline industry, which suffered massive losses because people stopped flying in reaction to the 9/11 attacks, would be considered a tertiary victim. Finally, he identifies three groups that are involved in the terrorist context and arguably may be considered by some to be victims, namely: (1) the terrorist himself; (2) law enforcement and other operations personnel; and (3) the mass media.[20]

More recently, Letschert and Van Ammerlaan proposed a similar typology for victims of terrorism,[21] which Letschert and Van Boven later extended to include mass victimization.[22] Like Crelinsten, their typology includes primary, secondary and tertiary victims. However, they define these categories very differently to Crelinsten. Letschert and Van Boven's typology encompasses only three groups: (1) *primary victims*; (2) *secondary victims*; and (3) *tertiary victims*. They equate primary victims to direct victims. Secondary victims are considered the dependants and family of the direct victims as well as first responders (those who are first to respond to a situation, such as ambulance personnel and police). Tertiary victims are 'all others not listed under primary and secondary victims'.[23]

Like Crelinsten's typology, Letschert and Van Boven's differs from most other typologies, which focus exclusively on the person who directly

[18] Ibid., at 192. [19] Ibid., at 193. [20] Ibid., at 195.

[21] R. M. Letschert and V. C. van Ammerlaan, 'Compensation and Reparation for Victims of Terrorism', in R. M. Letschert, I. Staiger and A. Pemberton (eds.), *Assistance to Victims of Terrorism: Towards a European Standard of Justice* (Dordrecht: Springer, 2010).

[22] R. M. Letschert and T. van Boven, 'Providing Reparation in Situations of Mass Victimization: Key Challenges Involved', in R. M. Letschert, R. Haveman, A. M. de Brouwer and A. Pemberton, *Victimological Approaches to International Crimes: Africa* (Antwerp: Intersentia, 2011) at 153–84.

[23] Ibid., at 162.

underwent the victimization, namely, the direct victim. Both their typologies include several types of victims in relation to the same crime. However, the typology of Crelinsten, as well as that of Letschert and Van Ammerlaan, was developed for victims of terrorism. While war crimes can terrorize large groups they are different to other terrorist acts in that they are repetitive in their nature. A terrorist event may be a single event (e.g., 9/11) or a series of events, but war crimes are continuous and committed on a regular basis while war is on-going.

The typology by Letschert and Van Boven focuses on victims of international crimes and is, therefore, preferable to that of Crelinsten and Letschert and Van Ammerlaan. However, their typology does not allow one to analyse and understand victims' needs in relation to each type of victim adequately. For example, Letschert and Van Boven use the term secondary victims to identify two very different groups of victims: indirect victims and first responders.[24] Family members who suffer the loss of a loved one will likely have different needs than first responders who may not have witnessed the crime but arrived on the scene soon after the victimization and witnessed the carnage and human suffering. Their third group, tertiary victims, is ill-defined and essentially groups together many different types of victims whose only common characteristic is that they are neither primary nor secondary victims. Gross violations of human rights, such as genocide, which target entire social groups (e.g., ethnic or religious groups), may be felt by all members of the social group regardless of whether or not they or their family members were actually the direct target of a particular act of violence.[25] Therefore, a more refined typology for victims of war crimes, which is victim-focused and based on a psychological or physical relationship to the relevant crimes, needs to be developed.

Proposed typology

Definitions concerning who is a victim must not be limited to the direct victims of crime. We need to include both individuals and groups that have suffered harm as well as their family members and communities. In the following section we will present a typology of victims which takes

[24] Ibid., at 162.

[25] J. Westermeyer and M. Williams, 'Three Categories of Victimization Among Refugees in a Psychiatric Clinic', in J. M. Jaranason and M. Popkin (eds.), *Caring for Victims of Torture* (Washington, DC: American Psychiatric Association, 1998) at 61–87.

into account the diverse mix and types of victims. Our typology is based on one's emotional or psychological proximity to the victimization and as such allows us to better understand the possible consequences of the victimization in order to address victims' needs.

The proposed typology consists of four categories: (1) direct victims; (2) indirect victims; (3) secondary victims; and (4) tertiary victims.

1. The *direct victim* is the person who is unlawfully killed, disappeared, injured or tortured.[26] Those persons have directly suffered the effects of war crimes either by death or by undergoing physical or psychological abuse, or by otherwise being unlawfully arrested or detained or by undergoing discriminatory actions or other forms of atrocities.[27]
2. *Indirect victims* are those who are linked to direct victims in such a way that they too suffer as a result of that link.[28] They are often the family members of a direct victim, who 'experience extreme hardship and pain because of the suffering of a family member or by being punished because of their connection to that person – through serious socio-economic deprivation, bereavement, the loss of a breadwinner, missed educational opportunities, family breakdown, police intimidation or humiliation'.[29] For example, a mother can suffer moral damage from the loss of a son, as well as material damage if she was economically dependent on him.[30] Indirect victims may undergo even greater stress than the direct victims themselves, by virtue of the fact that the latter's coping mechanisms have been fully activated to deal with the situation while the former feel totally helpless and useless.[31] Indirect victims may also suffer PTSD following the victimization of a loved one, even though they were nowhere near the crime when it occurred. Recognition of this fact is reflected in the definition of PTSD, which is found in the new, fifth, revision of the Diagnostics and Statistics Manual (DSM) of the American Psychiatric Association.[32] According to the DSM, one

[26] REDRESS, *Implementing Victims' Rights: A Handbook on the Basic Principles and Guidelines on the Right to a Remedy and Reparation* (London, March 2006), available at www.redress.org/downloads/publications/Reparation%20Principles.pdf (accessed 29 November 2011).

[27] L. Huyse, 'Victims', in D. Bloomfield, T. Barnes and L. Huyse, (eds), *Reconciliation after Violent Conflict: A Handbook* (Stockholm: International IDEA, 2003) at 54–66.

[28] Crelinsten, above note 17, at 193.

[29] Huyse, above note 27, at 54–5.

[30] REDRESS, above note 26, at 18.

[31] Crelinsten, above note 17, at 193.

[32] American Psychiatric Association (APA), Posttraumatic Stress Disorder (2013), available at www.ptsd.va.gov/professional/PTSD-overview/dsm5_criteria_ptsd.asp (accessed 13 June 2014).

of the criteria for developing PTSD is learning that a traumatic event occurred to a close family member or close friend. Other terms used to refer to this group of victims includes 'secondary victims'[33] and 'co-victims'.[34] However, in line with Crelinsten, we prefer the term indirect victims.

3. *Secondary victims* are persons who have suffered harm in intervening to assist victims in distress or witnessed the victimization.[35] This category is comprised of bystanders, who may well include neighbours, friends and family of direct victims, who may have been traumatized because of what they witnessed, as well as first responders, such as the police and paramedics.[36] Research on PTSD has established that witnessing violence can be a source of trauma and, hence, this has long been included in the definition of PTSD.[37] Trauma among first responders and other professionals in regular contact or a professional relationship with victims is often referred to as 'vicarious traumatization'.[38] The new, fifth revision of the DSM, recognizes recurring exposure to the effects of victimization, which could apply to first responders, as a potential trigger for PTSD.[39] These victims often do not directly experience the crime, only its aftermath.
4. *Tertiary victims* refers to community members. For example, entire communities can be stricken with fear following the systematic use of violence by armed groups.[40] When victimization is hate-motivated, this has been found to enhance the impact of crime and increase trauma.[41] Persons who belong to the targeted social group may suffer

[33] R. Condry, 'Secondary Victims and Secondary Victimization', in S. G. Shoham, P. Knepper and M. Kett (eds.), *International Handbook of Victimology* (CRC Press, 2010) at 219–49; see also Letschert and Van Boven, above note 22.

[34] Armour, above note 16, at 109. [35] Crelinsten, above note 17, at 193–4.

[36] J. M. Wemmers, 'War Crimes', in B. Fischer and S. P. Lab (eds.), *Encyclopedia of Victimology and Crime Prevention* (Thousand Oaks, CA: Sage Publications, 2010) at 1051.

[37] APA, above note 32, at 1.

[38] L. McCann and L. Perlman, 'Vicarious Traumatization: A Framework for Understanding the Psychological Effects of Working with Victims', (1990) 3 *Journal of Traumatic Stress* 131; L. J. Schauben and P. A. Frazier, 'Vicarious Trauma: The Effects on Female Counsellors of Working with Sexual Violence Survivors', (1995) 19 *Psychology of Women Quarterly* 49.

[39] APA, above note 32, at 1. [40] Crelinsten, above note 17, at 193.

[41] J. M. Wemmers, L. Lafontaine and L. Viau, 'Racial Victimization in Canada', in J. Winterdijk and G. Antonopoulos (eds.), *Racist Victimization* (Aldershot: Ashgate, 2008) at 43–66.

> extreme fear and trauma, which inevitably affects their quality of life.[42] Individuals who are not direct or indirect victims but simply members of the victimized community can also suffer trauma.[43] For example, in a study involving 286 refugees following their flight from their country of origin, it was reported that only 5.6 per cent of the sample had directly experienced victimization and another 22 per cent had experienced impersonal assault (e.g., air raids). Most of the refugees in the study (72.4 per cent) had not experienced direct victimization or direct threat of harm in their home country and yet they were suffering from severe trauma. The fear of harm or threat was at the basis of the decision to flee from their country of origin.[44]

When victimization is widespread, as is the case during war, any one individual may fall under several categories of victim simultaneously. For example, a person may have been the direct victim of crime as well as a witness to the victimization of others (secondary victimization), as well as the family member of someone who was victimized (indirect victim), in addition to being a member of the victimized community (tertiary victimization).[45] Research on multiple victimization shows that the effects of each discrete victimization are cumulative.[46] Hence, in the case of war crimes, where members of the population may have suffered multiple victimizations both directly and indirectly, trauma will be widespread. In a context where multiple victimization is the norm it does not make sense from a mental health perspective to focus only on a specific direct victimization and ignore the rest. This point will be illustrated in the following discussion on victims' needs.

42 E. Hauff and P. Vaglum, 'Vietnamese Boat Refugees: The Influence of War and Flight Traumatization on Mental Health on Arrival in the Country of Resettlement: A Community Cohort Study of Vietnamese Refugees in Norway', (1993) 88 *Acta Psychiatrica Scandinavica* 162; see also C. R. Brewin, B. Andrews and J. D. Valentine, 'Meta-Analysis of Risk Factors for Posttraumatic Stress Disorder in Trauma-Exposed Adults', (2000) 68 *Journal of Consulting and Clinical Psychology* 748; R. Strobl, 'Becoming a Victim', in S. G. Shoham, P. Knepper and M. Kett (eds.), *International Handbook of Victimology* (CRC Press, 2010) 3, at 19.

43 Y. Danieli, D. Brom and J. Sills, 'The Trauma of Terrorism: Contextual Considerations', in Y. Danieli, D. Brom and J. Sills (eds.), *The Trauma of Terrorism: Sharing Knowledge and Shared Care. An International Handbook* (Binghamton, NY: Haworth Maltreatment and Trauma Press, 2005) at 1–17.

44 Westermeyer and Williams, above note 25, at 77.

45 Wemmers, above note 36, at 1051.

46 M. Shaw, 'Time Heals All Wounds?', in G. Farrell and K. Pease (eds.), *Repeat Victimization. Crime Prevention Studies*, (Monsey, NY: Criminal Justice Press, 2001) at 165–97.

Victims' needs

In order to understand victims' needs, one first needs to know how the victim was affected by his or her victimization. While each victim and victimization is different, research has established that the consequences of victimization for direct victims fall under four general categories: (1) emotional impact; (2) physical effects; (3) financial consequences; and (4) social effects. These effects can be both short and long term.[47]

With the exception of physical effects due to injury, these categories can apply equally across all types of victims. All types of victims can suffer emotional, social and financial effects as a result of the crime committed against them. They may also suffer physical symptoms (e.g., sleeplessness) as a result of psychological trauma. Although physical injury may, however, be suffered by secondary victims such as good Samaritans or first responders who are injured while trying to help the direct victim, in general indirect victims and tertiary victims will not suffer physical injuries.

The effects of wartime victimization can be long term. The children of first-generation victims may suffer trauma as a result of what happened to their parents. Studies have demonstrated that second generation victims may also display deep hurt and bitterness, which is a problematic heritage that can threaten the future of an entire society.[48] Even children who were not born at the time of the victimization may develop symptoms. The transmission of trauma across generations is referred to as 'secondary traumatization'.[49]

As a result of the psychological, social and financial consequences of wartime victimization victims may develop psycho-social, financial and sometimes medical needs. If left untreated, these needs may continue to exist long after the direct victim has died. In wartime, the vast number of victims and victimizations means that the aforementioned needs may seem endless, especially as it is sometimes difficult to know just where to start.

The exponential needs of victims in wartime mean that it is necessary to prioritize victims' needs. In the context of war, Wemmers and De

[47] Wemmers, above note 6, at 57–64; see also J. Shapland and M. Hall, 'What Do We Know about the Effects of Crime on Victims?', (2007) 14 *International Review of Victimology* 175.

[48] Huyse, above note 27, at 55.

[49] A. Baranowsky, M. Young, S. Johnson-Douglas, L. Williams-Keeler and M. McCarrey, 'PTSD Transmission: A Review of Secondary Traumatization in Holocaust Survivor Families', (1998) 39 *Canadian Psychology* 247; Y. Danieli, *International Handbook of Multigenerational Legacies of Trauma* (New York, NY: Plenum Press, 1998) at 3.

Brouwer mention that victims will focus first on their basic *physiological needs.*[50] Based on Maslow's pyramid of needs,[51] they contend that victims' primary needs are food, water and medical care. Studies have shown that in the earliest stages following the experience of victimization, reparation is simply not a priority, not even an issue, for victims.[52] Victims need to be able to eat and to sleep. Moreover, there is a pressing need for those who are injured to receive medical care.[53] In the absence of these basic resources the individual's survival is threatened. Yet, in wartime, access to medical care can be difficult and with the war comes the risk of famine as farmers are afraid to go out and work in their fields. This has been shown to be the case in countries such as the Democratic Republic of Congo (DRC)[54] and Somalia.[55]

Once victims' primary daily needs are met, they *need safety and security.* Victims are afraid of victimization in general, and re-victimization by their aggressor in particular.[56] Fear of victimization is not unique to direct victims but runs across all categories of victims. In wartime, victims fleeing the on-going violence often live outside their homes. Many find refuge in refugee camps. For example, the on-going violence in Syria has forced some 2 million people to flee their homes and register as refugees in neighbouring countries such as Egypt, Turkey, Lebanon, Jordan and Iraq. Another 4.25 million Syrians are estimated to be internally displaced within their country.[57] War victims are vulnerable and at risk of re-victimization. According to a 2013

[50] J. M. Wemmers and A. M. de Brouwer, 'Globalization and Victims of Crime', in R. M. Letschert and J. J. M. van Dijk (eds.), *The New Faces of Victimhood: Globalization, Transnational Crimes and Victims' Rights* (Dordrecht: Springer, 2010) at 279–302.

[51] A. H. Maslow, *Toward a Psychology of Being* (2nd edn, New York, NY: Van Nostrand Reinhold, 1968).

[52] REDRESS, *Torture Survivors' Perceptions of Reparation – Preliminary Survey* (Aldridge Print Group, 2001), available at www.redress.org/downloads/reparation/TSPR.pdf (accessed 30 November 2011).

[53] K. Johnson, J. Scott, B. Rughita, M. Kisielewski, J. Asher, R. Ong and L. Lawry, 'Association of Sexual Violence and Human Rights Violations with Physical and Mental Health in Territories of the Eastern Democratic Republic of the Congo', (2010) 304 *Journal of the American Medical Association* 553.

[54] *Mail and Guardian*, 'LRA spreads fear and threat of famine in DRC', Mail and Guardian-online, 2009, available at http://mg.co.za/article/2009-09-01-lra-spreads-fear-and-threat-of-famine-in-drc (accessed 13 June 2014).

[55] T. Parry, 'Somalia Famine: The Level of Suffering is Beyond our Imagination', *Mirror*, 22 July 2011, available at www.mirror.co.uk/news/uk-news/somalia-famine-the-level-of-suffering-is-beyond-143247 (accessed 9 December 2013).

[56] Wemmers and De Brouwer, above note 50, at 288.

[57] UNHCR, 'Syria Situation' (UNHCR, 2013), available at www.unhcr.org/pages/5242d8fa6.html (accessed 10 December 2013); see also UNHCR, 'The Future of Syria: Refugee Children

UN High Commission for Refugees (UNHCR) study, 50 per cent of the externally displaced Syrian refugees are children, many of whom are separated from their families. Unaccompanied by a caregiver, these children are at risk of exploitation and further victimization. Victimization can heighten vulnerability and victims need safety and security for themselves and their loved ones.

Next is the *need for belonging and acceptance*. People need to feel loved and accepted by the people around them. Direct victims of war crimes may feel rejected by their families and their communities. For example, girls enlisted in armed forces are often used as 'bush wives'. If and when they are released, they often have small children. Upon release, however, these girls are often rejected by their families and their communities.[58] Victim support aims to rehabilitate victims and reintegrate them into their communities. This includes psychological help and support for direct victims, such as would enable them to function in society. However, in order to promote the acceptance and support of the direct victims by their families as well as their community, indirect and tertiary victims require rehabilitation as well.

The next level of need identified by Maslow is *self-esteem*, which includes the respect of others. It is important to bear in mind that self-esteem is not only based on the individual and personal characteristics but is also an integral part of one's social group.[59] This is where the individual and the group come together. Belonging to a group that is evaluated positively makes us feel good about ourselves. The social group is particularly salient in war crimes because they are often the target of attack (e.g., national, religious or ethnic groups).[60] It is hard to feel good about belonging to a group that is looked down upon by others. Sensing that others do not respect your social group and with it, your culture, can lead to feelings of inferiority and helplessness.[61]

in Crisis' (UNHCR, 2013), available at https://s3-eu-west-1.amazonaws.com/unhcr-campaigns/childrensreport/Future-of-Syria-UNHCR-v13.pdf (accessed 16 June 2014).

58 S. Mackay and D. Mazuana, *Où sont les filles?* (Montreal: Droits et Démocratie, 2004), at 42.

59 M. A. Hogg, 'Social Identity Theory', in P. Burke (ed.), *Contemporary Social Psychological Theories* (Stanford, CA: Stanford University Press, 2006) at 112–26.

60 J. M. Wemmers, 'Victims' Need for Justice', in R. M. Letschert, R. Haveman, A. M. de Brouwer and A. Pemberton, *Victimological Approaches to International Crimes: Africa* (Antwerp: Intersentia, 2011) at 145–52.

61 See Hogg, above note 59.

Repairing victims

Using our typology we have identified different groups of victims and their possible needs. But is our typology useful in the context of international criminal law and, in particular, reparation? Reparation can mean many different things. The UN Basic Principles and Guidelines on the Right to a Remedy and Reparation for Victims of Gross Violations of International Human Rights Law and Serious Violations of International Humanitarian Law (hereafter the 'Guidelines') provide an extensive description of the goals and the forms of reparation based on the needs of victims of these particularly serious crimes. According to Article 15 of the Guidelines, the aim of reparation is 'to promote justice by redressing gross violations of international human rights law or serious violations of international humanitarian law'. The various forms of reparation are defined in Articles 19 to 23, which include restitution, compensation, rehabilitation, satisfaction and guarantees of non-repetition. The Rome Statute of the ICC provides the possibility of reparation for victims of war crimes. Article 75 of the Rome Statute states that reparation includes compensation, restitution and rehabilitation and, while it does not name other forms of reparation, it does not exclude them either. Nor does the Statute provide further details on which precise victims are entitled to reparation. In the following sections reparation will be discussed and critiqued in light of the needs of the different groups of victims of war crimes.

Physiological needs

Responding to victims' basic physiological needs (as the term was used by Maslow to underline his pyramid of needs) is not a task of the criminal justice system. Victims require this kind of care immediately and cannot wait until justice has run its course, or after the courts, domestic and international, have reached pertinent decisions. Moreover, the 1949 Geneva Conventions specify that such aid should be available to *all* people, regardless of whether they are victims or offenders. The Trust Fund for Victims (TFV) was created together with the ICC by the Rome Statute. It was established for the benefit of victims within the jurisdiction of the ICC and their families. The TFV aims to directly address and respond to victims' physical, psychological or material needs. This is the very purpose of humanitarian aid, which should be provided by humanitarian organizations to anyone in need. Humanitarian aid should not differentiate between victims and offenders. However, such services cannot be considered reparation, and victims are sensitive to this distinction. According to a 2011 UN report, the projects funded by the TFV in the DRC are not seen as a form of reparation.[62] This is because there is no official recognition of harm. While according to the Guidelines rehabilitation can include medical aid, victims view reparation as something that recognizes the harm suffered and is, therefore, not available to everyone.[63] Thus, one must make a distinction between reparation and humanitarian aid. Medical assistance should be available to all on the basis of humanitarian grounds under the 1949 Geneva conventions, in addition to customary international law. Programmes that do not limit access to victims are not considered reparation.

The need for safety and security

Guarantees of non-repetition may provide victims, both individually and collectively, with a sense of security and protection from further victimization. However, apart from detaining offenders, it is not within the mandate of the ICC to impose national measures designed to promote guarantees of non-repetition. While the prosecution of war criminals is considered in the Rome Statute's preamble as a means to attain peace and security,[64] so far it is difficult to assess the real contribution of the ICC to the establishment of peace and security. Insofar as the ICC can apprehend and detain war criminals, the Court can contribute to the victims' sense of safety. Besides specific deterrence, the ICC may have a general deterrent effect by restraining potential war criminals from committing new crimes. However, the ICC is not particularly successful in deterring war criminals.[65] While we cannot exclude the possible deterrent effect of

[62] UN, Report of the Panel on Remedies and Reparations for Victims of Sexual Violence in the Democratic Republic of Congo to the High Commissioner for Human Rights (March, 2011), available at www.ohchr.org/Documents/Countries/CD/DRC_Reparations_Report_en.pdf (accessed 16 June 2014).

[63] J. M. Wemmers, 'Regaining Trust: The Importance of Justice for Victims of Crimes against Humanity', (2014) 20 *International Review of Victimology* 101.

[64] See the preamble to the ICC Statute, which reads: '*Determined* to put an end to impunity for the perpetrators of these crimes and thus to contribute to the prevention of such crimes.'

[65] A. Manirabona, 'La Cour Pénale Internationale et la Prévention des Atrocités en Afrique: Le Difficile Passage de la Rhétorique à la Réalité', (2010) 69 *Revue du Barreau* 277; C. W. Mullins and D. L. Rothe, 'The Ability of the International Criminal Court to Deter Violations of International Criminal Law: A Theoretical Assessment', (2010) 10 *International Criminal Law Review* 771.

the Court, the on-going hostilities in situations such as the DRC[66] and the Central African Republic[67] suggest that any such effect is limited in its scope.

In addition, the activities of the Court may put victims in danger. For example, victim-witnesses who are viewed as collaborating with the Court may be at risk of violence from opposition forces and their supporters. Direct victims, eye-witnesses (secondary victims) and their families (indirect victims) may be at risk of retaliation. Stover provides extensive evidence of how direct victims and secondary victims who participated as witnesses at the International Criminal Tribunal for the former Yugoslavia, as well as their family members (indirect victims), experienced fear, threats of violence and intimidation from other community members due to their collaboration with the Tribunal.[68] The international community, however, can play an important role in the establishment of guarantees of non-repetition. Through the provision of development funds from national governments it can strengthen the criminal justice system of countries in post-conflict recovery. For example, those funds may help a war-torn country, such as the DRC, cope with training law enforcers as well as criminal law reform. Moreover, through the complementarity principle, which recognizes the primary responsibility of domestic criminal courts with respect to investigating and trying offenders, the ICC may also contribute to the promotion and the strengthening of the rule of law in war-torn countries.[69]

Satisfaction may also contribute to the victims' sense of safety and security. According to the Guidelines, satisfaction consists of measures designed to reinstate the dignity of victims by putting an end to the violations and acknowledging the harm suffered by them. When crimes are publicly recognized, victims may feel validated and, therefore, consider it is less likely that such crimes will be committed again in the future. Public acknowledgement validates the victims' experiences and recognizes their

[66] Médecins Sans Frontières, 'Providing Emergency Assistance to Thousands of Congolese Refugees Following Attack in North Kivu', (2013), available at www.msf.ca/news-media/news/2013/07/providing-emergency-assistance-to-thousands-of-congolese-refugees-following-attack-in-north-kivu/ (accessed 10 December 2013).

[67] A. Harding, 'Central African Republic: Where Have all the People Gone?', *BBC News*, available at www.bbc.co.uk/news/world-africa-25195929 (accessed 10 December 2013).

[68] E. Stover, *The Witnesses: War Crimes and the Promise of Justice in the Hague* (Philadelphia, PA: University of Pennsylvania Press, 2005).

[69] M. Wierda, 'Stocktaking: Complementarity', in International Center for Transitional Justice, *The Rome Statute Review Conference: Briefing* (June 2010), available at http://ictj.org/sites/default/files/ICTJ-RSRC-Global-Complementarity-Briefing-2010-English.pdf (accessed 10 December 2013).

suffering. This is relevant for all groups of victims, including indirect and tertiary. Truth commissions can play a great role in victims' search for satisfaction. For example, in Canada it was victims groups, consisting of both direct and indirect victims, which asked for the creation of a Truth and Reconciliation Commission regarding the Indian Residential Schools.[70] By uncovering the truth, the commissions recognize victimization and validate victims' suffering. However, when a truth commission fails to uncover the truth this may augment the victims' sense of insecurity. While the DRC established a truth commission in 2003 following political deal-making during the transitional government, the commission has been a total failure. It has been unable to collect a single witness statement or open a single enquiry. Its lack of success is due to the fact that some of the commissioners were drawn from the warring groups alleged to have been actively involved in the mass atrocities which they were meant to be investigating. This seriously undermined the legitimacy of the commission from the outset.[71]

Restitution can also help re-establish a sense of security for direct and indirect victims. The non-governmental organization (NGO) REDRESS correctly notes that 'restitution is especially important where the obligation breached is of a continuing character: thus in a case of unlawful detention or disappearance, for example, the authorities must end the situation by producing the victim'.[72] Yet, the ICC has no direct power to compel combatants to release persons unlawfully detained or to bring back those who have disappeared. The ICC may only exert an indirect effect by its ability to deter war criminals and, as we have mentioned, the ICC is not particularly successful in this respect. Sometimes restitution will be impossible. For example, restitution is not necessarily feasible in the case of sexual violence, physical injuries, torture or the loss of family members. In such cases, other forms of reparation might be preferable.

The need for belonging and acceptance

According to the Guidelines, rehabilitation includes medical and psychological care as well as legal and social services. However, as pointed out earlier, in order to be considered reparation it is essential that

[70] P. Regan, *Unsettling the Settler Within: Indian Residential Schools, Truth Telling and Reconciliation in Canada* (Vancouver, BC: UBC Press, 2011).

[71] IRIN, 'Analysis: Justice Still Remote for Victims of Atrocities in DRC' (IRIN, 2010), available at www.irinnews.org/report/90736/analysis-justice-still-re.mote-for-victims-of-atrocities-in-drc (accessed 10 December 2013).

[72] REDRESS, above note 26.

rehabilitation services are reserved for victims. Thus, while immediate medical aid is not considered reparation, non-essential medical procedures such as plastic surgery can be considered reparation when they are reserved for victims. Recognition of one's status as a victim should determine access to such services.

However, the recognition of victims should not be limited to direct victims and should include indirect and secondary victims as well as tertiary. In the context of war, all categories of victims can suffer trauma. In order to accept the direct victims back into their communities it is important that indirect victims and other community members receive support in coming to terms with their trauma as well. Rehabilitation can focus on the individual or the group. For example, while they implicate individuals, measures that focus on group membership and the needs of the group can stimulate collective rehabilitation among group members.[73] Collective healing is at the heart of transitional justice. It refers to a variety of measures, both judicial and non-judicial, implemented in order to redress the suffering following mass violence.[74] While individual and collective healing are two distinct processes, they are also related. Each individual is also a member of one or more social groups. Victims are often aware of this distinction between their personal needs and those of the group.[75] The individual's social identity is the linking pin between individual and collective processes.[76] Belonging to groups – in particular, a group that is valued by others – is important for how we feel about ourselves.

The ICC, which is currently dominated by a largely individualized approach to victims, is unable to recognize many of these categories of victims.[77] In its decision establishing the principles and procedure to be applied to reparation in the *Lubanga* case the ICC seems to insist on direct and, to some extent, indirect victims. The TFV, however, is not burdened by the same limitations. It can offer reparation to victims in cases where the Court cannot. Recognition of the situation as one that

73 Wemmers, above note 60.

74 W. Lambourne, 'Transitional Justice and Peacebuilding after Mass Violence', (2009) 3 *The International Journal of Transitional Justice* 28.

75 B. Hamber, *Transforming Societies after Political Violence: Truth, Reconciliation and Mental Health* (Dordrecht: Springer, 2009).

76 Wemmers, above note 60, at 149.

77 F. Mégret, 'The Case for Collective Reparations before the International Criminal Court', in J. M. Wemmers (ed.), *Reparation for Victims of Crimes Against Humanity* (New York, NY: Routledge, 2014) at 171–89.

falls within the competence of the Court should be sufficient to allow the recognition of victimized groups.[78] Thus, while the ICC has only completed one trial after ten years of operation and the only offender convicted by the Court, Thomas Lubanga Dyilo, was deemed by the Court to be insolvent, the TFV has invested in projects for some war victims in the DRC. These projects include psychological support, physical rehabilitation, and material support related to sexual violence.[79] Insofar as these projects recognize victimization, they can be an important source of reparation for victims.

Self-esteem needs

Compensation has an important practical and symbolic value for victims. Its symbolic value lies in its recognition of the victim as a valued or worthy member of society. Because of its symbolic value, compensation can help restore victims' social standing. However, it is important that victims see that compensation is distributed fairly across other sufferers.[80] Perceived inequality between victims can lead to secondary victimization. Moreover, compensation should not be limited to direct victims. As we have seen, indirect victims and secondary victims can also suffer serious trauma. While all categories of victims may wish to seek compensation for their losses, ultimately, however, the sheer magnitude of the losses suffered in wartime makes full compensation unrealistic. To illustrate, in the DRC no fewer than 5.4 million people are believed to have died since the outbreak of the war in that country and the conflict is still on-going.[81] Besides all the practical problems mentioned above, it is simply impossible ever to have enough resources to provide compensation to each and every victim. Ordering compensation for victims while knowing that they will never actually receive it is not an option either. Therefore, compensation will necessarily be limited in scope. But how

[78] G. Bitti, 'Les Droits Procéduraux des Victimes Devant la Cour Pénale Internationale', (2011) 44 *Criminologie* 64.

[79] The Trust Fund for Victims, *Recognizing Victims and Building Capacity in Transitional Societies* (2010), available at www.trustfundforvictims.org/sites/default/files/imce/TFV%20Programme%20Report%20Spring%202010.pdf (accessed 11 December 2013).

[80] B. Feldthusen, O. Hankivsky and L. Greaves, 'Therapeutic Consequences of Civil Actions for Damages and Compensation Claims by Victims of Sexual Abuse', (2010) 12 *Canadian Journal of Women and the Law* 66.

[81] International Rescue Committee, *Mortality in the Democratic Republic of Congo: An Ongoing Crisis* (2007) at 16, available at www.rescue.org/sites/default/files/resource-file/2006-7_congoMortalitySurvey.pdf (accessed 16 June 2014).

does one limit compensation to certain groups without creating inequality between victims? These problems highlight the importance of other non-monetary, collective forms of reparation for victims.[82]

Restitution can also provide direct and indirect victims with a sense of validation and respect. Following the definition of restitution found in the Guidelines, the ICC can, for example, insist that the offender return stolen property that has not been consumed or destroyed. The restitution of civil and political rights is an example of collective reparation which falls outside the jurisdiction of the ICC but can be used by states. For example, an effective form of restitution may be the recognition of citizenship to those who fled their country of origin as refugees, thus allowing them or their children (including those born abroad) to return home. This is also consistent with the obligations of states against rendering their nationals stateless.

Satisfaction can reflect recognition and respect by others for the victim and the victimized group. Public acknowledgement offers all victims of the event support by providing them with recognition and validation of their victimization. Such recognition may help re-establish victims' self-esteem and the value of their social group.[83] Recognition can be achieved in many different ways: a formal apology from the head of state; a public monument in memory of the victims; a nation-wide day of remembrance. Criminal prosecution of those suspected of having committed war crimes is also a form of recognition that is valued by victims. While it may be imperfect, victims place great importance on the criminal prosecution of offenders.[84] The ICC was created in order to put an end to impunity. In addition, the ICC follows the complementarity principle and encourages domestic courts to prosecute suspected war criminals as well, thus allowing maximum reach. These various forms of recognition complement one another and, therefore, in order to maximize healing, should be used together.

A summary of the above discussion is found in Table 12.2. Specifically, it provides an overview of victims' need for reparation across the different types of victims identified in our typology of victims. For each type of victim, it lists the various forms of reparation with respect to each of the different types of needs experienced by victims. By recognizing these different types of victims and their needs, the ICC (including the TFV) can better understand the impact of its work on victims and effectively use reparation to help restore justice for victims.

[82] See Mégret, above note 77. [83] See Wemmers, above note 63, at 105.
[84] Ibid., at 104–5.

Table 12.2: *Overview of types of victims by victims' needs in relation to reparation*

	Direct victim	Indirect victim	Secondary victim	Victimized community
Physiological needs	Humanitarian aid	Humanitarian aid	Humanitarian aid	Humanitarian aid
Safety and security	Guarantees of non-repetition Satisfaction Restitution	Guarantees of non-repetition Satisfaction Restitution	Guarantees of non-repetition Satisfaction	Guarantees of non-repetition Satisfaction
Belonging and acceptance	Rehabilitation	Rehabilitation	Rehabilitation	Rehabilitation
Self-esteem needs	Satisfaction Compensation Restitution	Satisfaction Compensation Restitution	Satisfaction Compensation	Satisfaction

Conclusion

The typology developed and presented in this chapter allows us to better understand the consequences of victimization and, therefore, to better meet the needs of victims. Our typology reflects the growing awareness that victimization does not only affect the direct victim. It identifies four different groups of victims, all of which can be impacted by the same crime. Moreover, we need to bear in mind multiple victimizations and the fact that any one individual may fall under numerous categories.

Our typology highlights how important it is that the ICC also considers other groups in addition to direct victims. From a victimological standpoint there is no reason to limit the Court to direct victims, as other groups are equally affected by crime and, in some cases (for example, indirect victims), they may be even more strongly impacted by the crime than the direct victims. Moreover, multiple victimizations make the distinction between direct victims and other groups seem somewhat arbitrary. To do so fails to reflect the reality of war crimes.

Finally, our typology helps to better understand the different needs of victims of war crimes and crimes against humanity and how the ICC can meet these different needs. Clearly, the ICC suffers many limitations. It is very slow and tends to focus on individual victims (direct and indirect) at the expense of secondary and tertiary victims. The Court must bear in mind its impact on the community of victims. Its ability to recognize situations and validate victims' suffering is very important to victims' recovery both individually and as a group. In addition, the TFV is a vital tool that allows the Court to help a broad range of victims.

INDEX